SCRIBING THE CENTER

THE SOCIETY OF BIBLICAL LITERATURE
MONOGRAPH SERIES

Number 49
SCRIBING THE CENTER
Organization and Redaction in Deuteronomy 14:–17:13

by
William S. Morrow

William S. Morrow

SCRIBING THE CENTER

Organization and Redaction in Deuteronomy 14:1–17:13

Scholars Press
Atlanta, Georgia

SCRIBING THE CENTER

Organization and Redaction in Deuteronomy 14:1–17:13

by

William S. Morrow

Library of Congress Cataloging in Publication Data
Morrow, William S.
Scribing the center : organization and redaction in Deuteronomy 14:
1–17:13 / William S. Morrow.
p. cm. — (Monograph series / Society of Biblical Literature;
no. 49)
Includes bibliographical references (p.).
ISBN 0-7885-0064-3 (cloth: alk. paper). — ISBN 0-7885-0065-1
(pbk. : alk. paper)
1. Bible. O. T. Deuteronomy XIV, 1–XVII, 13—Criticism,
Redaction. I. Title. II. Series: Monograph series (Society of
Biblical Literature) ; no. 49.
BS1275.2.M67 1994
222'.15066—dc20 94-23617
CIP

Printed in the United States of America
on acid-free paper

To Ruth

Ecclesiastes 4:9–12

Contents

ABBREVIATIONS

The following list of abbreviations supplements those found in the Society of Biblical Literature's "Handbook for Editors and Authors" (1992).

A	Adverbial (limited to locatives in time and space)
Av	Action verb
B	Bound
BH	Biblical Hebrew
c.	clause
cc.	clauses
Cl.	clause
CNc	Complex Noun clause
Co	Coordinated / Coordination
C.1	Coordinating conjunction
C.2	Subordinating conjunction
D	Deixis
Dist	Distance
Dtn	Deuteronomic
Dtr	Deuteronomistic
E	Ellipsis
ET	Emended Text
ex par	ex parallelis locis
F	Free
f.	feminine
Imp	Imperative (clause)
Inf	Infinitive (clause)
Gen	Geniza fragment
IVc	Inverted Verbal clause
K	Cataphoric referent
K#	Kennicott Ms (e.g., K^{69})
L	Lexical reiteration
M.#	Mediated referent
m.	masculine
Ma	Matching
N.#	Non-mediated referent
Nc	Noun (verbless) clause
N	Nominalized clause
NP	Noun phrase
Np	Noun phrase neither S, O, or A
O	Object
P	Prepositional phrase
Pa	P equivalent to A
Part	Participial clause
Pc	P governing a clause
Pet	*pətûḥâ*
pl	plural
Po	P equivalent to O
PP	Prepositional phrase
Pred	Predicate
res	resumed
Pr.1	Pronominal reference which is S in the clause.
Pr.2	Pronominal reference which is O of either a V or P
S	Subject
s	singular
Set	*sətûmâ*
SP	Samaritan Pentateuch
Sres	Noun phrase resuming a non-contiguous S
Sub	Substitution
Sv	Stative verb
Syr	Peshiṭta
TJ	Targum Pseudo-Jonathan
TN	Targum Neofiti

TO	Targum Onqelos
V	Verb
Vc	Verbal clause
Vg	Vulgate
V+O	V with O as pronominal suffix
WA	"Appendix 1" in Weinfeld, *Deuteronomy and the Deuteronomic School*
wyqtl	Vc in *wayyiqṭôl* form
wqtl	Vc in *wəqāṭal* form
x	Marker of negation (e.g., xVc = negated verbal clause)
>	Lacking in
2mpl	second person masculine plural
2ms	second person masculine singular
3mpl	third person masculine plural
3ms	third person masculine singular

Acknowledgments

This book would not have not have been written without help from many people. First and foremost, I would like to acknowledge the support and patience of my life partner Ruth and our children Ernest and Evelyn.

An earlier version of this study was defended as a doctoral thesis for the Department of Near Eastern Studies, University of Toronto in 1988. I would like to thank Prof. Paul Dion and Prof. J. W. Wevers for their inspiration and supervision of that dissertation, and Prof. Ernest Clarke for his scholarly encouragement. I am grateful to the following agencies and institutions for aiding my doctoral research: The Social Sciences and Humanities Research Council of Canada Doctoral Fellowship programme (1984-1986); The Board of Ministry, The Presbyterian Church in Canada (1986); The Ontario Graduate Scholarship programme (1986-1987). A portion of the study on Deut 15:1–6 first appeared in my article "The Composition of Deut 15:1–3" in *Hebrew Annual Review*.

This book is the result of a thorough methodological revision of my doctoral thesis which also extends its textual horizons. I am grateful to Prof. Edward F. Campbell Jr., the former editor of the Society of Biblical Literature Monograph Series, for accepting it for publication, and to the readers of the manuscript who made many valuable suggestions for its improvement. Responsibility for the views expressed in this book, however, remains mine.

Part One

The Organization of Deuteronomy 14:1–17:13

Chapter One

Exegetical Method and Textual Unity in Deuteronomic Instructions

This book reports the results of two interests that have motivated my research. In the first place it contains a description of immanent organizational principles used in the composition of a portion of biblical law. This description is based on the results of an exegetical procedure which reflects my second interest. I offer here an attempt at a method of exegesis which is responsive to various insights of text linguistics but which does not obligate the exegete to fully commit to a particular school of linguistic theory. Many of the instructions in Deut 14:1–17:13 focus on journeys to the legitimate cult center. Others are meant to circumscribe the behavior of the community which must make such journeys. Here I describe the organizational techniques used by the scribes who wrote and edited them. Therefore, I have called this book *Scribing the Center: Organization and Redaction in Deuteronomy 14:1–17:13.*

The book is organized so that readers may read my conclusions regarding immanent organizational principles before scrutinizing the detailed evidence on which they are based. Therefore, I have divided the book into two parts corresponding to its subtitles. Chapter Two concludes Part One by describing the organizational principles used in Deut 14:1–17:13 in particular, and in Deuteronomy 12–18 in general. It restates and assumes the redaction critical conclusions of the exegetical study found in Part Two (Chapters Three to Six). The result, perhaps, is a book which is somewhat more repetitive than it could be. But its present form seems preferable to obliging the reader to wade through a rather technical discussion looking for a summary of key conclusions regarding the organization and composition of the text.

The selection of Deut 14:1–17:13 for investigation is somewhat arbitrary. I would defend it now on the grounds that the results of my studies, I think, illuminate not only the organization of this span of text, but also of Deuteronnomy 12–18 as a whole—fully half of Deuteronomy 12–26. When I began, I started with 14:1 because it seems to introduce a section of materials which are mostly related to cultic practice but which end in an interlocking structure, including a span of legal and administrative material beginning in 16:18.[1] Hence, the text possesses indications of some sort of relative unity as well as manifesting several problems of order prominent in past discussions of the arrangement of Deuteronomy 12–26: It is crucial to any account of the relationship between the current disposition of instructions and pre-deuteronomic materials. It spans the division between cultic (14:1–16:17) and legal institutions (16:18–20; 17:2–13) which many topical divisions of Deuteronomy distinguish. It contains materials which have often been regarded as intrusive (e.g., 14:1–21; 15:1–18; 16:21–17:1). Finally, it also touches on the issue of *Numeruswechsel* (14:1–21).[2]

A plausible account of the organization of the mixture of cultic, humanitarian, and legal instructions in Deuteronomy 12–26 has proven difficult to obtain.[3] This well-known problem has been given new light thanks to a number of discussions of immanent organizational techniques used in biblical law which have appeared in the past two decades, in part influenced by the work of Petschow on Codex Hammurabi and the Laws of Eshnunna.[4] Kaufman used related principles in an attempt to articulate a detailed connection between the Decalogue in Deut 5:6–21(18) and Deut 12:1–25:16.[5] Similar techniques were invoked by Braulik in his account of the relationship between Deuteronomy 12–26 and the Decalogue.[6] The heuristic value of such principles is also evident in a study by Rofé who notes that the use of associative techniques similar to those found in Babylonian law are evident both in Deuteronomy and in the Temple Scroll from Qumran.[7] More recently, Levinson has also expressed optimism about the possibilities of dis-

---

[1] G. Braulik, "Zur Abfolge der Gesetze in Deuteronomium 16,18–21,23. Weitere Beobachtungen," 65.

[2] The programmatic importance of these issues for an account of order in Deuteronomy 12–25 is set forth by H. D. Preuss in *Deuteronomium*, 103–44; see especially p.107.

[3] See, e.g., the rather pessimistic conclusions of A. C. Welch, *The Code of Deuteronomy*, 23; E. W. Nicholson, *Deuteronomy and Tradition*, 33; Preuss, *Deuteronomium*, 108; and S. D. McBride, "Polity of the People: The Book of Deuteronomy," 239.

[4] H. Petschow, "Zur Systematik und Gesetzestechnik im Codex Hammurabi"; and "Zur 'Systematik' in den Gesetzen von Eschnunna." For indications of Petschow's influence, see B. Levinson, *The Hermeneutics of Innovation: The Impact of Centralization upon the Structure, Sequence, and Reformulation of the Legal Material in Deuteronomy*, 14–77; and B. Levinson, "Calum Carmichael's Approach to the Laws of Deuteronomy," 229. For an example related to laws in Exodus, see V. Wagner, "Zur Systematik in dem Codex Ex 21,2–22,16."

[5] S. A. Kaufman, "The Structure of the Deuteronomic Law," 108–14.

[6] G. Braulik, "Die Abfolge der Gesetze in Deuteronomium 12–26 und der Dekalog," 257–58.

[7] A. Rofé, "The Order of the Laws in the Book of Deuteronomy," 285.

covering immanent organizational principles in the instructions of Deuteronomy, though he is critical of the work of Kaufman, Rofé, and Braulik, and their use of Petschow's results.[8]

But however promising the approaches of the researchers cited above may be, such investigations are dependent on the perception of a certain degree of literary unity in the text studied. Textual organization implies the arrangement of a number of clauses or rows of clauses into a meaningful discourse. Traditionally, biblical scholarship has investigated textual organization as part of a concern to discover clues about the way in which the extant text was composed. Often signs of grammatical and semantic inconsistencies are taken as indications that the text's present form is a result of some history of editorial activity. It is the task of *literary-criticism* (= *Literarkritik*) to detect the various strata which such clues suggest. It is the task of *redaction criticism* to account for the composition of such an edited text in terms of its chronological development.

The exegetical method used in this book aims at arriving at a redaction-critical statement of the text's composition. Its major tools are the techniques of literary-criticism. It is expected that the use of these critical procedures will throw light on the principles used in the organization of any original composition as well as subsequent expansions and editions. In many ways, therefore, the exegetical methods used here (and the questions asked of the text) are traditional ones. What novelty this study brings to the techniques of literary- and redaction criticism is through application of some insights about the nature of textual organization drawn from the area of modern linguistics known as *discourse analysis*.

It is hardly news that a number of modern exegetes have insisted on the need to integrate recent insights into the nature of textual unity with more traditional methods of biblical criticism. But, as late as 1991, Cotterell and Turner note with dismay that discourse techniques seem to have made little impact on published exegetical studies outside of those for biblical translators.[9] Certainly, the use of such an exegetical program is uncommon in the study of biblical instructions.[10]

An important influence on my understanding of textual unity is found in Halliday and Hasan's concept of textuality:

> A text is best regarded as a SEMANTIC unit: a unit not of form but of meaning . . . A text does not CONSIST of sentences; it is REALIZED BY, or encoded

[8] Levinson, *The Hermeneutics of Innovation*, 76–77.

[9] P. Cotterell and M. Turner, *Linguistics and Biblical Interpretation*, 30.

[10] But see, e.g., G. Braulik, *Die Mittel deuteronomischer Rhetorik*, and T. Seidl, *Tora für den »Aussatz«–Fall*.

> in, sentences. If we understand it in this way, we shall not expect to find the same kind of STRUCTURAL integration among the parts of a text as we find among the parts of a sentence or clause. The unity of a text is the unity of a different kind.[11]

In other words, textual unity is a property of what Halliday and Hasan call *cohesion*. Cohesion occurs where the interpretation of some element in the discourse is dependent on that of another. The one presupposes the other in the sense that it cannot be effectively decoded except by recourse to the element it presupposes or refers to. When this happens, a relation of cohesion is set up and the two elements, the presupposing and the presupposed, are thereby (at least potentially) integrated into the text.[12]

The concept of cohesion is mainly a semantic one: it refers to relations of meaning that exist within the text, and that define its string of utterances as text. Such semantic relationships can manifest themselves structurally by grammatical and lexical references which connect clauses or sentences in the text. Structural cohesive relations are established by pronominal reference, substitution, ellipsis, conjunction, and lexical reiterations.[13]

A major influence on my application of discourse principles to biblical exegesis comes from Wolfgang Richter's proposals in *Exegese als Literaturwissenschaft* (1971). This book represents a pioneering attempt to integrate traditional methods of critical biblical study with insights from modern linguistics. Richter's fundamental principle is that a description of a text's linguistic structure (*Form*) ought to discipline one's interpretation of the contents of the text (*Inhalt*).[14] In this regard, the book won approval from reviewers for its attempt to distinguish itself from methods of exegesis which base their judgments on more intuitive grounds.[15]

Richter has also been justly criticized.[16] And although I acknowledge a debt to Richter, particularly with respect to his insights on the description of textual form, this book does not follow many other aspects of his exegetical program. In the first place, whereas Richter insists on the need for an analysis of textual structure after literary-critical study, I follow those who insist on the need for a synchronic description of textual structure prior to literary-critical analysis.[17] For the same reason, a description of the text's

---

11 M. A. K. Halliday and R. Hasan, *Cohesion in English*, 2.

12 Ibid., 4.

13 Ibid., 29.

14 W. Richter, *Exegese als Literaturwissenschaft*, 32–33.

15 See F. Langlamet, Review of Richter, *Exegese*, 275; J. W. Rogerson, Review of Richter, *Exegese*, 117.

16 See, e.g., N. Lohfink, Review of Richter, *Exegese*.

17 See P. E. Dion, "Deutéronome 21,1–9: Miroir du dévelopment légal et religieux d'Israël."

relationship to various sorts of literary parallels on the phrase, clause, and clause row levels of textual organization also precedes literary-critical analysis. A systematic description of the nature of these relationships can also discipline literary-critical investigation.

My use of Richter is most unqualified with respect to describing textual structure. The system of formal grammatical and lexical references which contribute to a text's cohesion may be called the text's *outer structure*. The semantic relationships between its clauses may be called its *inner structure*. The goal of structural analysis is to arrive at a description of inner structure. Since elements of outer structure often indicate relations of meaning between various clauses, an analysis of outer structure ought to precede an analysis of inner structure in order to control the description as fully as possible.[18]

But there is a distinction to be maintained between the relations of meaning which hold together items in a text and the explicit expression of those relations within a text. This has been pointed out by Brown and Yule:

> Few would dispute that it is necessary that such relations be postulated within a discourse which is capable of being interpreted coherently. What is questionable is whether the explicit *realization* of these relations is required to identify a text as text.[19]

In other words, a text may possess a cohesion which is not structurally apparent. There are texts which possess semantic unity despite the absence of contextual references of either a grammatical or lexical nature. Recent work on discourse analysis points to the role of extra-textual context (exophoric context) as a determining factor in making sense of a series of utterances, namely, giving them *texture*.[20] Hence, one may not be able to determine why a particular span of discourse has texture just by describing its properties of structural reference (endophoric context).

A problem that arises in discourse analysis of the Bible, therefore, is that a full description of the texture of a biblical text depends on a knowledge of both its exophoric and endophoric contexts. But access to the original exophoric context is usually incomplete or missing when reading the Bible. To be sure, biblical exegesis has often concerned itself with exophoric context. The results of these efforts appear in descriptions of the *Sitz(e) im Leben* of particular genres of literature. But such a description falls short of determining the original external communication context for a particular

---

[18] Richter, *Exegese*, 78.

[19] G. Brown and G. Yule, *Discourse Analysis*, 195.

[20] Cotterell and Turner, *Linguistics and Biblical Interpretation*, 94–95.

text. The best that can usually hoped for in the case of biblical texts is to control one's intuitions about the semantic relationships which connect the utterances of the text by a description of the way they manifest themselves in the endophoric context of the text. But often only approximate descriptions of texture can be achieved.

Intuitions about semantic relationships are also at work in literary-critical investigations. Literary-critical inquiry searches for inconsistencies which suggest that the present text is a modification of some older form or context. Many of these inconsistencies manifest themselves as cases in which a logical relationship in the text's semantic references appears to break down.[21] In other words, literary-criticism frequently concerns itself with inconsistencies in the text's inner structure. As such, literary-critical method deals with apparent breaches in the cohesion of the text, both within itself and with other texts. How to control such observations?

I follow Richter in focusing on the clause-level of textual organization in both the description of outer and inner structure.[22] Clauses are the medium in which textual utterances are typically expressed. They form the building blocks of larger spans of discourse. Clause-level phenomena are also the discourse features most capable of structural (syntactic) analysis. They provide the bases for a controlled description of the endophoric context of the text. It is possible that this evidence will not be enough to satisfy all questions about semantic unity. Because of this, and since the exophoric context is so difficult to determine for biblical texts, a conservative approach is warranted in terms of a perception of literary-critical inconsistencies. In other words, unless there is evidence to the contrary, the text's unity should be assumed.[23] This is an additional argument for the need to begin with synchronistic analysis. But even within these strictures, a description of textual unity at the clause-level should provide data sufficient both to aid and control the literary-critical process to a significant extent.

My choice of clause-level phenomena also reflects another exegetical interest, namely, to develop a method which, while linguistically responsible, does not require the exegete to describe the discourse structure of the text apart from its interface with syntactic features. This is a desideratum, I believe, for researchers who, like myself, consider themselves to be students of biblical literature first, and linguists second. A description of clause-level

---

21 These are described in detail by Richter in *Exegese*, 51–62. For an overview, see Langlamet, Review of Richter, *Exegese*, 277–78.

22 Richter, *Exegese*, 78.

23 For examples of cases in which I have applied this principle, see my decision to connect 14:21b with the composition of 14:21a and to relate 15:1–3 to the composition of 14:28–29 in the absence of syntactic evidence to connect them with 15:7–18.

phenomena in terms of textual structure and meaning should provide insights into textual unity, even without describing the full range of textual pragmatics. I invite readers to reflect on whether my partial description of discourse structure was adequate for the purposes of this study. I hope that my work will aid others in the study of the relationship between linguistic analysis and exegesis.

The analysis of outer structure amounts to a description of its formal techniques of cohesion on the clause-level of textual organization. Two considerations emerge with respect to the description of formal cohesion:

a) There are correlations between predication type, clause structure and communication function. Similar clause patterns can indicate structural arrangements and the progression of textual meaning. By the same token, a break in such a pattern can indicate a shift in the way the text's meaning is organized.[24]

b) Insights concerning textual organization can be also controlled by observing the arrangement created by the text's system of structural references between clauses. A description of this system of references occurs below (pp. 39–42). This program was pursued in the present study by describing the text's formal reference system using an adaptation of the categories of Halliday and Hasan in *Cohesion in English*. A systematic presentation of this evidence appears in the Appendix.

Readers familiar with Richter's program for the description of outer structure will note a significant absence. I have not compiled statistical information in order to describe style. First, we have yet to hear from Richter as to what span of homogeneous text is necessary before meaningful statistical results can be obtained.[25] Secondly, the statistics he recommends tend to focus on word-level phenomena.[26] This study is focused on clause-level phenomena.

Following an analysis of outer structure, one can describe the text's inner structure. This is an abstract description of the communication function of the text's clauses and sections. It is accompanied by a commentary explaining how various factors of outer structure contribute to the inner structure of the text.[27]

---

[24] See P. J. Nel's review of H. Irsigler, *Ps 73–Monolog eines Weisen*, 174. A similar theme is sounded by M. P. O'Connor (*Hebrew Verse Structure* §10.5) in his observation of the prominence of heavy clauses at junctures in batch and stave organization.

[25] Nel, Review of Irsigler, *Ps 73*, 174.

[26] Richter, *Exegese*, 88-89.

[27] See the examples in ibid., 104-11.

In view of the priority of inner structure as an indicator of textual cohesion, the adequacy of my descriptions of inner structure needs some defense. I have not, in fact, provided a full mapping of semantic relationships within each clause row. This is justifiable, in my opinion, given the decision to focus inquiry on phenomena capable of syntactic description, namely, above the word-level of clause syntax. But even the clause constituent analysis which accompanies the transcriptions provides only a partial semantic mapping of clause-level syntagms. This decision was made in order to provide access to vital details of structure and meaning at the level of clause syntax without having to make a full commitment to any particular theory of clause syntax (e.g., transformational-generative linguistics, tagmemics, case grammars). This is another desideratum, in my opinion, for researchers who wish to use linguistic categories as an aid to exegesis rather than as an end in themselves.

The initial interest of this study is to investigate the literary integrity (or literary unity) of units of semantic cohesion called *clause rows* in Deut 14:1-17:13. The exegetical method used is described in detail in Chapter Three and each clause row is analyzed in Chapter Four. Each text is first established and presented in transcription and translation. This yields the evidence for an analysis of structure. The search for parallels is another important step prior to literary criticism. It must be born in mind that textual parallels can be either structural, semantic or both. Parallels on the level of structure are important since they point to a common trait of composition which may escape the reader who concentrates only on similar contents. Considerations for finding such textual parallels follow principles articulated by Richter.[28]

Analysis of the text's structure and relationships with other texts furnishes evidence which can control investigations about its literary unity. But putative difficulties in the text's system of meaning relations may solve themselves or appear even more acute in the light of a larger context. A distinction is made, therefore, between literary-critical problems which can be solved by evidence at the clause row level and evidence which can only be adduced when a larger span of texts to which the clause row belongs has been identified. Consequently, certain literary-critical problems are identified whose solution must be deferred until a determination of sequential relationships between clause rows has been made.

Chapter Five follows the individual clause row analyses. This chapter, in fact, represents an extension of literary-critical investigation to contexts above the individual clause row. Aspects of structure and parallelism are

---

[28] Ibid., 137-41

used to connect various portions of the text into *clause row sequences* and to distinguish various spans of discourse in terms of structure, content and style. The identification of these larger contexts also allows for a discussion of literary-critical difficulties which could not be solved at the clause row level of textual organization.

The manner in which these sequences of clause rows are redactionally related is the subject of Chapter Six. The conclusions reached in Chapter Six form the basis for describing immanent organizational principles which appear in the various clause row sequences (and their expansions). A description of these techniques appears in Chapter Two.

Chapter Two

LITERARY ORGANIZATION IN DEUTERONOMY 14:1–17:13

This chapter relies on the results obtained from the investigation of the literary unity of Deut 14:1–17:13 undertaken in Part Two. It will begin by reporting those results and then describe the literary organization of 14:1–17:13 based on them. The description will proceed in two parts. First, the techniques used to organize the primary layer in 14:22–17:10 will be described. Secondly, the techniques used to relate the secondary materials in 14:1–17:13 to the primary layer will be described. On this basis, an overview of the arrangement immanent in the present disposition of Deut 12:1–18:22 will be proposed.

Layers of Composition in Deuteronomy 14:1–17:13

A redaction history of Deut 14:1–17:13 can only be indicated in general terms. The reason for this is that the evidence uncovered in this study is not sufficient to determine the diachronic relationships between all of the materials which are secondary to the primary layer. The following broad redactional stages suggest themselves:

Primary layer. This span of text consists of the basic Dtn form of 14:22–23a, 24aα.aβ.b, 25–27aα.b, 28–29; 15:1–3, 19–23; 16:1–11, 13–20; 17:8–10. Outside of 14:1–17:13, other texts which belong to this layer include 12:13–19 and 18:1–8 more or less in their present forms. This span of material may be called the *mqwm sequence*, because its primary concern is with actions and journeys connected to the "place which Yahweh your God chooses." It cites a large amount of pre-Dtn material including: 14:22; 15:2aβ.b; 15:19*; 16:1aα.b*, 3aα, 3aβ*.b, 4a, 4b, 8*, 9–10aα, 13, 16aα.b, 19. The writer of the *mqwm* sequence did not take many pains to smooth over inconsistencies between his own formulations and the traditions he used. It would appear that he was conscious that he was citing such material (cf. 15:2; 16:19) and that he viewed his own program as one in continuity with their interests. Nevertheless, it is evident that the *mqwm* sequence is composed as a commentary on 12:13–19 and that its organization is not dependent on a single, pre-existing text or tradition.

Secondary redactions. As a rule, these texts are interested in describing the nature of the society that organizes itself around the *mqwm*. They are particularly interested in promoting cultural solidarity and distinctiveness. Diachronic discriminations within this group are difficult. This group includes 14:1–21; 14:23b; 15:4–6 (which is later than 15:7–18); 15:7–18; 16:12; 16:21–17:7; 17:11–13.

Copyists' additions. There are a number of small expansions which likely come from the later transmission tradition: *hšswʿh* in 14:7a; *whdyh* in 14:13; the bird names with *ʾt* in 14:12–18; 14:24aγ; 14:27aβ; 17:5aγ.

The Organization of the mqwm Sequence

The clause rows of the *mqwm* sequence in 14:22–17:10 include 14:22–23a, 24aαβ, 24b–27aα, 27b; 14:28–29; 15:1–3; 15:19–23: 16:1–8; 16:9–11; 16:13–15; 16:16–17; and 16:18–20 + 17:8–10. They are organized by the principles:

a) movement from the general to the particular[1]
b) chronology
c) arrangement by social group
d) association through the repetition of clauses, syntactic structure, and phrases
e) association by use of *Privilegrecht* traditions.

These principles are described below. Aside from (e), they are similar to patterns of organization found in Mesopotamian law identified by Petschow. These include the chronological principle, organization by importance or social importance, organization by frequency (the general situation being stated first), and organization by similar theme or catch word.[2]

a) Movement from the General to the Particular

The *mqwm* sequence examines the meaning of the requirements of a principle clause row in 12:13–19. This is demonstrated by the parallels which exist between the clause rows in the *mqwm* sequence and phraseology found in 12:13–19. Deut 12:13–19 is a Dtn statement which articulates the principle that no legitimate sacrificial action is to take place outside the *mqwm*. The

[1] This Dtn technique was observed previously by C. Carmichael in *The Laws of Deuteronomy*, 94–96. But, my account of its use in the *mqwm* sequence is often at variance with his.

[2] Petschow, "Zur Systematik und Gesetzestechnik im Codex Hammurabi," 170–71.

implications of this command for Israel's cultic and social life are subsequently explored in the *mqwm* sequence.

The sequence of 14:22–27 and 15:19–23 is a reflection of the requirement of *mʿśr dgnk wtyršk wyṣhrk wbkrt bqrk wṣʾnk* in 12:17. These two clause rows take the general instruction of 12:17 and explore its particulars. A number of rules regarding the cultic use of the *mqwm* are articulated in 16:1–17. They give particular focus to the general command to sacrifice only at the *mqwm* (cf. 16:5–6 and 12:17–18). It appears that the Dtn writer conceives of the three festivals mentioned as the context in which the people will discharge their required cultic activities at the *mqwm* as well as any voluntary offerings (16:10b, 17; cf. 12:17b).

The technique is also apparent in the relationship between 14:22–27; 28–29; 15:1–3; and 15:19–23. A general principle dealing with both tithes and firstlings is articulated in 14:22–27. The writer examines some specific implications of this principle in 14:28–29 (tithes) and 15:19–23 (firstlings). While a second mention of firstlings in 15:19–23 seems redundant after 14:23a, this clause row is meant to emphasize that blemished firstlings which cannot be driven to the *mqwm* come under the rules of profane slaughter in 12:15–16. Since 15:19–23 and 14:22–27 belong to the same layer of the text, the reader is probably meant to understand that compensation for a defective firstling is expected at the cult under the rules of 14:24–27.

Before dealing with the firstling problem, however, the tithing principle itself is explored from the point of view of social justice. The Dtn tithe law evidently will have an adverse effect on *personae miserae* who do not live near the *mqwm*. Deut 14:28–29 is written to deal with this problem.[3]

Movement from general to particular also defines in part the placement of 16:18–20. Interests of special groups are examined after interests of the group as a whole (cf. the placement of 14:28–29). By the same token, the interests of the special group of judges and their relationship to the *mqwm* are taken up after the interests of the group as a whole *vis à vis* the *mqwm* have been addressed. The placement of 16:18–20 also reflects a subclass of the movement from general to particular found in the movement from common to uncommon. The whole group commonly is engaged in fixed-time cultic celebrations (cf. 16:11, 14). It is less common for members of the group to journey to the *mqwm* on legal business.

The technique of stating a general principle and then developing it in detail is also found in the form of 14:22–27; 15:19–23; and 16:18–20 + 17:8–

[3] H. Jagersma, "The Tithes in the Old Testament," 127.

10. In these cases, a general principle is stated in the beginning of the clause row (14:22–23a; 15:19–20; 16:18–20). What follows is a conditionally introduced unit which examines a special case related to the general principle (14:24–27; 15:21–23; 17:8–10).

b) Chronology

The chronological principle explains why tithes and firstlings, which are annual offerings (*šnh šnh* cf. 14:22; 15:20), are placed before the row of festival regulations in 16:1–17 which affect thrice-yearly journeys. The chronological order between 14:22–27 and 14:28–29 is connected to the concern for the socially disadvantaged. Having established the principle in 14:28–29, 15:1–3 follows the triennial institution with a septennial institution for a similar purpose. The three pilgrim festivals in 16:1–15 are chronologically arranged.

Chronological considerations also affect the disposition of 16:18–20 + 17:8–10. The opposition between the group of institutions ending in 16:1–17 and 16:18–20 is that between those fixed in time and those not fixed in time. Evidently, the single largest category of cultic journey which was not fixed in time was that for the purposes of justice. For that reason, 16:18–20 follows 16:1–17. Unlike, the cultic regulations, however, the relationship with the *mqwm* is established only in the If-You construction of 17:8–10.

c) Organization by Social Group

The disposition of 14:28–29 with respect to 14:22–27 has been noted by Braulik: 14:22–27 concern *ʾth wbytk* and 14:28–29 concern the cause of those with a lower social status.[4] Another case of organization in this mode is implied in the fact that 16:18–20 precedes 18:1–8 in the *mqwm* sequence. It is assumed that the addressees of the *mqwm* sequence are not priests. Priestly concerns are addressed after those of the addressees (cf. the order of 12:18, 19 and 14:26bβ.27*).

d) Association by Repetition

Various repeated phrases and vocabulary help the cohesion of the clause rows in the *mqwm* sequence (see pp. 195–96). For example, the principle of association by repetition of clause elements and catchword helps to explain the placement of 15:1–3. Although the repetition is not exact, 14:28–29 and 15:1–3 are linked by the catchword phrase *mqṣh* / *mqṣ*. Repetitions also link

---

[4] Braulik, "Die Abfolge der Gesetze in Deuteronomium 12–26," 264.

clause rows in the *mqwm* sequence with 12:13–19. Besides the phrase-level repetitions which clause rows in the *mqwm* sequence share with 12:13–19 (see p. 196), the following syntactic parallels should be noted:

14:22–27. This clause row shares three structural parallels to 12:17–18:

1) the unusual word order of 14:23a where V and O are separated by an adverbial expression.

2) 14:24aβ has a 3ms pronominal suffix which resumes a plural referent (14:23aβ), as does the verb found in 12:18.

3) The motif of "eating before Yahweh in the place which he chooses" is found in 12:18; 14:23a and alluded to in 14:26bα. Deut 12:18 and 14:26 are parallel because both possess the pattern "eat before Yahweh . . . and rejoice."

16:1–8. Deut 16:5, 6 are related in the same way as 12:17–18: *lʾ twkl . . . šʿryk . . . ky ʾm . . . (h)mqwm.*

e) Association using Privilegrecht traditions

A *Privilegrecht* is a series of prescriptions and prohibitions which are given to the people in direct address either by Yahweh or his representative. Texts likely derived from pre-Dtn *Privilegrecht* traditions include 14:22; 15:19*; 16:1aα.b*, 3aα, 3aβ*.b, 4a, 4b, 8*, 9–10aα, 13, 16aα.b, 19. Such traditions have most obviously had an influence on the disposition of the festival laws in 16:1–17. This order is a traditional one as the parallels show. Reference to *Privilegrecht* tradition might also explain why 16:1–8 follows 15:19–23. An association of firstling and *mṣwt* laws can be found in Exod 13:1–16; 34:18–20. This association may be operative even if the prescriptive material used by the Dtn writer in 15:19 and 16:1–8. circulated independently.

The association of legal and cultic instructions is not uncommon in *Privilegrecht* traditions. The provisions of 14:28–29 and 16:18–20 can also be related to the articulation of the *Privilegrecht* which typically contains provisions for social justice as well as cultic obligations. Their placement, however, is not determined by a particular *Privilegrecht* tradition.

One can only speculate as to why the Dtn writer chose to use a selection of various independent traditions instead of only one. The tensions between 14:22 and 16:13 point to the probability that he did not have one cohesive pre-Dtn text which touched on all of the issues he wanted to address. It is difficult to be sure how the pre-Dtn traditions were available to the Dtn writer. The large number of citations suggest that the Dtn writer wanted his readers to identify his work as one in continuity with previous venerable institutions. A related explanation for the citation of pre-Dtn materials can be also advanced: The Dtn writer may be striving for an archaic effect, since *Privilegrecht* traditions typically relate their contents to the time of Moses. It would be important for a cultic innovator to show continuity with older traditions as well as to indicating how his program demands a new perspective for traditional practices.

Organization in Expansions of the mqwm Sequence

Clause Row Sequences

The model most helpful for explaining the placement of 14:1–21; 15:4–6, 7–18; 16:21–17:7 has been set out by Rofé. It is typical for those wishing to supplement ancient legal texts to do so at the beginning or end of a section of relevant material.[5]

14:1–21. Before addressing the placement of 14:1–21, it is necessary to state the case for seeing 14:21b as an intrinsic part of this clause row sequence. The text of 14:1–21 in its present form both begins and ends with a non-Dtn instruction (vv. 1, 21b). Identifiable Dtn motifs occur inside (vv. 2, 3, 21a). The structure of 16:1–8 is comparable, although 14:1–21 does not belong to the *mqwm* sequence. Deut 16:1 begins with a non-Dtn element (v. 1*) which is subsequently developed with Dtn terms; the text also ends with non-Dtn material in 16:8*. Therefore, a text like 14:1–21 has an analogue of sorts in Dtn composition. This means that the fact that 14:21b stands outside the inclusio created by 14:2, 21a does not necessarily argue for the presence of v. 21b as a secondary expansion of v. 21a.

Deut 14:21b was obviously understood as a food taboo at the time of its placement in 14:21b. It also belonged to the polemic against non-Israelite culture.[6] In the light of the literary ambiguities which surround the meaning and placement of 14:21b in this context, it is best to regard the clause as an original part of the composition of 14:1–21.

Two problems emerge when 14:1–21 is considered in the light of its larger context. First, 14:1–2 does not owe its present position to formal or lexical associations with the context of Deuteronomy 13. Secondly, it is not obvious why the writer of 14:1–2 then moved to classes of foodstuffs in 14:3–

---

5 Rofé, "Order of the Laws," 221.

6 E. Axel, "Zur Herkunft und Sozialgeschichte Israels. 'Das Böckchen in der Milch seiner Mutter,'" 167.

21. The motif of *twʿbh* is commonly associated with questions of apostasy in Deuteronomy, but there is no other Dtn context in which apostasy is conceived in terms of the violation of food laws.

Attempts to explain the presence of 14:3–21 in its current context typically focus on the motifs of *twʿbh* and holiness. Both 14:1–2 and vv. 3–21 deal with actions which concern these categories and, for that reason, they are mentioned together.[7] Such explanations, however, ignore the concrete problem of the text. Actions which are *twʿbh* are discussed in a number of places in Deuteronomy. The question is, why food here?

It appears that the presence of 14:3–21 is not dependent on the context which is prior to these verses, but on the context which follows it. In other words, 14:3–21 owe their position in the text to the fact that their writer was aware of the presence of a context dealing with foodstuffs which began with 14:22. The progression from food law in 14:3–21 to 14:22–27 can be explained by the assumption that the Dtn writer knew of 14:22–27 when 14:3–21 was composed. This mode of association can be contrasted with the principles of composition evident in the *mqwm* sequence. There is no evidence in the *mqwm* sequence of material preposed to the context which dictates its placement.

The connection between 14:1–2 and 14:3–21 lies in the notion of being a holy people. This entails the need to avoid contact with death (14:1, cf. the treatment of the *nblh* in 14:21a) and uncleanness. They are, therefore, to be distinct from other cultures. Deut 14:21a points to the use of food laws as a means to distinguish the *ʿm qdwš* from the *gr* and *nkry*. Differences in funerary practices would also contribute to the expression and production of Israel's separateness.[8]

In conclusion, Deut 14:1–21 can be regarded as a construction whose concern for separateness fits in between the anti-idolatry polemic in Deuteronomy 13 and the following concern for food offerings in 14:22–27. The placement of 14:1–21 is largely governed by the context of 14:22–27. Deut 14:22–27 deals with food consumption at the *mqwm*. The concern of 14:3–21 is that the chosen people maintain their holiness by strict observance of food laws. It was more convenient to insert 14:3–21 before 14:22 than to interrupt the relationships of 14:22–15:3. The same writer also regarded the avoidance of certain funeral customs as a mark of distinction. Deut 14:1–2 probably was placed before 14:3–21 because the context which gave rise to the insertion involved food (14:22–27).

---

[7] For example, Kaufman, "Structure," 127–28; Rofé, "Order of the Laws," 228.

[8] I owe this insight to a communication from Prof. P. E. Dion, University of Toronto.

The establishment of the context in which the insertion of 14:1–21a has been made allows judgments about the function of 14:21b in the discourse. Deut 14:21b has connections both with food taboos (as its current context indicates) and the rules of sacrifice (as its Exodus parallels indicate). Therefore, its placement in 14:21b between the rules of food consumption (14:21a) and rules for sacrifice (14:22–27) is not fortuitous. It is a transitional law which mediates between the context of 14:3–21a and what follows.

It has been suggested that 14:1–2 is a transitional law also.[9] If so, it functions primarily on an implicit combination of themes explored in Deuteronomy 13 and 14:3–21a. There are no structural or lexical links between the laws of 14:1–2 and Deuteronomy 13. But the juxtaposition of the themes of death and separation from the other nations in 14:1–2 might be a connecting link which leads from the context of Deuteronomy 13 to 14:3–21. Therefore, the position of 14:1–2 is analogous to 14:21b and suggests a similar strategy of composition in the placement of both.

15:7–18. It is likely that 15:7–18 followed directly on 15:1–3 at some point in the transmission of the text. But 15:7–11 and 12–18 do not belong to the *mqwm* sequence; they are secondary to it. They have been placed directly after the context they are related to. Associations between 15:7–11 and 15:1–3 appear in the repetition of the term *šmṭh* in 15:9. Another seven year institution of release is discussed in 15:12–18, a clause row composed by the same hand which wrote 15:7–11.

A particular problem in understanding the organization of 15:7–11 lies in determining the principles for the placement of 15:12–18. This clause row has some thematic relationships with 15:7–11 because of the motif of seven years (cf. 15:9, 12, 18). The question is whether any other principles are at work in connecting them.

It has been suggested that 15:1–23 is organized by motifs derived from the book of Exodus.[10] There are important associations between the core of 15:19 and Exod 13:1–16. These, however, are not merely associations by content but also associations of vocabulary and syntax. Visible signs of linkage with this same portion of the Exodus account are not apparent in 15:11–18. In fact, even the Exodus allusions in 15:9 (cf. Exod 22:24) and 15:12–18 (cf. Exod 21:2–6) are not in order. Therefore, it is not likely that

---

9 Rofé, "Order of the Laws", 228.

10 See, e.g., C. Carmichael, *Law and Narrative,* 83–85; Rofé, "Order of the Laws," 229.

Exodus motifs provide an explanation for the arrangement of materials within Deut 15:1–23.

Kaufman suggests that 15:1–19 shows an arrangement of subjects by their socioeconomic priority. In the case of 15:1–19, the progression is supposed to be "freemen-slaves-animals".[11] Organization by socioeconomic priority also appears in the Codex Hammurabi[12] and in the *mqwm* sequence (14:28–29).

The presence of socioeconomic arrangement in Deuteronomy is not always as clear as Kaufman represents it. Of the cases he cites, the lists breakdown as follow:

5:14	family, slaves, animals, stranger
15:1–18	free citizens, slaves, animals
16:11, 14	family, slaves, Levite-stranger-orphan-widow
19:1–22:8	institutions, free citizens, criminals, animals
24:8–25:4	Moses (levitical priests), non-poor debtor, poor debtor-hireling, indigent (stranger-orphan-widow), criminal, animal.[13]

These lists do not reveal in each case whether the arrangement is original or a redactional device. In favor of the second possibility: if *gr* in 5:14 belongs to the class of "indigents" (cf. 16:11, 14), then one notes a shift in position with respect to animals in the order of 24:8–25:4. Secondly, Eslinger has noted a thematic relationship between the laws of 25:4–12 which is enhanced by a chiastic structure. Carmichael has noted a chiastic arrangement which enhances the common concerns of the laws in Deuteronomy 21.[14] The analyses of Eslinger and Carmichael suggest inner relationships in these passages which claim a priority over the pattern in which Kaufman believes they participate. In this regard, it is also noteworthy that while 5:14; 16:11, 14 involve classes engaged in a single activity, this is not true of the examples in Deuteronomy 15; 19ff.; 24f.

The pattern which Kaufman has discovered is not exact enough to prove his hypothesis that 15:1–23 is a unified composition. Deut 15:19–23 belongs to the *mqwm* layer whereas 15:7–18 do not. Nevertheless, the arrangement of the lists of subjects in 5:14; 16:11, 14 is suggestive. In these lists, persons

---

[11] Kaufman, "Structure," 132–33.

[12] Petschow, "Zur Systematik und Gesetzestechnik im Codex Hammurabi," 171.

[13] Kaufman, "Structure," 132–33, 135, 141.

[14] L. Eslinger, "More Drafting Techniques in Deuteronomic Laws," 222–23; C. Carmichael, "A Common Element in Five Supposedly Disparate Laws," 139.

which belong to the household unit (in the order of family members, then slaves) are listed before those who do not (i.e., the Levite, the stranger, etc.). The transition from 15:7–11 to 15:12–18 is related to the concern to deal with slaves after dealing with free men. This is an arrangement by socioeconomic priority.

16:21–17:7. Deut 16:21–17:7 interrupts the more primary connection of 16:18–20 with 17:8–10. The relationships of 16:21 to its context are primarily cataphoric. There is a formal connection between 16:21–17:1 and 16:19 because of the threefold prohibition structure in each. It is also likely that 16:21 is linked to 16:19aα by the device of paronomasia (cf. *lʾ tṭh* in 16:19aα and *lʾ tṭʿ* in 16:21a).[15] Deut 16:21–17:1 acts to introduce 17:2–7 which concerns laws of evidence in the cases of idolatry *bšʿryk* (17:5). This insertion was made probably for thematic reasons. It is appropriate to address laws of evidence for cases in the cities before appeals to the *mqwm* are considered (17:8–10).

Deut 17:2–7 is noteworthy for its extensive intertextual references to Deuteronomy 13 which it appears to recapitulate and revise. It has often been suggested that 17:2–7 has been displaced from an original context in Deuteronomy 13.[16] This view has been thoroughly examined by Levinson and dismissed. The pericope has not been mechanically severed from an original context in Deuteronomy 13, but is designed to exegetically reformulate the conception of juridical powers found in 13:7–12. The indicator of this intentional revision is to be found in the contrast between 13:10aβ.b and 17:7. All hint of summary execution has been excised from the text of 13:10 in its revision in 7:7, which demands considered legal investigation which explicitly excludes the use of a single witness.[17]

Deut 17:2–7 is appropriate in its context given its concern for careful juridical investigation of such the charge of apostasy. Those most concerned with such exact legal procedure are the judges mentioned in 16:18–20. The imitation of the *Richterspiegel* form in 16:21–17:1 assigns the crime of apostasy to the purview of provincial judges. This represents another refinement to the context of Deuteronomy 13, because the identity of the investigators (cf. 13:13–18) is not established. Since the offense is considered

---

[15] Kaufman, "Structure," 155.

[16] See Preuss, *Deuteronomium*, 108.

[17] Levinson, *Hermeneutics of Innovation*, 380. See also P. E. Dion, "Deuteronomy 13: The Suppression of Alien Religious Propaganda in Israel during the Late Monarchical Era," 162.

to take place *bʾḥd šʿryk* (17:2) the provisions in 17:2–7 logically precede 17:8–10.

Redactionally, the placement of 16:21–17:1 after 16:18–20 and before 17:2–7 creates a particular interlocking structure with 16:1–17 which has been described by Rüterswörden and Braulik.[18] Rüterswörden's view depends on the claim that the linkage between 16:18–17:1 has at its core a cohesive clause row. This opinion is not supported by my study. Nevertheless, the pattern appears in the present disposition of the text:

16:1–17	cult	A
16:18–20	law	B
16:21–17:1	cult	A
17:2–7	law	B

Therefore, the transitional interests of 16:21–17:1 are clear. This includes not only cataphoric references to 17:2–7 but also repetition of phraseology from the cultic instructions such as 12:31 and 15:21.[19]

A comparison of the techniques of arrangement used in the secondary materials with those used in the *mqwm* layer is difficult because there are fewer clause rows, and they cannot be assumed to all come from the same hand. The use of repetitions and catchwords, and arrangement by socio-economic importance are the only two of the five principles of organization in the *mqwm* layer also used in the placement of secondary materials.

A feature not found in the *mqwm* sequence is the creation of transitional laws. Deut 16:21–17:1 creates an interlocking transitional structure between 16:18–20 and 17:2–7. Here, there here are structural similarities between 16:21–17:1a and the prior instructional context (cf. 16:19) as well as the prior theme: the cult (cf. 15:21); but there are also vocabulary links between 17:1 and 17:4, 5. Less formal bridging structures appear in 14:1–2 and 14:21b.

Additions to Clause Rows

Two forms of clause row additions can be identified:

a) There are exhortatory or paraenetic additions in 14:23b; 14:27aβ; 15:4–6; 16:12; and 17:11–13 (all of these have intertextual references to other contexts in Deuteronomy);

---

[18] U. Rüterswörden, *Von der politischen Gemeinschaft zur Gemeinde*, 29; Braulik, "Zur Abfolge der Gesetze in Deuteronomium 16,18–21,23," 64.

[19] Braulik, "Zur Abfolge der Gesetze in Deuteronomium 16,18–21,23," 71–72.

b) Glosses from parallel texts occur in 14:7a; 14:13; the bird names modified by *ʾt* in 14:12–18; 14:24aγ; 17:5aγ.

The large paraenetic discourse of 15:4–6 shows connection to its context by repetition as well as grammatically through the use of a conjunction. Deut 15:4–6 has been inserted between 15:1–3 and 7–11. Its contribution to the context is as a commentary on the *šmṭh* instructions. The juxtaposition of the word *ʾbywn* in 15:4 with *šmṭh* legislation suggests the writer of 15:4–6 was aware of the fallow year tradition in Exod 23:11. The word *ʾbywn* is uncommon in the Pentateuch. It is confined to Exod 23:6, 11; Deut 15:4, 7, 9, 11; 24:14. The rarity of the use of *ʾbywn* and its appearance in two contexts which seek to establish septennial institutions for the relief of the socially disadvantaged is striking. It indicates that the time frame in 15:1 was connected to other sabbatical traditions by the writer of 15:4–6.

Deut 17:11–13 is an extensive paraenetic addition to 17:8–10 connected by various repetitions. The intention of this paraenesis is to encourage obedience to the instruction of the central authorities and to sanction disobedience with capital punishment. Thus, there are formal relationships between 17:11 and 17:2–7 (cf. 17:7 and 17:11–12) as well as with 17:8–10.

Other exhortatory or motivational elements are connected to their contexts principally by conjunctions: 14:23b; 16:12. The least grammatically integrated text is 14:27aβ. This is a repetition of terms found 12:19. Its integration in the context is made by the referential value of the pronominal suffix on *tʿzbnw*.

The Literary Logic of Deuteronomy 12:1–18:22

A reasonable solution to the present disposition of Deut 12:1–18:22 can be made on the observation that the instructions of the *mqwm* sequence in 14:22–18:8 develop the principle articulated in Deut 12:13–19. They are addressed to three classes which can be divided according to social membership:

a) 2ms instructions which *all* of those addressed by the *mqwm* sequence are required to observe (14:22–15:3, 19–23; 16:1–17);

b) 2ms instructions which *some* of those addressed by the *mqwm* sequence must observe (16:18–20 + 17:8–10), namely, those who are appointed as judges and court officials.

c) 3ms instructions for a group to which *none* of the second person addressees of the *mqwm* sequence belong (18:1–8), namely, members of the priestly tribe.

In other words, a major principle which governs the organization of the *mqwm* sequence is that of *all, some, and none*, based upon membership in social groups in Israel. This inner logic is used by the various clause rows of the *mqwm* sequence in 14:22–18:8 as they develop the primary command (12:13–19) to centralize sacrifice at the place Yahweh will choose. This division can be extrapolated to embrace all of 12:1–18:22. There are three major blocks of material in 12:1–18:22 based on the backbone of *mqwm* instructions and organized by the principle of all, some, and none: 12:1–16:17; 16:18–17:20; 18:1–22.

The writer of the *mqwm* sequence recognizes two tribal divisions in Israel: those who traditionally received a patrimony of land during the conquest, and the priestly tribe which did not. Throughout the 2ms instructions, it is clear that the writer does not consider members of the priestly tribe to belong to the group of 2ms addressees. By the same token, the clause row which addresses the rights of the priests and Levites in 18:1–8 is the only one in the *mqwm* sequence in which the majority of instructions are predicated in the third person (except for the 2ms instruction to the offerer in v. 4). Some members of the land-holding tribes, however, hold a special office which will bring them into occasional contact with the legitimate cult center other than during regular pilgrimages. They are those appointed from the group of 2ms addressees as judges and officers. Hence the logic of arrangement by social location: instructions relevant to all the 2ms addressees precede instructions addressed to some from this group. These are followed by instructions to that part of Israel which has the least affinity with the land-owning tribes of Israel—the priestly tribe.

An account of the logic of the present disposition of 12:1–18:22 can begin with the observation that Deut 12:2–19 consists of three clause rows whose major concern is to limit legitimate sacrifice to "the place which Yahweh chooses." The first two clause rows are written in the 2mpl (vv. 2–7, 8–12). Each ends with the instruction *wśmḥtm lpny yhwh ʾlhyk* and includes a list of subjects for that verb (12:7aβ, 12). Deut 12:13–19 is written in the 2ms. These instructions conclude with a parallel list of subjects (12:18a), ending with a *wśmḥt* clause in 12:18b and a demand to look after the Levite, who also ends the list of subjects in 12:12. These three clause rows, therefore, represent a thrice repeated demand to confine all legitimate sacrifice to the "place which Yahweh chooses": the *mqwm*.

Other clause rows which mention the *mqwm* seek to develop this primary demand and explore its various implications. These clause rows include 12:20–28; 14:22–27; 15:19–23; 16:1–8; 9–12; 13–17; 16:18–20 + 17:8–13; and

18:1–8. One relationship which exists between this material and the primary commands in 12:2–19 is that between general commands (12:2–19) and particular developments of it in subsequent *mqwm* instructions. Not all these developments are of the same order in terms of the structure of the text. Dtn instructions tend to develop a theme in some detail before returning to a more primary element in the sequence. For example, 14:22–27 and 15:19–23 show an equivalency in terms of topic: eating sacred imposts at the *mqwm*. But before taking up 15:19–23, the writer first explores the subtheme of care for persons disadvantaged by the regulations of 14:22–27 in 14:28–29. This in turn leads to 15:1–3.

The contents of 12:2–19 show that restriction of legitimate sacrifice to this single cult place carries a number of implications. First, all sacrifice outside the legitimate site is considered idolatrous and alien to the values of Israelite culture. Secondly, provisions must be made for the profane slaughter of animals used for food. Thirdly, there are socially disadvantaged persons who must be cared for by those who are obligated to bring their offerings to the legitimate cult site.

The major concerns of Deut 12:20–13:19 are to address the need to avoid illegitimate sacrifice. This can be seen from the way in which Deuteronomy 11, 12, and 13 are formally linked to each other as well as from their contents. There is a frame attaching Deuteronomy 12 to Deuteronomy 11 consisting of 11:31–32 and 12:1, 29. This frame is of a piece with both 12:2–7 and 12:29–31. Deut 12:28; 13:1, 19 link Deut 13:2–18 with Deuteronomy 12.[20] In these frames, Torah observance is closely linked to the need to avoid idolatry and apostasy. The order of discussion in Deut 12:20–13:19 proceeds from legitimate to illegitimate practices. The concern for profane slaughter is treated in 12:20–28, which develops a theme found in 12:13–19. The text then addresses the issue of illegitimate sacrifice and idolatry in 12:29–13:19, a theme which its frame links with the material in 12:2–12.

Deut 14:1–21 develops the concerns of the framework linking Deuteronomy 12 and 13. Since idolatry is associated with death (cf. 13:6, 10, 16), the concern to avoid death frames Deuteronomy 14, as it occurs in 14:1, 21a (i.e., the *nblh*). With prohibitions which touch on both food preparation and illegitimate cultic rites, 14:1–21 acts as a transitional section between Deuteronomy 13 and 14:22–27.

---

[20] Dion, "Deuteronomy 13," 158.

Deut 14:22–27; 15:19–23; 16:1–17 all deal with required journeys to the legitimate cult center. They look past the intervening material to 12:13–19 to develop other implications of the choice of the single cult place after the prohibition against illegitimate sacrifice has been explored in detail. The journeys of 14:22–27; 15:19–23; and 16:1–17 are determined by the agricultural calendar or portions of it. There are journeys that happen annually (14:22–27; 15:19–23) and thrice annually (16:1–17). Probably the annual imposts of 14:22–27 and 15:19–23 were brought during one of the thrice annual festivals of 16:1–17.

Special provisions appear in 14:28–29 to ameliorate social hardships that may be caused by the transport of all tithes to the cult place. This is followed by a seven-year institution also calculated to provide relief for the poor. The pattern running between 14:22–15:6 is one year, three years, and seven years. Rules related to financial relief at the end of seven years follow in 15:7–11 and 15:12–18 which are arranged by order of socioeconomic priority. The theme of relief of the disadvantaged stemming from the demands of 14:22–27 is examined in detail in 14:28–15:18 before returning to the mention of another annual impost related to the *mqwm* (15:19–23), which goes back to 14:22–27 and ultimately to 12:17–18.

The theme of journey is also prominent in 17:8–10; 18:1–8. These journeys, however, are not determined by the agricultural year or cultic calendar. Deut 16:18–20 contain various details which signal a shift in topic. Formal elements include the use of a preposed object in 16:18a,[21] and the unusual redundancy of the terms *bkl šʿryk* and *lšbṭyk*. The motif of the tribal distribution of the addressees is found previously in the *mqwm* sequence only in 12:14. Therefore, the vocabulary of 16:18 indicates a shift in topic which looks past the festival regulations of 14:22–16:17 to the first clause row of the sequence, 12:13–19.

There can be no question that 16:18 introduces a new block of material, in effect, a new kind of journey. Another indication of the fact that this legislation shows itself conscious of a new beginning in the explication of 12:13–19 is probably to be found in the presence of 16:21–17:7. These latter verses reiterate the responsibility of the judges to control those who might practice illegitimate cultic acts. So, there is an analogue between the discussion of legitimate and illegitimate actions as described in 16:18–17:7 and the development of 12:13–19 by 12:29–13:19.

---

[21] Braulik, "Zur Abfolge der Gesetze in Deuteronomium 16,18–21,23," 64.

Deut 16:18–20 distinguishes itself not only topically from what precedes, but also chronologically. In the case of litigation, the journey is not determined by chronological necessity, but occurs on an ad hoc basis. Therefore, another polarity mediating 14:22–16:17 and 16:18–20 is that between events fixed and non-fixed with regard to time. The ad hoc nature of the journey is clear from 17:8–13. Since the relationship between 16:18–20 and 17:8–13 participates in the pattern of movement from the general situation to the special case, the provisions of 16:18–20 precede those of 17:8–13. But the connection between 16:18–20 + 17:8–10 and prior journey instructions is found in 17:8–13. This pattern continues in the next *mqwm* text: 18:1–8. Here also, instructions for the journey to the *mqwm* occur in the conditional subsection and are not fixed with regard to time (18:6–8).

Concern for special groups inside the body politic is not unprecedented in the *mqwm* sequence, as 14:28–15:6 shows. Their interests and relationships emerge as topics worthy of definition, primarily in connection with journeys to the *mqwm*. The special interests of judge and Levite come to the fore when journeys not fixed by time are discussed. Judges come before Levites because of the possibility of overlap between the primary group of addressees and the group of judges. Evidently, it is assumed that the majority of the persons addressed by the *mqwm* sequence will not journey to the *mqwm*, outside fixed times of cultic observance. But the situation is different when difficult legal disputes arise. Ad hoc journeys can be expected in such events, whether the class of parties resorting to the *mqwm* was then restricted to the judge group or involved the complainant and defendant as well.

Organization from common to uncommon in terms of social position is characteristic of the material running from 16:18–18:22. The first group, consisting of officers and judges, is drawn from the same group as are addressed by 2ms instructions in other *mqwm* rows because 2ms instructions predominate in 16:18–20. The king mentioned in 17:14–20 belongs to the same group although he is mentioned in the 3ms. The king is to be chosen "from the midst of your brethren" *mqrb ʾḥyk*. The book of Deuteronomy is notable for its efforts at social leveling.[22] As a member of one of the tribes of land-owning Israel, it is understandable why the rules for the king precede those for members of the priestly tribe (18:1–8). As a much rarer office holder among the land-owning tribes, it is logical why the king follows the judges.

---

[22] J. G. McConville, *Law and Theology in Deuteronomy*, 19.

The association between the priest and the diviners in 18:9–13 also rests on the movement from regular to irregular, including legitimate to illegitimate. In this case, the movement goes from a group of legitimate cultic mediators to a group of illegitimate cultic mediators (18:9–13). There is a parallel in the structure of 16:18–17:7 and 18:1–13. In both cases, notices about a particular office holder represent some new juncture in the movement of the *mqwm* sequence. The motif of tribal affiliation in 18:1 recalls the vocabulary of 16:18 and 12:14. In both cases, the relationship with 12:13–19 implies the need to avoid illegitimate cultic activities, cf. 12:29–13:19, 16:21–17:7, and 18:9–13.

The last legitimate member of the Israelite community is presumably also the rarest and least identified with the predominant group of 2ms addressees: the prophet. Presumably this sort of second Moses (cf. 18:15, 18) is expected to be a member of the priestly tribe. This is suggested by the fact that 18:14–22 follows instructions to the priests in 18:1–8, that references to the prophet are also in the third person (cf. 18:15, 20, 21), and by the traditional tribal affiliation of Moses, although the phrases *mqrbk m'ḥyk* in v. 15 are ambiguous (see also v. 18 and cf. 17:15). In any event, the prophet is characterized by a unique capacity to perceive the *dbr yhwh* which is not given to ordinary cultic functionaries. Hence the organization of Deuteronomy 18 moves from the common (vv. 1–13) to the uncommon type of cultic intermediary (vv. 14–22) and from the legitimate (vv. 1–8, 14–19) to the illegitimate (vv. 9–13, 20–22).

The preceding description provides a basis for proposing a rationale behind the present arrangement of all of Deuteronomy 12–18. The fact that the principle of "all, some, and none" does not seem to continue into Deuteronomy 19–25 suggests some kind of literary tension between chapters 12–18 and the composition of what follows. Such literary tensions can be explained on the model of Braulik's thesis that Deuteronomy 19–25 has been organized by a *relecture* of Dtn law using the Ten Commandments which did not affect the organization of Deuteronomy 12–18 to the same degree.[23]

---

[23] Braulik, "Die Abfolge der Gesetze in Deuteronomium 12–26," 271–272.

Part Two

The Redaction of Deuteronomy 14:1–17:13

Chapter Three

A Method for Analyzing Literary Unity in Clause Rows

The goal of this method is twofold. First, it intends to describe the literary form of a given clause row. Second, it intends to analyze the clause row for evidence that an earlier, literary form of the text has been modified. Evidence for such modification typically occurs where a logical relationship between a referential item and its referent appears to break down. Consequently, a description of the references in a given text on the levels of clause and clause constituent structure provides a control for the discovery of such inconsistencies. Referential inconsistencies may occur within a particular clause row or become apparent through a study of structural and semantic parallels to other texts.

Clause Row Identification

The term clause row is roughly analogous to the concept of paragraph in English. But I have refrained from using a technical term to denote this level of textual organization since it remains a matter of debate as to what larger units of syntax in BH beyond the clause consist of, or ought to be called.[1] Nevertheless, it can be shown that the text does fall into collections of clauses which are connected by shared vocabulary and grammatical referents.

Identification of clause rows for preliminary investigation follows the spacing used in standard manuscripts of the MT. The MT has been transmitted with a system of spacing known as the *pətûḥôt* (Pet) and the *sətûmôt* (Set). Recent research has argued that the use of these divisions in the Torah is principally governed by considerations of sense and content.[2] The present system may have been standardized as early as the first century CE in the case of the Torah.[3]

---

[1] F. I. Andersen, *The Sentence in Biblical Hebrew,* 23. The unit of grammatical analysis above the clause level is called *Satzreihe* in German; see Richter, *Exegese,* 86.

[2] C. Perrot, "Petuhot et Setumot," 81.

[3] J. M. Oesch, *Petucha und Setuma,* 364.

The system of Pet and Set is not worked out thoroughly in narrative prose. Therefore, the identification of clause rows for preliminary analysis in BH prose or in other unmarked material would have to proceed on a different basis. But these text divisions do appear regularly in the legal materials.[4] They tend to correspond to shifts related to the object which is the theme of the actions commanded. This is a good criterion for dividing texts involving procedural discourse.[5] As the oldest attested divisions on record, these ancient clause row distinctions were taken as the information units to be initially examined.

Aesthetic concerns, however, can affect the disposition of Set units. In the case of 14:1–21, preference for the number three seems to have prevented a distinction between the instructions regarding clean birds in 14:11–18 and the *nblh* in 14:21a. A division of 14:3–8; 9–10; 11–20; 21 would have resulted in four sections related to unclean food rather then three, although elsewhere the Set tradition is assiduous in separating distinct objects. For example, 16:21 and 16:22 are separated despite the fact that they are coordinated by *waw*. Another case occurs in the division of festival rules in 16:1–17. On the basis of chronology and theme, a case can be made for the division 16:1–8; 9–12; 13–15; 16–17. The present divisions of 16:1–8; 9–12; 13–17 seem to be justified by the preference for threefold subsections as also occur in 14:3–21. An explanation will be given when deviation from the Set tradition seems called for.

Transcription and Translation

The clause rows of Deut 14:1–17:13 are reproduced in transcription and translation. The transcribed text is based on the edition of BHS. Where text-critical evidence suggests that a shorter text can be recovered than the one attested in MT, that text is presented in the transcription. Nevertheless, this does not imply a diminution of the value of the later text. In keeping with recent discussions on the relationship between the *traditum* and the *traditio*, evidence of the work of the *traditio* is not dismissed simply as later glossing, but is accorded its significance as a distinct and important stage in the composition of the text.[6]

---

[4] Perrot, "Petuhot et Setumot," 91.

[5] R. E. Longacre, "The Discourse Structure of the Flood Narrative," 98.

[6] See M. Fishbane, *Biblical Interpretation in Ancient Israel*, 42.

A transcription is used to display the understanding of the exegete regarding clause syntax.[7] The transcription used here is only of the consonantal text. This is due to the fact that my exegetical method concerns itself mainly with analysis at the constituent level of clause structure (as opposed to word-level phenomena). The translation is meant to act as a kind of philological commentary on the transcription and, along with the accompanying notes, serves as a justification for my understanding of various details of the clause structures of Deut 14:1–17:13.

Clause Level Analysis. A clause is defined as a grammatical construction which possesses a *clause predicator*, either a verbal or, in the case of the so-called verbless clause, a nominal group functioning as a clause predicator.[8] A single clause, therefore, consists of all the phrases or words related to each other by a clause predicator. Ideally, each clause should occupy its own line. But this is not possible because of the phenomenon of embedded nominalized clauses as well as because of space limitations. There is no intention to break up clauses in order to aid the study of rhetorical devices such as parallelism, although certain word clusters or phrases, often punctuated by pausal forms, are accorded some linear relationships in the transcription.

The Class column, which is closest to the transcribed text, classifies each clause in terms of its type of predication. The following classes of clause predication in BH are distinguished:

a) Verbal Clause (Vc): the clause predicator is a verbal (V) appearing as the first constituent in the clause. A negated Vc is indicated by the symbol: xVc.

b) Inverted Verbal Clause (IVc): the verbal clause predicator is not the first constituent in the clause. A negated IVc is indicated by the symbol: xIVc.

c) Verbal Clauses in Sequence (*wqtl* / *wyqtl*): In view of their distribution in Deut 14:1–17:13, it would be incorrect to consider uncoordinated Vc constructions in independent (free) clauses on par with *wqtl* clauses. Free, positive Vc constructions unmarked by *waw* are rare and have the form of the free infinitive (14:21aδ; 15:2aβ; 16:1), the imperative (15:9aα), or the indicative verb form modified by the free infinitive (14:22; 15:8a, 10aα, 14). Such Vc constructions always play a more significant part in the structure of the discourse than *wqtl* clauses.

---

[7] W. Richter, *Transliteration und Transkription*, 3.

[8] This definition is taken from W. Richter, *Grundlagen einer althebräischen Grammatik* 3, §2.1.2.1.2.3.

d) Noun Clause (Nc): the clause is a verbless clause.

e) Complex Noun Clause (CNc): the clause in question consists of a fronted clause constituent (other than the subject) before a clause in which it does not appear as an argument.[9]

f) Participle (Part): the clause predicator is a participle. Other exegetes tend to reduce Part clauses to a type of Vc or Nc.[10] From the point of view of surface analysis, however, Part clauses are formally distinct.

g) Infinitive (Inf): this is a special type of Vc construction in which the clause predicator is an infinitive. Depending on the clause, the predicator may be either a free or bound Inf.

h) Imperative (Imp): the clause predicator is an imperative. The only example in Deut 14:1–17:13 occurs in 15:9aα.

This schema falls short of more abstract and systematic models of analysis which seek to reduce clause typology to variants of either the class of verbal clauses or nominal clauses. One reason I have not done this is to facilitate the analysis of clause row structure. It is clear that a shift in clause types is an important element in the composition of rows of instructions. For example, Part constructions are not randomly placed in a span of clauses (cf. 15:11, 15) but appear at important junctures in the flow of discourse. The second reason I have resisted reduction of clause typology to a more systematic model is due to my attempt to avoid identification with any particular school of syntactic abstraction.

Fundamental to the description of clause class in BH is the distinction between the class of Free clauses (F) and Bound clauses (B). B clauses are signaled by the use of morphemes which are traditionally described in the grammar of BH as subordinating conjunctions or particles, e.g., *ky*, *ʾm*, *lmʿn*, etc. These bound structures can be regarded as the constituents of sentences whose predicate is in an F (independent) clause. By way of contrast, F

---

9 The term "Complex Noun clause" comes from E. Talstra, "Text Grammar and Hebrew Bible 1," 169–70. The definition used here is that given for "focus marking" in O'Connor, *Verse Structure*, 306–7. The definition of what constitutes a CNc is a grey area in BH grammar. Talstra would identify this construction on formal grounds whenever a nominal group precedes a verb in a clause, even if it is only a case of a fronted subject. For this study, however, cases of fronted constituents which fall short of the definition of O'Connor will be described as IVc following the discussion of Richter in *Grundlagen* 3:223–24.

10 For Part clauses as Vc, see O'Connor, *Verse Structure*, §3.2.4. For Part clauses as Nc, see Richter, *Grundlagen* 3:12, 79, 84.

clauses are not subordinated to another predication structure.[11] F clauses can be linked by coordination (Co) with other F clauses in the text. Special cases of Co include the clause sequence patterns known as the *wyqtl* and *wqtl* types.[12]

There are also clauses which are embedded in their respective sentences to a different degree than B clauses. That is, they are not imbedded in another clause structure simply by the presence of a subordinating conjunction.[13] These clauses are nominalized clauses, classified here by the symbol N. Clauses in the N class include those used to modify a nominal group (mainly of the *ʾšr* type), participial constructions which govern an object (including a pronominal suffix acting as the object) or prepositional phrase while modifying a clause constituent, clauses standing as an object or subject of a clause predicator (including direct quotation), as well as bound Inf clauses. Where a clause is embedded in another clause, acting in effect as if it were a nominal, this is noted by indenting the embedded clause in the transcription. Apart from embedded clauses, no attempt is made to distinguish clauses on the basis of parataxis or hypotaxis in the transcription. This lack of distinction is typical in published transcriptions.[14] Clauses which contain N clauses are sometimes referred to herein as *complex* clauses, as opposed to *simple* clauses which do not contain embedded clauses. This distinction can be important in a typological description of clause row structure.

F and B clauses are identified by verse number (e.g., 15:1; 16:10). If there is more than one F or B clause in the verse, then the verse divisions suggested by the Masoretic accents are also used (e.g., 15:7a, 7bα, 7bβ). N clauses are marked by the prime sign as well as by the relevant Masoretic verse division (e.g., 16:10aβ'). Where more than one N clause is found in a verse division, the prime sign is doubled or even tripled (e.g., 16:9b''; 15:5b'''). An explanation will be offered where the clause divisions in the transcription are in conflict with the system of punctuation in the MT.

Clause Constituent Analysis. The second column beside the transcription describes each clause according to its constituent structure. Any Hebrew

---

11 S. Dempster, *Linguistic Features of Hebrew Narrative*, 28–29.

12 Talstra, "Text Grammar and Hebrew Bible 1," 170–72.

13 This distinction in types of clause subordination is based on F. I. Andersen, *The Hebrew Verbless Clause in the Pentateuch*, 29.

14 See, e.g., the model transcriptions of Richter throughout *Transliteration und Transkription*; also, the transcription of Deuteronomy 4 by Braulik in the endpapers of *Die Mittel deuteronomischer Rhetorik*.

clause possesses a surface structure which can be represented with a few symbols. At the most basic level, these consist of symbols such as NP (noun phrase), PP (prepositional phrase), and V (verbal). An interest of traditional phrase structure grammars, as well as many newer approaches, is to resolve the ciphers NP, PP, and V into more elaborate systems of semantic relationships.[15]

My attempt at representing constituent structure is a hybrid system of structural and semantic categories. At its base are the symbols NP, PP and V. At the same time, however, I also want to describe cohesive relationships between clauses. Therefore, common semantic functions such as subject (conventionally = agent), object (conventionally = patient, or direct complement), and adverb (locatives) emerge as important ones to note. Grammarians generally recognize these common semantic functions, although they systematize them differently. Such a hybrid system is useful because it presents a good deal of information about syntactic structure in a reasonably abbreviated form. At the same time, marking only some but not all constituents by their semantic functions avoids privileging a particular grammatical theory as the preferred description of all Hebrew syntactical phenomena.

The syntagm object is indicated in a number of fashions:

O the object is a noun phrase ungoverned by a preposition;
Po the object is governed by a preposition;
V+O the object occurs as a pronominal suffix on the verb.

An adverb is often defined as a time, place, or manner phrase. Here, the syntagm adverb is restricted to time and space phrases (locatives). There is evidence that manner phrases can be resolved into more than one syntagm.[16] Consequently, manner phrases are marked by either Np (for a noun phrase which does not belong to the syntagms S, O, or A) or P (if governed by a preposition). Adverbial phrases are identified by the symbols A or Pa, depending on whether they are governed by a preposition or not.

In the case of the large number of prepositional phrases (P), it was advisable to distinguish certain classes of P in order to point out that not all

---

15 This is clearly the case, e.g., in Richter's grammar (*Grundlagen* 3:41). Richter's system of syntagms is a set of semantic slots derived from the concepts of dependency grammar with which to classify various combinations of V, NP, and PP constructions.

16 Ibid. Nevertheless, I have not followed Richter in distinguishing between locatives and dislocatives. Insistence on formal grounds for establishing structural repetitions made this distinction unnecessary.

cases of P fill the same grammatical slot or govern the same kind of construction. The description distinguishes the following cases from the general class P:

Pa the preposition governs an adverb, a time or place indicator;
Po the preposition governs the object of the verb;
Pc the preposition governs an N clause, usually predicated by an Inf.

Clause Row Structure

Each analysis of clause row organization begins with a description of elements implicated in the structural cohesion of the clause row. This system of formal references I have called outer structure. These references are used to propose relationships between strings of clauses in terms of their communication function, or what I have termed inner structure. As a result, the clause row can be divided into various sections. The discussion ends with a synthesis of these observations made in a tabular form.[17]

Outer Structure. Structural cohesion can be considered to be a function of grammatical and lexical references which organize the text. The following scheme of references draws on the work of the systemic-functional linguist M. A. K. Halliday:[18]

- A. Grammatical
  - 1. Structural (clause conjunctions)
    - a) Dependence
    - b) Coordination
  - 2. Nonstructural
    - a) Anaphora
      - i) deictics and submodifiers
      - ii) pronouns
    - b) Substitution
      - i) verbal
      - ii) nominal
- B. Lexical
  - 1. Repetition of item
  - 2. Occurrence of item from same lexical set

Halliday's category of grammatical structural indicators of clause row cohesion can be readily applied to BH. A detailed account of the categories he classifies as grammatical, but nonstructural, is set out by Schneider.[19] The virtue of Schneider's system is that it is specifically interested in clause row cohesion in BH prose. Typically, a text of BH carries both anaphoric and

[17] Richter, *Exegese*, 82–98.

[18] M. A. K. Halliday, "Descriptive Linguistics in Literary Studies," 72.

[19] W. Schneider, *Grammatik des biblischen Hebräisch*, §§52–54.

cataphoric referents. In other words, the reader is oriented at each step of a continuous, running text by observing and combining various indicators of meaning and relationship. These signs may point backwards to already mentioned material (anaphoric) or forward to anticipate new material (cataphoric). Among the word groups which possess these reference functions on a grammatical level are (a) pronouns, suffixes, and nouns used as pronouns; (b) deictic particles and conjugation morphemes; and, (c) the article.[20]

A list of the indicators of structural cohesion within the clause rows of Deut 14:1–17:13 appears in the Appendix. The descriptive criteria are adapted from those used by Halliday. Arranged by the clause rows marked in the MT, the chart is concerned with cohesion within clause rows and does not consider cohesion above the clause row level. It uses the following categories:

Cl. Clause. The clauses listed are the F and B clauses in the text. Cohesive items in N clauses are considered to belong to the larger clause structure in which they occur.

Ties. Each clause with a cohesive item is considered to be formally tied to the clause row. The number of ties for each clause are counted in this column.

Cohesive item. Each cohesive item is identified as it appears in the text. So, for example, the inseparable conjunction *w* is cited along with the word it is attached to. Cohesion is considered to involve grammatically identifiable parts of speech, such as conjunctions and pronominal references, ellipsis, matching between contiguous clauses, and repetition between nominals and verbals showing similar form and grammatical embedding.

Type. Cohesive items are classified using the criteria adapted from Halliday and Hasan in *Cohesion in English*. The abbreviations used are:

C.1 Coordinating conjunction.

C.2 Subordinating conjunction.

Pr.1 A pronominal reference used as the subject of the listed clause.

Pr.2 A pronominal reference used as the object of a verbal or preposition in the listed clause.

D Deictic reference (e.g., the article).

E Ellipsis of a verbal or nominal used as a clause constituent.

---

[20] Ibid., 231–32.

Sub Substitution. The word *kn* in 15:17b is an example of clause substitution.

Ma Matching of clause constituent structure in contiguous clauses.[21] Examples include 14:8bα, 8bβ; 14:9b, 10a; 15:6bγ, 6bδ; 16:7bα, 7bβ; 16:19aα, 19aβ, 19bα.

L Lexical reiteration. Repetition of lexical items and the presence of words with similar semantic associations contribute to clause cohesion.[22] I have adapted Halliday and Hasan's model in the interests of structural description by limiting its use to items identical on either the clause level or clause constituent level of discourse. Lexical cohesion between non-contiguous clauses is allowed in this analysis because all other forms of formal reference (with the exception of matching) also occur between non-contiguous clauses.

Two forms of lexical reference are taken into account: repetition and collocation. Lexical repetition in Deut 14:1–17:13 involves both verbs and nouns. Repeated nomina may differ in number, state or suffixation (but not definiteness). Repeated verbals possess the same *binyan* but may differ in person and affixation.[23] Pronoun repetition was not considered to be a category of lexical cohesion. Repetition between repeated nomina was not considered structural if the preposition was not the same. An exception was made in the case of the syntagm O, where the identity of O and Po was allowed (cf., e.g., 15:6bα and 15:6bγ).

Another kind of lexical cohesion is the phenomenon Halliday and Hasan call reiteration by collocation.[24] This category includes synonyms and antonyms which are identical in constituent structure and embedding. Similar phenomena are known in the analysis of BH poetry through the concept of the breakup of stereotypical word pairs, or "coloration."[25] Such features can also be observed in BH prose.[26]

---

[21] Matching is a prominent feature of clause row cohesion in biblical poetry. See O'Connor, *Verse Structure*, §1.5.6. But Dempster also found matching playing a part in the structural organization of BH narrative prose; see *Linguistic Features of Hebrew Narrative*, 85.

[22] Halliday and Hasan, *Cohesion in English*, §6.2.

[23] O'Connor, *Verse Structure*, §4.1.

[24] Halliday and Hasan, *Cohesion in English*, §6.4.

[25] See O'Connor, *Verse Structure*, §5. O'Connor's categories have been extended and qualified by P. E. Dion in *Hebrew Poetics*2, §6.2.

[26] Y. Avishur notes that "although the phenomenon of word pairs is dominant in Ancient Semitic poetic verse, it is not absent in prose." See his *Stylistic Studies of Word-*

Dist Distance. This column refers to the number of F and B clauses between the occurrence of an item and its reference.[27]

1 The reference and the presupposed item occur in contiguous clauses.

N.# The reference and the presupposed item are separated (non-mediated) by at least one clause. N.2 marks a reference two clauses away from its referent, separated by one clause, etc.

M.# The reference occurs in a string of contiguous clauses (mediated). M.1 marks the first cohesive item in a string one clause away from its referent. M.2 marks the second reference, now distant from the antecedent by two clauses, etc.

K The reference is cataphoric. Because clauses, rather than sentences are the basic unit of analysis, my use of the category of K for marking coordination is not the same as Halliday and Hasan's. The particle *ky* is considered cataphoric when it marks the protasis of a conditional construction.[28]

Presupposed item. This column refers to the item presupposed by the cohesive item. Conjunctions are regarded as having an entire clause as the cohesive reference. Exact lexical repetitions are considered to be self evident and are not usually listed in this column when only one clause apart.

Inner Structure. The tabular model of clause row organization at the end of the discussion of discourse structure involves a typology of the communication function of the clauses in the clause row.[29] The typology uses a terminology which also occurs in discussions of the genre membership of various kinds of BH instructions. It is important, therefore, to be able to distinguish the concern of the description of inner structure from the discussion of parallels below. While generic terminology is used to describe

---

Pairs in Biblical and Ancient Semitic Literatures, 1.

27 My analysis of distance differs from that of Halliday and Hasan (cf. *Cohesion in English*, 339). They mark distance as a function of the number of clauses intervening between a referential item and its referent. I have found it simpler to mark the number of clauses the referential item is away from the one carrying the referent.

28 Cf. Halliday and Hassan, *Cohesion in English*, §5.6. They consider conditional particles to operate at the sentence level of grammatical organization and not above. It is above the sentence level that the reference system described in *Cohesion in English* is supposed to work.

29 This form of analysis is related to Richter's concept of inner structure. According to Richter (*Exegese*, 92), the aim of a description of inner structure is to work out the deep structure (*Tiefen-Struktur*) of the small unit.

individual clauses as elements of inner structure, it is left to the discussion on parallels to determine if the organizational model identified in the clause row belongs to a generic pattern or not.

Determination of the communication function of individual clauses relies to a large extent on the work of transcription and translation. This makes it possible to distinguish clauses of instruction and motivation, and so forth. To distinguish between the various types of instructions present, I have given them labels which are meant to reflect the form of their main clause predicator. Clauses with positive verbal commands in the regular Imperfect are called *prescriptions*. Instruction clauses having the form of *lʾ* with the regular Imperfect are called *prohibitions*. The majority of the instructions or laws in Deut 14:1–17:13 can be described with these terms. Other positive commands are described by their predication structure and the word prescription; for example, *Infinitive prescription* (14:21aδ; 16:1) or *Jussive prescription* (15:3b) in the case of the short Imperfect. Verbless clauses used as instructions are called *Nominal prescriptions* (14:4–6a, 12–18*; 16:8bα).

The basis for this terminology rests on Richter's distinction between the paradigms *Imperativ* / *Vetitiv* (imperative/vetitive) and *Gebot* / *Prohibitiv* (prescription/prohibition) in BH. Richter accorded to each of these paradigms a different genre assignation and literary function. In his opinion, whereas the imperative/vetitive paradigm in the *Mahnspruch* form (i.e., with motive clauses) was basically used for the education of the children of the upper classes, the prescription/prohibition paradigm was used in short series (originally without motive clauses) to proclaim codes of ethical behavior.[30] Richter has been criticized for this generic distinction, even if the formal differences are generally recognized.[31] In using such terminology, I take no position on Richter's thesis of a distinct cultural function for the prescription/prohibition paradigm as opposed to the occurrence of the imperative/vetitive paradigm. This is a complex issue which only indirectly affects this study. In Deut 14:1–17:13 there are only one imperative (15:9a), one short Imperfect (15:3b), and no vetitives. The generic significance of 15:3b, 9aα will be discussed in the analyses below.

An important lexical feature which affects the analysis of inner structure is found in the distinction between Active verbals (Av), Stative verbals (Sv), and *hyh* constructions. It can be shown that the presence of Sv clauses is a semantic shift which has discourse functions. Hence, observations of Sv clauses are important for the description of inner structure. The Sv category

---

[30] W. Richter, *Recht und Ethos*, 190.

[31] W. M. Clark, "Law," 113.

of verbs is not formally distinct from the Av category, but it is semantically distinct. Sv verbs denote nominal ideas or are related to adjectival formations.[32] In Deut 14:1–17:13, the list includes all instances of the verbs *ḥyh, ykl, yrʾ, qrb (qal), qšh, rbh, śbʿ, śnʾ,* and *śmḥ*.[33] The verb *hyh* is given a class by itself. Semantically, it does not belong clearly to either the Av or the Sv category. However, since the Av clauses are by far in the majority, the occurrence of either an Sv or *hyh* construction is a significant contrast from the norm.

Another important indication of inner structure is the presence of rhetorical devices which promote clause row cohesion. This includes the discovery of constructions such as *ring structure*, *inclusio*, and *chiasmus*. In order to be considered structurally significant, only arrangements which interface with the clause constituent level of clause construction are considered.

An organizational model for each clause row is suggested in a summary table. Registered beside each clause number is a description of its communication function. Then there appears a record of its class taken from the Class column of the transcription. This provides a view of the grammatical context of clause communication function and emphasizes its relationship to the outer structure of the clause row. If analysis discloses important divisions within the discourse of the clause row, they are also recorded.

Parallels

As with the synchronistic description of clause row organization, this methodological step seeks to be descriptive while avoiding overly abstract schemes of classification. The term parallel is preferred to the use of the terms genre or *Gattung* for two reasons. First, the term parallel is used because of the range of materials considered. Structural parallels at the clause or clause row level hold first place of importance. But relevant parallels in phraseology at the clause constituent level and content parallels will also be identified. Second, the terms genre or *Gattung* have no common definition in scholarly literature. The method of genre analysis used here is but one of several.

---

[32] Richter, *Grundlagen*, 1:70–71.

[33] The inclusion of *śmḥ* in this group may be justified by considering the fact that a participle does not appear in the *qal*. Instead one encounters an adjectival form (e.g., 16:15).

A description of inner structure will show that a clause row possesses a particular way of organizing its contents. One concern in the search for parallels is the identification of parallels to the model of organization described. In the study below, the clause rows of Deut 14:1–17:13 will be investigated for evidence of stereotypical patterns of composition. Such work will provide additional criteria for the evaluation of literary-critical problems and prepare the way for a discussion of relationships between clause rows. As in literary-critical investigation, it should be recognized that the study of parallels can proceed on more than one level of discourse. Properly, one should keep the investigation of the parallels of clause rows distinct from the investigation of the genre of the text in which they are implicated. The text itself, as opposed to its clause rows (or small units), may participate in a different layer of discourse and may possess a separate genre membership. At this stage of investigation, it is premature to make an observation about the genre of the whole text. This task must await a synthesis of observations made about its parts.

In selecting comparative texts, I have taken seriously Fohrer's distinction between isolated incidences of the "apodictic" speech form in conversation and extended texts composed in the same.[34] This study recognizes Fohrer's distinction but has not confined itself to seeking only rows of large numbers of prescriptions and prohibitions. In seeking comparative texts, I have concentrated on texts which contain at least two contiguous prohibition or prescription forms, the minimum number for a "row" as defined by Gerstenberger.[35] The study of structural parallels will accept the thesis that second person prescriptions and prohibitions typically circulated in rows. Many of these have been identified by Gerstenberger and his results will be among those invoked in this study.

This study also accepts the existence of a form of construction called the "If-You" instruction (cf. 14:24–26; 15:7, 12, 13, 16–17, 21; 17:8–9). These texts have a similar construction. The protasis is in the third person and the apodosis is in the second person. The apodosis may either have the form of a prescription (15:12), a prohibition (15:7, 13, 21), or a *wqtl* form (14:25–26; 15:16–17; 17:8–9).

Gilmer's monograph presents a detailed argument for the existence of a genre of biblical law he calls the "If-You Law," to which he claims the texts listed above belong.[36] Among Gilmer's reviewers there seems to be general

---

[34] G. Fohrer, "Das sogennante apodiktisch formulierte Recht und der Dekalog," 51.

[35] E. Gerstenberger, *Wesen und Herkunft des 'apodiktischen Rechts,'* 86–87.

[36] H. W. Gilmer, *The If-You Form in Israelite Law*, 48, 57.

approval for the thesis that a genre such as the If-You formula exists in the biblical material. However, there is considerable dissent as to the relationship between the If-You formula and so-called apodictic law. Some hold, along with Alt, that the If-You form is a secondary derivative of apodictic style and of no great age in BH traditions.[37] But the works of Richter and Gerstenberger point to a widespread use of second person instruction language for the teaching of duties in the clan, court, and cult.[38] Despite the fact that neither Richter or Gerstenberger address the issue of the If-You law, conclusions about the cultural function of the If-You formula similar to those suggested for prescriptions and prohibitions are justified. There is no warrant for the assumption that the If-You formula is simply a secondary evolution of a legal form which was originally always in the third person.[39]

The search for parallels also deals with certain questions of content. These include semantic parallels to the contents of particular clause rows, vexed problems of communication function on the clause level, and stereotypical formulae on the phrase level of composition.

The most important phrase level concern is the identification of stereotypical deuteronomic language. The identification of Dtn texts assumes the presence of a reliable guide as to what may be considered Dtn style. Here I follow research which recognizes an intimate relationship between Dtn expressions and the theological outlook of the book of Deuteronomy. Research from this perspective has been summarized by Preuss in a chapter entitled, "*Sprache, Stil und Theologie des Deuteronomiums.*" Dtn style is

---

[37] A. Alt, "The Origins of Israelite Law," 88, 93. See the following reviews of Gilmer: B. F. Batto, 117; H. J. Boecker, 428; R. Knierim, 113.

[38] Richter, *Recht und Ethos*, 190.

[39] Such evidence affects theories about the origins of the If-You laws which D. Patrick has labeled "casuistic law governing primary rights and duties" ("Casuistic Law Governing Primary Rights and Duties," 181, 183–84). As opposed to remedial casuistic law, Israelite casuistic law governing primary rights and duties has some unique features. These include the tendency towards second person address and the addition of motive clauses. Patrick views the presence of these features as a secondary development in the history of Israelite law which is illustrated by the shift from the earlier law in Exod 21:2–6 to the parallel in Deut 15:12–18. In the Dtn version the law has been recast in personal address and the definitions of the slave's rights (Exod 21:3–4) replaced with an admonition to furnish the slave with produce when he leaves. The law has moved away from technical law towards moral law, a type of change characteristic in Deuteronomy. Patrick's thesis owes much to Alt's analysis of the Covenant Code which recognized only one original class of casuistic law: that framed entirely in the third person. See Alt, "Origins of Israelite Law," 88, 93; cf. Patrick, ibid., 183.

considered a function of a characteristic rhetoric which is organized around several major topics: *Gott und seine Verehrung* (pp. 177f.), *Israel* (pp. 182f.), *Israel und seine Geschichte* (pp. 185f.), *Israels Land* (pp. 191f.), and *Gesetz und Gehorsam* (pp. 194f.).

One might assume that with such a definition of style a means might be developed to aid the recognition of Dtn composition elements in the laws of Deuteronomy. This would entail the development of lists of characteristic Dtn usages and vocabulary items. Such lists do, in fact, exist. They are a product of the recognition that in the Pentateuch what distinguishes Deuteronomy from other writings is a number of characteristic phrases, vocabulary, and rhetorical motifs. Lists of these have been drawn up independently by Weinfeld and Wevers.

According to Weinfeld, Deuteronomy is the primary witness to a unique literary style "distinguished by its simplicity, fluency, and lucidity (which) may be recognized both by its phraseology and more especially by its rhetorical character."[40] The main content of this style is not an employment of new idioms and expressions, but of a specific jargon related to a few basic, theological tenets:

1. The struggle against idolatry
2. The centralization of the cult
3. Exodus, covenant, and election
4. The monotheistic creed
5. Observance of the law and loyalty to the covenant
6. Inheritance of the land
7. Retribution and material motivation[41]

Characteristic phrases in Deuteronomy related to each of these topics are listed by Weinfeld in the first appendix to *Deuteronomy and the Deuteronomic School.*[42]

A second catalogue comes as a result of Wevers's work as editor of the critical text of Deuteronomy in the Göttingen Septuagint. According to Wevers,

> The most obvious characteristic of the book of Deuteronomy is its repetitive style. The book is filled with phrases and clauses that recur again and again with slight modification. Copyists were of course thoroughly familiar with these

---

40 M. Weinfeld, *Deuteronomy and the Deuteronomic School,* 1.

41 Ibid. Weinfeld lists other categories found only in deuteronomistic literature.

42 Ibid., 320–49.

> formulaic expressions with the result that parallel passages have played havoc with textual transmission.[43]

Wevers provides his readers with a list of 56 different categories of "formulaic pieces of text" found in Deuteronomy with stylistic characteristics notable enough to put pressure on the copying tradition.[44]

In the study below, appeal will be restricted to Weinfeld's list. While Wevers's list is a valuable catalogue of phrases favoured by the Dtn writer(s), the lists are not as restricted to cataloguing what are peculiarly or exclusively Dtn usages, expressions, and concerns as are those of Weinfeld. In the analysis which follows, elements of Dtn style identified in Appendix I of Weinfeld will be cited by the abbreviation WA followed by the page number (e.g., WA p. 324). As a rule, when appeal is made to the presence of Dtn vocabulary, the appeal will usually be made for inclusive reasons, not exclusive reasons. That is, a passage which contains no phraseology of the kind identified in WA as Dtn is not necessarily non-Dtn. It will not be supposed here that a Dtn text must contain at least one of the formulaic expressions identified by Weinfeld. On the other hand, it will be assumed that a passage which contains vocabulary unique to Deuteronomy and which is listed in WA has signs of Dtn origin.

Literary Unity

Literary-critical analysis is used to discuss the literary cohesion of the clause row with respect to signs of unified or composite composition. The discussion uses the prior examination of structure and parallels to other texts for evidence. These observations are used to control the perception of semantic inconsistencies typically appealed to in literary-critical analysis. Many of these inconsistencies manifest themselves as cases in which a logical relationship between a referential item and its referent seem to break down. Classes of literary-critical criteria include:

a) non-structurally integrated doublets and repetitions;
b) tensions and contradictions in content, vocabulary usage, and syntax;
c) the presence and absence of similarly constructed phrases;
d) parallels with other biblical texts.[45]

---

43 J. W. Wevers, *Text History of the Greek Deuteronomy*, 86.

44 Ibid., 86–99.

45 These are described in detail in Richter, *Exegese*, 51–62. For an overview, see Langlamet, Review of Richter, *Exegese*, 277–78.

Although commentaries continue to appear on Deuteronomy, comprehensive and methodical studies of the literary-critical problems in Deuteronomy 12–26 (let alone 14:1–17:13) are not common. Recent, detailed treatments of all of Deuteronomy 12–26 include those of Merendino (1969), Nebeling (1970), and Seitz (1971).[46] Merendino's discussion continues to be influential;[47] however, it has been deservedly criticized for its overly fine division of the laws into various redactional layers.[48] In addition, Merendino seems to be concerned to discover as much pre-Dtn material as possible—so much so that he seems to ignore the extent that Dtn composition may be implicated in the formation of the laws in Deuteronomy 12–26.[49] Similar criticisms may be directed against the unpublished doctoral dissertation of Nebeling. Nebeling also identifies a great deal of pre-Dtn material and minimizes the possible role of Dtn composition.[50] Specific reservations may be registered about their handling of the key formula *hmqwm ʾšr ybḥr yhwh* and assumptions they share about the meaning of the adjective *deuteronomic* (see below). A further charge which may be leveled against both Merendino and Nebeling arises out of the synchronistic analysis of the text. The present form of the text reveals a concern for composition in paragraphs or clause rows which suggests a degree of organization and cohesion greater than that proposed by either Nebeling or Merendino.

In the course of the following analysis, my own opinion most often confirms that of Seitz. One reason for this is that Seitz shows a greater respect for the kind of paragraph structure which synchronistic analysis shows to be a feature of the text in its present form. On the other hand, in some cases Seitz is the least detailed since his discussion of Deuteronomy 12–26 is part of his larger discussion of the development of the book as a whole.

---

46 R. P. Merendino, *Das deuteronomische Gesetz*; G. Nebeling, *Die Schichten des deuteronomischen Gesetzeskorpus*; G. Seitz, *Redaktionsgeschichtliche Studien zum Deuteronomium*.

47 See, e.g., his influence on J. Halbe's analysis of 16:1–8 ("Passa-Massot im deuteronomischen Festkalendar," 151–52, 161); within A. D. H. Mayes's discussion of 14:1–17:13 see *Deuteronomy*, 239, 245, 248, 258, 260, 266, 267; J. G. McConville (*Law and Theology in Deuteronomy*) cites Merendino over Seitz 6 to 3.

48 F. Langlamet, Review of Merendino, *Gesetz*, 587; Mayes, *Deuteronomy*, 224.

49 Langlamet, Review of Merendino, *Gesetz*, 592.

50 For example, Nebeling finds five strata: A, B, C, D^1, D^2 in 14:22–16:15. Only the last two are to be considered deuteronomic (*Schichten*, 252–54). Within this schema, e.g., Nebeling would consider all of 15:19–23 to be pre-Dtn despite the appearance of such motifs as the *mqwm* formula, the demand to eat *lpny yhwh* and the presence of imagery associated with the permission for profane slaughter in Deuteronomy 12.

Certain of his discussions require more attention (e.g., 14:1–21; 16:9–17:1). Moreover, Seitz has been criticized for his lack of form-critical sophistication as well as for failing to spell out the criteria used to reach his conclusions.[51]

All three authors show detailed knowledge of the positions of previous scholarship and have assimilated prior viewpoints where they have seen fit. Readers wishing for an overview of the various opinions expressed before 1969 on literary-critical problems in Deut 14:1–17:13 are referred especially to the discussions of Merendino *ad loc.* A schematic overview of past scholarship is also provided by Seitz.[52] There is no comprehensive review of the arguments of Merendino, Nebeling, or Seitz with respect to their literary-critical analyses of Deuteronomy 12–26, let alone 14:1–17:13, to date.[53] Accordingly, the views of these three authors will figure prominently in the text below and in accompanying notes. Moreover, because these three scholars have already made full use of the scholarship which preceded them, the chapter remains most closely involved with scholarship touching on 14:1–17:13 since 1969. Interest will be focused on recent special studies including those of Weinfeld (1972), Rofé (1975), Halbe (1975), Kaufman (1978–79), McConville (1981), Rüterswörden (1988), and the commentary of Mayes (1979), who also is in dialogue with the views of Merendino, Nebeling, and Seitz.[54]

A major requirement in this investigation is an adequate definition of the adjective *deuteronomic*. Should one understand this term as a literary, or historical referent, or both? In the following discussion, I shall argue that what is by definition Dtn must be understood primarily as a literary, not an historical, phenomenon. For the purposes of this book, Dtn refers strictly to literary formulae attested in Deuteronomy. The adjective *deuteronomistic* (Dtr) will refer to formulas in related literary strata in the Former Prophets and the prose sermons in Jeremiah.[55]

The priority of a literary approach to the question as to what may be considered Dtn can be illustrated by appeal to the literary-critical value of the *mqwm* formula.

---

[51] R. Hals, Review of Seitz, *Studien*, 282; W. Richter, Review of Seitz, *Studien*, 143.

[52] Seitz, *Studien*, 92–95.

[53] The latest review of past literary-criticism on Deuteronomy 12–25 appears in Preuss, *Deuteronomium*, 103–144. The nature of the series in which Preuss is writing limits him to cataloguing major problems and past and current consensus on their resolution.

[54] To this list should now be added E. Reuter, *Kultzentralisation: Entstehung und Theologie von Dtn 12* (1994). Unfortunately, this book came to my attention too late for its results to be considered in this study.

[55] See Weinfeld, *Deuteronomy*, 4; Mayes, *Deuteronomy*, 41.

There are five major variants of the *mqwm* formula:

a) *hmqwm ʾšr ybḥr yhwh ʾlhyk lškn šmw šm*[56]
b) *hmqwm ʾšr ybḥr yhwh ʾlhyk lśwm šmw šm*[57]
c) *hmqwm ʾšr ybḥr yhwh bʾḥd šbṭyk*[58]
d) *hmqwm ʾšr ybḥr yhwh ʾlhyk bw*[59]
e) *hmqwm ʾšr ybḥr yhwh*[60]

Of these five, it appears that the long form with *lśwm* is likely a Dtr variant of the Dtn formulation with *lškn*.[61] But apart from this, there are no indications which can determine the literary or historical priority of the remaining four.

There is widespread agreement that the formula *hmqwm ʾšr ybḥr yhwh* is a phrase with a history of usage and development. It has been suggested that the phrase was originally used without the extension *lškn šmw šm*.[62] But more recently, it has emerged that the short forms *hmqwm ʾšr ybḥr yhwh* (*bw*) represent abbreviated allusions to one of the longer formulas. This opinion may now claim the support of Lohfink's exhaustive study of 1984. He concludes that the short forms are abbreviated references to the long form with *lškn*.[63]

The failure of the variants in the formula *hmqwm ʾšr ybḥr yhwh* as a literary-critical criterion constitutes an important objection to the understanding of the adjective Dtn as principally an historical referent. Merendino regards only those passages which seem to him to be products of the redaction of Deuteronomy associated with the Josianic reform as Dtn. Nebeling regards as Dtn the material belonging to his fourth and fifth layer which he

---

56 Deut 16:2, 6, 11; 26:2; 14:23 occurs without the divine name. Deut 12:11 appears in the 2mpl and conflates this formula with formula (d).

57 Deut 12:21; 14:24. Deut 12:5 appears in the 2mpl and conflates this formula with formula (a).

58 Deut 12:14; I consider this as a separate variant following the discussion of B. Halpern, "The Centralization Formula in Deuteronomy," 35.

59 Deut 12:18; 14:25; 16:7; 17:8.

60 Deut 12:26; 15:20; 16:15; 17:10; 18:6. Deut 16:16 and 31:11 occur without the divine name.

61 Seitz, *Studien*, 213; Halpern, "Centralization Formula," 32; N. Lohfink, "Zur deuteronomischen Zentralisationformel," 298. Related forms with *lśwm* appear in Dtr contexts, but a formula with *lškn* is absent in Dtr texts, although an allusion to the motif occurs in Jer 7:12; see WA p. 325.

62 In this regard, see the literature surveyed by Seitz in *Studien*, 212–14.

63 Lohfink, "Zentralisationformel," 326. For a survey of past literature supporting this viewpoint see ibid., 299–300.

believes dates to c.700 BCE or later. In both cases Merendino and Nebeling rely on presumed indicators present in the formula *hmqwm ʾšr ybḥr yhwh* to buttress their arguments. A key distinction made by both is the appearance of a short form without the infinitival phrase *lškn šmw šm*.[64]

In fact, variants of the *mqwm* formula do not possess literary-critical value (with the possible exception of the formula with *lśwm*). It is clear that the short form without *lškn šmw šm* appears in Dtn texts which belong to various literary strata. For example, it is the shortest form of all which occurs in Deut 31:11, although this is generally admitted to be a late addition to the book of Deuteronomy.[65] Deuteronomy 16 offers another good case for disputing the literary-critical value of the *mqwm* formula. The *mqwm* formula appears with the infinitival complement in 16:11, but in the shorter form in 16:15. However, apart from the variation in *mqwm* formula, there is evidence that the Dtn elements in 16:11, 14–15 belong to the same layer of the text since they share several stylistic traits. Seitz is correct in denying that the addition or removal of the infinitival phrase *lškn šmw šm* can be controlled by literary-critical principles.[66] Moreover, the same ambiguity is also true of the variation between *ʾšr ybḥr yhwh lškn šmw šm* and *ʾšr ybḥr yhwh bw*. These formulas occur side by side in 16:6, 7. Unnoticed by most commentators is the presence of a chiasmus between 16:5–7 which suggests an artful composition by a single hand.

Finally, as a general principle, it seems excessively wooden to deny the possibility of stylistic variation in a book noted for its sophisticated rhetoric. Several other phrases or formulas appear in various slightly altered versions throughout Deuteronomy.[67] These observations tell against the use of variants in the style of Dtn phrases as reliable criteria for diachronic distinctions. Diachronic distinctions within Dtn material must be demonstrated by reference to other, more reliable literary-critical factors.

An important assumption which needs to be addressed is the meaning of the *mqwm* formula in the legislation where it occurs in Deuteronomy.

---

64 Merendino, *Gesetz*, 382–87, 402 especially p. 387; Nebeling, *Schichten*, 34–38, 296.

65 Seitz, *Studien*, 193–94. The secondary nature of Deuteronomy 31 is discussed in Mayes, *Deuteronomy*, 375; it is also admitted by more conservative scholars such as G. T. Manley (*Deuteronomy*, 162) and M. H. Segal (*The Pentateuch*, 97). The same short formula as in 31:11 also occurs in 16:16.

66 Seitz, *Studien*, 193, 221.

67 E.g., the bestowal formula *ʾšr yhwh ʾlhyk ntn lk* may be applied to *ʾrṣ*, *ʾdmh*, *šʿryk*, and *ʿryk* (Wevers, *Text History of the Greek Deuteronomy*, list #10, pp. 88–89). Note also the variants in the formula *ʾšr yšbʿ* (ibid., list #1, p. 86) and the variants possible for the formula "the one who is in your gates" (ibid., list #44, p. 97).

Outside Deuteronomy a phrase close to the *mqwm* formula may refer to a plurality of sites (Exod 20:24). The question here is the meaning of the *mqwm* formula in Deuteronomy: does it mean a single cult center? Although this is maintained by most commentators, there has always been a small but steady stream of commentators who have denied that a sole legitimate sanctuary is signified in Deuteronomy. It is necessary to inquire, therefore, what one may assume about the history of Israelite religion and the meaning of the *mqwm* formula prior to beginning a literary-critical analysis in Deut 14:1–17:13.

Arguments in favour of the *mqwm* denoting a plurality of cult sites typically point to the ambiguity of 12:14, the instructions in Deuteronomy 27 and the Dtn use of singulars of class.[68] According to Segal, the singular usage "the place" is a regular use of the singular in the Pentateuch to signify a class of object. So, in the phrase "and the Levite, and the stranger, and the orphan etc." (e.g., 14:28; 16:11, 14), the singular denotes not singular individuals but singular classes of individuals. Therefore, the singular "place" in Deuteronomy does not exclude a plurality of legitimate sanctuaries. Only at a later stage in history was the Dtn command about the place chosen by God interpreted as being fulfilled exclusively in Jerusalem and its temple.[69] Contra Segal, it must be noted that Deuteronomy never uses the particle *kl* before *mqwm*, despite the fact that *kl* is prominent in Dtn style, and despite the fact that it appears in Exod 20:24, a key text in Segal's argument. It is significant that Deuteronomy does not use the one small indicator which would clinch the argument of Segal and others like him.

The meaning of the *mqwm* formula has been recently addressed by Halpern. The evidence favors the view that the word *mqwm* refers to one place in Deuteronomy if one reads the book as it now stands.[70] What is apparent is that the *mqwm* is regarded as a place where *kl yśrʾl* can gather (e.g., 31:11). The same observation also applies to Deuteronomy 27.[71] What gives Deuteronomy 27 its legitimacy is the presence of *kl yśrʾl* (27:9). However, there is no evidence that any cultic activity possesses validity in Deuteronomy apart from the possible participation of *kl yśrʾl* in one place.

---

68 Among recent commentators, see, e.g., Segal, *The Pentateuch*, 87–88; McConville (*Law and Theology*, 28–29); and G. J. Wenham, "Deuteronomy and the Central Sanctuary," 114–15. For scholarship with this opinion prior to Segal, see Halpern, "Centralization Formula," 22; and Manley, *Deuteronomy*, 132.

69 Segal, *The Pentateuch*, 87–88.

70 Halpern, "Centralization Formula," 22–23.

71 M. G. Kline, *Treaty of the Great King*, 82.

The centrality of the *mqwm* is also evident in 17:8–9 which suggests a supreme court, and Deut 18:6–8 which maintains the right of all Levites *mʾḥd šʿryk mkl yśrʾl* to go *ʾl hmqwm ʾšr ybḥr yhwh* to minister.

Nevertheless, Halpern has suggested that one cannot arbitrarily assume that every level of Deuteronomy legal formulation invested the *mqwm* with the idea of a single sanctuary. His chief evidence is the phrase *bʾḥt šbṭyk* in 12:14 which he believes implies the possibility of more than one cult place.[72] There is, however, a parallelism in terminology between the context of 12:14 and other *mqwm* passages which Halpern seems to have missed. I refer to the contrast between "the place which Yahweh chooses" (singular) and "your gates" (plural). This contrast may be found between 12:14 and 12:15; cf. 17:8 and 18:6. There is no reason to believe that the contrast in 12:14–15 means something different from these clearer references to a single (central) cult place. I conclude that the evidence of Deuteronomy favors the conception that the "place which Yahweh chooses" is one place and that this is a valid presupposition for literary-critical investigation.

At the same time, it is necessary to resist the easy assumption that what is meant by the Dtn *mqwm* formula is Jerusalem. This identity may be implied by the phrase *lškn šmw šm* as well as the election motif,[73] but it remains implicit in Deuteronomy at best. On closer reflection, this datum is provocative. Whatever relationship the book of Deuteronomy may have had to events in Israelite history, the *mqwm* is never explicitly identified with the capital of Judah. Therefore, as a starting point for literary-criticism, I ally myself with those who remain agnostic about the necessary relationship between Deuteronomy and any identifiable historical events which might have been centered in the capital of Judah.[74] In fact such agnosticism is required not only by the details of Deuteronomy itself but also by current thought in literary interpretation. It is illegitimate to begin by using an historical construction as the key to interpretation of a particular piece of biblical literature.[75] The book deserves to be approached from its own vantage point before its place in history is examined or determined.

---

[72] Halpern, "Centralization Formula," 35–38; the apparent ambiguity of 12:14 is also admitted by Mayes, *Deuteronomy*, 227.

[73] Nebeling, *Schichten*, 38; Merendino, *Gesetz*, 393; Lohfink, "Zentralisationformel," 297.

[74] Mayes, *Deuteronomy*, 102–3; McConville, *Law and Theology*, 155; C. Houtman, "Ezra and the Law," 114.

[75] This point is made at length by M. Weiss (*The Bible from Within: The Method of Total Interpretation*, 7–12, 39) in his discussion of a valid approach to BH poetry.

A priori assumptions about the dependency of a Dtn text on some other biblical text are a related concern. In the analysis below, parallelism and agreement between Dtn regulations and other contexts in BH will often be identified. In many cases, it will be claimed that there is a common tradition underlying the material found in the Dtn context and other texts. In some cases, the Dtn text can even be characterized as a modification of an existing tradition or text. It is tendentious, however, to begin with the assumption that where several witnesses are present, one text is necessarily older than the others and the source for them. This ought to be a conclusion of literary-critical investigation, not a starting point. This affects a priori assumptions such as those about the relationship between the so-called Covenant Code in Exod 20:19–23:19 and the legislation in Deuteronomy 12–26. This study is not based on preconceived opinions about the relative age of parallel material in Exodus, Leviticus, Numbers, and Deuteronomy. Such assumptions are invalid presuppositions for literary-critical investigation, which proceeds from a synchronistic analysis of textual organization.

Chapter Four

LITERARY UNITY IN THE CLAUSE ROWS OF DEUTERONOMY 14:1–17:13

§1 Deut 14:1–2

The instructions of Deut 14:1–2 are concerned with actions of mourning. This observation is sufficient to set them apart topically from other instruction rows in the context of Deuteronomy 13–14.

Transcription and Translation

1a	bnym ᵓtm lyhwh ᵓlhykm	F:Nc	Pred S P
1bα	lᵓ ttgddw	F:xVc	V
1bβ	wlᵓ tśymw qrḥh byn ʿynykm lmt	CoF:xVc	V O Pa P
2a	ky ʿm qdwš ᵓth lyhwh ᵓlhyk	B:Nc	Pred S P
2b	wbk bḥr yhwh	CoB:IVc	Po V S Pc P
2b'	lhywt lw lʿm sglh	N:Inf	V P Po
	mkl hʿmym ᵓšr ʿl pny hᵓdmh		

14:1] You are children belonging to Yahweh your God.[1] You shall not lacerate yourselves or make a bald spot on your scalp[2] for the dead, [2] because you are a people consecrated to Yahweh your God, and you Yahweh has chosen out of all the peoples which are upon the face of the earth to become his specially treasured people.

Clause Row Structure

The clauses of v. 1 form a row marked by 2mpl references. Clause 1bα is connected to c.1a by the pronominal subject in the verb. Co and pronominal reference connect c.1bβ to c.1bα. The Set tradition connected v. 1 and v.

[1] Semitic languages have different constructions for distinguishing alienable and inalienable possession. See W. Diem, "Alienable und inalienable Possession im Semitischen," esp. pp. 228, 283. In BH *lamed* is used to indicate alienable possession (R. J. Williams, *Hebrew Syntax*, §270)—a nuance which the translation of *lyhwh* as "belonging to Yahweh" reflects.

[2] The idiom *byn ʿynykm* connotes a larger area of the skull than simply the forehead. This may be inferred from the parallelism between *qdqd* and *bn ʿnm* in Ugaritic in the speech of Kothar addressed to the weapons of Baal (**2**. *iv*. 21, 26 following Herdner's numbering). See also Y. Avishur, "Expressions of the Type *byn ydym* in the Bible and Semitic Languages," 127.

2 by interpreting the *ky* clause in c.2a as a modifier of c.1bβ. This tradition is supported by the repetition *lyhwh ʾlhykm / lyhwh ʾlhyk* which connects cc.1a and 2a. Clause 2b is connected to c.2a by Co and pronominal reference to the subject *ʾth*. Consequently, c.2b continues the clause modification marked by *ky* in c.2a.

Deut 14:1a, 2a and 2b are motive clauses.[3] The lack of a conjunction between c.1a and c.1bα is significant. There is no correspondence between the vocabulary of c.1a and the lexical set of mourning terms (*gdd, qrḥ*) in cc.1bα, 1bβ. It is typical for motive clauses not to be closely connected in vocabulary with the instructions or laws they accompany.[4] The similar constituent structure (Pred S P) of cc.1a and 2a also suggests that c.1a plays a similar role in the discourse. Hence, it has an explanatory function not far removed from the function of c.2a where *ky* can be assigned a causal value. The inner structure of 14:1-2, therefore, shows an envelope construction with statements of motivation surrounding prohibitions:

1a	Motive clause	F:Nc	2mpl
1bα	Prohibition	F:xVc	
1bβ	Prohibition	CoF:xVc	
2a	Motive clause	B:Nc	2ms
2b	Motive clause	CoB:IVc	

Parallels

14:1-2. Deut 5:6–11 (=Exod 20:2–6) shows a similar inner structure. Like 14:1–2, these verses are also set apart by Set in the manuscript tradition. Deut 5:6 is a verbless motive clause.[5] It is followed by a row of prohibitions (vv. 7–9a) and concludes with motivation introduced by the particle *ky*. Unlike 14:1–2, there is no change in the number of the subject.

14:1a. Clause 14:1a is a verbless motive clause asyndetically preposed to the prohibitions it modifies. This is an unusual construction in the Pentateuch. Besides the parallel in Deut 5:6, other examples of asyndetic verbless motive clauses preposed to prohibitions may be found in Lev 18:7bα, 11a, 15bα; 23:36bγ.[6] These parallels are structurally distinct from Deut 14:1a because they appear in the middle of a span of related discourse and not at the beginning. A parallel to the position and structure of 14:1a occurs in Neh 8:9 where the asyndetic motive clause *qdš hwʾ lyhwh ʾlhykm* is

---

[3] P. Doron, "Motive Clauses in the Laws of Deuteronomy," 71.

[4] H. Rücker, *Die Begründungen der Weisungen Jahwes im Pentateuch*, 16–17.

[5] R. Sonsino, *Motive Clauses in Hebrew Law*, 231.

[6] As analyzed by Sonsino, ibid., 229–49.

preposed to two negative instructions. The verbal instructions of Neh 8:9 also use 2mpl references, but they are vetitives, not prohibitions.

14:1b. Gerstenberger has identified a number of originally paired prohibitions in BH literature. Examples formally similar to 14:1b may be found in Exod 23:2a–2b; 18a–18b; Lev 19:13aα–13aβ; Deut 24:17a–17b.[7]

The contents of 14:1b mention stereotypical mourning actions listed in similar terms in Jer 16:6. Semantic (but not syntactic) parallels to these prohibitions appear in Lev 19:27–28; 21:5. Lev 19:27–28 belongs to a row of six prohibitions found in vv. 26–28 and marked as a unit by the (likely secondary) motive clause *ʾny yhwh*.[8] The prohibitions in Lev 19:27–28a forbid shaving oneself and slashing oneself on behalf of the dead—the reverse order of the injunctions in Deut 14:1. They are written in the 2mpl with the exception of v. 27b which appears in the 2ms. Lev 21:5 is written in the 3mpl and addressed to priests. It shows a vocabulary link to 14:1a by the use of the root *qrḥ* but, like Lev 19:27–28, forbids shaving before slashing. It is accompanied by a motivational element in Lev 21:6 which appeals to the sanctity of the priests to their God—a motif which has an analogue in Deut 14:2.

14:2. Deut 14:2 consists of two motive clauses, the first an Nc introduced by the *ky* particle and the second a Vc coordinated with it by *waw*. These clauses have different subjects. An exact parallel to 14:2 appears in 7:6, except that the second clause follows the Nc asyndetically in 7:6. Other examples of the form of 14:2 occur in Exod 29:28aβ.b, Lev 21:23b and Deut 12:23aβ.b.

The contents of 14:2 have the following phrases which are connected to Dtn rhetoric:

ʿm qdwš Found also in 7:6; 26:19; 28:9. This phrase is confined to Deuteronomy in BH. Its closest analogues are *ʿm (h)qdš(k)* in Isa 62:12; 63:18; Dan 12:7.[9]

ʿm sglh Found also in 7:6; 26:18. This phrase is confined to Deuteronomy in BH. The closest analogue occurs in Exod 19:5: *whyytm ly sglh*.[10]

hyh lw / lyhwh lʿm Found also in 4:20; 7:6; 26:19; 27:9.[11]

---

[7] Gerstenberger, *Apodiktischen Rechts*, 88.

[8] K. Elliger, *Leviticus*, 249.

[9] See WA p. 328.

[10] See WA p. 328. For a discussion of its affinities with treaty terminology see Weinfeld, *Deuteronomy*, 226–227.

[11] See WA p. 327. According to Weinfeld (*Deuteronomy* 80–81), the phrase is rooted in marriage adoption terminology. It belongs to a pattern of covenant thinking well attested

Literary Unity

A compositional distinction between v. 1 and v. 2 suggests itself because v. 1 is written in the 2mpl and v. 2 in the 2ms. There is no use of Dtn clichés in 14:1 and a significant parallel to 14:1a occurs outside the Dtn/Dtr corpus in Neh 8:9. But caution is required because it is apparent that number change (*Numeruswechsel*) is not always evidence of a different hand in the book of Deuteronomy.[12] Therefore, an opinion about the literary integrity of 14:1 with v. 2 depends on a conclusion about the meaning of the change in number in 14:1–2. Such an opinion can be best controlled when the text is implicated in a larger span of Dtn composition (see Chapter 5).

It has been claimed that prohibition rows originally circulated without motive clauses.[13] But Sonsino's examination of motive clauses in Mesopotamian law argues against such a sweeping conclusion.[14] This study does not proceed with a priori assumptions as to whether prohibitive rows were originally composed with or without motive clauses. The possibility has to be examined on a case by case basis.

A question arises as to whether the motive clause in 14:1a is a Dtn addition to the prohibitive row in 14:1b.[15] The source of the imagery of 14:1a is disputed. Deuteronomy has recognizable relationships with two kinds of literature which appeal to father-son imagery: wisdom literature and treaty language.[16] Weinfeld has suggested a connection with prophetic rhetoric (e.g., Hos 11:1; Jer 31:9, 20).[17] Such postulates, however, have to be controlled by the observation that the addressees of 14:1a are referred to as *bnym*. References to the people of Israel as the *bnym* of God or Yahweh occur, e.g., in Deut 32:19-20; Hos 2:1; Isa 1:2, 4; 30:1, 9; 43:6; 45:11; 51:18; 63:8; Jer 3:14, 22; 4:22; Ezek 16:21; 23:4. This usage seems to be derived from viewing Israel and Judah as the spouses of Yahweh (Hos 2:1; Ezek

---

in Deuteronomy but not confined to it.

[12] Mayes, *Deuteronomy*, 35.

[13] See, e.g., Richter, *Recht und Ethos*, 190. Gerstenberger (*Apodiktischen Rechts*, 55) generally agress with this conclusion, although he allows for exceptions, e.g., motivational elements in place of sanctions in some formulations of *Sippenethos*; see ibid., 113.

[14] Sonsino, *Motive Clauses*, 209–10.

[15] Gerstenberger,*Apodiktischen Rechts*, 32.

[16] For treaty usage see F. C. Fensham, "Father and Son as Terminology for Treaty and Covenant," pp. 133–34. J. W. McKay ("Man's Love for God in Deuteronomy and the Father/Teacher-Son/Pupil Relationship," 427–32) has shown the likelihood that the father and son imagery applied to Israel's relationship with Yahweh in 8:5 arises from a combination of wisdom and treaty motifs (cf. Deut 1:31; 32:5, 19).

[17] Weinfeld, *Deuteronomy*, 368–69.

16:21; 23:4), or Zion as Yahweh's spouse (a motif prominent in Isaiah).[18] Therefore, although the imagery of 14:1a may have affinities to Dtn ideology because of a common connection to the Zion tradition, its phraseology cannot be limited to Dtn/Dtr compositions. Further discussion on the origins of 14:1a depends on the meaning of the number change between vv. 1 and 2.

Lohfink has suggested that the relationship between 7:6; 14:2; and 26:18–19 is best explained by the theory of direct dependency of both 7:6 and 14:2 on the phraseology of 26:18–19. This would account for the expansionary character of 7:6 and 14:2 as well as the repetition of key terms and their direct association in 7:6; 14:2. But Lohfink considered the evidence inconclusive. This was because he could not determine what the *k'šr* clause in 26:18 referred to, and because he believed that the parallel phrases in Exod 19:5–6 appeared in a context which showed influence from the Dtn tradition.[19]

Since Lohfink's study, evidence has emerged which reinforces the likelihood that the formula *k'šr dbr* in 26:18–19 refers to Exod 19:5. The phrase regularly occurs in the book of Deuteronomy as a citation formula for material found elsewhere in the Pentateuch.[20] The meaning of the *k'šr* clauses in 26:18–19 has been recently explored by Skweres, who has reiterated the case for seeing the direction of influence from Exod 19:5 to Deut 26:18. The parallelism of *ʿm sglh* and *ʿm qdwš* in Deut 26:18, 19 can be explained as a derivation of the terms *sglh* and *gwy qdwš* in Exod 19:5, 6.[21] It is likely, therefore, that the composition of 26:18-19 is dependent on Exod 19:5.

The composition of 7:6 and 14:2, however, cannot be solely dependent on 26:18–19. Repetition of the phrase *sglh mkl hʿmym* is shared between 7:6; 14:2 and Exod 19:5 but not with 26:18–19. Lohfink's conclusion about the dependence of 7:6 and 14:2 on Deut 26:18–19 is probably correct. But it would appear that the expansionary nature of 7:6 and 14:2 is due, in part, to knowledge of the rhetoric of Exodus 19 independent of the context of 26:18–19.

---

18 See J. J. Schmidt, "The Motherhood of God and Zion as Mother," 564–67.

19 N. Lohfink, "Dt 26, 17–19 und die 'Bundesformel,'" 546. Others insist that the context in Exodus 19 cannot be the source of the Dtn language in Deut 26:18–19; see Mayes, *Deuteronomy*, 184–85.

20 See J. Milgrom, "Profane Slaughter and a Formulaic Key to the Composition of Deuteronomy," 3–4. By contrast, inner Dtn citations are indicated by the formula *'šr 'nky mṣwh;* see Fishbane, *Biblical Interpretation*, 164.

21 D. E. Skweres, *Die Ruckverweise im Buch Deuteronomium*, 176–78.

The question of the relationship between 7:6 and 14:2 will be temporarily set aside in dealing with the literary formation of 14:1-2. It will be taken up when the significance of the repetition between 14:2a and 14:21aε can be discussed in the next chapter. In terms of the present study, it is clear that existing parallels point to 14:2 as a text connected to Dtn tradition and rhetoric.

§ 2 Deut 14:3-21

This section comprehends five clause row units transmitted in three Set divisions: 14:3–8; 9–10; 11–20, 21a, 21b. The motif which combines the first four is repetition of forms of the verb *ʾkl* having as its objects: clean and unclean land animals (vv. 4–8), water creatures (vv. 9–10), flying creatures (vv. 11–20), and animals found dead (v. 21a). The Set tradition included v. 21b with v. 21a, presumably on the understanding that v. 21b is also a food rule. Elsewhere, however, a shift in topic can occasion a new Set division, cf. 17:1. The meaning of the position of v. 21b will be examined when a larger context for discussion can be established. The literary features of each of the subdivisions of 14:3–21 will be described first, before turning to a general discussion of their literary unity.

§2.1 Deut 14:3–8

Transcription and Translation

3	lʾ tʾkl kl twʿbh	F:xVc	V O
4–6a	zʾt hbhmh	F:Nc	S Pred Sres
4a'	ʾšr tʾklw	N:Vc	V
	šwr śh kśbym wśh ʿzym		
	ʾyl wṣby wyḥmwr wʾqw wdyšn wtʾw wzmr		
	wkl bhmh		
6a'	mprst prsh	N:Part	V O
6a''	wšsʿt šsʿ šty prswt	CoN:Part	V O O
6a'''	mʿlt grh	N:Part	V O
	bbhmh		
6b	ʾth tʾklw	F:IVc	Po V
7a*	ʾk ʾt zh lʾ tʾklw	CoF:xIVc	Po V P
	mmʿly hgrh wmmprysy hprsh [ET]		
7bα	ʾt hgml wʾt hʾrnbt wʾt hšpn	F:[xIVc]	Po [V]
7bβ	ky mʿlh grh hmh	B:Nc	Pred S
7bγ	wprsh lʾ hprysw	CoB:xIVc	O V
7bδ	ṭmʾym hm lkm	F:Nc	Pred S P
8aα	wʾt hḥzyr	CoF:[xIVc]	Po [V]
8aβ	ky mprys prsh hwʾ	B:Nc	Pred S
8aγ	wlʾ grh	CoB:[xPart]	O [V]
8aδ	ṭmʾ hwʾ lkm	F:Nc	Pred S P
8bα	mbśrm lʾ tʾklw	F:xIVc	Po V
8bβ	wbnbltm lʾ tgʿw	CoF:xIVc	Po V

14:3] You shall not eat any loathsome thing. [4] The following are the animals which you may eat: ox, sheep and goat, [5] deer, gazelle, antelope, ibex, addax, oryx, and mountain sheep,[1] [6] i.e., any beast in the animal world which divides the hoof so as to make a cleavage into two hooves, which is a cud-chewer. That you may eat. [7] However, the following you may not eat among those which are cud-chewers and divide the hoof: [you may not eat] the camel, the hare, and the hyrax[2] because they are cud-chewers but they do not divide the hoof, they are unclean for you; [8] and [you may not eat] the swine because it divides the hoof but it is not a cud[-chewer], it is unclean for you. You shall not eat any of their flesh, nor shall you touch their carcasses.

14:4–6a. The phrase *bbhmh* is taken as one of the modifiers of the noun phrase *wkl bhmh*. Therefore, it is not considered to be a clause constituent.

14:6a'. The phrase *šty prswt* is identified as a double object on analogy with the use of the double object to mark what the direct complement of the verb is made into.[3]

*14:7a**. *hšswʿh* > SP
καὶ ὀνυχιζόντων ὀνυχιστῆρας LXX
mṭlpy ṭlpyʾ TO

The LXX reading seems to be based on a different parent text than the MT. Supporting evidence is found in TO, a version whose relationship to its parent text is quite conservative. Evidently SP preserves a shorter text which was subsequently expanded—in one manner as witnessed by the MT and in another attested by TO and LXX. The source for the variants was likely 14:6.

14:7bα, 8aα. There is a resumption of the Po *ʾt zh* of 14:7a* in 14:7bα, 8aα. The Po construction identifies 14:7bα and 14:8aα as objects of the verb gapped from 14:7aα (*lʾ tʾklw*). These gapped prohibitions are qualified by two series of *ky* clauses closed off in each case with an asyndetic Nc (cc. 7bβ–7bδ; 8aβ–8aδ).

14:8aγ. Deut 14:8aγ is analyzed as a Vc with an ellipsis of the verbal *mʿlh*. The negative *lʾ* is unusual in an Nc construction. The parallelism between cc.7bα–7bδ and cc.8aα–8aδ and the chiastic inversion of the *prsh* and *grh* nomenclature suggests that *mʿlh,* which appears in c.7bβ, is also to be understood in c.8aγ.

This inference depends on the assumption that *mʿlh* is singular in c.7aγ. A plural form of c.7aγ is found in the SP and many versions since a plural

[1] Not all of the animals in v. 5 can be identified with certainty. The list here follows the suggestions of G. Cansdale, *Animals of Bible Lands*, 82.

[2] Ibid., 129–31.

[3] B. Waltke and M. O'Connor, *Introduction to Biblical Hebrew Syntax*, §10.2.3c.

antecedent for *hmh* might be expected. Where this is not the case in BH, the antecedent is usually a collective noun such as "generation," or "nation" (e.g., Deut 32:20, 28). Nevertheless, the construction in the MT is not ungrammatical. In nominal sentences the predicate adjective is sometimes uninflected if it precedes the subject, cf. Ps 119:137.[4] A similar phenomenon can be observed in Arabic.[5]

Clause Row Structure

The Set division contains one clause written in the 2ms (v. 3) followed by a span of clauses written in the 2mpl (vv. 4–8). Clause 7a* is the central member of a tightly organized structure found in vv. 4–8. The only link between c.3 and c.4–6a is the repetition *tʾkl / tʾklw*. By contrast, various devices of coreference connect vv. 4–8 besides the repetition of *tʾklw* in cc.4a', 6b, 7a*, and 8bα.

The word *zʾt* in 14:4–6a is a cataphoric reference pointing forward to *hbhmh*. The theme is continued by 14:6b which reveals its relationship to c.4–6a by the pronominal suffix on the prepositional phrase *ʾth*. Clause 14:6b and c.7a* are linked by the conjunction *ʾk* creating a construction Andersen calls an "exclusive sentence."[6]

Clause 7a* has links with c.4–6a through deixis on the nouns *hgrh* and *hprsh*. Elements of structural repetition, ellipsis, and reference link c.7a* with the following cc.7aβ–8aβ. In 14:7bα, 8aα the object phrase *ʾt zh* of 14:7a* is resumed with the verbal ellided. Both c.7bα and c.8aα are qualified by a series of subordinate clauses closed off in each case with an Nc. Repetition (*ṭmʾ*), chiasmus of forms of the phrases *hprys prsh* and *mʿlh grh* in cc.7bβ, 7bγ; 8aβ, 8aγ,[7] and verbal ellision (c.7bβ and c.8aγ) reinforce the parallelism of cc.7bβ, 7bγ, 7bδ; 8aβ, 8aγ, 8aδ. The object of c.7a*, which is expounded by cc.7bα–8aδ, is recapitulated by the pronominal references in cc.8bα, 8bβ. The matching constituent structure (Po V) of cc.8bα, 8bβ aids the conclusion of this unit.

---

[4] A. B. Davidson, *Hebrew Syntax*[3], §116 R3; cf. S. R. Driver, *Deuteronomy*[3], 161. Driver suggests that the *he* on *mʿlh* is a "rare orthographic variant" for the expected *yod*, citing Gen 47:3 and 1 Chr 23:24 as parallel cases. But Davidson's observation will also explain the syntax of Gen 47:3 (contra GKC §145r which seems inconsistent on this point). In the case of 1 Chr 23:24, *ʿśh hmlʾkh* appears to be a kind of frozen form which appears also in the singular in Ezra 3:9 and Neh 2:16 (both plural contexts).

[5] W. Wright, *A Grammar of the Arabic Language*[3] Vol. 2 §152bj.

[6] F. I. Andersen, *The Sentence in Biblical Hebrew*, 174.

[7] The possibility of a previous chiasmus between the terms of cc.6a', 6a''' and c.7a is not mentioned here due to the fact that elements in question vary in their state of definiteness.

The evidence suggests the following model of inner structure:

3	Prohibition	F:xVc	2ms
4–6a	Nominal prescription	F:Nc	2mpl Positive instruction
6b	Prescription	F:IVc	
7a*	Prohibition	CoF:xIVc	2mpl Negative instruction
7bα	Prohibition	F:(xIVc)	Prohibited class 1
7bβ	Motive clause	B:Nc	
7bγ	Motive clause	CoB:xIVc	
7bδ	Motive clause	F:Nc	
8aα	Prohibition	CoF:(xIVc)	Prohibited class 2
8aβ	Motive clause	B:Nc	
8aγ	Motive clause	CoB:(xPart)	
8aδ	Motive clause	F:Nc	
8bα	Prohibition	F:xIVc	Summary instructions
8bβ	Prohibition	CoF:xIVc	

Parallels

14:3 Gerstenberger includes 14:3 among a number of single Prohibitions which he believes originally circulated independently of their present context (cf. Exod 20:16; 23:6; Deut 19:14a, 15aα; 23:16; 24:14a; 25:4).[8]

14:4–8 A similar structure and contents appear in Lev 11:2b–8. Elements prominent in 14:4–8 are also common in other ritual instructions. As an introduction to instructions, examples of *zh / zʾt* followed by an *ʾšr* clause appear in Exod 25:3; 29:1; Num 28:3; Ezek 45:13. Asyndetic phrases with a structure similar to *ṭmʾ hwʾ lkm* are found, e.g., in Exod 12:11 and Lev 16:31. Since distinctions between what is holy and common are part of the diagnostic function of priestly instruction,[9] the structure and contents of 14:4–8 suggest a genre of ritual texts with the cultural function of priestly instruction for the laity.[10]

§2.2 Deut 14:9–10

Transcription and Translation

9a	ʾt zh tʾklw mkl ʾšr bmym	F:IVc	Po V P
9b	kl	F:IVc	O V
9b'	ʾšr lw snpyr wqśqśt tʾklw	N:Nc	Pred S
10a	wkl	CoF:xIVc	O V

[8] Gerstenberger, *Apodiktischen Rechts,* 32, 88.

[9] P. J. Budd, "Priestly Instruction in Pre-Exilic Israel," 4.

[10] G. Liedke, *Gestalt und Bezeichnung alttestamentlicher Rechtssätze,* 198.

10a'	ʾšr ʾyn lw snpyr wqśqśt lʾ tʾklw	N:xNc	Pred S
10b	ṭmʾ hwʾ lkm	F:Nc	Pred S P

14:9] You may eat the following out of everything which is in the water: Everything which has fins and scales you may eat; [10] but everything which lacks fins and scales you are not to eat. It is unclean for you.

14:10′. There is disagreement about the analysis of *ʾyn*. O'Connor, following Andersen, considers *ʾyn* to be equivalent to a clause predicator and assigns it the status of a verbal in his constituent analysis; but Richter considers *ʾyn* as a particle which does not fill a syntagmatic slot.[11] Richter is followed here (and in 14:27b, 29aα) because *ʾyn* may be viewed as the bound noun in a construction in which the P *lw* is acting as the free nominal. As a bound nominal, *ʾyn* is operating below the clause constituent level and cannot be accorded the ranking of clause predicator.

Clause Row Structure

The cataphoric use of *zh* in 14:9a marks the boundary of the Set division. The clause row proceeds as a series of three commands in the IVc form followed by a Nc statement. Repetition of both vocabulary (*tʾklw* and *lw snpyr wqśqśt*) and clause structure (O V) serve together with Co to effect a close cohesion between cc.9b, 10a. The connection of 14:9b, 10a is also augmented by their structure: in contrast to the other two clauses in the text, 14:9b, 10a are two complex clauses. They are framed by the two simple clauses in cc.9a, 10b.

The parallelism of 14:9b, 10a shows that these two clauses are meant to draw out the implications of an initial command in 14:9a. Deut 14:10b acts in a similar manner as cc.7bδ, 8aδ in the clause row above. It signals the end of the span of discourse and provides a motivation for the preceding commands.

The evidence suggests the following model of inner structure:

9a	Prescription	F:IVc	General instruction
9b	Prescription	F:IVc	Positive implication of c.9a
10a	Prohibition	CoF:xIVc	Negative implication of c.9a
10b	Motive clause	F:Nc	

---

11 O'Connor, *Verse Structure*, 304; Andersen, *Sentence in Biblical Hebrew*, 82–83; Richter, *Grundlagen*, 3:173–74.

Parallels

This text has formal and semantic parallels in Lev 11:9–12. The Leviticus text is more expansive than the Dtn text and uses the evaluation *šqṣ* (Lev 11:10b, 11a, 12) where Deut 14:10b uses *ṭmʾ*.

§2.3 Deut 14:11–20

Transcription and Translation

11	kl ṣpwr ṭhrh tʾklw	F:IVc	O V
12–18*	wzh	CoF:Nc	S Pred Sres
12'	ʾšr lʾ tʾklw mhm	N:xVc	V P
	hnšr whprs whʿznyh		
	whdʾh wʾt hʾyh lmynh [ET]		
	wʾt kl ʿrb lmynw		
	wʾt bt hyʿnh wʾt htḥms wʾt hšḥp wʾt hnṣ lmynhw		
	ʾt hkws wʾt hynšwp whtnšmt		
	whqʾt wʾt hrḥmh wʾt hšlk		
	whḥsydh whʾnph lmynh whdwkypt whʿṭlp		
19a	wkl šrṣ hʿwp ṭmʾ hwʾ lkm	CoF:CNc	S (Pred S)
19b	lʾ yʾklw	F:xVc	V
20	kl ʿwp ṭhwr tʾklw	F:IVc	O V

14:11] Every clean bird you may eat. [12] But the following[12] are some of the ones you may not eat:[13] the eagle, the griffon vulture, the bearded vulture, [13] the black vulture?, the various kinds of kite, [14] all the various kinds of raven, [15] the eagle owl, the kestrel?, the gull?, the various kinds of hawk, [16] the little owl, the great-horned owl?, the barn owl?, [17] the light owl?, the Egyptian vulture, the fish owl?, [18] the stork, the various kinds of heron?, the hoopoe, and the bat. [19] Also every winged swarmer is unclean for you. They are not to be eaten. [20] Every clean flying thing you may eat.

---

[12] The gender of *zh* is not to be pressed because of its lack of agreement with *ṣpwr* in 14:11. Such a neutral usage for *zh* is attested elsewhere in BH; see P. Joüon, *Grammaire de l'hébreu biblique*, §143a.

[13] The list of birds in vv. 12–18 follows the identifications suggested by J. Feliks in *The Animal World of the Bible*. Feliks is particularly valuable because of his appeal to the ancient translation traditions contained in the Vss and rabbinic sources. Even so, not all these birds are readily identifiable. Question marks are added to those names which are considered least certain according to the study of Cansdale (*Animals of Bible Lands*, 175–176). Cansdale's work must serve as a caveat to the results of both Feliks and G. R. Driver in "Birds in the Old Testament 1: Birds in Law." For a critique of Driver's identifications (which appear in the NEB) see Cansdale, *Animals of Bible Lands*, 141.

14:13. whr'h w't h'yh whdyh MT
w't hd'h w't h'yh SP, Gen, K186,489,567,633
καὶ τὸν γύπα καὶ τὸν ἰκτῖνα LXX

Both *r'h* in v. 13 and the parallel reading *d'h* in Lev 11:14 are *hapax legomena*. Talmudic tradition assumed that these four words could be resolved into two synonymous pairs *d'h / dyh* and *'yh / r'h*, or that all four were synonyms for the same species.[14] But the similarity of the lists in Deut 14:13 and Lev 11:14 suggests that one of these texts is in error. This is possible, since *dalet* and *reš* can be easily confused in all scripts from paleo-Hebrew through to Herodian times. Even if all of the witnesses for *hd'h* have corrected the text in favor of the Leviticus reading, they are still of value for pointing out a philological problem in Deut 14:13 as well as its most likely solution. That is: *hr'h* is a corrupt version of the reading preserved in Lev 11:14.

The note in BHS is incorrect in suggesting that the LXX can be retroverted to the same Hebrew text represented by the SP. Judging from the Hexapla, Origen believed that the LXX attested to a shorter text without *whd'h*, since he added the phrase καὶ τὸν ἴξον to the beginning of v. 13 on the basis of the translation of Aquila. It is evident that Origen regarded γύπα as a translation for *'yh*, since the Hexapla transposed the LXX so that γύπα would correspond to *h'yh* in Lev 11:14.

One may conclude that at one time there were two shorter texts for Deut 14:13:

a) there was the text *whd'h w't h'yh lmynh* attested by the SP and Lev 11:14;[15]

b) Greek witnesses suggest a text containing the pair *h'yh* and *hdyh*.

The MT may be viewed as a conflation of these two shorter texts. The extant Hebrew witnesses are to be preferred over the LXX in a case where both readings appear equally credible.

14:19. The phrase *wkl šrṣ h'wp* in 14:19a does not belong to the list found in vv. 12–18. If it did, then the verbless clause in v. 19aβ would resume all of the members of the list in vv. 12–18. This is unlikely because of its singular number, cf. *ṭm'ym hm lkm* in 14:7aδ. Consequently, v. 19a is best analyzed as

---

14 Feliks, *The Animal World of the Bible*, 67; see *b. Hul* 63b.

15 The presence of *'t* in SP is also secondary. SP has evidently leveled the variation in vv. 12–18 by attaching *'t* throughout. See TO for support of the MT.

a CNc where *kl šrṣ hʿwp* is a focus marker for a clause in which it does not appear as an argument.

Clause Row Structure

Deut 14:11–20 is marked by an inclusio involving c.11 and c.20. The matching constituent structure of these two clauses marks the parallelism between them as does the interchange of the terms *ṣpwr ṭhwrh* and *ʿwp ṭhwr*—an example of cohesion by lexical reiteration. The prescriptions concerning what may be eaten (cc.11, 20) frame two instructions concerning what may not be eaten (cc.12–19, 19b). The structure of 14:11–20, therefore, can be viewed as a chiasmus in which c.11 = c.20 and variations on *lʾ ʾkl* appear in both vv. 12 and 19b.

The coordination of 14:19a is ambiguous. Sonsino believes that v. 19aβ is a motive clause.[16] But the previous philological discussion disclosed that v. 19a is best considered as one clause belonging to the type CNc. This suggests that the *waw* is acting as a conjunction on the clause level and not merely to connect v. 19aα with the list of nouns ending in v. 18. As such, all of v. 19a has the function of a motive clause preposed to v. 19b.

The evidence suggests the following model of inner structure:

11	Prescription	F:IVc	Initial instruction
12–18*	Nominal instruction	CoF:Nc	Forbidden class 1
19a	Motive clause	CoF:CNc	Forbidden class 2
19b	Prohibition	F:xVc	
20	Prescription	F:IVc	Recapitulation

Parallels

14:11–20 This text shows close structural and semantic parallels with Lev 11:13–23. As was the case for 14:4–8, 9–10, this includes the use of *zh* / *zʾt* introductory phrases (Lev 11:13, 21) and repetitive uses of valuations of uncleanness: *šqṣ . . . lkm* (Lev 11:13, 23).

§2.4 Deut 14:21a

Transcription and Translation

21aα	lʾ tʾklw kl nblh	F:xVc	V O
21aβ	lgr ʾšr bšʿryk ttnnh	F:IVc	P V+O
21aγ	wʾklh	CoF:wqtl	V+O
21aδ	ʾw mkr lnkry	CoF:Inf	V [O] P
21aε	ky ʿm qdwš ʾth lyhwh ʾlhyk	B:Nc	Pred S P

16 Sonsino, *Motive Clauses*, 256.

[21] You are not to eat anything which has died a natural death. You shall give it to the resident alien who is in your gates and he shall eat it;[17] or sell [it] to a foreigner. For you are a people consecrated to Yahweh your God.

Clause Row Structure

This clause row begins with a prohibition in the 2mpl (c.21aα) and continues with 2ms commands. Clause 21aβ shows a relationship with c.21aδ through the conjunction *ʾw* and also lexical reiteration through the parallelism of *lgr / lnkry*. Therefore, the *wqtl* clause in c.21aγ does not belong to the same level of discourse as cc.21aβ, 21aδ. Deut 14:21aβ, 21aδ are the two primary commands which develop the thought of 14:21aα. Clause 21aγ contemplates an action consequent on the command of 14:21aβ.

The notes to the translation indicate that Deut 14:21aγ has the syntax of a result clause. But this does not mean that it provides the grounds for a particular action.[18] In 14:21a the addressee is called upon to ensure the disposal of the *nblh*. Deut 14:21aβ, 21aδ develop the principle in c.21aα by indicating acceptable alternatives: one may give the *nblh* to a *gr* so it will be consumed, or it may be sold to a *nkry*. The real ground for such actions is the B clause in 14:21aϵ.

The evidence suggests the following model of inner structure:

21aα	Prohibition	F:xVc	Instruction	2mpl
21aβ	Prescription	F:IVc	Implication 1	2ms
21aγ	Result clause	CoF:wqtl		
21aδ	Infinitive prescription	CoF:Inf	Implication 2	
21aϵ	Motive clause	B:Nc		

Parallels

14:21a. This clause row consists of three instructions having the typology: "don't do this with *X*, do this with *X* or do that with *X*." Such a structure is not found in the examples listed by Gerstenberger as original series of three-row instructions.[19] Outside of Deut 14:21a, the conjunction *ʾw* is not normally used to link parallel prescriptions. A somewhat similar construction does occur in Exod 19:13a. In Exod 19:13aβ the conjunction *ʾw* links two positive instructions for breaking the prohibition in Exod 19:13aα.

---

[17] Sonsino (ibid., 71) construes the *wqtl* construction in 14:21aγ with a causative nuance. JPSV considers the clause to be a purpose clause. But if it is not simply a further instruction consequent on 14:21aβ, then 14:21aγ is best taken as a result clause. See T. J. Meek, "Result and Purpose Clauses in Hebrew," 40.

[18] Contra Sonsino, *Motive Clauses*, 250, 267.

[19] Gerstenberger, *Apodiktischen Rechts*, 88.

In Deut 14:21a *ʾw* joins two prescriptions which are alternative ways of realizing the prohibition expressed in 14:21aα. Exod 19:13, unlike Deut 14:21, is framed in the third person. Although the evidence is limited, it suggests that the second person instruction row found in 14:21a is not stereotypical.

14:21aα. Semantic parallels to the prohibition of consumption of *nblh* in c.21aα occur in Lev 22:8 and Ezek 44:31.[20] Both of these are directed toward the priesthood. Lev 11:40 and 17:15 provide ritual remedies for the consumption of the animals which have been found dead. All four passages suggest that the origin of the prohibition against eating the *nblh* is to be found in circles which composed and transmitted priestly torah.

14:21aβ–ϵ. Typical motifs of Dtn rhetoric are found in the 2ms section of v. 21a:

c.21aβ *hgr ʾšr bšʿryk*.[21] This is a specific instance of the wider description of *personae miserae* in Deuteronomy as "the one(s) in your city"; see, e.g., 14:27; 16:11, 14. This epithet for the *personae miserae* is confined to Deuteronomy, except for Exod 20:10.

c.21aα *ʿm qdwš* This clause is parallel to 14:2a. See the discussion on that verse.

§2.5 Deut 14:21b

Transcription and Translation

21b	lʾ tbšl gdy bḥlb ʾmw	F:xVc	V O P

You shall not boil a kid in its mother's milk.

Clause Row Structure

21b	Prohibition	F:xVc

Parallels

Gerstenberger considers 14:21b to be a member of the genre of independent prohibitions.[22] While there is little doubt that such a genre exists, the question is whether 14:21b belongs to it. A case can be made for

[20] G. Bettenzoli ("Deuteronomium und Heiligkeitsgesetz," 388) also would associate 14:21aα with the literary unit of 14:4–20.

[21] Found also in 14:29; cf. 5:14(=Exod 20:10); 24:14; 29:10; 31:12.

[22] Gerstenberger,*Apodiktischen Rechts*, 68.

the original membership of 14:21b in a series of festival injunctions now found in Exod 23:18–19; 34:25–26.[23]

The Literary Unity of Deut 14:3–21

A distinction in sources in vv. 3–21a is suggested by the presence of texts in the 2ms and 2mpl. This distinction is given support by the observation that most of the elements written in the 2mpl have a common generic parallel while those in the 2ms do not. It is likely that a Dtn writer provided v. 3 as an introduction to vv. 4–21aα and developed v. 21aα with the 2ms material in cc.21aβ–21aε. It is difficult to determine if 14:21b is original to the composition of 14:21 or added later.

14:3. Deut 14:3 has no close semantic or structural parallels outside Deuteronomy. It is probably a Dtn composition because the word *twʿbh* is practically confined to Deuteronomy in the Pentateuch, and it is recognized as being a part of its characteristic vocabulary.[24] In 14:3, *twʿbh* refers to something which can be eaten. This use of *twʿbh* is unusual both in Deuteronomy and in other biblical literature. Usually *twʿbh* refers to a person (Deut 18:12a; 22:5; 23:19; 24:4; 25:16) or a practice (Deut 12:31; 13:15; 17:4; 18:9, 12b; 20:18; 32:16) which is abominable to Yahweh. Nevertheless, there are five contexts in which *twʿbh* refers to an object in Deuteronomy: 7:25, 26; 14:3; 17:1; 27:15. The contexts of these references show that *twʿbh* may refer to inadmissible cultic objects (7:25, 26; 27:15) or animals (17:1).

The prohibition in 14:3 may either forbid the consumption of the product of an action which is *twʿbh* (e.g., food offered to an idol) or the consumption of something which makes one *twʿbh* (e.g., unable to participate in the cultic community). The second possibility is more likely given the context of 14:4–8. Deut 14:3 gives an explicitly religious classification to the list of unclean and clean animals which follows. It is on the basis of their acceptability to the worship of Yahweh that the animals are distinguished.[25] It appears that 14:3 is meant to act as a title introducing the contents of 14:4–20. What the text of 14:4–20 brands as *ṭmʾ* the Dtn writer calls *twʿbh*.

---

[23] A. Schoors, "Literary Phrases," 32.

[24] Contra F. Horst, *Das Privilegrecht Jahwes*, 73, 152. See WA p. 323. Outside Deuteronomy, in the legal portions of the Pentateuch, *twʿbh* only occurs in Lev 18:22; 20:13 (pl. in Lev 18:26, 27, 29, 30). These texts are concerned with sexual misconduct.

[25] Mayes, *Deuteronomy*, 239.

14:4–21aα. A literary pattern linking vv. 4–21aα has been described by Zakovitch in his examination of the numerical sequence three-four in the Hebrew Bible. In this sequence, the first three elements are parallel while the fourth element is related but distinct in some way.[26] So, in 14:4–21aα, the first three sense units deal with food categories which may be either clean or unclean (vv. 4–8, 9–10, 11–20*) but the fourth category is one which is entirely unclean (v. 21aα).[27]

14:4–20. Merendino has suggested that at the core of 14:4–20 are the lists of fauna and accompanying commands in vv. 4–5, 12b–18, 19b. Around this the rest of the material in 14:4–20 has accumulated in two discernible stages of composition: a) vv. 6, 9 b) vv. 7–8; 10; 11, 12a, 19a, 20.[28] Against this reconstruction are indicators of cohesion such as those noted above. Verses 6–7 show clause row cohesion by lexical repetition (*tʾklw*), deixis, and chiasmus (*prsh, grh*). As for v. 10a, it shows cohesion with v. 9b both by its similar constituent structure and by structural repetition (*tʾklw*). Secondly, in the earliest layer of Merendino's reconstruction (vv. 4–5; 12b–18, 19b), there is no technical term for uncleanness. In fact, Merendino's reconstructed core is devoid of indicators pointing to the cultic concerns implicit in the compilation of these lists. He has evidently decided on some other ground that the text in 14:11–20 was originally an animal list which has been developed in this particular fashion. But this hypothesis is uncontrollable.

A reconstruction proposed by Bettenzoli also founders because of inattention to details of clause row cohesion. According to Bettenzoli, vv. 7–8, 10–19 distinguish themselves from a core of vv. 4–6, 9 both by their usage of the article and by the use of the terms "clean/unclean."[29] But the indefinite use of *grh* and *prsh* is found not only in 14:6, but also in 14:7b, 8a. Secondly, there are structural relationships between v. 9b and v. 10a which are ignored by separating them. Finally, Bettenzoli does not note that the phrases of the type *ṭmʾ hwʾ lkm* act as punctuating devices to subsections in the overall description. In summary, an earlier literary form of vv. 4–20 cannot be determined from the text.

Deut 14:4–21aα is not dependent on the parallel text in Leviticus 11. For example, although Lev 11:2b–8 is quite similar in structure and vocabulary to 14:4–8, compared to Lev 11:2b–3a Deut 14:4 is longer because of its list of ten names of clean animals. But Lev 11:4b–8 contains a longer version of the

---

26 Y. Zakovitch, *The Numerical Pattern Three-Four in the Hebrew Bible*, II.

27 Ibid., xxvi.

28 Merendino, *Gesetz*, 84–89.

29 Bettenzoli, "Deuteronomium und Heiligkeitsgesetz," 388.

instructions of 14:7–8. Unlike Deut 14:7a*, Leviticus qualifies each of the named animals by motivations similar to Deut 14:7bβ–7bδ, deliberately achieving variation by changing the form of the verb. The description of the pig is longer in Lev 11:7 because of the appearance of the phrase *šsᶜ šsᶜ* and a well-formed clause using *grh*. Finally, the summary instructions found in 14:8b are qualified by a repetition of the motive clause "they are unclean for you" in Lev 11:8b.

It can be argued, therefore, that Lev 11:2–8 and Deut 14:4–8 are both expansionary with respect to each other. As the expansions are not found in the same place, it is best to conclude that Lev 11:2–8 and Deut 4–21aα represent independent recensions of a common tradition. A similar opinion has been expressed by Moran in answer to the attempt by Rendtorff to derive the food laws in Deut 14:4–21aα from the parallel in Leviticus. He notes in particular that the list of clean animals in 14:4–5 is unique to the Dtn context, and the term *šqṣ* as the evaluation assigned to unclean water and winged creatures (cf. Lev 11:9–23) is absent.[30]

*14:12–18**. Blau has suggested that the nouns in vv. 12–18 are to be regarded as nouns in apposition to the object of the verb *tʾklw* in 14:12a'. In such a case, he claims it is acceptable for members of a list of objects to vary in their modification by *ʾt*.[31] This is doubtful. A survey of lists of three members or more in Deuteronomy which contain *ʾt* as an object marker reveals that the preference is clearly for all members of the list to have identical modification (cf. 2:33; 3:2, 24; 4:19, 43; 5:24[21]; 7:11; 11:6; 26:7; 28:20; 30:15). An exception to this rule is found in 12:6, which can be schematized in the following fashion: a+b +*ʾt*– c +*ʾt*– d +e+f+g. The list is split roughly in thirds with the nouns modified by *ʾt* in the middle third. But this pattern is not parallel to 14:12–18* since in the twenty member list there follows a sequence of four names without *ʾt*, eight names with *ʾt*, two names without *ʾt*, two names with *ʾt*, and four names without *ʾt*.

---

30 W. L. Moran, "The Literary Connection between Lv 11,13–19 and Dt 14,12–18," 272–273; cf. R. Rendtorff, *Die Gesetze in der Priesterschrift*, 45.

31 J. Blau, "Zum Gebrauch von את vor den Nominativ," 12. Blau also suggests that the *wʾt* construction can be used as a variant on the conjunction (ibid., 16). He claims that this usage is attested in texts where a list is in the S grammatical slot. Nevertheless, close examination of his examples finds no parallels to the construction in 14:12–18 (cf. Num 3:26; Jos 17:11; 1 Sam 17:34; 26:16; 1 Kgs 11:25; Isa 57:15; Jer 27:8). This is similar to the suggestion of Merendino (*Gesetz*, 87), who points to the way the subjects *ʾt hṣby wʾt hʾyl* are marked for the Nifal form *yʾkl* in Deut 12:22. But 12:22 is not close to the pattern in 14:12b–18 either.

The situation in Deut 14:12–18* is a grammatical peculiarity. The haphazard use of *ʾt* is a breach in syntax which suggests the possibility of interpolation. It is likely that the context of vv. 12–18 has been supplemented by material from Leviticus 11, as suggested by Moran. One may suppose that the original list in vv. 12–18 contained only the ten unclean birds not modified by the preposition *ʾt*. This would yield a list of ten unclean birds corresponding in number to the ten clean animals in 14:4–5. The birds modified by *ʾt* were supplied when 14:4–20* was supplemented under the influence of Leviticus 11.[32]

14:21a. Clause 21aα is distinct in origin from cc.21aβ–21aϵ. Parallels in syntax and genre draw cc.20 and 21aα together. Formal indicators of this rest on the use of the 2mpl person in c.21aα and its structural connections with 14:20 through repetition (*tʾklw*) and matching constituent structure (V O). The use of the 2ms number suggests a distinction between c.21aα and cc.21aβ–21aϵ. This is supported by the lack of generic parallels for the structure of 14:21a and by the fact that it is only the 2ms portion which uses Dtn clichés. Therefore, Deut 14:21aβ–ϵ is best viewed as a Dtn composition built ad hoc on 14:21aα.

14:21b. This text is a literal equivalent of Exod 23:19b; 34:26b. Its lack of topical or formal cohesion with v. 21a and its parallels with texts in Exodus suggest that 14:21b may be a gloss which was not originally part of the composition which produced 14:21.[33] In other words, it is debatable whether the Dtn hand responsible for 14:21a also appended 14:21b. This problem will be addressed below when an attempt will be made to identify a more extensive Dtn text original to the hand which composed 14:21aβ–ϵ. This may yield more evidence about the use of non-Dtn materials made by the writer of 14:21aβ–e.

[32] Moran, "Literary Connection," 275–76.

[33] Merendino, *Gesetz*, 88–89.

§3 Deut 14:22-29

The topic which links the clause rows divided by the Set tradition into 14:22–27 and 14:28–29 is the tithe of produce (vv. 22, 28). The clause rows are distinguished, however, by their chronological references: *šnh šnh* in v. 22 as opposed to *mqṣh šlš šnym* in v. 28.

§3.1 Deut 14:22–27

Transcription and Translation

22	ʿśr tʿśr ʾt kl tbwʾt zrʿk	F:Vc	V Po
22'	hyṣʾ hśdh šnh šnh	N:Part	V O A
23a	wʾklt lpny yhwh ʾlhyk bmqwm	CoF:wqtl	V P Pa O
23a'	ʾšr ybḥr	N:Vc	V Pc
23a''	lškn šmw šm	N:Inf	V O A
	mʿśr dgnk tyršk wyṣhrk wbkrt bqrk wṣʾnk		
23b	lmʿn tlmd	B:Vc	V Pc
23b'	lyrʾh ʾt yhwh ʾlhyk kl hymym	N:Inf	V Po A
24aα	wky yrbh mmk hdrk	CoB:Vc	V P S
24aβ	ky lʾ twkl	B:xVc	V O
24aβ'	śʾtw	N:Inf	V+O
24aγ	ky yrḥq mmk hmqwm	B:Vc	V P S
24aγ'	ʾšr ybḥr yhwh ʾlhyk	N:Vc	V S Pc
24aγ''	lśwm šmw šm	N:Inf	V O A
24b	ky ybrkk yhwh ʾlhyk	B:Vc	V+O S
25a	wntth bksp	CoF:wqtl	V [O] P
25bα	wṣrt hksp bydk	CoF:wqtl	V O P
25bβ	whlkt ʾl hmqwm	CoF:wqtl	V Pa
25bβ'	ʾšr ybḥr yhwh ʾlhyk bw	N:Vc	V S Po
26a	wntth hksp bkl	CoF:wqtl	V O P
26a'	ʾšr tʾwh npšk	N:Vc	V S
	bbqr wbṣʾn wbyyn wbškr wbkl		
26a''	ʾšr tšʾlk npšk	N:Vc	V+O S
26bα	wʾklt šm lpny yhwh ʾlhyk	CoF:wqtl	V A P
26bβ–27a*	wśmḥt ʾth wbytk	CoF:wqtl	V S
	whlwy ʾšr bšʿryk [ET]		
27b	ky ʾyn lw ḥlq wnḥlh ʿmk	B:xNc	Pred S P

14:22] You must scrupulously tithe all the yield of your seed which springs up in the field[1] year by year. [23] And you shall eat the tithe of your grain, new wine, and oil, and the firstlings of your herd and your flock in the presence of Yahweh your God in the place where he chooses to have his name dwell so that you may learn to revere Yahweh your God for all time. [24] But if the journey is too long for you so that[2] you are unable to bring them,[3] if the place where Yahweh chooses to set his name is too far for you when Yahweh your God prospers you, [25] then you shall exchange [them] for silver, keep the silver securely in your hand,[4] travel to the place which Yahweh your God chooses, [26] and buy with the silver anything which your appetite craves: beef, mutton, wine, intoxicating drink, or anything which your appetite craves. Then you shall eat there in the presence of Yahweh your God and rejoice, you, and your household, [27] and the Levite who is in your gates since he has no portion or patrimony together with you.

14:23a. The Pa *bmqwm* is an indicator of place. It might be seen as standing in apposition to *lpny yhwh ʾlhyk*. But the phrase *bmqwm* is accorded independent status in the clause constituent analysis. This is because the phrase *lpny yhwh ʾlhyk* modifies a proper name, a personal referent. Therefore, although both phrases can be interpreted as indicators of place (see the discussion on *lpny yhwh ʾlhyk* below), the P *lpny yhwh ʾlhyk* probably belongs to a different syntagmatic slot than the Pa *bmqwm*.

14:24aγ. The translation assumes that cc.24aα, 24aγ are variant conditionals. The syntax of c.24aγ is ambiguous. Its parallelism with c.24aα would be clear if it had been introduced with the formula *wky*. Without Co it could be taken as a subordinate clause following c.24aβ (cf. NRSV). But evidence that 14:24aγ is not subordinate to 14:24aα or 14:24aβ is found in the fact that the verb in both cc.24aα, 24aγ has the semantic class Sv. This is a rare type of predication in the discourse of Deut 14:1–17:13. The fact that

[1] When associated with *yṣʾ*, the object can connote the place from which something goes out (Joüon, *Grammaire*, §125n), see Gen 44:4; Exod 9:29, 33. The translation here is in opposition to RSV "which comes forth from the field" which must assume an analysis like that of A. B. Ehrlich and suppose that the participle really refers to *tbwʾh* although it agrees in gender with the nearer noun (*Randglossen*, 2:292). Against this concept is the observation that the attributive adjective or participle in BH agrees with the gender of the noun it modifies in BH with very few exceptions (Joüon, *Grammaire*, §148).

[2] The particle *ky* can introduce a clause of result (GKC §166b).

[3] The resumption of a plural antecedent by the 3ms pronominal suffix is not unprecedented in Deuteronomy. It is clearly occurring in the form *tʾklnw* in Deut 12:18 referring to the list of sacrifices in Deut 12:17. The LXX has translated the pronoun with a neuter plural pronoun in both 12:18 and 14:24.

[4] Literally, "and you shall bind the silver in your hand." The idea here is to ensure that the money is not to be spent along the way but only at the holy precincts (Ehrlich, *Randglossen*, 2:292).

cc.24aα, 24aγ share Sv predication suggests a parallelism between them in terms of their function in the discourse.

14:27a. lʾ tʿzbnw > K69, LXX

This situation cannot have arisen due to the ordinary kinds of scribal error. The agreement of K69 with the LXX is noteworthy. Although K69 often has variants due to errors in the transmission tradition, the situation does not fit the major categories to which its variants may be assigned (i.e., various kinds of expansions). At this point, K69 seems to be a survival of the same text type represented by the LXX.[5]

Andersen has attempted to account for the MT by describing *lʾ tʿzbnw* in 14:27a as an "adjunctive clause," that is, one which sits rather loosely in a passage which would otherwise flow quite smoothly without it.[6] But this is the only example of such a construction which he adduces from the legal portions of the Torah. The separation of the explanatory clause in v. 27b from its referent—the Levite in v. 27aα—is syntactically peculiar.[7] See the parallel found in 14:29a which contains the same qualification of the Levite. Apparently, *lʾ tʿzbnw* is a gloss which has entered the text at some late stage in the transmission of the text.

Clause Row Structure

Deut 14:22–27 is dominated by clauses in the *wqtl* form. In 14:23 a *wqtl* clause develops the thought of 14:22. This is followed by a *lmʿn* clause in 14:23 which is bound to it. After a series of four *ky* clauses in 14:24, the clause row proceeds as a series of *wqtl* clauses in 14:25–26bβ. The appearance of *wntth* in 14:25a may be considered as a case of the so-called *waw* of the apodosis.[8]

The distinction between 14:22–23 and 14:24–27 is marked by a shift in the kind of verb used. Two Sv clauses mark the beginning of the conditional in 14:24 (cc.24aα, 24aγ). Consequently, one may suggest that the function of the conjunction *waw* in 14:24aα is not to coordinate at the clause level but at the clause row level. That is, the *waw* in 14:24aα serves to join two subsections within the clause row.

The initial clause row of vv. 22–23 and the conditionally introduced structure of vv. 24–26 are also connected by repetition and reference to a

---

5 See the discussion of the relationship between K69, the LXX, and the SP by J. Hempel, "Innermasoretische Bestätigungen des Samaritanus," 268.

6 Andersen, *Sentence in Biblical Hebrew*, 93.

7 Seitz, *Studien*, 195–96.

8 Joüon, *Grammaire*, §176.

common object. Clause 14:24aβ is related grammatically to c.23a by the pronominal suffix on *śʾtw*. It is also necessary to supply the object suffix on *śʾtw* to complete the sense of the verb in c.25a, so the contents of 14:24–25a also can be related to the construction of 14:22–23. The use of the reference word *šm* in c.26bα is noteworthy. This adverbial is acting as a circumstantial demonstrative reference:[9] *šm* substitutes for the phrase *bmqwm* and combines with the repetition of *wʾklt* and *lpny yhwh ʾlhyk* in c.26bα to refer back to c.23a.

The only *wqtl* clause with an Sv as a predicate is c.26bβ–27a*. This construction stands outside the inclusio created by the repetition between c.23a and c.26bα. Consequently, the inner clause row structure of 14:22–27 discloses a tripartite division: a) an initial prescription sequence (vv. 22–23), followed by b) a conditionally introduced prescription sequence (vv. 24–26bα), and c) a concluding command in vv. 26bβ–27:

22	Prescription	F:Vc	General instruction	
23a	Prescription	CoF:wqtl	(vv. 22–23)	
23b	Motive clause	B:Vc		
24aα	Conditional	CoB:Vc	Special case	Protasis
24aβ	Causal statement	B:xVc	(vv. 24–26bα)	
24aγ	Conditional	B:xVc		
24b	Temporal statement	B:Vc		
25a	Prescription	CoF:wqtl		Apodosis
25bα	Prescription	CoF:wqtl		
25bβ	Prescription	CoF:wqtl		
26a	Prescription	CoF:wqtl		
26bα	Prescription	CoF:wqtl		
26bβ–27a*	Prescription	CoF:wqtl	Summary instruction	
27b	Motive clause	B:xNc		

Parallels

14:22–27. Two major genres can be identified in this clause row: a prescription row in 14:22–23 and an If-You instruction in 14:24–26bα. The use of a prescription qualified by an If-You construction is a generic pattern. An analogue is found in the structure of the altar law in Exod 20:24–26. Exod 20:24 contains an initial instruction consisting of a prescription developed by a *wqtl* form. In Exod 20:25aα an instruction for a related matter is introduced by a conditional which has as its apodosis the prohibition in Exod 20:25aβ. A second prohibition follows in Exod 20:26. Other examples of this structure occur in Exod 13:13a (= Exod 34:20a) and Deut 15:19–23.

---

9 Halliday and Hasan, *Cohesion in English*, 57–58.

14:22. The use of the free Inf to reinforce a finite verb is common in BH, but the position of this construction in 14:22 is remarkable. In most of the directive material in the Pentateuch, the Inf V combination occurs as a prescription balancing a prohibition (e.g., Lev 19:17; Deut 13:10; 15:8, 14; 20:17; 21:23; 22:7; 23:22). The Inf V construction also appears within rows of instructions to mark some sort of shift in the discourse (e.g., Gen 17:13; Exod 21:19; Deut 7:2; 17:15; 24:13).

Cases in which an Av construction in the form Inf V stands at the head of an unconditional instruction sequence are rare. Within the materials known conventionally as law in the Pentateuch, the construction occurs in this position only in Deut 12:2 and 14:22. But 12:2 is not altogether analogous because it follows an introductory injunction in Deut 12:1. Other comparable contexts involve the verb *ydʿ* in a solemn injunction to pay attention at the beginning of a span of discourse, as in Gen 15:13; 1 Sam 28:1. The position of 14:22 probably made it especially marked for the first readers of 14:22–27.

14:23–27. A number of Dtn phrases appear in vv. 23–27. Besides the *mqwm* formula (14:23, 24, 25), such Dtn vocabulary includes:

c.23b *lmd lyrʾh*; See also 4:10; 17:19; 31:12, 13.[10]

c.24b *ybrkk yhwh ʾlhyk*; Lohfink identifies the verb *brk* as a *Leitwort* in the instructions for the tithe (cf. 14:29b), the *šmṭh* year, firstlings, and the festivals.[11] The motif of Yahweh's blessing on a second person pronominal object occurs in a number of different constructions:

wbrkk 7:13; 15:18, 24:13; 28:8; 30:16;
governed by *ky* 2:7; 14:24; 15:4, 6, 10; 16:15;
governed by *lmʿn* 14:29; 23:21; 24:19;
governed by *kʾšr* 15:14; 16:10.

Weinfeld considers the motif of Yahweh's blessing to be a characteristic Dtn cliché.[12] The closest analogue to 14:24b occurs in 16:15.

c.26b *wśmḥt*. This prescription is confined almost entirely to Deuteronomy in the Pentateuch. The closest analogues to 14:26b are in 16:14 and 26:11 (a 2mpl equivalent occurs in 12:7). A longer formula *wśmḥt*

---

10 WA, p. 332.

11 N. Lohfink, *Das Hauptgebot*, 83.

12 WA, p. 345

lpny yhwh ʾlhyk occurs in 12:18; 16:11; 27:7 (2mpl parallels occur in 12:12 and in Lev 23:40).[13]

c.27a *hlwy ʾšr bšʿryk*. Found also in 12:12 (2mpl), 18; 16:11. The phrase is a particular instance of the Dtn cliché "the one who is in your gates."

c.27b *ʾyn lw ḥlq wnḥlh ʿm(k)*. Cf. 10:9; 12:12 (2mpl); 14:29; 18:1. The closest analogue to 14:27b is in 14:29a. Outside Deuteronomy the combination *ḥlq wnḥlh* is attested in BH only in Gen 31:14.

14:23a. The development of prescriptive instructions by *wqtl* forms is typical in BH, e.g., Exod 23:10b, 11aβ; 29:3a; Lev 23:36bβ; Deut 12:3 (2mpl); 14:28b; 16:2.

14:23b. The use of *lmʿn* motive clauses to modify instructional contexts with second person referents in the Pentateuch is disproportional. The majority appear in Deuteronomy. See Exod 13:9; 20:12 (= Deut 5:16); 23:12; Lev 23:43; Num 15:40; 27:20; Deut 4:1, 40; 5:14, 33[30]; 6:2, 18; 8:1; 11:8, 9, 21; 12:25, 28; 13:18; 14:23, 29; 16:3, 20; 17:19; 22:7; 23:21; 25:15; 29:5, 8; 31:12.[14]

*14:26bβ–27a**. According to Sonsino, instructions of the *wśmḥt* type belong to a class of expression called *paraenesis*, a type he distinguishes from either "law" or "motive clause." Prior to Sonsino, the question of paraenesis in Deuteronomy has been addressed most fully by Lohfink. Sonsino, however, embraces many more constructions than Lohfink. For example, Lohfink does not regard expressions with *wśmḥt* as paraenesis.[15]

Sonsino's distinction between paraenesis and law confuses form with cultural function, a point not characteristic of Lohfink's more conservative list of paraenetic sections in Deuteronomy 5–28. Sonsino would like to distinguish between instructions which are embedded in narrative and address an ad hoc situation from those of durative value for the community. Only the latter are to be admitted to the generic category he calls "law."[16]

Such a distinction rests on a typology of communication function not based on grammatical grounds. Structural analysis suggests that 14:26bβ–27a* is an instruction of value for both the original prescription row in 14:22–23 and the special case in 14:24–26bα. In both cases, it is related to the

[13] Ibid., p. 346.

[14] Sonsino (*Motive Clauses*, 103) counts 18 examples in his corpus of which 11 are in Deuteronomy.

[15] For example, Lohfink (*Hauptgebot*, 94) sees paraenetic expressions in Deuteronomy 14–16 only in 15:4–6 and 16:12, 20. Cf. Sonsino, *Motive Clauses*, 66–69.

[16] Sonsino, *Motive Clauses*, 77.

sequence *ʾkl… śmḥ* which occurs also in 12:7(2mpl), 18; 27:7. But there are no syntactic indications that its value or force as an instruction differs substantially from the other *wqtl* clauses in 14:23–26.

Literary Unity

14:22. A tension exists between the sense of v. 22 and v. 23, since the former enjoins only the tithing of grain rather than the triad of grain, new wine, and oil. It is clear from other contexts that the harvest which comes out of the field is grain by definition (see Gen 47:24). According to Exod 23:10–11, field, vineyard, and olive orchard are three distinct classes of agricultural land, with *zrʿ* being the typical activity for the field. This distinction in land types also appears in Lev 25:3–4 (where *śdh* and *krm* are distinguished); 27:30 (compare *zrʿ hʾrṣ* and *pry hʿṣ*); Deut 24:19–21; 28:38–40.

Merendino assumes the phrase *hyṣʾ hśdh* is an explanatory gloss on the phrase *tbwʾt zrʿk* in v. 22a from the hand of the redactor of v. 23, who entered the reference to the three types of agricultural products in v. 23aβ.[17] But the phrase *hyṣʾ hśdh* merely reinforces the intent of v. 22a which enjoins the tithing of field crops only. Had a redactor wished to strive for a more inclusive formulation, then he could have resorted to a qualification using *hʾrṣ* (cf. *tbwʾt hʾrṣ* Lev 23:39; or *mʿśr hʾrṣ* Lev 27:30). There is no reason for reducing v. 22 to a shorter, more original form.

14:23. The view that *wʾklt lpny yhwh ʾlhyk* once appeared in c.23a in a literary layer without the *mqwm* formula is incorrect.[18] Seitz has previously noted the characteristic use of the phrase *lpny yhwh* as an indicator of place in Deuteronomy.[19] It is also necessary to recognize that the phrase "to eat before Yahweh" is unique to Deuteronomy in BH. Elsewhere in the Pentateuch the closest analogue is *ʾkl lḥm lpny hʾlhym* in Exod 18:12 (cf. Ezek 44:3; 1 Chron 29:22). Levitical instructions always talk of eating *bmqwm qd(w)š* (Lev 6:9, 19; 7:6; 24:9) or *bmqwm ṭhwr* (Lev 10:14). Moreover, the four other texts in Deuteronomy having *ʾkl lpny yhwh ʾlhyk* either explicitly link this phrase with the *mqwm* formula (12:18; 15:20) or with the adverb *šm* which refers to a previous mention of the *mqwm* formula (12:7; 14:26). Therefore, there are no grounds for dissociating the *mqwm* formula from the appearance of the phrase *ʾkl lpny yhwh* in 14:23, or for concluding that these phrases represent different layers in the composition of Deuteronomy.

---

17 Merendino, *Gesetz*, 96–97, 165.

18 Contra Merendino, *Gesetz*, 97; A. Rofé, *Introduction to the Book of Deuteronomy*, 35.

19 Seitz, *Studien*, 191; see 1:45; 4:10; 9:18, 25; 10:8; 12:7, 12, 18; 14:23, 26; 15:20; 16:11; 18:7; 19:17; 24:4; 26:5, 10, 13; 27:7; 29:9, 14.

The most detailed reasoning for seeing v. 23aα as originally composed without the object phrase in v. 23aβ ("the tithe of your grain, etc.") is given by Seitz. Besides the fact that the exclusion of v. 23aβ would alleviate the tension between v. 22 and v. 23aα, Seitz points to the unusual word order in v. 23a where V is separated from O by a prepositional phrase, and the fact that v. 23aβ contains an exact repetition of phrases in 12:17. Moreover, he argues that Deuteronomy often uses the verb *ʾkl* with no explicit object.[20]

The evidence is against Seitz. It is clear that v. 23 is composed by a writer familiar with Dtn rhetoric. Therefore, one may appeal to the syntax of the verb *ʾkl* as it generally appears in Deuteronomy. The verb *ʾkl* appears in Deuteronomy 76 times in the Qal. It is used absolutely in nonfinite forms three times: 4:24; 9:3; 31:17.[21] Excepting 14:23, *ʾkl* appears in the Qal governing a direct object or a prepositional phrase as object equivalent 57 times. The verb *ʾkl*, therefore, is normally transitive in the Qal in Deuteronomy. Five patterns may be distinguished in the 15 times in which the finite verb does not govern an object:

i) *ʾkl* does not take a direct object when it occurs in the formulaic sequence "eat and be sated" (6:11; 8:10, 12; 11:15; 14:29; 26:12; 31:20).

ii) A second pattern is "sacrifice *X* and eat" (12:21; 27:7), of which 16:7 is a variant: "sacrifice *X*, cook, and eat."

iii) A third pattern is found in 2:6, 28: "buy food and eat." Although the vocabulary is somewhat different, 14:26, "exchange silver (for food) and eat," also belongs with this group.

iv) A fourth pattern occurs in 12:7, "bring *X* and eat."

v) Finally, 4:28 occurs in an extended intransitive context describing idols and their lack of animate facilities.

In 14:23, *wʾklt* neither occurs as part of a well attested formula ("eat and be sated") or in an extended intransitive context where its role is clearly defined (cf. 4:28). The second, third, and fourth patterns listed above may be characterized as transitive patterns, since in these cases what is eaten appears explicitly as the object of a verbal in a prior clause. However, in v. 23 it is not the harvest, which is the explicit object of v. 22, but the tithe of the harvest which is to be eaten. Hence, v. 23 stands outside any other pattern in which a finite form of *ʾkl* appears with no object in Deuteronomy.

---

20 Ibid., 194.

21 I would translate *whyh lʾkl* in 31:17 literally as "and there shall be a devouring"; see the LXX.

Seitz seeks to reinforce his thesis about the original structure of v. 23aα by pointing to the unusual word order of the verse. But v. 23a is not without parallels. In 26:5, 13 the phrase *lpny yhwh ʾlhyk,* which acts as a place designator in Deuteronomy, divides O from V. In both cases, the contexts require the offerer to say a liturgical formula "before Yahweh your God," the O in each case being the words of the formula. These actions must take place at the place which Yahweh chooses (26:2). The most important parallel occurs in 12:17 in which the verb *lʾkl* is separated from the objects *mʿśr dgnk wtyršk wyṣhrk wbkrt bqrk wṣʾnk* etc. by a prepositional phrase equivalent to an adverb of place. In this case, *bšʿryk* serves as the opposite of the place which Yahweh chooses.

In summary, while it is possible that the verb *ʾkl* can be used absolutely in Deuteronomy, one should normally expect an object. The likelihood of this in v. 23a is increased by considering the syntax of *wʾklt* in v. 23 compared to other contexts with no explicit object in Deuteronomy. Moreover, the syntax whereby O is separated from V is not unique to 14:23 in Deuteronomy.

With a singular suffix on the infinitive *śʾtw* in 14:24aβ, the two antecedents in v. 23aβ (tithes and firstlings) do not seem to harmonize. Some critics assume that the phrase *bkrt bqrk wṣʾnk* was not originally part of the object of *wʾklt.*[22] The problem of the plurality of objects in v. 23aβ has already been adumbrated in the notes to the translation above. The construction in v. 23a is not unique in Deuteronomy. A plural antecedent for the suffix on *tʾklnw* is also indicated in the context of 12:18. The suffix on *śʾtw* in v. 24 may have a plural referent as well.

Arguments can be advanced both in favor and against the presence of *bkrt bqrk wṣʾnk* in 14:23a. These invariably appeal, however, to assumptions about the larger context of 14:23–27. For example, against the original inclusion of the firstlings is the observation that the surrounding context concerns only the tithing of agricultural goods (vv. 22, 28). Other contextual arguments may tell in its favor. These are derived from a consideration of the related instructions in 12:17–18 and 15:19–23. For example, there is no mention of the issue of compensation for the secular consumption of an unclean firstling in 15:21–23. The theological issue would be less acute if one assumed that the legislation in vv. 23–27 was intended to state a general principle which the writer in 15:20–23 felt need not be repeated.

In conclusion, the legitimacy of the firstling reference in v. 23aβ depends on a discussion of clause row relationships which is premature at this stage in the exegetical process. The issue will be reexamined in the next chapter.

---

22 For example, Merendino, *Gesetz,* 100.

14:23b. Deut 14:23b is problematic because of the context in which it appears. The idea of the fear of Yahweh is common in Deuteronomy, but the concept of learning to fear Yahweh is confined to 4:10; 14:23; 17:19; 31:12, 13. None of these formulations is identical, although they have similarities in word order or vocabulary. The motif of learning the fear of Yahweh typically occurs as an admonition in a context calling for observance of all of Yahweh's Torah (see 4:9a; 17:19b; 31:12bβ). This context is missing in 14:22–27. This difficulty will be reconsidered in the next chapter where it will be possible suggest a larger context for consideration.

14:24–26. Evidence for an original unity between 14:24–26 and 14:22–23 is indicated by generic parallels. There are parallels to the structure whereby a general instruction is followed by an If-You formula which addresses a special case. Secondly, there are important cohesive ties between v. 23 and vv. 24–26, including the envelope structure created by the repetitions between v. 23 and v. 26.

The most cogent argument of Merendino for literary-critical distinction between v. 23 and vv. 24–26 is the similarity between the phrase *t'wh npšk* in 14:26a and 12:20 (which he regards as secondary to the context of 12:21–28).[23] But even if Merendino is correct in his assumption that 12:20 is secondary to the context of 12:21–28, it does not follow that the repetition of the idiom *t'wh npšk* in v. 26a is evidence of composition by the same hand. Nor should one conclude that because 14:26 comes after 12:20 that the direction of influence must be from 12:20 to 14:26 and not vice versa. Out of eleven occurrences of the verb *'wh* in the Piel in BH, *npš* is found as the subject nine times (the parallels in 2 Sam 3:21; 1 Kgs 11:37 are especially noteworthy).[24] In other words, *t'wh npšk* is a fairly common idiom having to do with appetitive desire. The fact that a common expression concerned with appetite occurs in two contexts having to do with the consumption of food should not be too surprising; it need not be regarded as evidence of composition by the same hand.[25]

Merendino thinks the redactor who created v. 26bα took the vocabulary of v. 23a and repeated it in v. 26bα at the end of his supplement before the original ending of *wśmḥt* in order to round out the text. The repetition of *'kl lpny yhwh* is a proper object for literary-critical investigation. In this case, the

---

23 Merendino, *Gesetz*, 98–99.

24 Deut 12:20; 14:26; 1 Sam 2:16; 2 Sam 3:21; 1 Kgs 11:37; Isa 26:9; Mic 7:1; Job 23:13; Prov 21:10.

25 See the analogous discussion on *'wt npš* in Weinfeld, *Deuteronomy*, 2.

repetitive demand to "eat before Yahweh" seems to belong to a chiastic structure on the semantic level:

A	v. 23aα	*ʾkl lpny yhwh bmqwm*
B	v. 23aβ	foodstuffs
B'	v. 26a	foodstuffs
A'	v. 26bα	*ʾkl šm* (=*bmqwm*, cf. v. 25) *lpny yhwh*

In fact, there would be no perceived problem with the position of v. 26bα if it were not followed by the *wśmḥt* clause in v. 26bβ, which seems to be a demand covering not only 14:24–26 but also 14:23 as well. But this observation cannot be pressed since it is typical of *wśmḥt* commands to come toward the end of a section of discourse in Deuteronomy (see 12:18; 16:11; 26:11).

The list of subjects in 14:26bβ can also be viewed as original to v. 26.[26] A similar construction appears in 15:20. Furthermore, the phrase "you and your household" is common in BH (e.g., Gen 45:11; 1 Sam 25:6; 2 Kgs 8:1; Jer 38:17).

Rofé believes that vv. 24–26 are secondary to the Dtn layer in v. 23 because of c.14:24aγ: *ky yrḥq mmk hmqwm ʾšr ybḥr yhwh ʾlhyk lśwm šmw šm.* The clause occurs verbatim in 12:21, in a context (12:20–28) which Rofé sees as secondary to 12:13–19. He associates the latter text with the composition of v. 23a.[27] There are reasons for suspecting the originality of c.24aγ in v. 24. But there is no internal evidence against an original unity between v. 23 and vv. 24–26 even if c.24aγ is original to the context.

Without prejudice to the originality of 12:20–28 in Deuteronomy 12, the question remains whether c.24aγ is an interpolation in 14:24 or integral to it. At this point Richter's distinction between doublets with literary-critical value and repetitions with structural value is germane. Structurally valid repetitions, as opposed to doublets, occur in similar positions, are often found in the context of other repeated clauses, and show the same or similar constructions in their various manifestations.[28] In other words, the possibility that c.14:24aγ is a repetition with structural value must be addressed.

---

[26] Contra Merendino, *Gesetz*, 99.

[27] Rofé, *Introduction*, 35. As an ancillary argument, Rofé suggests that the writer of 14:23 could not have anticipated the problems his legislation would create. But other *mqwm* legislation also contains provisos of this kind where there can be no question of secondary intervention in the Dtn sections, e.g., 15:20–23 which Rofé considers is by one hand (ibid., 44).

[28] Richter, *Exegese*, 55.

Syntactically, the appearance of v. 24aγ overloads the context by creating a string of 4 *ky* clauses—most unusual in BH. In fact, there are no other examples analogous to the string of 4 *ky* clauses in v. 24 in the Pentateuch. Moreover, Broide's work suggests that Dtn sentence style favours tripartite clause patterns.[29] Deut 14:24 would fit in to this pattern well without v. 24aγ. Therefore, the presence of v. 24aγ indicates a breach of syntactic expectations with regard to biblical writing in general and Dtn composition in particular.

As noted above, c.24aα and c.24aγ appear to be variant conditionals with regard to meaning. As a verbatim repetition of a clause in another context, v. 24aγ is suspect according to the methods of literary–criticism. The redundancy and syntactical difficulties created by v. 24aγ suggest that it is an interpolation into v. 24 rather than a repetition which has structural value in this context.

The Literary Unity of 14:22–27

There is widespread agreement that v. 22 is traditional material which v. 23 is expanding—an opinion I also would support.[30] The core of v. 23 consists of the clause *wʾklt lpny yhwh ʾlhyk bmqwm ʾšr ybḥr lškn šmw šm* followed by an object in v. 23aβ. The phrase *bkrt bqrk wṣʾnk* in v. 23aβ and the *lmʿn* clause in v. 23b require further consideration.

Deut 14:24–27 forms a cohesive unit into which two insertions have been made: vv. 24aγ, 27aβ. There are structural indications of an original literary unity between 14:24–27 and 14:23. As well there are parallels to its inner structure which consist of an initial prescription row followed by a conditionally introduced special case. The suffix on *śʾtw* in 14:24aβ recalls the object of 14:23aβ. A chiastic construction involving the repeated demand to eat in the presence of *yhwh* (vv. 23a, 26bα) also serves to draw vv. 23–27 together.

§3.2 Deut 14:28–29

Transcription and Translation

28a	mqṣh šlš šnym twṣyʾ	F:IVc	Pa V Po
	ʾt kl mʿśr tbwʾtk bšnh hhwʾ		

---

[29] I. Broide, *The Speeches in Deuteronomy: Their Style and Rhetoric Devices*, III; cited in Braulik, *Die Mittel deuteronomischer Rhetorik*, 4.

[30] Merendino, *Gesetz*, 103; Rofé, *Introduction*, 35; Seitz, *Studien*, 19; Mayes, *Deuteronomy*, 245; Nebeling, *Schichten*, 76.

28b	whnḥt bšʿryk	CoF:wqtl	V [O] Pa
29aα	wbʾ hlwy	CoF:wqtl	V S
29aα'	ky ʾyn lw ḥlq wnḥlh ʿmk	N:xNc	Pred S P
	whgr whytwm whʾlmnh ʾšr bšʿryk		
29aβ	wʾklw	CoF:wqtl	V
29aγ	wśbʿw	CoF:wqtl	V
29b	lmʿn ybrkk yhwh ʾlhyk	B:Vc	V+O S P
	bkl mʿśh ydk		
29b'	ʾšr tʿśh	N:Vc	V

14:28] At the end of a three-year period you must take out all the tithe of your yield in that year and deposit [it] in your gates. [29] Then the Levite (since he has no portion or patrimony together with you), the resident alien, the orphan, and the widow who is in your gates must come, eat, and be satisfied so that Yahweh your God will bless you in all the work in which your hand is engaged.

14:28a. The phrase *bšnh hhwʾ* is a modifier of the noun *tbwʾtk*. Therefore, this chronological reference is not functioning at the clause constituent level.

14:29aa'. The similar clause in 14:27b is analyzed as a B clause. But the juxtaposition of 14:29aα' to *hlwy* creates a discontinuous subject in c.29aα. In fact, c.29aα' is not motivating the instruction as such, but justifying the inclusion of one of the nouns in the subject list. Therefore, c.29aα' is a word modifier, rather than a clause modifier. Such a clause may be described as an "internal motive clause."[31]

Clause Row Structure

This clause row begins with a clause in the IVc (v. 28a) structure which is continued by *wqtl* clauses (vv. 28b–29a). The close connection between the actions commanded in cc.14:28a, 28b is reinforced by the ellipsis of the object in 14:28b. The only Sv appears in v. 29aγ. This construction serves to mark the end of the *wqtl* sequence.

The translation assumes that 14:29a is a series of three *wqtl* instructions continuing the mood of 14:28b. The placement of the motive clause in 14:29b reinforces this perception. The actions in 14:28 may be seen as those that the addressee is required to ensure so that he may obtain the blessing promised in 14:29b.

The evidence suggests that 14:28–29 manifests the following inner structure:

28a	Prescription	F:IVc

[31] Sonsino, *Motive Clauses*, 75.

28b	Prescription	CoF:wqtl
29aα	Prescription	CoF:wqtl
29aβ	Prescription	CoF:wqtl
29aγ	Prescription	CoF:wqtl
29b	Motive clause	B:Vc

Parallels

The clause row structure belongs to the genre of prescription row discussed above with respect to 14:22–23. Deut 14:28–29a possesses the form of a prescription followed by *wqtl* clauses. A similar form to 14:28–29a, in which a IVc prescription clause is continued by *wqtl* clauses in the second and then third person, occurs in Exod 23:11.

The following phrases are associated with Dtn rhetoric:

c.28b *bšʿryk*

c.29aα *hgr whytwm whʾlmnh ʾšr bšʿryk* This is a variant of the Dtn motif "the one who is in your gates." See the discussion on 14:21aβ.

c.29b *lmʿn ybrkk yhwh ʾlhyk . . . bkl mʿśh ydk* As noted with regard to 14:23b, the *lmʿn* motive clause is characteristic of Dtn composition. Here it contains a variant of the Dtn motif of Yahweh's blessing on a 2ms pronominal object (see 14:24b). The phrase *mʿśh yd(y)k* occurs as an indirect object of Yahweh's blessing in 2:7; 14:29; 15:10; 16:15; 24:19.[32]

Literary Unity

It is Merendino's opinion that v. 28b is a later insertion in the complex of vv. 28a, 29* (without *hlwy*) which he associates with a layer to which v. 22 is also supposed to belong.[33] But there are no indicators of composite literary activity in Deut 14:28–29. The *wqtl* construction in 14:28b is a logical continuation of v. 28a. The phrase *bšʿryk* in v. 28b finds its explanation as the opposite of the *mqwm*, a contrast which is attested elsewhere in Deuteronomy, see 12:17–18; 15:20; 16:5–6 (cf. 14:23). One finds the familiar Dtn motif of *personae miserae* "in your gates" in v. 29a. Deut 14:29b has a number of signs of Dtn composition including *lmʿn* motivation and a variant of the well-attested Dtn motif of Yahweh's blessing on the 2ms addressee. Consequently, v. 29 has vocabulary links not with v. 22, which is evidently a non-Dtn formulation, but with formulas typical of Dtn composition, including the one found in v. 28b.

---

32 See WA, p.345 and Seitz, *Studien*, 275.

33 Merendino, *Gesetz*, 102–3.

§4 Deut 15:1–11

This section comprises two clause rows distinguished in the Set tradition: 15:1–6 and 15:7–11. They show a relationship through repetition of the phrase *yhyh bk ʾbywn* (vv. 4a and 7a). The theme of the *šmṭh* (v. 2 and v. 9) also appears in both clause rows.[1]

§4.1 Deut 15:1–6[2]

Transcription and Translation

1	mqṣ šbʿ šnym tʿśh šmṭh	F:IVc	Pa V O
2aα	wzh dbr hšmṭh	CoF:Nc	S Pred
2aβ	šmwṭ kl bʿl mšh ydw	F:Inf	V S O
2aβ'	ʾšr yšh brʿhw	N:Vc	V P
2bα	lʾ ygś ʾt rʿhw wʾt ʾḥyw	F:xVc	V Po
2bβ	ky qrʾ šmṭh lyhwh	B:Vc	V O P
3a	ʾt hnkry tgś	F:IVc	Po V
3b'	wʾšr yhyh lk ʾt ʾḥyk	N:IVc	S V P P
3b	tšmṭ ydk	CoF:IVc	O V O
4a	ʾps ky lʾ yhyh bk ʾbywn	B:xVc	V P S
4b	ky brk ybrkk yhwh bʾrṣ	B:Vc	V+O S P
4b'	ʾšr yhwh ʾlhyk ntn lk nḥlh	N:Part	S V P O Pc
4b''	lršth	N:Inf	V+O
5	rq ʾm šmwʿ tšmʿ bqwl yhwh ʾlhyk	B:Vc	V Po Pc
5b'	lšmr	N:Inf	V Pc
5b''	lʿśwt ʾt kl hmṣwh hzʾt	N:Inf	V Po
5b'''	ʾšr ʾnky mṣwk hywm	N:Part	S V+O A
6a	ky yhwh ʾlhyk brkk	B:IVc	S V+O Pc
6a'	kʾšr dbr lk	N:Vc	V P
6bα	whʿbṭt gwym rbym	CoF:wqtl	V O
6bβ	wʾth lʾ tʿbṭ	CoF:xIVc	S V
6bγ	wmšlt bgwym rbym	CoF:wqtl	V Po
6bδ	wbk lʾ ymšlw	CoF:xIVc	Po V

15:1] At the end of a seven-year period, you are to observe a remission.[3] [2] And the following is the procedure for the remission: every creditor must remit his personal loan

[1] For other treatments of Deut 15:1–11 as unit see, e.g., Seitz, *Studien*, 167–71, and J. M. Hamilton, *Social Justice and Deuteronomy*, 8–19.

[2] Portions of this study were previously published in W. Morrow, "The Composition of Deut 15:1–3."

which he lent to his countryman. He is not to press his countryman nor his kinsman for payment, for a remission of Yahweh has been proclaimed. [3] You may press the foreigner for payment, but you are to make your hand let go of the claim you have on your kinsman. [4] Except that, there is not to be a poor person among you, for Yahweh will richly bless you in the land which Yahweh your God is giving you as an inheritance to possess [5] if only you will really heed Yahweh your God by diligently observing all of this commandment which I am giving you today. [6] When Yahweh your God blesses you as he has promised you, then you will lend to many nations, but you yourselves will not have to borrow; you will rule over many nations, but they will not rule over you.

15:2. Deut 15:2aβ.b is a difficult construction which has given rise to a number of translations.[4] The root *nšh* denotes an interest bearing loan secured by distrained property or collateral held by the creditor.[5] The syntax of *nšh b* in Deut 24:10 makes it clear that the object of *nšh* is the loan itself and that *b* refers to the borrower. The same syntax is implied in 15:2aβ' where *ʾšr* resumes *mšh ydw* as the object of *yšh*.[6]

An understanding of the meaning of *mšh ydw* follows from the inferences of comparable phrases such as *mtnt ydw* in Deut 16:17; *mmšlt ydw* in Jer 34:1; and *ṣʾn ydw* in Ps 95:7. These passages show that *mšh ydw* is a transformation of *mšh* modified by the 3ms pronominal suffix. The word *ydw* refers to the one who has control of the bound noun. See also phrases such as *trmt ydk*, *mʿśh ydk*, and *mšlḥ ydk* which are common in Deuteronomy (e.g., 12:17; 14:29; 15:10; 16:15).

The translation assumes that *mšh ydw* is the object of the verb *šmwṭ*, the phrase *kl bʿl* being the subject. Normally, in BH one expects *bʿl* to be qualified by a bound formation (e.g., *bʿl ʾšh*; *bʿl byt*). But the position (favored by North among others) that *kl bʿl mšh ydw* is one bound phrase is difficult to sustain. This phrase would be a transformation of the phrase "every holder of his loan," which is redundant. Here I assume that it is possible for *bʿl* to stand without qualification in a context where it is clear what *bʿl* refers to (cf. Lev 21:4).[7] If *bʿl* cannot stand without qualification in

---

3 Philological study cannot determine whether the word *šmṭh* denotes a complete cancellation of the debts involved or only a one year suspension of payment, hence the neutral translation "remission." The translation of *tʿśh* as "observe" follows Merendino's observation that the construction here is similar to 16:1, 10, 13 where *ʿśh* is used to predicate festival observance (Merendino, *Gesetz* , 107). Other indications of festival observance are contained in the vocabulary of 15:2bβ; see the discussion on parallels.

4 For surveys of past scholarship see R. North, "YAD in the Shemiṭṭa-Law" and A. Cholewínski, *Heiligkeitsgesetz und Deuteronomium*, 218–19.

5 M. Gibeathi, "The Remission of Money in the Test Of Implementation," 172–73.

6 Contra North, "YAD in the Shemiṭṭa-Law," 199.

7 Horst (*Privilegrecht Jahwes*, 61) also understood *bʿl* in this way.

this context, then one should consider a conjectural emendation of the text and suppose that an original *kl bʿl mšh ʾt mšh ydw* was corrupted through haplography.[8]

15:3. The subject of *tšmṭ* is "you" as in c.15:3a. Both the RSV and the JPSV assume that it is *ydk*. But this means that the Hifil of *šmṭ* would have the same meaning as the Qal. Unfortunately, 15:3b contains the only attested use of a Hifil of *šmṭ* in BH. The word occurs most often in the Qal and, without further evidence available, one should assume that the Hifil is meant to give a causative nuance to the Qal as it does typically. Hence, it is best to regard the subject of *tšmṭ* as "you" and the verb as governing two objects.

The second object of *tšmṭ* is c.3b' *ʾšr yhyh lk ʾt ʾḥyk*. (The translation of v. 3b is changed from the one I published in "The Composition of Deut 15:1–3.") It follows from the syntax of v. 2a that what is to be released is the loan that is the object of the idiom *nšh b* (see c.2aβ'). Therefore, it is the loan placed with *ʾḥyk* rather than *ʾḥyk* itself that is best taken as the second object of *tšmṭ*.

15:4a. Clauses of the type *lʾ yhyh* appear in Deuteronomy both as statements (7:14; 11:17; 18:22; 23:11, 23; 28:65) and as prohibitions (5:7; 18:1; 22:5; 23:18; 25:13, 14). The *lʾ yhyh* clause in 15:4a is to be regarded as a prohibition because it is governed by the conjunction *ʾps ky*. A survey of the use of this conjunction reveals that it most often introduces an exception which does not alter the mood of the preceding statement (see Num 13:28; Judg 4:9; Amos 9:8).

Clause Row Structure

Deut 15:1–6 begins with a string of 6 independent clauses (cc. 1, 2aα, 2aβ, 2bα, 3a, 3b) of which only one (c.2bα) is modified by a subordinate clause (c.2bβ). There is linkage between 15:1 and 2aα through Co. Cohesion between c.2aα and what follows in v. 2aβ.b is indicated by the cataphoric use of *zh* in v. 2aα. The repetition of *šmṭh* in v. 2bβ creates a tie with c.1. Verse 2 is unusual in this clause row in that it contains no 2ms references. The clauses in vv. 3–6 show cohesion through consistent references to the 2ms addressee.

The *ky* clauses in 15:4–6 merit special attention. The only clause in vv. 1–6 with the verb *hyh* is not randomly placed. It occurs in the *ʾps ky* clause of v. 4. Thus a disjunction between the contents of v. 3 and vv. 4–5 is indicated not only by the conjunction but also by verb type.

---

[8] See the apparatus of BHS and Merendino, *Gesetz*, 108.

A popular solution to the syntax of 15:4–5 views c.4a as an apodosis of a conditional construction whose protasis is 15:5, Deut 15:4b being viewed as an intervening parenthetical remark (cf. LXX, Rashi, Ibn Ezra, JPSV, RSV). Against such a view, note that the two other instances of *rq ʾm* in BH both introduce a protasis whose apodosis occurs in the clause immediately before (cf. 1 Kgs 8:25 [=2 Chron 6:16] and 2 Kgs 21:8 [=2 Chron 33:8]). Secondly, 15:5 shows parallelism with 15:4b in the form of its main clause predicator. Both have finite verbs reinforced by the free Inf. This feature makes it difficult to regard 15:4b as merely parenthetical to 15:5 (see NRSV). Moreover, no other instance of a conditional with a protasis introduced by *ʾm šmwʿ tšmʿ(w)* contains such a parenthesis, hence such a view of 15:4b is unprecedented in the closest parallels in BH (see Exod 15:26; 19:5; 23:22; Deut 11:13–14; 28:1; Jer 17:24; Zech 6:15).

The identification of the verb in c.4a as a prohibition clarifies the structure of the bound clauses in vv. 4b–6a. Deut 15:4b introduces a conditional construction found in cc.4b–5 which is bound to 15:4a by the conjunction *ky* and which acts as a justification for the prohibition in 15:4a. The following *ky* construction in 15:6 consists of a temporal clause in the protasis with the apodosis coordinated with it in the *wqtl* form. Deut 15:6 is an exposition of the meaning of Yahweh's blessing mentioned in 15:4b. The relationship of 15:4b with v. 5 as apodosis and protasis is heightened by the repetition of the emphatic verbal construction occurring in vv. 4b, 5a. In v. 6b an interlocking order of IVc and *wqtl* types may be discerned. There is a chiastic match between 15:6bγ, 6bδ in constituent structure (V Po).

The inner structure of 15:1–6 has the following model:

1	Prescription	F:IVc	Instruction		
2aα	Cataphoric nominal clause	CoF:Nc	Exposition		
2aβ	Infinitive prescription	F:Inf	Details A	v. 2aβ.b	
2bα	Prohibition	F:xVc		(third person)	
2bβ	Motive clause	B:Vc			
3a	Prescription	F:IVc	Details B	v. 3	
3b	Jussive prescription	CoF:IVc		(second person)	
4a	Prohibition	B:xVc	Exception		
4b	Statement	B:Vc	Motivation for v. 4a		Apodosis
5	Conditional	B:Vc			Protasis
6a	Temporal clause	B:IVc	Exposition of v. 4b		Protasis
6bα	Statement	CoF:wqtl			Apodosis
6bβ	Statement	CoF:xIVc			
6bγ	Statement	CoF:wqtl			
6bδ	Statement	CoF:xIVc			

Parallels

15:1. The phrases *mqṣ* in 15:1 and *mqṣh* in 14:28 may be considered as stylistic variants. They differ in BH usage in that *mqṣ* only governs time words whereas *mqṣh* governs space as well as time words. Usually *mqṣh* governs time words in narrative statements (Gen 8:3; Jos 3:2; 9:16; 2 Sam 24:8; 1 Kgs 9:10; 2 Kgs 8:3; 18:10; Ezek 3:16; 39:14). The phrases *mqṣh* and *mqṣ* are not otherwise attested in the texts usually considered to comprise biblical law.

15:2–3. A parallel to the syntax of 15:2–3 occurs in Lev 6:7–11. Lev 6:7b is introduced by the formula *wz't twrt hmnḥh* in Lev 6:7a (cf. Deut 15:2aα). The first instruction is predicated by a free Inf (Lev 6:7b, cf. 15:2aβ). The text proceeds as a series of coordinated instructions predicated by finite verb forms in Lev 7:8–9. A related prohibition follows in Lev 6:10a (cf. Deut 15:2bα) ending with explanatory clauses in Lev 6:10b (cf. Deut 15:2bβ). Finally, a further set of clarificatory instructions is found in Lev 6:11 (cf. Deut 15:3).

15:2aα 15:2aα belongs to clauses of the type used in instruction contexts to introduce sections of third person instructions. Examples include, Exod 12:43; Lev 6:2, 7, 13, 18; 7:1, 11; Num 4:4, 31; 6:13; Deut 19:4.[9]

15:2aβ.2bα. Third person Vc constructions predicated only by an infinitive absolute are rare in BH.[10] Although the infinitive absolute occurs as a predicate in context in several texts in Deuteronomy (5:12, 16; 13:16b; 14:21; 16:1; 24:9; 25:17), these are all in second person contexts. The use of the free Inf as a clause predicator in a third person context in Deuteronomy is unique to 15:2.

A parallel to the syntax of 15:2aβ.2bα in Lev 6:7b–10 is noted above. Another text which shows some structural parallels to 15:2aβ.2bα is the instructions to the priests about those who may be admitted to the *psḥ* in Exod 12:43–47. The text begins with the formula *z't ḥqt hpsḥ* (Exod 12:43aβ) and proceeds as a set of instructions using the Imperfect indicative in the

---

[9] S. Talshir ("The Detailing Formula *wzh hdbr*") has labeled the formula *zh hdbr* as "the detailing formula" and attempted to identify a genre of texts on the basis of its occurrence. The texts she points to include the Siloam inscription; Jos 5:3b–7; 1 Kgs 9:15–22; 11:26b–28; and the legal texts of Exod 28:41–29:46; Deut 15:1–2; 19:3b–5. But these texts lack important structural similarities including genre membership and degree of embedding in their contexts. See the discussion in Morrow, "The Composition of Deut 15:1–3," 122–23.

[10] A free Inf predicates third person contexts in Num 15:35; in the prophetic utterances of 2 Kgs 3:16b and possibly Ezek 21:31 (*hsyr*); Ps 17:5 and wisdom instructions such as Prov 12:7; 13:20 (reading the *ketîb*); 17:12; 24:4, 5, 23b; 28:21.

third person. The instructions in Exod 12:43b–45 are arranged in antithetical parallelism (cf. 15:2aβ.bα). The subjects of the first two instructions (Exod 12:43b, 44) are marked by the noun *kl* (cf. *kl bʿl* in 15:2aβ).

Deut 15:2aβ.2bα belong to the genres of third person prescription and prohibition.[11] Legal instructions or decrees in an unconditional form in the third person are not unknown in ANE literature.[12] One connected with debt release appears in the Old Babylonian edict of Ammi-ṣaduqa.[13] Neo-Assyrian documents suggest that the same kind of proclamation as that of Ammi-ṣaduqa was also issued in later eras of Mesopotamian history.[14] There is evidence for influence of this practice on other cultures in the ancient Near East.[15]

15:2bβ. The motive clause in 15:2b provides important evidence for the cultural function of the instructions in 15:2aβ.b. Note the following parallel:

Isa 61:2	*qrʾ šnt rṣwn lyhwh*
Deut 15:2b	*qrʾ šmṭh lyhwh*

The verb *qrʾ* is used regularly as a verb of proclamation for institutions such as the *drwr* (Lev 25:10; Isa 61:1; Jer 34:8, 15, 17), sacred assemblies including the *ḥg* (Exod 32:5), *ʿṣrh* (Joel 1:14; 2:15), *mqrʾ qdš* (Lev 23:21), *mwʿd* (Lev 23:2, 37; Lam 1:15), and fasts (I Kgs 21:9, 12; Jer 36:9; Jonah 3:5; Ezra 8:21; 2 Chron 20:3).

The BH examples cited above all have as their cultural function the proclamation of a cultic or religious occasion. A cultic function also seems indicated for 15:2aβ.b because the *šmṭh* is *lyhwh*. Compare Exod 32:5 where the reader is told that Aaron proclaimed (*qrʾ*) *ḥg lyhwh mḥr* and Jehu's proclamation in 2 Kgs 10:19: *zbḥ gdwl ly lbʿl*. Either a cultic or royal figure may have issued a proclamation such as 15:2aβ.b. Aaron is the functionary in Exod 32:5. It is the elders who proclaim the fast in 1 Kgs 21:9. In 2 Kgs 10:20 the proclamation for the *ʿṣrt* comes from Jehu, whereas Jer 34:8 attributes the proclamation of *drwr* to Zedekiah.

15:3. An unusual feature of 15:3 is the appearance of the short Imperfect (the so–called jussive) in v. 3b. There is no evidence that variation between

---

[11] For a discussion and examples of these genres, see Richter, *Recht und Ethos*, 77, 90–91.

[12] A. Marzal in "Mari Clauses Part II," 507 lists the following examples: Laws of Eshnunna §§15, 16, 51, 52; Codex Hammurabi §§36, 38, 39, 40, 187; Edict of Ammi–ṣaduqa §12´; Middle Assyrian Laws §40, F2.

[13] F. Kraus, *Ein Edikt des Königs Ammi-ṣaduqa von Babylon* §I, 16'–17'.

[14] J. Lewy, "The Biblical Institution of Dᵉrôr in the Light of Akkadian Documents," 30.

[15] K. Balkan, "Cancellation of Debts in Cappadocian Tablets from Kültepe," 33.

instructions in the prescription and jussive forms is usual in BH. If textual error is ruled out, a case may be found in the parallelism between *tšyb* and *tšb* in Gen 24:6, 8. Sporadic appearances of the jussive in texts which normally use the indicative may be observed in Deut 28:8(*yṣw*), 21 (*ydbq*), and 36 (*ywlk*).[16] Cases of variation between prohibition and vetitive instructions are more common (see, e.g., Exod 12:9–10; 23:1; Lev 10:6; 11:43; 19:4, 29).

There is a visible motif of Dtn composition in v. 3: this is the opposition between *ʾḥyk* and the *nkry*. This opposition also appears in Deut 17:15 and 23:2 and is implied in 14:21a; it is a characteristic Dtn concern.[17]

15:4–6. The following Dtn phrases occur in 15:4–6:

v. 4	*ky brk ybrkk lyhwh*[18]
v. 4	*(hʾrṣ) ʾšr yhwh ʾlhyk ntn lk nḥlh lršth*[19]
v. 5	*tšmʿ bqwl yhwh ʾlhyk*[20]
v. 5	*lšmr lʿśwt*[21]
v. 5	*hmṣwh hzwt*[22]
v. 5	*ʾsr ʾnky mṣwk hywm*[23]
v. 6	*ky yhwh ʾlhyk brkk*[24]
v. 6	*kʾšr dbr lk*[25]

16 S. R. Driver, *A Treatise of the Use of the Tenses in Hebrew*³ §§56–58, especially §58.

17 Mayes, *Deuteronomy*, 248.

18 No other Dtn context has the verb *brk* emphasized by the free infinitive. Phrases close to 15:4 are found in 14:24b; 15:10; 16:15. Although the indirect object of *ybrkk* is frequently marked by *b* as in *bkl tbwʾtk* (16:15), *bkl mšlḥ ydk* (15:10), *bkl mʿśh ydk* (14:29; 16:15; 23:21; 24:9) 15:4 is unique in having the land as the object of *b* in the blessing formula. See WA, p. 345.

19 This is a long variant of the Dtn bestowal formula. See WA, p. 341. Deut 25:19 matches 15:4 exactly. Other contexts with a long form read the formula with *nḥlh* (4:21; 19:10; 24:4; 26:1; cf. 20:16; 21:23) or *lršth* (5:31[28]; 12:1: 19:2, 14; cf. 21:1) but not both.

20 Found also in 13:19; 28:2, 15; 30:10. The finite verb *šmʿ* strengthened by the free Inf occurs in 15:5 and 28:1. Outside Deuteronomy, cf. Exod 15:26; 23:22.

21 An infinitival variant of the Dtn phrase "to guard and to do," see WA p.336. Texts similar to 15:5 are found in 28:1, 13, 15; 32:46; cf. 17:19; 24:8.

22 See WA, p. 338. Found also in 6:25; 11:22; 19:9; 30:11.

23 Found also in 4:40; 6:6; 7:11; 8:1, 11; 11:8; 13:19; 19:9; 27:10; 28:1, 13, 15; 30:2, 8, 11, 16. See WA, p. 356.

24 An unusual form of the divine blessing motif. See the note on 14:24 for general references; cf. 2:7.

25 The conjunction *kʾšr* is a favorite in Dtn style. The clause is also found in 9:3; 12:20; 28:18; 29:12 and in 2mpl in 1:11; 11:25. For analagous uses of *kʾšr dbr (yhwh)* see 1:21; 2:1; 6:3, 19; 10:9; 18:2; 26:19; 27:3; 31:3. The Dtn function of this clause has been examined by

The conditional in 15:4b–5 is bound to 15:4a by the particle *ky* and acts as a motivation for the prohibition in 15:4a. The protasis of the condition has the form *ʾm šmwʿ tšmʿ*. It has parallels in Exod 15:26; 19:5; 23:22; Deut 11:13; 28:1; Jer 17:24; Zech 6:15. It is noteworthy that all of the analogous texts in the Pentateuch occur in contexts outside the texts usually designated as law. Their literary function is found within the preamble or conclusion of the speech of the covenant mediator to a proclamation of law.

Another sign of the connection of 15:4b–5 and speeches of the covenant mediator is to be found in the phrase *ʾšr ʾnky mṣwk hywm*.[26] This phrase belongs to a genre of similar phrases in Deuteronomy which Lohfink has called the "promulgation formula" (*Promulgationssatz*). According to Braulik's study, the adverbial expression *hywm* is never used in this formula when the speaker is Yahweh. Therefore, it calls to mind the speeches of the covenant mediator. The role of *hywm* in the promulgation formula has been described by de Vries. This phrase is used to emphasize the fact that the lawgiver is confronting his addressees with a situation which demands their decisive commitment.[27]

Deut 15:4–6 contains a number of passages with correspondences to other texts in Deuteronomy. There are significant similarities between 15:4a (*lʾ yhyh ʾbywn bk*) and 15:7a (*ky yhyh ʾbywn bk*); 15:5b and 28:1, 13b; and 15:6 and Deut 28:12b, 13aβ. Although the blessing of 15:6 is similar to the blessing in 28:12b, this motif does not appear to be a traditional motif of treaty blessings or curses. It is likely related to the Dtn motif of material reward.[28] The opposite situation is used as a curse in 28:43–44. Its presence in Deut 28:43–44 is apparently not due to a borrowing from ANE treaty language but reflects a concern for chiastic composition.[29]

Milgrom in "Profane Slaughter and a Formulaic Key to the Composition of Deuteronomy."

[26] The closest parallels to the formula in 15:5 occur in 8:11; 27:1(2mpl), 10; 28:1a, 15a; 30:2a, 8, 11a. Although the formula occurs frequently in Deuteronomy, only these texts have the phrase *hywm* ending at the clause boundary. Within Deuteronomy 12–26 the formula and its variants appear only in 12:11(2mpl), 14, 28; 13:1(2mpl), 19; 15:5; 19:9. It is more frequent in the prologue and epilogue of the book. See WA, p. 356.

[27] Lohfink, *Das Hauptgebot*, 59–63; Braulik, "Die Ausdrücke für 'Gesetz,'" 42; S. J. de Vries, "The Development of the Deuteronomic Promulgation Formula," 315.

[28] Weinfeld, *Deuteronomy*, 310.

[29] Ibid., 119.

Literary Unity

15:1. There is widespread support for the thesis of Horst that 15:1 is a non-, and pre-Dtn law.[30] Horst justifies his opinion by the supposition that Exod 23:10–11 and Deut 15:1 address the same concern.[31] The verb *šmṭ* occurs in both Exod 23:11 and Deut 15:2, and the noun *šmṭh* is etymologically related to *šmṭ*.

In response, one may cite Barr's critique of the etymological approach to lexical meaning. Function in context is the primary ground for determining the meaning of individual words; merely because words are etymologically related does not mean that they refer to the same thing.[32] The noun *šmṭh* does not appear outside Deuteronomy in BH and those contexts (15:1, 2[bis], 9; 31:10) must constitute the primary ground for determining what it means. In its biblical contexts, the noun *šmṭh* functions as the designation of an economic institution or activity related to the suspension or cancellation of debts. Deut 15:1 has in common with Exod 23:11 the concept of a seven-year period. But the name *šmṭh* and the custom involved in 15:1–3 cannot be transparently derived from Exod 23:10–11.

15:2. There are reasons for believing that 15:2aβ.b has a different origin from its surrounding context in vv. 1, 3. One indication of this is the function of the phrase *wzh dbr hšmṭh* in 15:2aα. Judging from its genre, the intention of the formula in 15:2 is to introduce a span of legal discourse in the third person as it does typically. In the context of Deut 15:1–3, the device of 15:2aα is intended to integrate the third person command in 15:2aβ.b into the second person context of v.1. Deut 15:2aα looks to be signaling a citation.[33] A second indicator is that the use of the free infinitive as a clause predicator in a third person context is atypical in Dtn syntax.[34]

15:3. Deut 15:3 can be contrasted to 15:2aβ.b in terms of syntax and function. To be noted in 15:3 is not only the change in person from 15:2 but also the *binyan* of the verb *tšmṭ*—Qal in v. 2aβ, Hifil in v. 3b. The mood of

30 Mayes, *Deuteronomy*, 246–47; Merendino, *Gesetz*, 107; Nebeling, *Schichten*, 82; Seitz, *Studien*, 167–68; Weinfeld, *Deuteronomy*, 223–24.

31 Horst, *Das Privilegrecht Jahwes*, 56–57.

32 J. Barr, *The Semantics of Biblical Language*, 107, 158–59.

33 Gerstenberger, *Apodiktischen Rechts*, 31.

34 Merendino (*Gesetz*, 107–9) is of the opinion that the composition of 15:2aβ.b underwent two stages: a) 15:2aβ* excluding the *ʾšr* clause (which he amends to read *kl bʿl mšh ʾt mšh ydw*); b) 15:2aβ'.b (beginning with the *ʾšr* clause). But there are no literary-critical factors which can be discerned in favor of such a view, even if the emendation is accepted.

the verb *tašmeṭ* is in the short prefixed conjugation (Jussive). It is more difficult to determine the mood of the verb *tgś* in v. 3a. Despite the fact that it is coordinated to 15:3b, it may be in the indicative as the positive counterpart to *lʾ ygś* in v. 2b.

In terms of function, v. 3 reads as a commentary added to v. 2aβ.b, granting permission to exact debts incurred by foreigners (v. 3a) but enjoining its addressees to release their countrymen from obligation (v. 3b). Its Dtn origin is indicated by the contrast between *ʾḥyk* and the *nkry*. Dtn composition also knows of the substitution of short Imperfects for indicative forms. Seitz has noted a chiastic arrangement of verbs based on the roots *šmṭ* and *ngś* in vv. 2–3.[35] This chiastic scheme affects the disposition of clause types as well since vv. 2bα = 3a in constituent structure. Evidently 15:3 has been designed by the Dtn writer to link up with the patterns of v. 2.

In summary, it appears that not all materials in the clause row come from the same source. The nearest parallel to 15:1 in terms of its time formula is Dtn (14:28a). The putative relationship between 15:1 and Exod 23:11 rests on a dubious etymological argument. Formal considerations in the context argue for a distinction between the composition of the 3ms references in 15:2 and the 2ms references in the rest of the clause row. Certainly (and here many commentators would agree), it is probable that v. 3 is a Dtn composition.[36] There is a good case, therefore, for assuming that non-Dtn material in 15:1–3 is confined to v. 2aβ.b. This clause row has been taken from some older source by the author of 15:1–3 and integrated into the present context by the phrase *wzh dbr hšmṭh* in v. 2aα.

Another device which may be involved in the integration of v. 2aβ.b into its present context is the phrase *wʾt ʾḥyw* in the clause *lʾ ygś ʾt rʿhw wʾt ʾḥyw*. Based on the paraphrase in the LXX, Talmon has suggested that the double reading in 15:2b is a result of conflation. Since *rʿhw* occurs in the phrase *brʿhw* in 15:2a and *ʾt ʾḥyw* appears below in 15:3, at some point in the transmission of the text these readings could have combined in 15:2b.[37] But from a grammatical point of view, the *waw* in the phrase *wʾt rʿhw* is identified traditionally as the *waw explicativum*.[38] It is possible that the phrase *wʾt ʾḥyw* may have been added by the author of Deut 15:1–3 as a means of further

---

35 Seitz, *Studien*, 169.

36 Ibid., 168.

37 S. Talmon, "Double Readings in the Masoretic Text," 168.

38 See D. W. Baker, "Further examples of the *waw explicativum*." Among uses in legal material he notes *wšsʿt šsʿ* in 14:6 (ibid., 132).

integrating the text of 15:2aβ.b into its current context. As such, it would serve to explicate the identification of *rʿhw* with the preferred Dtn term.

Originally Deut 15:2aβ.b may have been part of a royal proclamation of *drwr*. It can be argued that the character of 15:2aβ.b as a decree of *drwr* is implied by the use of *qrʾ* in 15:2bβ. Moreover, the contents of 15:2aβ.bα concern some kind of debt release, which suggests that 15:2aβ.b belongs to an equivalent to the institutions of *mišarum* and *anduraru* decreed by Mesopotamian monarchs. It is likely that similar practices also were known in ancient Israel.[39]

The mystery of the origins of 15:2aβ.b deepens, however, when the closest biblical parallels to the syntax of 15:2aβ are surveyed. There is no evidence that the kind of formulation found in 15:2aβ was characteristic of the royal court. Instead, it is best located in priestly torah. Such a cultic context does not seem to be analogous to the Mesopotamian parallels which are represented as royal decrees. The cultic ties of 15:2aβ are reinforced by the motive clause in 15:2bβ which declares that the *šmṭh* is *lyhwh*. But such strong ties to priestly and cultic language need not preclude the involvement of a royal figure in such a proclamation in Israel. There is evidence that royalty had certain priestly functions in pre-exilic times in Israel and Judah (see, e.g., 2 Sam 8:15; 1 Kgs 9:25; 13:1). It is possible that the *šmṭh* decree was made in Israel by a royal figure who used a torah form (cf. Lev 6:7) in order to undergird the decree with divine (cf. Deut 15:2bβ) as well as civil authority (cf. 2 Kgs 10:20; Jer 34:8).

It is likely that the author of Deut 15:1–3 incorporated 15:2aβ.b into his own legislation in order to show continuity with the older tradition of *drwr*. The motive clause in 15:2bβ suggests that this particular kind of *drwr* probably had the name *šmṭh* in pre-Dtn times and that the term as used in 15:1 is dependent on this older context. The writer of 15:1–3 provided the institution of *drwr* with an important innovation in order to create an effective measure for the periodic relief of the disadvantaged. The Dtn writer's choice of a seven-year time period was likely influenced by his knowledge of a sabbatical year tradition related to that attested in Exod 23:10–11.[40]

15:4–6. Deut 15:4–6 show affinities with speeches of the covenant mediator which fall outside the articulation of the kind of specific

---

[39] N. Lemche, "The Manumission of Slaves—the Fallow Year—the Sabbatical Year—the Jobel Year," 40–41.

[40] S. A. Kaufman, "A Reconstruction of the Social Welfare Systems of Ancient Israel," 282.

stipulations represented by 15:1–3. A sign of the connection between 15:4–6 and such contexts is indicated by the phrase *k'šr dbr lk* in 15:6a. The likely referents of this passage have been studied by Skweres. It is probably not referring simply to the promised blessing in 15:4b. In Skweres' opinion, the best candidate is Deut 7:12–15, although it is not possible to prove it.[41] According to Milgrom, the phrase *k'šr dbr lk* is often used in Deuteronomy to cite sources outside the book.[42] But the most logical source is the list of blessings in Deuteronomy 28. Deut 15:6bα.β paraphrases 28:12b and 15:6bγ.δ approximates the sense of 28:13a.

There is a semantic tension between 15:4–6 and assumptions about the continuing presence of the poor implied by the need for the *šmṭh* law in 15:1–3.[43] This gives the contents of 15:4–6 a somewhat polemical relationship to the foregoing 15:1–3. The structure of both vv. 1–3 and vv. 4–6 also reinforces the perception that these verses have little intrinsic relationship. There is little structural linkage between them. The presence of *'ps ky* seems to be a kind of patching device meant to hold two small units together which are not closely connected. A decision as to whether the cohesion of 15:1–3 and 4–6 is secondary or not will be made after the clause row sequences in Deut 14:1–17:13 have been identified. Then it will be more apparent if such a mixture of genres as that presently found in 15:1–6 is a likely feature in the sequence of clause rows to which 15:1–3 most probably belongs.[44]

§4.2 Deut 15:7–11

Transcription and Translation

7a	ky yhyh bk 'bywn m'ḥd 'ḥyk b'ḥd š'ryk b'rṣk	B:Vc	V P S P
7a'	'šr yhwh 'lhyk ntn lk	N:Part	S V P
7bα	l' t'mṣ 't lbbk	F:xVc	V Po
7bβ	wl' tqpṣ 't ydk m'ḥyk h'bywn	CoF:xVc	V Po P
8a	ky ptḥ tptḥ 't ydk lw	CoF:Vc	V Po P
8b	wh'bṭ t'byṭnw dy mḥsrw	CoF:Vc	V+O O
8b'	'šr yḥsr lw	N:Vc	V P
9aα	hšmr lk	F:Imp	V P
9aβ	pn yhyh dbr 'm lbbk bly'l	B:xVc	V S P A Pc

---

[41] Skweres, *Rückerweise im Buch Deuteronomium*, 38.

[42] Milgrom, "Profane Slaughter," 3–4.

[43] Seitz, *Studien*, 169.

[44] The opinion that 15:4–6 is secondary is generally held; see Mayes, *Deuteronomy*, 246; Merendino, *Gesetz*, 110–11; Nebeling, *Schichten*, 84; Seitz, *Studien*, 169.

9aβ'	l'mr	N:Inf	V O
9aβ''	qrbh šnt hšbᶜ šnt hšmṭh	N:Vc	V S
9aγ	wrᶜh ᶜynk b'ḥyk h'bywn	CoB:wqtl	V S P
9aδ	wl' ttn lw	CoB:xVc	V P
9bα	wqr' ᶜlyk 'l yhwh	CoB:wqtl	V P P
9bβ	whyh bk ḥṭ'	CoB:wqtl	V P S
10aα	ntwn ttn lw	F:Vc	V P
10aβ	wl' yrᶜ lbbk	CoF:xVc	V S Pc
10aβ'	bttk lw	N:Inf	V P
10b	ky bgll hdbr hzh ybrkk yhwh 'lhyk bkl mᶜśk wbkl mšlḥ ydk	B:IVc	P V+O S P
11a	ky l' yḥdl 'bywn mqrb h'rṣ	B:xVc	V S Pa
11b	ᶜl kn 'nky mṣwk	CoF:Part	S V+O Pc
11b'	l'mr	N:Inf	V O
11b''	ptḥ tptḥ 't ydk l'ḥyk lᶜnyk wl'bynk b'rṣk	N:Vc	V Po P

15:7] If there is a poor person among you, one of your kinsmen, in one of your gates, in your land which Yahweh your God is giving you, do not harden your heart or shut your hand to your poor kinsman. [8] On the contrary, you must generously open your hand to him and you must liberally lend him the amount sufficient to cover the needs which he has. [9] Watch out lest there come into your mind the vain thought, "The seventh year, the year of remission, is close at hand"; and then you ill-regard your impoverished kinsman, do not give to him, and he appeals to Yahweh because of you, and you incur guilt. [10] You really must give to him; and let not your heart begrudge it when you give to him, for on account of this action Yahweh God will bless you in all your activities, and in every personal enterprise.[45] [11] Since a poor person will not disappear from the land, accordingly I am giving you a command: "You must generously open your hand to your kinsman, to your needy and your poor in your land."

15:7a. The constituent analysis for 15:7a assumes that the phrase *m'ḥd 'ḥyk* is a modifier of the Subject *'bywn*. For that reason, it is not recognized as a clause constituent. Similarly, the phrase *b'rṣk* is also a modifier.

15:11b. It is assumed that the prepositional phrases *lᶜnyk wl'bynk* stand in apposition to the P *l'ḥyk*. As modifiers, they are not separate clause constituents.

---

45 Literally, "in every enterprise of your hand." Given the observation that there are plural forms in the text written defectively (15:10, 18) what is the likely interpretation of the form of *ydk* in 15:10? The preference in this part of Deut is for the singular in bound constructions where *yd* is the free noun; see 14:29; 15:2; 16:10, 17. Consequently, the vocalization of 15:10 is likely that of a singular form in pause.

Clause Row Structure

Following the protasis in 15:7a, there appears a row of clauses in two coordinated series (cc.7bα, 7bβ and cc.8a, 8b) ending in c.8b. Within this span, matching constituent structure (V Po P) and repetition (*ʾt ydk*) connect the last prohibition in v. 7b with the first prescription in v. 8a. The two prohibitions in cc. 7bα, 7bβ are connected by the lexical collocation of *ʾt lbbk* and *ʾt ydk,* a formulaic word pair which also occurs in Isa 13:7 and Job 31:27. The pattern is broken in 15:9aα by the appearance of an Imp clause. Clause 9aα is followed in c.9aβ by a B clause introduced by *pn*, which is developed by an extended series of *wqtl* forms ending in 15:9bβ. The *wqtl* pattern is broken by the appearance of 15:10aα, which is coordinated with 15:10aβ. This brace of F clauses is followed by B clauses in 15:10b, 11a. The final clause in 15:11b is connected to 15:11a by the anaphoric conjunction *ʿl kn*.

Unusual predication structures play important roles in the discourse. A new juncture in the instruction sequence is signaled by the occurrence of an Imp in c.9aα. The verb *hyh* marks the opening and conclusion of the span of result clauses in cc.9aβ–9bβ. The distinctive central section of admonition is, therefore, marked by an inclusio of *hyh* clauses which highlights the *šmṭh* context. In addition, the clause containing the *šmṭh* reference is predicated by an Sv. The final prescription in v. 10aβ is also an Sv and echoes the Sv which signaled the beginning of the *wqtl* sequence in v. 9aγ.

In Richter's view, a major role is played in clause row structure by passage to and from direct quotation.[46] The feature may be found twice (vv. 9, 11), both times as the object of the introductory phrase *lʾmr*. In 9aβ" the quotation contains the only explicit reference to the *šmṭh* context occurring above in 15:1–3. The appearance of quotation at the centre of 15:7–11 further highlights the *hšmr* sequence as the pivotal part of the clause row. The other quotation in 15:11 is also meant to connect with a prior context and works as an inclusio with 15:8.

A resumptive inclusio is created by the quotation in v. 11b, which is introduced by a Part—a distinctive and unusual clause pattern in the flow of F and B clause types in Deut 14:1–17:1. The reiteration of the demands of 15:8 in 15:11 augment the envelope form around v. 9; in addition, v. 11b has vocabulary relationships with v. 7a. Connections between the summary instructions in v. 10 and the central section in v. 9 are made by the lexical collocation of *wrʿh ʿynk* in c.9aγ and *yrʿ lbbk* in c.10aβ. Repetitions of the phrase structure *ntn l* connect all three sections (cc.7a', 9aδ, 10aα, 10aβ).

The inner structure of 15:7–11 may be described as:

---

[46] Richter, *Exegese*, 92.

7a	Conditional	B:Vc	Initial instruction	Protasis
7bα	Prohibition	F:xVc	(vv. 7–8)	Apodosis
7bβ	Prohibition	CoF:xVc		
8a	Prescription	CoF:Vc		
8b	Prescription	CoF:Vc		
9aα	Imperative	F:Imp	Central instruction	
9aβ	Result clause	B:xVc		
9aγ	Result clause	CoB:wqtl	(v. 9)	
9aδ	Result clause	CoB:xVc		
9bα	Result clause	CoB:wqtl		
9bβ	Result clause	CoB:wqtl		
10aα	Prescription	F:Vc	Recapitulation	
10aβ	Prohibition	CoF:xVc	(vv. 10–11)	
10b	Motive clause	B:IVc		
11a	Motive clause	B:xVc		
11b	Resumptive prescription	CoF:Part		

Parallels

15:7–8. Deut 15:7–11 begins with an If-You instruction. It belongs to the genre of casuistic laws governing primary rights and duties defined by Patrick. Most casuistic law is remedial: it describes the violation of someone's rights in the protasis and prescribes compensation or retaliation in the apodosis (e.g., Exod 21:22). There is a class of casuistic law which is not remedial, however. Laws such as Exod 21:2–6 do not describe a breach in the community requiring remedy but a right or duty with no provision for the correction of any violation of the law.[47]

As noted in the discussion on 14:22, prohibitions in BH instructions are often balanced by prescriptions reinforced with the free Inf. Examples which are formally similar to the construction of 15:7b, 8a would include, Exod 23:24; Deut 13:9b–10aα; 20:16–17; 21:23.

The following Dtn phrases occur in 15:7: *bʾḥd šʿryk*[48] and *hʾrṣ ʾšr yhwh ʾlhyk ntn lk*.[49] An analogue to the use of the word pair *ʾt lbbk* and *ʾt ydk* to connect c.7bα and c.7bβ occurs in 11:18. The phrase *ʿl ydkm* in 11:18bα

---

[47] D. Patrick "Casuistic Law Governing Primary Rights and Duties," 180–81; see also by the same author, *Old Testament Law*, 23–24. Among examples of the casuistic laws of primary rights and duties Patrick lists also Exod 21:7–11; 22:24–26; 23:4–5; Lev 25:8–55; Num 27:8–11; 36:6–9; Deut 15:7–11, 12–17[sic]; 21:10–14, 15–17; 22:1–4, 6–7, 8; 23:16–17, 20–21, 25–26; 24:5, 6, 10–11, 12–13, 19–21; 25:5–6.

[48] Found also in 16:5; 17:2; 23:17; cf. 18:6. This is a particular example of the Dtn motif *šʿryk*; see the note on 14:28.

[49] Found also in 1:25; 2:29; 3:20; 4:1, 21; 11:17, 31; 12:1; 15:4; 16:20; 17:14; 18:19; 19:14; 24:4; 25:19; 26:2; 27:2, 3. The use of the bestowal formula as applied to *ʾrṣk* in 15:7 has analogues in 19:2, 10; 26:2; cf. 21:23 (*ʾdmtk*). See WA, p. 341.

connects this clause with 11:18a through repetition by lexical collocation with the pair *ʿl lbbkm wʿl npškm*.

15:.9 Sonsino considers the Imp construction *hšmr lk pn* in 15:9 to be a form of paraenesis distinct from the character of law.[50] But it is a valid instruction form. The formula *hšmr lk pn* occurs in contexts which suggest that it can be used as a stylistic variant of the prohibition. In Gen 24:6 Abraham enjoins his servant not to return his son to the land of Haran. This injunction is first expressed in the form *hšmr lk pn tšyb ʾt bny šmh*, which opens the span of discourse in Gen 24:6–8. Abraham's concluding and parallel remark in Gen 24:8b is *rq ʾt bny lʾ tšb šmh*, a prohibition or vetitive.[51]

Other contexts in which the formula *hšmr lk pn* seems to be a stylistic variant for a prohibition occur in Gen 31:24; Deut 12:19; and Deut 6:12; 12:13. In this last example, the instruction in 12:14 contains a prescription linked to Deut 12:13 by the conjunction *ky ʾm*. Compare the sequence in Deut 16:5–6 where the prohibition of 16:5 is linked with the accompanying prescription in 16:6 by the same conjunction. The closest analogue to the structure of Deut 15:9 is found in Deut 8:11. Here the injunction *hšmr lk* is followed by two parallel *pn* clauses, the first in 8:11aβ.b and the second in 8:12. In the case of the second, the verb form of the *pn* clause in Deut 8:12aα is continued by *wqtl* forms in 8:12aβ–17. The evidence points to the conclusion that the formula *hšmr lk pn* is a kind of negative instruction related in nuance to the prohibition. Its currency with prescription language is implicated in texts such as Deut 6:12–13 and 12:13. Another text where the context is continued by a prescription appears in Exod 34:12–13.

There are indications that both *hšmr lk pn*[52] and the clause *whyh bk ḥṭʾ*[53] may be regarded as Dtn expressions.

15:10–11. Motivation also appears in 15:10b, 11a. Doron considers the combination of cc.10b, 11a to be a case of double motive clauses.[54] But

---

50 Sonsino, *Motive Clauses*, 68.

51 There is a textual problem in Gen 24:8b. The verb form *tšb* is a short Imperfect; SP reads *tšyb*.

52 Found also in 4:9, 23; 6:12; 8:11; 11:16; 12:13, 19, 30; 24:8. Outside Deuteronomy the construction *hšmr pn* occurs only in Gen 24:6; 31:24; Exod 34:12. According to Fishbane (*Biblical Interpretation*, 60–61), the particle *pn* is a characteristic stylistic element of Dtn rhetoric.

53 Found also in 23:22, 23; 24:15; cf. 21:22. WA, p. 356 considers this pattern to be characteristically Dtn as opposed to what is described as the "equivalent phrase in P," *nśʾ ʿwn*.

15:10b, 11a do not relate to the same clause. The main reason for regarding 15:10b, 11a separately is the presence of the *ʿl kn* construction in 15:11b. In Deuteronomy motivation associated with the *ʿl kn* construction is found in 5:15; 15:11, 15; 19:6–7; 24:18, 22. As Doron himself points out, the *ʿl kn* construction is not motivation in itself but it gives the opportunity to reiterate the law on the strength of the just stated motivation.[55] In 5:15; 15:15; 24:18, 22 the motivation is introduced by the *wzkrt* clause. In 19:6–7 the motive clause is the *pn* construction in 19:6. These examples lead one to expect *ʿl kn* to refer to one motivation not two. Therefore, it is best to regard 15:10b as the motive clause to 15:10a and 15:11a as the motivation for the reiterated instruction in 15:11b. A motive clause beginning with *bgll* in 18:12b also occurs following a prohibition (18:10–11).

The clause *ʿl kn ʾnky mṣwk lʾmr* can be regarded as a variation of the Dtn promulgation formula which appears in 15:5, 15.[56] The closest parallel to 15:11b is found in 19:7, where the formula *ʿl kn ʾnky mṣwk lʾmr* also introduces a reiteration of a previously stated instruction.[57]

The phrase *ybrkk yhwh ʾlhyk . . . (b)mšlḥ ydk* can also be regarded as part of the repertoire of Dtn rhetoric.[58]

Literary Unity

The unity of 15:7–11 has been called into question by both Merendino and Nebeling. They interpret the deliberate repetition of v. 8a in v. 11b as a redactional framing device which has been used by the author of vv. 9–11 to link this section with vv. 7–8. According to their view, vv. 7–8 were written prior to vv. 9–11, and the unity of vv. 7–8, 9–11 created by v. 11 is a secondary feature.[59] Seitz views 15:7–11 as an original unity.[60] There is no

---

[54] Doron, "Motive Clauses," 70–71.

[55] Ibid., 69.

[56] Braulik, "Ausdrücke für Gesetz," 41.

[57] A Dtn cliché, see WA, p. 357; found outside Deuteronomy only in Exod 34:11. Cases modified by *ʿl kn* include 15:11, 15; 19:7; 24:11, 22.

[58] See WA, p. 345.

[59] Merendino, *Gesetz*, 113; Nebeling, *Schichten*, 84. This is not to say that they agree in all details. Merendino sees vv. 7–9 and vv. 9–11 as composed in two stages following the composition of 15:3. Nebeling connects vv. 7–8 with the composition of 15:2 and vv. 9–11 with the composition of 15:3. A somewhat different position is taken by Bettenzoli ("Deuteronomium und Heiligkeitsgesetz," 393–95). He argues that vv. 2b–4; 7–8, 10, 12–14 originally formed a cohesive layer with a similar construction *Verbot, Gebot, Abschluß*. According to Bettenzoli, this construction was subsequently glossed by 15:5–6, 9, 11, 16–18.

[60] Seitz, *Studien*, 169–71.

unambiguous evidence outside 15:7–11 which can decide the issue.[61] The resolution of this question depends on whether there are other features of vv. 7–8, 9–11 which suggest that these two segments were composed at different stages.

If the presence of v. 11 is temporarily discounted, it is doubtful that a case can be made against the unity of vv. 7–10. In fact, vv. 7–10 apart from v. 11 reveal a cohesion which approaches the model of ring composition:

A	v. 7a	*ky* clause
B	v. 7b	prohibitions (2)
C	v. 8	emphatic commands (2)
D	v. 9	prohibitive
C'	v. 10a	emphatic command
B'	v. 10aβ	prohibition
A'	v. 10b	*ky* clause

From the point of view of structure, vv. 7–8 and v. 10 diverge from each other in that vv. 7–8 contain two prohibitives followed by two positive commands whereas in v. 10 there is only one of each kind. Nevertheless, the chiastic arrangement is not to be overlooked (v. 7b = v. 10aβ; v. 8 = v. 10aα), nor is the similarity of the constructions involved. Both vv. 7–8 and v. 10 share important motifs with v. 9. The prepositional phrase *mʾḥyk hʾbywn* in v. 7b is recapitulated by *bʾḥyk hʾbywn* in v. 9a. Similarly, the important motif *ntn lw* in v. 10aα.β is anticipated in v. 9aδ. Note also the various occurrences of *lbbk* in vv. 7b, 9a, 10a.

The *ky* clauses in vv. 7a, 10b can also be shown to share an unusual compositional feature. The double collocation *bʾḥd šʿryk bʾrṣ ʾšr yhwh ʾlhyk ntn lk* in v. 7a has bothered commentators who usually wish to remove either *bʾḥd šʿryk*,[62] *bʾrṣk*, etc.,[63] or both.[64] Behind the disquiet about v. 7a is the recognition that these phrases occur elsewhere in Deuteronomy in separate contexts.[65] In response, it may be noted that combinations of

---

61 Seitz, Merendino, Gesetz, and Nebeling all point to the inclusio made by *ʿl kn mṣwk lʾmr* in 19:7 as evidence for their positions. But Seitz sees 19:2a, 7 as the product of one hand (*Studien*, 113, 226), whereas Merendino (*Gesetz*, 202–3) and Nebeling (*Schichten*, 154) see evidence in 19:2 of two layers of composition, one of which (v. 2a) is pre–Dtn.

62 Seitz, *Studien*, 170.

63 Merendino, *Gesetz*, 111.

64 Nebeling, *Schichten*, 84.

65 The phrase *bʾḥd šʿryk* is found also in 16:5; 17:2; 23:17; cf. 18:6. The use of the bestowal formula as applied to *ʾrṣk* in 15:7 has analogues in 19:2, 10; 26:2; cf. 21:23 (*ʾdmtk*). See WA, p. 341.

similar phrases are not unprecedented in Deuteronomy.[66] There is a redundancy of a similar nature in v. 10b: *bkl mʿśk wbkl mšlḥ ydk*. This verse also has a combination of two phrases which appear elsewhere in Deuteronomy as variants of each other in the blessing motif: *mʿśh ydk*[67] and *mšlḥ ydk*.[68] It seems more than coincidence that two noteworthy instances of redundancy should occur in the *ky* clauses which frame vv. 7–10. The feature suggests a similar tactic of literary composition in both verses.

I conclude that vv. 7–10 are a unified structure which show signs of deliberate planning and composition. If one allows their unity, the question of the meaning of the redundancy in v. 11 becomes clearer. There is no redactional necessity for v. 11 as far as the structure of vv. 7–10 is concerned. Deut 15:11 owes its place, therefore, to aesthetic considerations. Seitz has noted this in his study, and uses it as a principal argument for the unity of vv. 7–11.[69] Deut 15:11 creates a consciously created envelope structure which at the same time acts as a summary (v. 11a) and gives a further rationale (v. 11b) for the preceding clause row. Not only does v. 11b reiterate elements in v. 8a, but also elements in v. 7 (*ʾḥyk, ʾbywn(k), bʾrṣk*). Note that both v. 7 and v. 11 contain the key word *ʾbywn* twice: once in the *ky* clause (vv. 7a, 11a) and once in the actual instruction (vv. 7b, 11b).

15:7b. Seitz, following Gerstenberger, suggests that v. 7b is older material incorporated into the Dtn composition of vv. 7–11.[70] Proof for or against such a thesis is hard to adduce. In terms of usage, *ʾmṣ lbb* occurs in the Piel elsewhere in BH only in Deut 2:30 and 2 Chron 36:13 (Hifil = Pss 27:14; 31:25). Of more weight is the occurrence of the phrase *ʾḥyk hʾbywn* in v. 7b. Although not confined to Deuteronomy, the use of the expression *ʾḥyk* to connote "your fellow Israelite" is a typical Dtn expression, as opposed to other laws in the Pentateuch where it is the exception.[71] The word *ʾbywn* is rare in the Pentateuch, but it appears mostly in Deuteronomy.[72] Therefore,

---

66 See, e.g., 17:2 *bqrbk bʾḥd šʿryk*; 19:14 *bnḥltk . . . bʾrṣ ʾšr* etc.; and especially 23:17 *bqrbk bmqwm ʾšr ybḥr bʾḥd šʿryk*.

67 The phrase *bkl mʿśh yd(y)k* is governed by *ybrkk* in 2:7; 16:15; 24:19; cf. 28:12. *bkl mʿśh ydk* also occurs in 30:9; *kl mʿśk* is unique to 15:7.

68 The phrase *bkl mšlḥ ydk* is governed by *ybrkk* in 23:21, cf. 28:8; *bkl mšlḥ ydk* also occurs in 12:7(2mpl), 18; 28:20.

69 Seitz, *Studien*, 170.

70 Ibid., 185.

71 E.g., 15:3, 12; 17:15; 22:1–4; 23:20, 21; 24:14; 25:3. Outside Deuteronomy only in Lev 19:17; 25:25, 35, 36, 39, 47. See Weinfeld, *Deuteronomy*, 229.

72 Exod 23:6, 11; Deut 15:4, 7(twice), 9, 11(twice); 24:14. In the Pentateuch, only Deuteronomy contains the formulaic word pair *ʿny wʾbywn*, 15:11; 24:14.

it is likely that the phrase *m'ḥyk h'bywn* in v. 7b is a Dtn coinage and, by implication, all of v. 7b as well.

§5 Deut 15:12–18

Transcription and Translation

12aα	ky ymkr lk ʾḥyk hʿbry ʾw hʿbryh	B:Vc	V P S
12aβ	wʿbdk šš šnym	CoB:wqtl	V+O A
12b	wbšnh hšbyʿt tšlḥnw ḥpšy mʿmk	CoF:IVc	Pa V+O P
13a	wky tšlḥnw ḥpšy mʿmk	CoB:Vc	V+O P
13b	lʾ tšlḥnw ryqm	F:xVc	V+O Np
14a	hʿnyq tʿnyq lw mṣʾnk wmgrnk wmyqbk	F:Vc	V P P
14bα	ʾšr brkk yhwh ʾlhyk	B:Vc	V+O S
14bβ	ttn lw	F:Vc	V P
15a	wzkrt	CoF:wqtl	V O
15a'	ky ʿbd hyyt bʾrṣ mṣrym	N:IVc	O V Pa
15a''	wypdk yhwh ʾlhyk	CoN:wyqtl	V+O S
15b	ʿl kn ʾnky mṣwk ʾt hdbr hzh hywm	CoF:Part	S V+O O A
16aα	whyh	CoF:wqtl	V
16aβ	ky yʾmr ʾlyk	B:Vc	V P O
16aβ'	lʾ ʾṣʾ mʿmk	N:xVc	V P
16bα	ky ʾhbk wʾt bytk	B:Vc	V O
16bβ	ky ṭwb lw ʿmk	B:Nc	Pred S
17aα	wlqḥt ʾt hmrṣʿ	CoF:wqtl	V Po
17aβ	wntth bʾznw wbdlt	CoF:wqtl	V [O] P
17aγ	whyh lk ʿbd ʿwlm	CoF:wqtl	V P O
17b	wʾp lʾmtk tʿšh kn	CoF:Vc	P V O
18aα	lʾ yqšh bʿynk	F:xVc	V P Pc
18aα'	bšlḥk ʾtw ḥpšy mʿmk	N:Inf	V Po P
18aβ	ky mšnh śkr śkyr ʿbdk šš šnym	B:Vcs	O V+O A
18b	wbrkk yhwh ʾlhyk bkl	CoB:wqtl	V+O S P
18b'	ʾšr tʿšh	N:Vc	V

15:12] If your Hebrew[1] kinsman sells himself to you (either male or female) and he serves you for six years, then in the seventh year you shall send him away from you as a free man.[2] [13] Moreover, when you send him away from you as a free man, you are not

---

[1] The term *ʿbry* is an ethnic designation in 15:12 applying to anyone who is an Israelite. This is proven by its association with *ʾḥyk* (Mayes, *Deuteronomy*, 250–51).

[2] *ḥpšy* is used mainly in the context of the manumission of slaves in BH. In Deut 15:12 it means a complete restitution of former status. This is also conceded by Lemche, who would prefer to interpret the nuance of *ḥpšy* differently in Exod 21:2 ("The Hebrew Slave," 142).

to send him away empty-handed. [14] You must generously provision him from your flock, your threshing floor, and your wine-press. Because Yahweh your God has blessed you, you must give to him [15] and remember that you were a slave in the land of Egypt and Yahweh your God liberated you. Therefore, I am commanding you this action today. [16] Now if he says to you, "I will not go away from you," because he prefers you and your household, as it is beneficial for him to be with you, [17] then you shall take an awl and put [it] through his ear into the door, and he will become a perpetual slave of yours. So shall you act with respect to your maidservant also. [18] It should not be hard in your eyes when you send him away from you as a free man; because he rendered you service for six years with double[3] a hired man's pay, and Yahweh your God will bless you in everything which you do.

15:12. Here, in v. 13 and in v. 18, *ḥpšy* is in apposition to the pronominal suffix of the verb. Consequently, it is not a clause constituent.

15:18. *mšnh śkr śkyr* is an appositional phrase of the kind which consists of a measure followed by the object measured.[4] The clause as a whole is translated by interpreting the verb *ʿbd* in the sense it has when it takes a double object, for example, "to serve someone with something" (e.g., Exod 10:26b).

Clause Row Structure

The clause row proceeds in three segments, two introduced by a conditional (vv. 12–15, 16–17) and a third (v. 18) which functions as the final member of an inclusio.

The first section consists of two coordinated conditional instructions in 15:12–15. Following the accentuation of the MT, the protasis of the conditional in v. 12 occurs in v. 12a and the apodosis in v. 12b. In contrast to c.12b, the subjects of cc.12aα, 12aβ are in the third person. The shift between 3ms in v. 12a and 2ms in v. 12b supports the division between the protasis and apodosis suggested by placement of the *ʾatnaḥ*. The Co of v. 13a connects its *ky* clause above the clause level and coordinates it with the preceding *ky* clause in v. 12a. The apodosis of c.13a is found in v. 13b. The conditionals of v. 12 and v. 13 are also related by repetition of the phrase *tšlḥnw ḥpšy mʿmk*. Following asyndetically on v. 13b is the F clause in v. 14a. A parallelism between the demands of 15:14a and 15:14bβ is suggested by the repetition of the phrase *lw*. Deut 15:15a is coordinated to v. 14bβ and has the form of a *wqtl* clause. Deut 15:15a is generally treated as a coordinated prescription by translators. At the same time, v. 15a provides motivation for the commands in 15:12–14 through its connection with v.

[3] J. Lindenberger, "How Much for a Hebrew Slave?" 482.

[4] See Driver, *Treatise on Tenses*[3], §194.

15b.[5] The sequence is ended by c.15b whose use of the substitution *ʿl kn* has a distinctive anaphoric value.

A new departure in the discourse is signaled by *whyh* in 15:16aα. What follows in 15:16aβ–17aγ is a conditional form with an apodosis introduced and developed by the *wqtl* construction. The Co of 15:17b also implicates it in this span of discourse. The procedural instructions introduced by c.17aα end in a clause with a form of *hyh*. The coordinated remark in 17b associated with this unit stands somewhat outside it as additional procedural commentary.

The Sv in 15:18aα signals a new departure in the discourse as does the change from second to third person in the clause predicator. This verse stands outside the conditional structure in 15:16–17 and by its vocabulary looks back beyond it to reiterate the demand expressed both in 15:12b and 15:13a. Accompanying the prohibition are two motive clauses. At the same time, there are connections between 15:18 and the third segment also. This becomes apparent when the sole direct quotation appearing in 15:12–18 is considered. This appears in 15:16aβ'. In Deut 15:16aβ' the statement reads *lʾ ʾṣʾ mʿmk*. In this form, it recalls the expressions of 15:12b, 13a with the same phrase; *mʿmk* occurs a fourth time in 15:18aα'.

The inner structure of 15:12–18 may be described as:

12aα	Conditional	B:Vc	Instruction 1 (v. 12)	Protasis
12aβ	Statement	CoB:wqtl		
12b	Prescription	CoF:IVc		Apodosis
13a	Conditional	CoB:Vc	Instruction 2 (v. 13)	Protasis
13b	Prohibition	F:xVc		Apodosis
14a	Prescription	F:Vc	Summary motivation	
14bα	Motive clause	B:Vc	(vv. 14–15)	
14bβ	Prescription	F:IVc		
15a	Prescription	CoF:wqtl		
15b	Resumptive statement	CoF:Part		
16aα	Introductory formula	CoF:wqtl	Special case (vv. 16–17)	
16aβ	Conditional	B:Vc		Protasis
16bα	Causal statement	B:Vc		
16bβ	Causal statement	B:Nc		
17aα	Prescription	CoF:wqtl		Apodosis
17aβ	Prescription	CoF:wqtl		
17aγ	Prescription	CoF:wqtl		

---

5 S. R. Driver, *Deuteronomy*[3], 183.

17b	Prescription	CoF:IVc	
18aα	Prohibition	F:xVc	Resumptive instruction
18aβ	Motive clause	B:IVc	
18b	Motive clause	CoB:wqtl	

Parallels

15:12–18. Deut 15:12–18 belongs to the genre of casuistic laws governing primary rights and duties (see the discussion on 15:7–8 above). A text similar in structure and content occurs in Exod 21:2–6.

15:13–14. These verses contain a matched pair of prohibitions in the form xIVc + Inf V. Similar cases were noted with respect to the form of Deut 15:7b–8.

15:14bα. The *ʾšr* clause in 15:14bα is a motive clause.[6] The causal use of *ʾšr* is characteristic of spoken style (cf. especially 1 Sam 15:15; 20:42).[7] The motif of Yahweh's blessing found in *brkk yhwh ʾlhyk* (cf. v. 18) belongs to the catalogue of Dtn clichés.[8]

15:15. The *wzkrt* motivation is a prescription which provides a reason for performing the action to which it is attached. According to Sonsino, there are three recurrent motive clauses introduced in combination with the particle *waw*:

1) *wbʿrt* "and you shall remove (the evil)"
2) *wzkrt* "and you shall remember"
3) *w . . . yšmʿw wyrʾw* "and . . . they will hear and fear"

All three are typical Dtn motifs.[9] There are numerous parallels to *wzkrt ky ʿbd hyyt bʾrṣ mṣrym* in Deuteronomy.[10]

Deut 15:15b is a form of the Dtn promulgation formula.[11]

---

[6] Doron, "Motive Clauses," 70.

[7] J. Macdonald, "Some Distinctive Characteristics of Israelite Spoken Hebrew," 167.

[8] See WA, p. 345. The variant of the blessing formula with *wbrkk* is found also in 7:13; 28:8; 30:16. For the root *brk* with *bkl ʾšr tʿśh* cf. 14:29; 28:20; for a parallel to 15:14 cf. 16:10.

[9] Sonsino, *Motive Clauses*, 71, 135.

[10] Found also in 5:15; 16:12; 24:18, 28; cf. 7:18; 16:3; 24:9. Deut 15:15 is paralleled almost exactly in 24:18. See WA, p. 327.

[11] For the related formulas see the note on 15:5; WA, p. 357. Deut 15:15b shows a similar formulation to 15:11; 19:7 and more exactly to 24:18, 22.

Literary Unity

According to Merendino, 15:12a.b, 13, 14a belong to a stratum apart from vv. 14b–15.[12] My studies do not lead to such a conclusion. It is correct that 15:12–14a belong together, but it cannot be proven that these verses belong to a different stratum of the text than vv. 14b–15. There is no question that 15:14b–15 do not add any material substance to the law of 15:12–14a. At issue is whether the presence of such rhetoric is appropriate to the composition of this law. An affirmative answer to this query can be made. There are no significant tensions in syntax or vocabulary which require the distinction of 15:14b, 15 from the preceding context, and there are indications that paraenetic concerns appear elsewhere in the clause row. Other observations favoring the integrity of 15:14b, 15 in its present context are repeated vocabulary (vv. 12b, 13, 18) and alternation between prohibitive and emphatic command (vv. 13b, 14a).

Deut 15:12–18 falls into three sections: vv. 12–15 (ending with the participial construction in v. 15); vv. 16–17 (indicated by *whyh*); and v. 18. In a manner similar to 15:11b, v. 18 has no direct relevance to vv. 16–17 but looks back to the first section by its reiteration of the motifs *šlḥ ḥpšy* (v. 18aα, see vv. 12b, 13), *ʿbdk šš šnym* (v. 18aβ, see v. 12a) and the blessing of *yhwh ʾlhyk* (v. 18b, seee v. 14b). Therefore, as a somewhat otiose demand, 15:18 has its principal value as a rhetorical device meant to encourage obedience to the prescriptions of 15:12–14; at the same time, it marks a span of discourse. Encouragement toward the obedience of the law and discourse marking are also functions of 15:14b, 15.

Seitz would like to discover a ring composition in vv. 13–15, 18 similar to what he sees in vv. 8–11. But the evidence is not strong. Rather, the most prominent feature of both texts is the envelope structure created by virtual repetition of important elements in the early portions of each clause row.

Seitz held vv. 16–17 to be a later addition to vv. 12–15, 18 on account of the difficult position of v. 18.[13] But Mayes has noted that v. 18 does not really go any better with 15:15 since 15:15 clearly concludes the preceding section. I follow Mayes in concluding that v. 18 is an overall summary to the two subsidiary sections in vv. 12–15, 16–17.[14] A further indication of cohesion between vv. 12–15 and 16–17 may be found by scrutinizing the speech of the prospective slave in v. 16aβ', *lʾ ʾṣʾ mʿmk*. Within Deut 14:1–17:13 the

---

[12] Merendino (*Gesetz*, 114) thinks that this section is pre-Dtn. Nebeling, (*Schichten*, 88) believes the formulation of 15:12–14a belongs to that of the author of 15:7–8*.

[13] Seitz, *Studien*, 172.

[14] Mayes, *Deuteronomy*, 252.

preposition *mʿm* is confined to 15:12, 13, 16, 18. It would appear that the speech in 16aβ' in its use of *mʿmk* has been composed to echo part of the significant phrase *šlḥ mʿmk* which appears in 15:12b, 13a, 18a (see the similar speech in Exod 21:5).

The contents of the formulations in 15:12–15, 18 raise the question of literary allusion to or dependence on known biblical parallels, specifically Exod 21:2–6. Both Seitz and Merendino hesitate at deriving the formulation of 15:12 from a parent text such as Exod 21:2. Their caution is based on the perception that the relationship mainly exists by means of allusions in content, not in structure or expression. Merendino and Seitz are more certain that 15:16–17 were literally dependent on a law like Exod 21:5–6. Deut 15:16 is parallel to Exod 21:5, and allusions to Exod 21:6 are contained in 15:17.[15]

The views of both Seitz and Merendino are predicated on their assumptions that 15:12–18 contain two or more distinct literary strata. However, the available evidence makes such a conclusion doubtful. Since the analysis above removes some possible objections to the inclusion of vv. 16–17 in the original form of 15:12–18, the presence of vv. 16–17 would lend credence to the view of literary dependency on Exod 21:2–6 in v. 12 also.[16] In view of the fact that many of the clauses in Exod 21:2–6 have no parallel in Deut 15:12–18, it probably cannot be proven that 15:12–18 is dependent precisely on the law in Exod 21:2–6. It can be reliably supposed, however, that the law in 15:12–18 is an adaptation of a law which contained clauses parallel to Exod 21:2, 5, 6. An account of the rationale for the Dtn revision will substantially follow that given by Weinfeld, whether or not the latter is justified in his certainty that Deut 15:12–18 is a revision of Exod 21:2–6 in its present form and context.[17]

---

15 Seitz, *Studien*, 171–72; Merendino, *Gesetz*, 114–15.

16 Mayes, *Deuteronomy*, 249.

17 Weinfeld, *Deuteronomy*, 282–83. See also the discussion by Fishbane, *Biblical Interpretation*, 211.

§6 Deut 15:19–23

Transcription and Translation

19a	kl hbkwr	F:IVc	O V P
19a'	ʾšr ywld bbqrk wbṣʾnk	N:Vc	V P
	hzkr tqdyš lyhwh ʾlhyk		
19bα	lʾ tʿbd bbkr šwrk	F:xVc	V P
19bβ	wlʾ tgz bkwr ṣʾnk	CoF:xVc	V O
20	lpny yhwh ʾlhyk tʾklnw	F:IVc	P V+O A Pa S
	šnh bšnh bmqwm		
20'	ʾšr ybḥr yhwh	N:Vc	V S
	ʾth wbytk		
21a	wky yhyh bw mwm psḥ ʾw ʿwr	CoB:Vc	V P S
	kl mwm rʿ		
21b	lʾ tzbḥnw lyhwh ʾlhyk	F:xVc	V+O P
22	bšʿryk tʾklnw hṭmʾ whṭhwr yhdw	F:IVc	P V+O Np P
	kṣby wkʾyl		
23a	rq ʾt dmw lʾ tʾkl	CoF:xVc	A Po V
23b	ʿl hʾrṣ tšpknw kmym	F:IVc	P V+O P

15:19] Every male firstling which is born in your herd and in your flock you shall consecrate to Yahweh your God. You shall do no work with the first born of your cattle, nor shall you shear the first born of your sheep. [20] In the presence of Yahweh your God you shall eat it, year after year,[1] in the place which Yahweh chooses, you and your household. [21] But if there be in it a blemish, lameness or blindness—any serious blemish, you shall not sacrifice it to Yahweh your God. [22] You shall eat it in your gates, the unclean and the clean together, just like a deer or a gazelle. [23] Only its blood you shall not eat. You are to spill it out on the ground like water.

Clause Row Structure

Deut 15:19a and 15:20 are complex clauses which envelop the prohibition row of v. 19b. Deut 15:19bα, 19bβ show cohesion through the lexical reiteration of *šwrk* and *ṣʾnk*. The only B clause in 15:21a contains the only instance of *hyh* in the clause row. This shift helps to mark the beginning of the conditional sequence. As such it effectively marks the transition from the general prescription in 15:20 to a section dealing with a special case running from 15:21–23. The prescriptions and prohibitions of vv. 21b–23 form an interlocking pattern.[2] Connections between c.20 and vv. 21–22 are

[1] C. Brockelmann, *Hebräische Syntax*, §129c.

[2] Seitz, *Studien*, 189.

reinforced by the repetition of *t'kl* (cc.20, 22, 23a) and the collocation of *bmqwm* and *bš'ryk* (cc.20, 22).

The inner structure of 15:19–23 may be described as:

19a	Prescription	F:IVc	General instruction	
19bα	Prohibition	F:xVc	(vv. 19–20)	
19bβ	Prohibition	CoF:xVc		
20	Prescription	F:IVc		
21a	Conditional	CoB:Vc	Special case	Protasis
21b	Prohibition	F:xVc	(vv. 21–23)	Apodosis
22	Prescription	F:IVc		
23a	Prohibition	CoF:xIVc		
23b	Prescription	F:IVc		

Parallels

15:19–23. The structure of 15:19–23 belongs to the same genre of instruction found in 14:22–27: initial instructions in 15:19–20 are qualified by a casuistic formula in 15:21–23. The following Dtn phrases are found in 15:19–23:

v. 19 *bqrk wṣ'nk*[3]
v. 20 *'kl lpny yhwh*[4]
v. 20 *hmqwm 'šr ybḥr yhwh*[5]

15:19. Gerstenberger thinks that 15:19b belongs to the genre of the prohibitive row and was originally independent of its present content.[6] Series of three instructions varying between positive and negative formulations are also possible. Such a series is likely found in Lev 19:15, although it is debatable whether the original form was Lev 19:15aα, 15aβ, 15aγ or Lev 19:15aβ, 15aγ, 15b.[7]

Literary Unity

Three separate opinions have emerged from recent study of 15:19: a) v. 19 is a wholly Dtn composition;[8] b) v. 19a is Dtn but v. 19b is pre-Dtn;[9] c) v.

[3] See the notes on 14:23, 26.

[4] See the notes on 14:23, 26.

[5] Equivalents to 15:20 occur in 12:26; 16:15; 17:10; 18:6. See WA, p. 324.

[6] Gerstenberger, *Apodiktischen Rechts*, 32.

[7] Ibid., 88.

[8] For example, Weinfeld, *Deuteronomy*, 215–16; Rofé, *Introduction*, 43; McConville, *Law and Theology*, 96.

[9] For example, Merendino, *Gesetz*, 119; Mayes, *Deuteronomy*, 253; Nebeling, *Schichten*,

19 is completely non-Dtn (except, perhaps, for the *ʾšr* clause in v. 19a).[10] Because of these variant reconstructions, v. 19 is best evaluated in the light of its context. It is advantageous to begin with a consideration of the composition of vv. 20–23.

15:20–23 Dtn style is clearest in v. 20 (cf. 14:23). At issue in the composition of vv. 20–23 is whether there are any detectable stages in the growth of the text.[11] Merendino has argued that the presence of the subjects in v. 20b *ʾth wbytk* is not original to the rest of v. 20. But there are no literary-critical factors which justify excising this noun phrase from the text. Naming of participants is common in other Dtn contexts (e.g., 12:15, 18; 14:26bα–27aα; 16:11, 14).

Merendino holds that 15:21 belongs to a stratum of 15:19–23 prior to the composition of 15:20 and that 15:21 is dependent on 17:1.[12] But it is improbable that 15:21a is dependent on 17:1a. The concept behind 15:21 and 17:1 is related to that expressed in Lev 22:17–25. But it is evident that 15:21 and 17:1 are more closely related to each other than either is to Lev 22:17–25. Although all three contexts share the phrase *yhyh bw mwm*, Lev 22:21 has a different word order. Moreover, in contrast to Leviticus 22, Deut 15:21 and 17:1 both use the phrase *zbḥ lyhwh ʾlhyk*. The analogous phrases are *hqryb lyhwh* in Lev 22:21, 22, 24 and *ntn lyhwh* in Lev 22:22.

The following equivalences may be established between 15:21 and 17:1: *yhyh bw mwm* in the same word order (15:21a; 17:1aβ) and *lʾ tzbḥ lyhwh ʾlhyk* (17:1aα; 15:21b reads *tzbḥnw*). A third proximity occurs between *kl dbr rʿ* (17:1aβ) and *kl mwm rʿ* (15:21aβ). Both phrases stand in apposition to *mwm* in their respective occurrences of *yhyh bw mwm*.

It is often assumed that 15:21 is dependent on the "older" 17:1a. This is argued because 17:1 is perceived to be the general principle on which the practical application of 15:21 is based.[13] However, if literary dependency exists between 15:21 and 17:1, indicators point to a possible dependency on 15:21 by 17:1. The interchange between *kl mwm rʿ* in 15:21 and *kl dbr rʿ* in 17:1a requires scrutiny. Given the possibility of dependence between the two

---

253.

[10] Seitz, *Studien*, 189–91; A similar opinion is held by von Rad, *Deuteronomy*, 108.

[11] For example, Nebeling (*Schichten*, 91) regards vv. 22–23 as stemming from a later hand than vv. 20–21. Merendino (*Gesetz*, 119–20) considers the original law to have been vv. 19b, 21. To this was added vv. 19a, 20 and subsequently vv. 22*, 23* with portions of vv. 22a, 23b added by a later stage of redaction.

[12] Merendino, *Gesetz*, 118–19; see also Mayes, *Deuteronomy*, 25.

[13] For example, Merendino, *Gesetz*, 156; Mayes, *Deuteronomy*, 253–54.

contexts, which one is primary? Whereas no particular point seems to be made if 15:21 substituted *kl mwm rʿ* for an original *kl dbr rʿ* other than to emphasize that a serious blemish is required for cultic exclusion, more can be said for a substitution the other way. It is noteworthy that, while *kl mwm rʿ* has no Dtn parallels, *kl dbr rʿ* has. In fact, out of 13 occurrences of variants of the phrase *dbr rʿ* in BH, five occur in Deuteronomy (13:12; 17:1, 5; 19:20; 23:10).[14] Outside 17:1 three of these occur in a context dealing with cultic apostasy: 13:12; 17:5; 19:20 (where the subject is a trial for *srh*).[15] One might conclude that a motive for changing the phrase *kl mwm rʿ* to *kl dbr rʿ* would be to aid the connection of 17:1a and the polemic against apostasy both with respect to 16:21–22 and to juridical contexts such as 17:5 (cf. 13:12; 19:20).

It is doubtful, therefore, that 15:21 is based on 17:1a. There are signs that v. 21 is probably drawing on older traditions but the evidence suggests that 15:21 owes its present form at least in part to a Dtn writer. One particular detail in 15:21a points to a specific Dtn adaptation of a general sacrificial principle: the specification of lameness and blindness (*psḥ ʾw ʿwr*) as examples of serious blemishes (cf. Lev 22:22, 24). These are precisely the kind of defects which would make it difficult to drive an animal to the *mqwm*. Hence, 15:21a implies an awareness of distance between the dwellings of the addressees and the cult place. There is no compelling reason to divorce 15:21b from the sphere of possible Dtn composition. The verb *zbḥ (lyhwh ʾlhyk)* governing an object is attested in Dtn passages such as 16:2, 5, 6.

As far as integrity with v. 20 is concerned, there are signs of stylistic similarity between vv. 20, 22. Deut 15:20, 22 both begin with a place indicator; in both verses the suffixed form of *tʾklnw* follows; and both verses name the participants involved (vv. 20b, 22b).[16] The prohibition against eating blood likely had a venerable history in Israel. However, its form in 15:23 and its association with 15:22 seem to reflect an accommodation to cultic values articulated in the laws on profane slaughter which are generally recognized as a Dtn formulation in 12:15 (see also 12:22).[17] Finally, the structure of 15:20–23 has formal parallels. Therefore, there are no significant literary-critical factors within 15:20–23 which would lead to the discovery of a small unit which is not informed by patterns attested in Dtn composition, nor are there indications of diachronic divisions within 15:20–23.

---

[14] Found also in Exod 33:4; Jos 23:15; 2 Kgs 4:41; Pss 64:6; 141:4; Qoh 8:3, 5; Neh 13:17.

[15] See the discussion of *srh* in Weinfeld, *Deuteronomy*, 99.

[16] Ibid.

[17] Weinfeld, *Deuteronomy*, 214; McConville, *Law and Theology*, 42–52.

15:19. Rofé argues that the law in 15:19–20 is a Dtn modification of the rites of Exod 22:28–29 because of cult centralization. As opposed to Exod 22:28–29, human firstlings do not appear in Deut 15:19 because they have no bearing on the issue of sacrifice and cult centralization. The Dtn writer has instituted the practice on a yearly basis (*šnh bšnh*, 15:20) and drawn up the rules in v. 19b to prevent the abuse of the firstling. Deut 15:21–23 is explained by recognizing the taboo concept inherent in the firstling sacrifice. According to Rofé, the firstling taboo can be handled by sacrifice in the required manner, or the taboo may be rendered inactive by a process of redemption or slaughter. Although the logical method might appear to be redemption following the tithe law in 14:22–27, the Dtn legislator has chosen the method of slaughter.[18]

An initial objection to the thesis of Rofé rests on a question of method. It is methodologically preferable to avoid appeal to other sources on the assumption of historical priority and attempt to answer the questions involved from a literary-critical viewpoint.

McConville points to the motif of "not working" in 15:19b as one which seems to indicate knowledge of the slave law in 15:12–18. A similar suggestion was made by Kaufman. Both use this apparent connection to support the thesis that 15:19 is a Dtn composition. As Kaufman notes, the association between Sabbath, the slave law, and the law on firstlings in Deuteronomy on the basis of the command *lʾ tʿbwd* was previously suggested by Ibn Ezra.[19] McConville also points to this relationship and notes that the idiom *ʿbd b* found in 15:19bα occurs in Lev 25:39, a context of slavery. He suggests that the command *lʾ tgz* in 15:19bβ may be a paronomasia on the command *lʾ tgś* in 15:3, thus strengthening the connection between 15:19 and 15:1–18.[20]

The evidence that *ʿbd b* is an idiom related to slavery is better than McConville represents it.[21] The idiom *ʿbd b* meaning "to do a task through the agency of someone" and connoting servitude is found in the Exodus story (Exod 1:14) and in several prophetic contexts (Isa 14:3; Jer 25:14; 27:7; 30:8; 34:9, 10; Ezek 34:27). However, this only means that the verb *ʿbd* occurs in several contexts with the *beth* of instrument governing a nominal with a human referent. Moreover, the perception of slave imagery in the phrase *ʿbd b* relies on the context in which it is found as much as on the fact that *beth* of

---

[18] Rofé, *Introduction*, 43.

[19] S. Kaufman, "The Structure of the Deuteronomic Law", 132.

[20] McConville, *Law and Theology*, 95–97.

[21] Ibid., 95.

instrument governs a person. The idiom *ʿbd b* also means "to work for (a wife)" (e.g., Gen 29:18, 20, 25; 30:26; Hos 12:13; cf. Ezek 29:20). Hence, the perception of a particular nuance of *ʿbd b* is heavily dependent on context. In Deut 15:19–23, the immediate context is that of firstlings, cult (v. 20f) and agricultural usage (v. 19bβ). The verb *ʿbd* is well attested in the sense of "to do agricultural work" (e.g., Gen 2:5; 3:23; 4:2; Deut 21:4 (Nifal); 2 Sam 9:10; Ezek 36:34 (Nifal); Zech 13:5; Prov 12:11; 28:19). Also, the idiom *ʿbd b* appears in Deut 21:3 in a context which is not overtly connected with slavery.[22] Significantly, the idiom *ʿbd b* does not appear in 15:12–18, although its use in 15:18 would have simplified the syntax of *mšnh*. Consequently, there is no indication that the association of v. 19 with 15:12–18 can be pushed beyond the mere occurrence of the verb *ʿbd*.

McConville's theory of paronomasia also rests on tenuous grounds. The pun he sees between *lʾ ygś, tgś* in 15:2–3 and *lʾ tgz* in 15:19b is disturbed by the distance between these texts. His ancillary argument, that these verses possess a common theme because both contexts restrict the worshiper from taking what is his by rights, is also debatable.[23] There is a difference between the background to 15:3 and 15:19. In 15:19 the relationship of the firstlings to Yahweh would seem to imply that the farmer has no proprietary interest to be overridden unlike the situation of the creditor. In summary, McConville has not proven that 15:19 necessarily shows features of composition in common with prior portions of Deuteronomy 15.

Weinfeld also conceives of 15:19 as a Dtn composition and sees in 15:19a "a command which openly contradicts the injunction of Lev 27:26." According to him, the text of 15:19 is also in conflict with the priestly rules in Num 18:11 which expressly forbid the redemption of the firstlings of clean animals. As Weinfeld sees it,

> The author of Deuteronomy . . . by ordaining that the owners consecrate their firstlings with the alternative of redemption if they find it too difficult to bring them to Jerusalem (14:23ff.) shows that he does not recognize automatic sanctity but only sanctity which derives from the express will of the consecrant.[24]

But there is no necessity to evaluate the command *tqdyš* in v. 19a as a Dtn polemic against ideas such as those registered in Lev 27:14–27. In arguing this point, Weinfeld requires the reader to read into *tqdyš* an understanding

---

22 Dion ("Deutéronome 21,1–9," 18–19) has examined this passage following the principles of Richter and concluded that 12:3 is not part of the Dtn stratum but prior to it.

23 McConville, *Law and Theology*, 96.

24 Weinfeld, *Deuteronomy*, 215.

derived from a particular context which is dealing specifically with free-will offerings and vows which are dedicated (*hqdyš* cf. Lev 27:14) to Yahweh. Note, however, that Lev 27:26–27 indicates that there is no choice in the matter of the holiness of the firstlings since they possess automatic sanctity. Also, it cannot be shown that Leviticus 27 is the only context in which the verb *hqdyš* makes sense of the consecration of firstlings. It is evident that the verb often requires the offerer to take an object from the profane sphere and to make it over into the sphere of the holy. Hence it is logically used of various vows and free-will dedications (e.g., Judg. 17:3; 2 Sam 8:11). But Yahweh can also consecrate to himself what is already his (e.g., firstlings and Levites, Num 3:11–13). Num 20:12 also shows that it is possible to promote the holiness of someone who is already holy (*lhqdyšny*).

Weinfeld's thesis demands that an opinion be formed about the likelihood that 15:19 does, or does not, conceive of the automatic sanctity of firstlings as well as its relationship to the thought world of other firstling legislation. In fact, the context of 15:19 is not devoid of indicators of automatic sanctity. This includes the prohibition against secular use of the firstlings in 15:19b and the exception clause in 15:21. In 15:21 the issue of exclusion is not one of intention but of physical conditions which result in automatic exclusion from the cult (cf. Lev 22:18–24). Moreover, automatic sanctity is implied in other instances of the root *qdš* which appear in Deuteronomy, including the verbs in 5:12; 22:9 and the adjective *qdwš* in 7:6 (= 14:2, 21; 26:19) and 23:15. Finally, as a vocabulary item, it may be questioned whether *tqdyš* (in the Hifil) has a good claim to be typical Dtn usage. Elsewhere, Deuteronomy prefers the sacrificial terms "bring," "slaughter," and "send up."[25] If Deuteronomy really meant to exclude the idea of automatic sanctity it could have used a less loaded vocabulary item. One may assume, therefore, that there is no philological barrier to an interpretation of the command in 15:19 which assumes a continuity of thought with other firstling traditions in BH.

In addition, there are important syntactic parallels with Exodus 13 which Weinfeld has not taken into account. These include a command in Exod 13:2 using a causative form of *qdš*,[26] and the apposition of the noun *zkr* to the description of the firstlings in Exod 13:12, 15:

v. 2 *qdš ly kl bkwr pṭr kl rḥm . . . bʾdm bbhmh ly hwʾ*
v. 12 *whʿbrt kl pṭr rḥm lyhwh*

---

[25] *hbyʾ* 12:6, 11; 23:19; 26:2, 10; *zbḥ* 15:21; 16:2, 4, 5, 6; 17:1; 18:3; 27:7; *hʿlh* 12:13, 14; 27:6.

[26] I assume no real shift in meaning between the incidence of the Hifil and the Piel in this connection.

wkl pṭr šgr bhmh ʾšr yhyh lk hzkrym lyhwh
v. 15 *ʿl kn ʾny zbḥ lyhwh kl pṭr rḥm hzkrym*

In Exod 13:12, 15 the appearance of a form of the noun *zkr* following the object of a verb of sacrifice is striking (cf. *kl hbkwr . . . hzkr* in Deut 15:19a). Weinfeld has not solved the problems in 15:19–23 by polemical appeal to another source. The context of 15:19–23 itself, the other uses of *qdš* in Deuteronomy, and significant syntactic parallels with Exod 13:2, 12, 15 speak against his analysis of the import of v. 19.

On the assumption that 15:19 does suppose the automatic sanctity of firstlings, a tension emerges between the proviso in vv. 21–23 and the requirement of 15:19–20. The corollary of the requirement in v. 19a is that its addressees are not to have any benefit of the use of the firstlings (v. 19b).[27] In 15:21, the addressees are allowed to obtain real benefit from the firstling in that they are allowed to have it as food.

It might be argued that that right is already implicit in 15:20, which commands the consumption of the firstling by the participants at the sanctuary. Nevertheless, the extraordinary nature of 15:21 stands out in comparison with the tithe, which is also *qdš* (26:13) and remains subject to cultic restrictions even in the year when it is not consumed at the *mqwm* (26:14). Secondly, the implication in 15:19 is that the *bkwr* is the property of Yahweh and therefore of his servants the priests, to whom the perquisites of the cult belong. According to 18:1–8, which also concerns the *mqwm* (18:5–6), the officiating priest has the right to the first fruits of sheep-shearing (cf. 15:19bβ) and part of the meat (18:3–4). The instruction in 15:21–23 denies any share of the firstling to the servants of Yahweh at the *mqwm*.

What underlies 15:20 is the subsumption of the sacrifice of the firstling to the model of the shared offering, the ordinary kind of sacrifice.[28] Like the tithe, a portion is to be eaten by the offerer and by the cultic functionary. In 15:21–23 the legislator has followed this logic through to deal with the problem of animals which cannot be driven to the *mqwm* because they are too crippled or perhaps even diseased. They can be eaten profanely, since they are not fit as sacrifices. However, the issue of compensation to the cult is not addressed, despite the fact that it logically flows from the inferences present in 15:19. It follows therefore, that 15:19 is in conflict with the main Dtn layer in 15:20–23.

---

27 P. C. Craigie, *Deuteronomy*, 240.

28 Rofé, *Introduction*, 48. By "shared offering" I mean the *zbḥ šlmym* also known as the "communion sacrifice" as described by R. de Vaux, *Studies in Old Testament Sacrifice*, 31–33.

The question arises as to why there is no mechanism of compensation for the firstling as for the tithe. Various explanations advanced seem unconvincing. McConville suggests that unclean firstlings, in effect, do not belong to Yahweh but are to be considered foreign.[29] However, other legislation belonging to the same thought world as 15:19 does not remove the claim of Yahweh on unclean firstlings (Lev 27:27; Num 18:15–17). The language involved in v. 19 clearly claims a proprietary interest in all firstlings by virtue of their firstling nature. Rofé assumes that the slaughter of the firstlings envisaged in 15:22 is a kind of *ʿrph*.[30] But this is not convincing, since the *ʿrph* ceremony is designed to destroy an animal so as to render it without benefit to the use of the owner. It is reserved for animals which are not to be eaten, such as the unredeemed firstling ass (e.g., Exod 34:19–20).[31] A ceremony which results in the use of the firstling as an ordinary meal does not adequately deal with the problem of taboo.

The implication of this line of reasoning is that all or a portion of 15:19 was not composed by the same hand as 15:20–23. The evidence suggests that 15:19 contains traditions which have been adapted by the writer of 15:20–23 but which do not originate with him or entirely suit his purposes. In this, the relationship of 15:19 to 15:20–23 is similar to the relationship between 14:22 and 14:23–27.

The conflict between 15:19 and 15:20–23 would be diminished to some degree if the presence of the phrase *bkrt bqrk wṣʾnk* in 14:23 is admitted as original (this has been pointed out by Weinfeld). I have purposely not appealed to this, since I have sought to explain 15:19–23 on its own terms as much as possible. If the mention of firstlings is original to 14:23, there is a still a significant doublet between 14:23 and 15:20 which requires an explanation. Both passages command the same action: the consumption of the firstling at the *mqwm*. Even given Carmichael's perception that the laws of 14:23; 15:20 are deliberately repetitious since they act as sub-sections of 12:17–18,[32] a third demand to eat the same thing at the *mqwm* is unusual. One must ponder why the demand to eat at the *mqwm* occurs a third time with respect to the firstlings.

The repetition of the command to eat the firstling in 15:20 is redundant after essentially the same command occurs in 12:18 and 14:23. Such a

---

[29] McConville, *Law and Theology*, 94–95.

[30] Rofé, *Introduction*, 43.

[31] C. M. Carmichael ("A Common Element in Five Supposedly Disparate Laws," 133) claims that *ʿrph* is a technique for bloodless slaughter. As such, it would render even clean animals inedible since the meat could not be drained of the blood.

[32] Carmichael, *Laws of Deuteronomy*, 88–89.

repetition would be acceptable, however, if it were necessary to incorporate traditional material in 15:19 into a Dtn composition. Another literary-critical factor which indicates that 15:19 has a separate origin from 15:20 is its parallelism with Exod 13:2, 12, 15. It is evident that both 15:19a and texts in Exodus 13 share common features in syntax. Nevertheless, the texts in Exodus 13 and Deut 15:19 are not so close as to support the view that one is dependent on the other.

Comparison with the framework of 14:22–27 is helpful as a model for explaining the cohesion of 15:19–23. In 14:22–27, it has been shown that an initial instruction in some degree of tension with the following context (v. 22) was expanded by a command to eat sacred imposts in the presence of Yahweh at the chosen place (v. 23). Following v. 23 comes a conditional construction which deals with a special difficulty which might arise in connection with the instruction in v. 23 (vv. 24–26). It is striking how similar the structure of 15:19–23 is to this model. An initial command, somewhat at variance with the following context (v. 19), is continued by a command to eat in the presence of Yahweh at the chosen place (v. 20). This instruction is followed by a conditional construction which deals with a special difficulty associated with the fulfillment of the command in v. 20 (vv. 21–23).

I conclude that 15:19 belongs to a tradition which has been used as the basis for the legislation in 15:20–23. A question which needs further attention is the unity of 15:19 itself. It is likely that it has been reworked by a Dtn writer because the *ʾšr* clause of v. 19a parallels other passages in Deuteronomy in the way in which it describes the livestock involved.[33] Like Exod 13:12–15, the wording of the tradition implicated in v. 19a may have originally concerned human beings as well as animals. As it came to the Dtn writer from tradition, the form of v. 19a was probably *kl hbkwr hzkr tqdyš lyhwh (ʾlhyk)*.[34]

Questions about the cohesion of 19b with v. 19a have also been raised.[35] Given the likelihood that v. 19a has been qualified by Dtn phraseology, one

---

[33] The phrase *bqrk wṣʾnk* is found also in 8:13; 12:6(2mpl), 17, 21; 14:23. Outside Deuteronomy modification of the phrase "cattle and sheep" with the 2ms suffix is not attested. The following texts have "your sheep and your cattle": (2ms) Gen 45:10; Exod 20:21; Jer 5:17; (2mpl) Exod 10:24; 12:32.

[34] Seitz, *Studien*, 190–91. Seitz would eliminate *hzkr* which he finds awkward in v. 19a as an adjective; this perceived difficulty disappears if *hzkr* is considered a noun (see BDB). A similar phrase appears in Num 3:41, 44. The likelihood that v. 19a goes back to a tradition containing *kl bkwr hzkr tqdyš lyhwh* is strengthened by the observation of the parallels mentioned in Exod 13:1, 12, 15.

[35] Merendino, *Gesetz*, 116–17; Seitz, *Studien*, 190–91.

cannot rule out the possibility that v. 19b might be a Dtn qualification also. Other firstling instructions indicate that sacrifice was to take place shortly after birth (Exod 22:29). But because the animals would have had to be mature enough to have been driven to the *mqwm*, the addressees of 15:20–23 would have faced the temptation to use their firstling animals for their own benefit. The most conservative literary-critical position to take with respect to 15:19 is to assume that non-and pre-Dtn material is confined to v. 19a.

§7 Deut 16:1–17

Deut 16:1–17 comprise three sections in the Set tradition: vv. 1–8, 9–12, 13–17. Their relationship is established in formal terms through repeated use of the verb *ʿśh* to predicate festival observance in 16:1a, 10, 13. Their relationship is also indicated by the summary instructions in v. 16 which names festivals either mentioned or alluded to in vv. 1–15. The division followed below deviates from the Set tradition in distinguishing vv. 16–17 as a separate clause row because v. 16 contains instructions valid for all three festival periods mentioned in vv. 1–8, 9–12, 13–15.

Investigations into the literary features of 16:1–17 inevitably raise questions of their relationships with similar biblical instructions. To facilitate comparison, lists of significant parallels to 16:1–17 are attached to §§ 7.1–4 in Figs. 1–4. The basis of selection has taken into consideration structure as well as content. To qualify for selection, the relevant parallels had to show similarity in syntax as well as vocabulary.

§7.1 Deut 16:1–8

Transcription and Translation

1aα	šmwr ʾt ḥdš hʾbyb	F:Inf	V Po
1aβ	wʿśyt psḥ lyhwh ʾlhyk	CoF:wqtl	V O P
1b	ky bḥdš hʾbyb hwṣyʾk yhwh ʾlhyk mmṣrym lylh	B:IVc	Pa V+O S Pa A
2	wzbḥt psḥ lyhwh ʾlhyk ṣʾn wbqr bmqwm	CoF:wqtl	V O P Ores Pa
2b'	ʾšr ybḥr yhwh	N:Vc	V S Pc
2b''	lškn šmw šm	N:Inf	V O A
3aα	lʾ tʾkl ʿlyw ḥmṣ	F:xVc	V P O
3aβ	šbʿt ymym tʾkl ʿlyw mṣwt lḥm ʿny	F:IVc	A V P O
3bα	ky bḥpzwn yṣʾt mʾrṣ mṣrym	B:IVc	P V Pa
3bβ	lmʿn tzkr ʾt ywm	B:Vc	V Po A
3bβ'	ṣʾtk mʾrṣ mṣrym kl ymy ḥyyk	N:Inf	V Pa
4a	wlʾ yrʾh lk śʾr bkl gblk šbʿt ymym	CoF:xVc	V P S Pa A
4b	wlʾ ylyn mn hbśr	CoF:xVc	V S Pa
4b'	ʾšr tzbḥ bʿrb bywm hrʾšwn lbqr	N:Vc	V Pa
5	lʾ twkl	F:xVc	V Pc Pa
5a'	lzbḥ ʾt hpsḥ	N:Inf	V Po P

	b'ḥd š'ryk		
5b'	'šr yhwh 'lhyk ntn lk	N:Part	S V P
6	ky 'm 'l hmqwm	CoF:IVc	Pa V Po Pa
6a'	'šr ybḥr yhwh 'lhyk	N:Vc	V S Pc
6a''	lškn šmw šm	N:Inf	V O A
	tzbḥ 't hpsḥ b'rb kbw' hšmš mw'd		
6b'	ṣ'tk mmṣrym	N:Inf	V Pa
7aα	wbšlt	CoF:wqtl	V [O]
7aβ	w'klt bmqwm	CoF:wqtl	V [O] Pa
7aβ'	'šr ybḥr yhwh 'lhyk bw	N:Vc	V S Po
7bα	wpnyt bbqr	CoF:wqtl	V Pa
7bβ	whlkt l'hlyk	CoF:wqtl	V Pa
8a	ššt ymym t'kl mṣwt	F:IVc	A V O
8bα	wbywm hšby'y 'ṣrt lyhwh 'lhyk	CoF:Nc	Pred S P
8bβ	l' t'śh ml'kh	F:xVc	V O

16:1] Observe the month of newly ripe grain, and hold a Passover festival in honor of Yahweh your God. For in the month of newly ripe grain Yahweh your God brought you out from Egypt by night. [2] And you shall sacrifice as a Passover offering to Yahweh your God sheep and cattle in the place where Yahweh chooses to have his name dwell. [3] Do not eat leaven with it. For seven days you shall eat unleavened bread with it, food in times of affliction (because in anxious flight you went out from the land of Egypt) so that you might recall the day of your exodus from the land of Egypt all the days of your life. [4] Moreover, leaven is not to be visible to you in any of your territory for seven days, nor is any of the flesh which you sacrifice at eventide on the first day to remain overnight until the morning. [5] You are not permitted to sacrifice the Passover offering in one of your gates which Yahweh your God is giving you. [6] But at the place where Yahweh chooses to have his name dwell you shall sacrifice the Passover offering in the evening, at sunset, the time of your departure from Egypt. [7] Then you shall boil [it], eat [it] in the place which Yahweh your God chooses, and in the morning you shall turn and go to your tents. [8] For six days you shall eat unleavened bread, and on the seventh day there shall be a solemn convocation in honour of Yahweh your God. You shall do no work.

16:1aα. Literally *ḥdš* means "new moon", although it often appears figuratively in the sense of "month" in BH. Literary-critical arguments on the meaning of *ḥdš* in 16:1 will be addressed below. There is little warrant for translating *'byb* as if it were a proper noun (e.g., JPSV, NEB, NRSV). The word *'byb* refers to mature grain on the stock which may be roasted (see Lev 2:14).[1] Hence, one may translate *'byb* as "newly ripe grain." Support for this translation may be obtained from the LXX translation of *'byb* in 16:1 as τῶν νέων. The LXX did not regard the word as a proper noun (see also the Vg).

---

1 *HALAT* 3, 4.

16:1aβ. The noun *psḥ* is translated differently in v. 1 and v. 2. Although it is possible for the verb *ʿśh* to connote the actual act of sacrifice (e.g., Lev 16:9; 17:9), the translation of *wʿśyt* is based on the observation of the Dtn formula *šmr . . . ʿśh* in cc.1aα, 1aβ.[2] The translation is also guided by the parallel expressions in 16:10, 13 where *ʿśh* is used in the sense of festival observance. This would suggest that *psḥ* in v. 1 means "the Passover festival," whereas the noun in v. 2 means "a Passover offering" as indicated by the verb *zbḥ*.

16:2. The phrase *ṣʾn wbqr* occurs throughout BH as a plural collective meaning either "sheep (including goats) and cattle" or, more generally, "livestock." The following texts best demonstrate the collective nuance of this phrase: Gen 20:14; 24:35; Exod 12:38; 2 Sam 12:2; 1 Kgs 8:5 (= 2 Chr 5:6); 2 Kgs 5:26; 2 Chr 18:2; 32:29. The same observation is also true for the parallel phrase *bqr wṣʾn*. In this light, it is surprising to see translations of this phrase in 16:2 such as: "the Passover sacrifice from the flock or from the herd" (NICOT, RSV); "a lamb, a kid, or a calf as a Passover victim" (NEB); "*als Passa Schafe oder Rinder*" (ATD).

Both here and in connection with 16:3, several translations seek to harmonize the sense in 16:1–8 with regulations found in other parts of the Pentateuch (e.g., Exod 12:1–20). In the case of 16:2, the available evidence does not allow this kind of harmonization. In the few texts where disjunction between *ṣʾn* and *bqr* is warranted, there are other indications of this nuance in the syntax, (e.g., Lev 22:21 and Deut 14:26). The nouns in the phrase *ṣʾn wbqr* complement each other, and it is improbable that the *waw* has disjunctive value in 16:2. Translations which reflect the sense of the text include: τὸ πάσχα . . . πρόβατα καὶ βόας (LXX); *als Passahopfer . . . Kleinvieh und Rindvieh* (KAT); "the Passover sacrifice . . . from the flock and the herd" (JPSV, NRSV).

16:3. The antecedent of *ʿlyw* is problematic, especially in v. 3aβ.[3] This phrase and its meaning will be discussed again at the level of literary unity. The translation recognizes an instance of the idiom *ʾkl ʿl* which is well

---

[2] See Wevers, *Text History*, 93–94.

[3] M. Dahood (followed by NICOT) has suggested that *ʿlyw* be translated as "in his presence" based on Ugaritic parallels (Review of *JPSV*, 283). Unfortunately, he cites no evidence for his position, and there appears to be no text with this meaning in BH. Alternately, Dahood commends a translation which construes *ʿlyw* as a spatial reference: *tu n'y mangeras pas de pain levé; durant sept jours, tu y mangeras des azymes* (ibid.). JPSV attempts to relieve the difficulty by translating the phrase in v. 3aβ as "for seven days thereafter." All of these suggestions are unconvincing.

attested as a technical term in the regulations of sacrifice, e.g., Exod 12:8; Num 9:11.[4] It carries the connotation of "to eat something together with something." The parallelism in the syntax of the two uses of *ʿlyw* in v. 3a (v. 3aα = V P O; v. 3aβ = A V P O) points to a meaning shared by both occurrences of this phrase:*ʿlyw* must mean substantially the same thing in each case. It has as its antecedent the noun *psḥ* in v. 2.

16:6. A problem of syntax is reflected in the accentuation of the word *šm* in v. 6b. One would have expected *šm* to be attached to the preceding *ʾšr* clause and take the place it usually occupies in this formula (cf. 14:23, 24; 16:2, 11). In fact there is no reason not to do so here. I read v. 6 as if the *zaqep* were over *šm* in v. 6a instead of over *šmw*. The present accentuation in the MT may have arisen from difficulty in understanding the force of the preposition *ʾl* in the phrase *ʾl hmqwm*. Properly, *ʾl* is an expression of motion (cf. 14:25). But it can be used in an especially pregnant construction to answer the question "where?"[5]

In the grammatical analysis of 16:6b, only one N clause is recognized: 16:6b' in which the infinitival clause is acting as the free nominal in a bound formation. Following the principles of O'Connor, the Inf in the phrase *kbwʾ hšmš* is not regarded as a clause predicator, since it is not governing a word which can be considered as its object.[6] Since both the phrases *kbwʾ hšmš* and *mwʿd ṣʾtk mmṣrym* stand in apposition to *bʿrb*, these three time phrases are considered to fill only one slot in the constituent analysis.

16:7. The word *bšl* is difficult in this context, especially in the light of Exod 12:9, where it is contrasted with the approved method of preparing the Passover meal.[7] Is there a case for seeing *bšl* as a comprehensive term for cooking including roasting?[8] In most contexts, there is no explicit indication as to what manner of food preparation the verb *bšl* connotes when it appears in the Piel. But those contexts which do mention the container in which the action connoted by *biššel* takes place are instructive. In all but one the vessel involved is clearly some kind of pot: *kly* Lev 6:21; 1 Kgs 19:21; *prwr* Num 11:8; *syr* 2 Kgs 4:38; Zech 14:21; 2 Chron 35:13b. Most illuminating are the four vessels mentioned in 1 Sam 2:14. Both BDB and *HALAT*3 are

---

[4] See BDB, 755.

[5] GKC, §119g; cf. 1 Kgs 8:30; 13:20; Jer 41:12.

[6] O'Connor, *Verse Structure,* §3.2.4.

[7] Inner biblical exegesis attempting to harmonize the contradiction between Exod 12:9 and Deut 16:7 seems to manifest itself in 2 Chron 35:12–13. See Fishbane, *Biblical Interpretation*, 135–36.

[8] As rendered, e.g., by KAT (p.131) and NICOT (p.244).

agreed that the *kywr*, *dwd*, *qlḥt*, and *prwr* are all types of cooking pots. The sole exception to this general picture, on first glance, would seem to be 2 Sam 13:9, where the cooking instrument associated with *bšl* (v. 8) is called *mśrt*, "pan" according to the RSV. Unfortunately, *mśrt* is a *hapax legomenon* in BH; but it seems that *HALAT*3 is correct in suggesting that it has a Middle Hebrew cognate in the word *msrt* (Aramaic *msrtʾ*) which Jastrow's dictionary identifies as "a mold for frying batter." Therefore, 2 Sam 13:9 does not prove an exception to the other texts cited. All of these texts show that the action connoted by *biššel* is a cooking process which takes place in some kind of vessel or container. I conclude that, as a general rule, *biššel* means "to cook in a container."

Can one assume that *bšl* connotes "roasting"? Not if roasting is conceived as the action of cooking something on a spit. It is explicitly contrasted with *ṣlh*, the roasting verb, not only in Exod 12:9 but also in 1 Sam 2:15. Moreover, *bšl* does not seem to be a baking action (see Exod 16:23). In a context such as Deut 16:7, where the cooking instrument is not specified, there is no warrant for the assumption that the *psḥ* is conceived as being prepared other than in a cooking pot—the same manner connoted by *bšl* when used of other sacrificial offerings (e.g., Exod 29:31; Ezek 46:20). In a cultic context, the cooking pot action commonly refers to "boiling" (see 1 Sam 2:13–15).

Clause Row Structure

Deut 16:1–8 begins with a Inf clause which is continued by a *wqtl* clause in c.1aβ. To this is bound the *ky* clause in v. 1b. The *wqtl* sequence, however, continues through to v. 2. Clauses 3aα, 3aβ follow asyndetically. Thereafter are found two B clauses in v. 3bα and v. 3bβ. The repetition of the time phrase *šbʿt ymym* in 16:3aβ, 4aα suggests that the coordination of 16:4a looks over the B clauses in 16:3b to the F clause 16:3aβ. In turn, 16:4b is connected to 16:4a. Deut 16:5 follows c.4b asyndetically; it is connected to 16:6 by the conjunction *ky ʾm*. In continuity with 16:6 are the *wqtl* clauses in 16:7aα, 7aβ, 7bα, 7bβ. Deut 16:8a follows c.7bβ asyndetically; it is coordinated with c.8bα to which is appended c.8bβ without Co.

Deut 16:1–8 is a clause row which breaks into two cohesive sections: a) vv. 1–4; b) vv. 5–8. Each of these shows a certain inner structure.

Deut 16:1aβ follows 16:1aα on the basis of the word pair *šmr . . . ʿśh*. The prohibition of 16:3aα is connected to the prescription in 16:3aβ by repetition, and 16:4b follows on v. 4a to create a pair of prohibitions. In 16:3b there is a pair of motive clauses. Lexical repetitions are prominent in binding cc. 3a–4a. These include cc.3aα, 3aβ (*tʾkl ʿlyw*), cc.3bα, 3bβ (*yṣʾt* /

ṣʾtk mʾrṣ mṣrym), and cc.3aβ, 4a (*šbʿt ymym*). This group is surrounded by the vocabulary of sacrifice in cc.2, 4b. Thus a pattern emerges whereby sacrificial regulations envelope a group of clauses which concern the consumption of unleavened bread for seven days. The phrase *ʿlyw* in c.3aα connects this clause with the sacrificial regulation of c.2 and makes c.3aα read as a regulation of sacrifice. Therefore, cc.3–4b seem to show a ring composition:

A	v. 3aα	sacrificial regulation
B	v. 3aβ	*mṣwt* regulation
C	v. 3b	Exodus memorial
B'	v. 4a	*mṣwt* regulation
A'	v. 4b	sacrificial regulation

This arrangement has not gone unnoticed.[9]

There is a chiastic arrangement between 16:5–7 which also operates on the semantic level:

A	v. 5	*šʿryk*	secular dwelling place
B	v. 6	*bmqwm*	
B'	v. 7a	*bmqwm*	
A'	v. 7b	*ʾhlyk*	secular dwelling place

Deut 16:5 signals a break from what has preceded by its use of an Sv, the only such verb in vv. 1–8. With 16:5–6 the reader encounters a closely related pair of prohibition and prescription connected not only by the coordinating conjunction *ky ʾm* but also by the repetition of the phrase *zbḥ ʾt hpsḥ*. What follows the prescription in c.6 is a series of coordinated prescriptions in the *wqtl* form of which the last three match formally in constituent structure (V Pa, cc.7aβ, 7bα, 7bβ). The noun *hpsḥ* links the clauses in vv. 5–7a either through repetition (cc.5, 6) or through ellipsis of the object (cc.7aα, 7aβ).

There is also linkage between the sections. Both contain notices of the nighttime celebration of the Exodus event (vv. 1b, 6), the fact that the cultic center for these rites is the *mqwm* (vv. 2, 5–6), the assumption that the *psḥ* is in essence a kind of cultic offering (vv. 4b, 7a), and the fact that the ceremonies described have as their context a seven-day ritual period involving the consumption of unleavened bread (vv. 3, 4a, 8).

The evidence suggests the following inner structure:

---

[9] See J. Halbe, "Passa-Massot im deuteronomischen Festkalender," 150; and Cholewínski, *Heiligkeitsgesetz und Deuteronomium*, 180.

1aα	Infinitive prescription	F:Finf	Passover Sacrifice &
1aβ	Prescription	CoF:wqtl	Maṣṣot Week (vv. 1–4)
1b	Motive clause	B:IVc	
2	Prescription	CoF:wqtl	
3aα	Prohibition	F:xVc	
3aβ	Prescription	F:IVc	
3bα	Motive clause	B:IVc	
3bβ	Motive clause	B:Vc	
4a	Prohibition	CoF:xVc	
4b	Prohibition	CoF:xVc	
5	Prohibition	F:xVc	The Place of Sacrifice
6	Prescription	CoF:IVc	(vv. 5–8)
7aα	Prescription	CoF:wqtl	
7aβ	Prescription	CoF:wqtl	
7bα	Prescription	CoF:wqtl	
7bβ	Prescription	CoF:wqtl	
8a	Prescription	F:IVc	
8bα	Nominal prescription	CoF:Nc	
8aβ	Prohibition	F:xVc	

Parallels

The following Dtn phrases are found in Deut 16:1–8:

v. 1 *šmr . . . ʿṣh*[10]
vv. 2, 6 *(h)mqwm ʾšr ybḥr yhwh lškn šmw šm*[11]
v. 3 *kl ymy ḥyyk*[12]
v. 5 *bʾḥd šʿryk*[13]
v. 5 *ʾšr yhwh ntn lk*[14]
v. 7 *(h)mqwm ʾšr ybḥr yhwh ʾlhyk bw*[15]

---

[10] The combination of *šmr . . . ʿśh* occurs mainly in general legal paraenesis (e.g. 4:6; 5:1, 32[29]; 6:3, 25; 7:12; 8:1; 11:32; 12:1; 13:1; 15:5; 16:12; 17:19; 26:19). But it also occurs with more specific referents in 17:10; 23:24; 24:8.

[11] Equivalent passages occur in 14:23; 16:11; 26:2; cf. 12:11.

[12] Though by no means confined to Deuteronomy, Wevers (*Text History*, 99) is correct in pointing out that phrases in which *ymym* occur are favorites of Dtn style: *kl ymy ḥyyk* 4:9; 6:2; 16:3 (cf. 17:19); *kl hymym* 4:10, 40; 5:26[23]; 6:24; 11:1; 12:1; 14:23; 18:5; 19:9; 28:29, 33; 31:13; *kl ymyk* 12:19; 23:7 (cf. 22:19, 29).

[13] See note on 15:7. Equivalent phrases occur in 15:5; 17:2; 23:17 (cf.18:6).

[14] See note on 15:4 and on 16:18; WA, p. 341.

[15] Equivalent passages occur in 12:18; 14:25; 17:8.

16:1–8. The clause row contains prescription and prohibition elements in combinations met previously. There are prescriptions developed by *wqtl* forms (16:1a, 2; 6–7) and prohibition-prescription pairs (16:3a, 5–6). Rows of third person prohibitions as in 16:4 are also generic in BH (e.g., Exod 13:7; Lev 21:4–5).

These instructions have been labeled by Kraus (along with others) as part of a cultic calendar.[16] Recently Fisher has taken Kraus to task for this as a result of his comparative study of cultic calendars in Ugaritic and BH. In Fisher's opinion, it is incorrect to speak of texts such as Exod 23:10–19; 34:18–26; Lev 23:4–44; and Deut 16:1–17 as "calendars." According to Fisher, the calendar form consists of: 1) time clause, 2) special element, 3) ordinary additional elements, the elements being offering instructions. On the basis of the Ugaritic parallels, only Numbers 28–29 possesses the structure of a calendar.[17]

Fisher's objection is substantial. Prescriptive instructions such as those in 16:1–8 probably did not have the same cultural function as the calendar in Numbers 28–29, which preserves technical information of interest to cultic functionaries. The addressees of Deut 16:1–8 seem to be worshipers or pilgrims coming to the cult center (16:5–7), not primarily cultic functionaries (i.e., priests).

16:1. The opening command in 16:1 is a free Inf (cf. 5:12; 14:21aδ; 15:2aβ).

16:3. In 16:3b there appear two motive clauses: a *ky* clause followed by a *lmʿn* clause. They are not coordinated, and one is not subordinate to the other. Analogous cases are not common; the closest are all in Deuteronomy. Deut 12:25; 13:18–19; 25:15–16 have double motivations which use a *lmʿn* clause (12:25bα; 13:18b; 25:15b) followed by an uncoordinated *ky* clause (12:25bβ; 13:19; 25:16) to motivate the preceding prohibition (12:25a; 13:18a; 25:15a). Unlike these examples, the *ky* clause in 16:3b precedes the *lmʿn* clause.

16:8 Similar patterns of second person prescriptions followed by a nominal prescription can be found using the six-seven motif in Exod 31:15 and Lev 23:3 (cf. Exod 35:2). These are Sabbath regulations. A *mṣwt* regulation in Lev 23:8 has the form of a *wqtl* prescription followed by an Nc prescription, but without the six-seven motif.

---

[16] H. J. Kraus, *Worship in Israel*, 26–36.

[17] L. R. Fisher, "Literary Genres in the Ugaritic Texts," 143–46.

Fig. 1. Structural Parallels between Deut 16:1–8 and Other Biblical Texts

Deut 16:1		šmwr	ʾt ḥdš hʾbyb . . .	[wqṭl] . . .	ky bḥdš hʾbyb	hwṣyʾk . . .
Exod 34:18	ʾt ḥg hmṣwt	tšmr	. . .	[command] . . .	ky bḥdš hʾbyb	yṣʾt . . .
Exod 23:15	ʾt ḥg hmṣwt	tšmr	. . .	[command] . . .	ky bw yṣʾt . . .	
Exod 12:17		wšmrtm	ʾt hmṣwt		ky bʿṣm hywm. . .hwṣʾty . . .	
Exod 13:3		zkwr	ʾt hywm hzh . . .		ky bḥzq yd	hwṣyʾ . . .

Deut 16:1aβ	wʿśyt	psḥ lyhwh ʾlhyk
Exod 12:48	wʿśh	psḥ lyhwh
& Num 9:10, 14		

Deut 16:1b	ky bḥdš hʾbyb		hwṣyʾk	yhwh ʾlhyk	mmṣrym lylh	
Exod 34:18	ky bḥdš hʾbyb		yṣʾt		mmṣrym	
Exod 23:15	ky bw		yṣʾt		mmṣrym	
Exod 12:17	ky bʿṣm hywm hzh		hwṣʾty	ʾt ṣbʾwtykm	mʾrṣ mṣrym	
Exod 13:9	ky	byd ḥzqh	hwṣyʾk	yhwh	mmṣrym	
Exod 13:3	ky	bḥzq yd	hwṣyʾ	yhwh ʾtkm	mzh	

Deut 16:3aα	lʾ tʾkl	ʿlyw	ḥmṣ
Exod 13:3	wlʾ yʾkl		ḥmṣ
Exod 23:18	lʾ tzbḥ	ʿl	ḥmṣ dm zbḥy
Exod 34:25	lʾ tšḥṭ	ʿl	ḥmṣ dm zbḥy

Deut 16:3aβ	šbʿt ymym	tʾkl	ʿlyw	mṣwt	
Exod 13:6a	šbʿt ymym	tʾkl		mṣwt	
& Exod 23:15					
& Exod 34:18					
Exod 12:15	šbʿt ymym			mṣwt	tʾklw
& Lev 23:6					

Deut 16:3bα		ky	bḥpzwn	yṣʾt mʾrṣ mṣrym
Isa 52:12		ky lʾ	bḥpzwn	tṣʾw
Exod 12:11	wʾkltm ʾtw		bḥpzwn	

Deut 16:3bβ	ʾt ywm	ṣʾtk mʾrṣ	mṣrym
Mic 7:15	kymy	ṣʾtk mʾrṣ	mṣrym
Deut 16:6	mwʿd	ṣʾtk	mmṣrym

Deut 16:4a	wlʾ yrʾh lk	śʾr bkl gbwlk	šbʿt ymym
Exod 13:7b	wlʾ yrʾh lk	śʾr bkl gbwlk	[time frame of "seven days" in v. 7a]

Deut 16:4b	wlʾ ylyn	mn hbśr ʾšr tzbḥ bʿrb bywm hrʾšwn	lbqr	
Exod 23:18	wlʾ ylyn	ḥlb ḥgy	ʿd bqr	
Exod 34:25	wlʾ ylyn		lbqr	zbḥ ḥg hpsḥ
Lev 7:15	lʾ ynyḥ	mmnw [bśr zbḥ twdt šlmyw]	ʿd bqr	
Exod 12:10	wlʾ twtyrw	mmnw [śh]	ʿd bqr	

Deut 16:6	tzbḥ	ʾt hpsḥ		bʿrb	kbwʾ hšmš
Num 9:5	wyʿśw	ʾt hpsḥ	brʾšwn bʾrbʿh ʿśr ywm lḥdš	byn hʿrbym	
Exod 12:6	wšḥṭw	ʾtw	kl qhl ʿdt yśrʾl	byn hʿrbym	
Exod 12:18			brʾšn bʾrbʿh ʿśr ywm lḥdš	bʿrb	tʾklw

Deut 16:7	wpnyt	bbqr	whlkt	lʾhlyk
Jos 22:4	pnw		wlkw lkm	lʾhlykm ʾl ʾrṣ ʾḥztkm
1 Kgs 10:13	wtpn		wtlk	lʾrṣh
Judg 18:21	wypnw		wylkw	
2 Kgs 5:12	wypn		wylk	
Deut 29:17	pnh . . .		llkt	lʿbd ʾt ʾlhy hgwym hhm
1 Sam 10:9	khpntw škmw		llkt	
1 Kgs 17:3	lk	mzh	wpnyt	

Deut 16:8a.b	ššt ymym . . . wbywm hšbyʿy
& Exod 23:12	
& Exod 31:15	
& Exod 35:2	
& Lev 23:3	

Deut 16:8b	wbywm hšbyʿy	ʿṣrt lyhwh ʾlhyk	
Exod 13:6b	wbywm hšbyʿy	ḥg lyhwh	
Lev 23:3	wbywm hšbyʿy	šbt šbtwn mqrʾ qdš	
Num 29:35	wbywm hšmyny	ʿṣrt	thyh lkm

Deut 16:8b	lʾ tʿśk		mlʾkh
Exod 20:10	lʾ tʿśh	kl	mlʾkh
& Deut 5:12			
Lev 23:36		kl	mlʾkt ʿbdh lʾ tʿśw
& Num 29:35			

Literary Unity

Literary-critical analysis of 16:1–8 is difficult. Among recent studies, support has been voiced for three different viewpoints on the genesis of 16:1–8:[18] a) 16:1–8 is based on a tradition originally containing *psḥ* regulations, and the *mṣwt* directions are secondary;[19] b) 16:1–8 is based on a tradition originally containing *mṣwt* regulations, and the *psḥ* directions are secondary;[20] c) both *psḥ* and *mṣwt* elements stood together in the same text originally but with no specific reference to each other.[21]

A great deal of scholarship on 16:1–8 has been directed at showing the historical relationships between 16:1–8 and other festival texts. It has been common to assume that *psḥ* and *ḥg hmṣwt* cannot belong to the same festival originally. But latterly Halbe has contributed significant evidence for the view that *psḥ* and *mṣwt* regulations are both associated with pastoral, nomadic practices. It is not plausible that *ḥg hmṣwt* belongs to a cycle of Canaanite harvest festivals both because of the timing and the features of the festival itself.[22] Whether Halbe is correct or not, his opposition to other critical viewpoints is at least a signal that no study on 16:1–8 can proceed with certainty on historical presuppositions about the priority of either *psḥ* or *ḥg hmṣwt* features in the traditions the text is based on.

One factor which emerges as more or less a constant in many critical discussions of 16:1–8 is emendation of the text. This occurs equally among treatments insisting on the priority of *psḥ* or *mṣwt* legislation as the background to the present composition. In view of the perplexities involved, emendations of portions of 16:1–8 must be regarded with suspicion, especially if they emerge as significant factors in literary interpretation. Does the text really not make sense as a cohesive unit in its current form? In order to highlight the difficulties and also render some account for the meaning of

---

18 For a survey of past scholarship, see Halbe, "Passa-Massot," 147–48.

19 For example, Seitz, *Studien*, 197; B. N. Wambacq, "Les Origines de la Pesaḥ israélite," 308–9; Cholewínski, *Heiligkeitsgesetz und Deuteronomium*, 178.

20 For example, Merendino, *Gesetz*, 145–46; Rofé, *Introduction*, 47; Mayes, *Deuteronomy*, 255.

21 For example, Nebeling, *Schichten*, 103. Nebeling regards the first pre-Dtn layer as a compilation of *mṣwt* and *psḥ* regulations corresponding to those in Exod 23:15, 18; 34:18, 25.

22 J. Halbe, "Erwägungen zu Ursprung und Wesen des Massotfestes," 324–26. Halbe's views have been well received in recent literature, see Mayes, *Deuteronomy*, 255; H. L. Ginsberg, *The Israelian Heritage of Judaism*, 53; McConville, *Law and Theology*, 102–3.

the text as it now stands, the sense of the text's more difficult clauses will be examined.

16:1aα. Auerbach has argued that *ḥdš hʾbyb* in 16:1 means "*der Neumond des abîb*." The importance of this insight for Auerbach is that he finds it helpful as a way of differentiating the ritual requirements of the *psḥ* and *mṣwt* feasts in Deuteronomy for historical purposes.[23] But Auerbach also contends that *ḥdš* always means "new moon" in pre-exilic BH texts and only means "month" in the post-exilic period.[24] This position cannot be sustained. For example, although Auerbach cites Ezek 45:17 as a text in which *ḥdš* means "new moon," the dating formulas of Ezek 45:18, 20, 21, 25 show that *ḥdš* can also mean "month." In principle, there is no objection to the thesis that *ḥdš hʾbyb* signifies the lunation of the moon associated with the green ears of barley; Auerbach is correct in asserting that this is the literal meaning of the phrase. What is objectionable is the assertion that no metaphorical use of *ḥdš* can be admitted in the context. Such a position goes beyond the available evidence. The traditional understanding of *ḥdš* as "month" in 16:1 can be equally argued.[25] No position on the association of *psḥ* and the *mṣwt* week in this text can be sustained which depends on an a priori understanding of the time frame in 16:1.

16:1aβ. The combination *šmr . . . ʿśh* in 16:1a is a significant pattern in v. 1 which has been overlooked by many commentators. The pattern is frequent in contexts of general exhortation in Deuteronomy, but it is occasionally applied as a demand for obedience to specific legal situations (e.g., 17:10; 23:24; 24:8; outside Deuteronomy, see Exod 31:16). These texts suggest that the use of the combination *šmr . . . ʾṣh* in 16:1a implies legal as well as festival observance. That is: it is implicit in 16:1a that the addressees are to comply with the ritual requirements associated with the *ḥdš hʾbyb* and Yahweh's *psḥ*.

16:2. Many wish to exclude the phrase *ṣʾn wbqr* in v. 2 as a later addition.[26] But the excision of this phrase from v. 2 makes what remains

---

[23] E. Auerbach, "Die Feste im alten Israel," 5.

[24] Ibid., 1.

[25] Cholewínski, *Heiligkeitsgesetz und Deuteronomium*, 183; Wambacq, "Origines," 306. J. B. Segal ("Intercalation and the Hebrew Calendar," 254–56) has pointed out that in the pre-exilic period one custom of month naming used the noun *ḥdš* followed by an ordinal number. According to Segal, this custom was only gradually abandoned in the post-exilic period in favor of month names borrowed from Mesopotamia.

[26] This is jettisoned as secondary by advocates of the "*mṣwt* first" position such as Halbe ("Passa-Massot," 152) and Merendino (*Gesetz*, 128–129); the "*psḥ* first" position such as

completely redundant vis à vis 16:5–6. Even if one were to accept a model of 16:1–7 following Halbe's putative ring composition, such redundancy is not apparent in other Dtn contexts where ring composition has been discerned, nor even in poetry where parallelism is cultivated more deliberately.[27] Without the phrase *ṣʾn wbqr*, 16:2 carries no information or vocabulary not conveyed in a more pointed fashion in vv. 5, 6. In other words, there seems to be no justification or literary function for v. 2 apart from its presentation of the species of *psḥ* offering.

Of importance is the meaning the author of v. 2 intended by the phrase *ṣʾn wbqr*. A number of exegetes have concluded that the import of v. 2 is that either cattle or sheep may be used as the *psḥ* animal, and they have drawn what seem to them to be appropriate inferences for the history of Passover based on comparisons with other texts.[28] Medieval commentators unpacked the meaning of this phrase with reference to the custom of offering festival sacrifices as well as the *psḥ* during the festival period inaugurated by *psḥ* itself (e.g., Ibn Ezra). A text for comparison is 2 Chron 35:7–15. Here v. 13 makes it clear that there were *qdšym* offered from the animals named in 2 Chron 35:7–9 (lambs, kids, and bulls) as well as the *psḥ* itself. Evidently, one is to assume that the lambs and kids are the *psḥ* and the bulls are the *qdšym*.[29] Nevertheless, this does not prevent the writer from referring to the collectivity of sacrificial animals as *psḥym* in 2 Chron 35:7, 8, 9. In Deut 16:2, however, *psḥ* remains in the singular. This fact makes a division between *ṣʾn* and *bqr* on the basis of *psḥ* and festival offerings unlikely.

The implications of the command in v. 2 become clearer in view of other evidence about the nature of the *psḥ* which can be gleaned from v. 7. Rather than anticipate that discussion, at this point it will suffice to reiterate the point made in the notes to the translation above: the meaning of v. 2 is that the worshipers are to sacrifice sheep and cattle as Yahweh's *psḥ*.[30]

Seitz, (*Studien*, 197); and emended even by the more conservative J. B. Segal (*The Hebrew Passover*, 205).

[27] J. Kugel, *The Idea of Biblical Poetry*, 8, 54–55. Seitz has detected ring composition in *mqwm* legislation in 12:13–19 (*Studien*, 211) and 17:9–11 (ibid., 203). According to Halbe, who posits a ring composition between vv. 1–7, v. 2 has as its counterpart vv. 5–6aα ("Passa-Massot," 153).

[28] For example, Mayes, *Deuteronomy*, 258; Rofé, *Introduction*, 48; Ginsberg, *Israelian Heritage*, 57; Weinfeld, *Deuteronomy*, 217; McConville, *Law and Theology*, 117.

[29] Ginsberg, *Israelian Heritage*, 58.

[30] McConville, *Law and Theology*, 116–17.

16:3aα. In 16:3aα, one may assume that *ʿlyw* has as is referent *psḥ* in 16:2.[31] Hence, the text uses 16:3aα as a *psḥ* regulation.

16:3aβ. The presence of *ʿlyw* in v. 3aβ has always given commentators difficulty. Like many others, Halbe believes it is without sense in the context but is present in the text because of scribal error: dittography under the influence of *lʾ tʾkl ʿlyw hmṣ* in v. 3aα.[32] While the thesis of textual corruption cannot be dismissed out of hand, it should be noted that the phrase is firmly anchored in the available textual witnesses. Halbe's thesis is one of last resort, and must be invoked only if there is no possibility of explaining the function of *ʿlyw* as a literary or redactional device.

In this connection, one ought to note that the referent of *ʿlyw* in v. 3aβ is ultimately *psḥ* in v. 2. In other words, the wording of v. 3aβ presupposes v. 2. One way to explain the construction in v. 3aβ might be to assume that festival offerings were offered over a seven-day period (cf. Lev 23:8) and that these were considered collectively as *psḥ* offerings. This seems unlikely, since there is no indication elsewhere in BH that *psḥ lyhwh* means other than a sacrifice associated with the *psḥ* ritual itself.[33]

Another, more likely, possibility springs from the observation that the preposition *ʿl* is used in 16:3aβ to connote association. If one takes *ʿlyw* in 16:3aβ to mean something like "along with it" or "in association with it"—a nuance not far removed from the meaning of *ʿlyw* in 16:3aα—then 16:3aβ is not without sense as it stands.[34] What it means is that in association with the *psḥ* sacrifice one is to observe a concomitant ritual entailing the consumption of unleavened bread for seven days. This clause follows plausibly as a explanation for the demand to eat unleavened bread in 16:3aα.

16:4b. Of key importance here is the phrase *bywm hrʾšwn*. From 16:4b the reader learns that there are special rules attached to the inaugural sacrifice of the first day. By implication sacrifices are to be offered in a festival context which extends beyond one day.

---

31 Seitz, *Studien*, 197.

32 Halbe, "Passa-Massot," 150.

33 Cf. Num 9:2–14. In Num 9:2, 4, 5, 6, 13 the sacrifice is referred to as *hpsḥ*. In Num 9:10, 14 the sacrifice is *psḥ lyhwh*, a referent subject to identical restrictions as *hpsḥ* mentioned in the same context. In Deut 16:2, 6 there is a similar alternation of *psḥ lyhwh* and *hpsḥ*. There are no grounds for assuming that both phrases do not have the same referent.

34 For this use of *ʿl* see, e.g., Exod 12:9; 35:22; Ezek 16:37; Hos 10:14; Amos 3:15.

16:5–6. The meaning of these clauses is not subject to much debate. Deut 16:5, 6 work together to demand that the *psḥ* sacrifice be made only in the chosen place. Of special interest is the emphasis on the time when the sacrifice is to be made: exactly at sunset, which the writer identifies as the time of the Exodus.

16:7aα.aβ. These *wqtl* clauses flow out of the demands in 16:5–6. Here, I wish to underscore the implications of these prescriptions for the conception of *hpsḥ*. In the notes to the translation, *bšl* is established as the cooking pot verb. There is no warrant for considering it a roasting term in this context.[35] Without further qualification in the cultic context, one may infer that the action enjoined on the addressees of 16:7aα is the preparation of the *psḥ* in a manner similar with the preparation of other sacrifices like the shared offering (i.e., boiling).

The identification of the *psḥ* with traditions involving the preparation of the typical shared offering is also enhanced by considering the meaning of c.7aβ. The prescription *wʾklt bmqwm* has as its analogues to similar prescriptions in 12:18; 14:23; and 15:20. Missing in 16:7aβ is the phrase *lpny yhwh*; however, the wording in 16:7aβ seems but a shorter variant of these fuller contexts. As such, the implication of 16:7aβ is that the *psḥ* will be consumed by the offerers like all the other offerings brought and sacrificed at the *mqwm*.

The integrity of v. 7a with the regulations of vv. 5–7 has been called into question. Halbe believes that v. 7b follows naturally on v. 6a and that v. 7a intrudes upon this relationship. The arguments that Halbe adduces for the removal of v. 7a are founded on those of Merendino.[36] First, Merendino distinguishes v. 7a because of the variant of the *mqwm* formula which appears there. This is an argument with no literary-critical controls, however. Merendino also argues that v. 7a shows a conceptual relationship with the insertion of *ṣʾn wbqr* in v. 2. This criterion is no longer applicable if *ṣʾn wbqr* is seen as integral to v. 2. Finally, Merendino's statement that v. 7a shows a concern to subsume the *psḥ* to the rules of the cult is no more applicable to v. 2 than to vv. 5–6, which are plainly concerned to confine the sacrifice of the *psḥ* to the *mqwm*. Below it will be argued that this is also the function of the contrast between the mention of *mqwm* in v. 7a and *ʾhlyk* in v. 7b.

---

[35] Further evidence of a contradiction between the terms of Exod 12:9 and Deut 16:7 appears in the terms of 2 Chron 35:12–13. According to Fishbane (*Biblical Interpretation*, 135–36), the writer of 2 Chronicles 35 is attempting to resolve the conflict between the two Pentateuchal contexts.

[36] Halbe, "Passa-Massot," 152; cf. Merendino, *Gesetz*, 133–34.

16:7ba.bβ. Along with others, Halbe has argued that v. 8 is a secondary addition to the context of vv. 1–7. In his opinion, the phrase *ʾhlyk* in v. 7b must refer to the worshipers' permanent dwellings.[37] Consequently, there is a tension between the injunction to return home in v. 7b and v. 8 which only seems operable if the worshipers remain by the cult site for the duration of the seven-day festival.

Deut 16:8 mandates an *ʿṣrt* on the closing day of the seven-day period for eating unleavened bread. The word *ʿṣrt* connotes a sacred assembly held at a shrine. It is a day especially appointed by authority and one which is to be observed in ritual cleanliness.[38] The *ʿṣrt* seems to involve many of the same religious duties characteristic of the more common word *ḥg*, including sacrifice (2 Kgs 10:19, 20). In the context of a pilgrimage festival, it seems to be a term for the closing day of the ceremonies (Lev 23:36). But Dtn thinking restricts legitimate sacrifice to the *mqwm*. Therefore, there is a tension between v. 7b and v. 8 if v. 8 demands that its addressees participate in a solemn assembly at the *mqwm*. After all, they just went home. I will argue here that, a) the idiom of v. 7b can be taken literally as well as figuratively, and b) that the *ʾṣrt* could be observed away from the place of sacrifice by work stoppage (see c.8bβ).

The use of the idiom *hlk . . . lʾhl* to connote a return to one's permanent place of residence in BH is clear. This concept occurs in Jos 22:4, 6 with the phrase *hlk ʾl ʾhl* and in Jos 22:8 with *šwb ʾl ʾhl*. The word *ʾhl* can be used as a figurative (sometimes archaic) term applied to permanent places of residency,[39] and this concept seems to be uniform in BH references which combine *hlk* and the phrase *lʾhl* (Judg 19:9; 20:8; 1 Kgs 8:66; 12:16[= 2 Chron 10:16]).[40]

As compelling as these data are, they must be considered in the context of Dtn usage. In Deuteronomy the people are conceived primarily as urban dwellers (*bšʿryk*) who occupy houses. In 6:11; 19:1 it is stated that the occupation of the land will involve the occupation of the former residents' cities and houses. In 7:26, the Israelites are forbidden to take any of what is *ḥrm* into their houses; and, in 26:13, which is related to the *mqwm* legislation

---

37 Halbe, "Passa-Massot," 148–49.

38 Segal, *Hebrew Passover*, 209.

39 For example, *ʾhl byty* Ps 132:3; *ʾhl dwd* Isa 16:5; Jerusalem = *ʾhl bt ṣywn* Lam 2:4; in Judg 20:8 *ʾhl* and *byt* occur in parallel clauses.

40 Hos 12:10 has been identified as a text which might suggest temporary tent dwellings at festival time (J. Pedersen, *Israel. Its Life and Culture*: vols. 3–4, 388). But (if the phrase *ymy mwʿd* in Hos 12:10 refers to a festival at all and not simply to the wilderness wanderings) the most likely festival referent is *skwt*, not *psḥ* or *ḥg hmṣwt*.

of 26:1–11, the worshiper is to certify that the holy offering has been removed *mn hbyt*. A comparison with the demobilization orders in Deut 20:5–8 and Jos 22:4–8 is also instructive. The operative word in Deuteronomy is *byt* not *ʾhl*. In fact, it is everywhere assumed in the laws contained in Deuteronomy that Israelites normally live in houses.[41] Outside 16:7, tents are specifically mentioned only in 1:27; 5:30[27]; 11:6; or in the phrase *ʾhl mwʿd* (Deuteronomy 31 *passim*). In the former cases, it is assumed by the narrative that the tents involved are those of the wilderness wandering—literal dwellings in a specific historical context.

If *ʾhl* refers to permanent residences in 16:7, it must be admitted that the usage is purely idiomatic since the referent *ʾhl* meaning "house" is conspicuous by its absence in the rest of Deuteronomy. Deuteronomy generally uses the word *ʾhl* only when it means a real tent. A consideration which is of importance here arises from the following question: Supposing that the Dtn writer had in mind temporary pilgrim residences, what other word is more à propos than "tent"? It is likely that a certain number of pilgrims to the *mqwm* would have pitched a tent in any event, even if the pilgrimage were only for one day. The term *hlk lʾhl* would be a natural expression if a writer had conceived of his addressees as living in temporary dwellings around a shrine.[42]

This ambiguity is not clarified by a study of the idiom *pnh . . . hlk*. This combination seems to have the connotation of to leave one place and go somewhere else. The contexts of Jos 22:4; 1 Sam 10:9 (= a variant: "to turn the shoulder and go"); 1 Kgs 10:13; and probably 2 Kgs 5:12 suggest a homeward journey. This is not true of Gen 18:22 or Judg 18:21. Deut 29:17 attests a metaphorical usage of the phrase to describe the action of apostasy.

The implication of 16:7b is that its addressees are to leave the *mqwm* in the morning and go to their dwellings. As such, the instructions in 16:7b most clearly maintain a distinction between the *mqwm* itself and the living quarters of the people. They do not tell the reader how far the journey is to be. As McConville points out, there is not only physical distance, but also metaphysical distance implied in this context.[43] That is: departure from the *mqwm* involves not only a concrete action but also passage from the realm of the holy (where cultic acts have their only legitimacy, see 12:17–18 and 16:5–

---

[41] Cf. 21:12, 13; 22:2, 8, 21; 24:1, 2, 3, 5, 10; 25:10, 14.

[42] Pedersen (*Israel* vol 3–4, 703) notes that in his time during *psḥ* and *mṣwt* the Samaritans were observed to live in tent camps on Mt. Gerizim; but he acknowledges that it is not certain if this is due to ancient tradition.

[43] McConville, *Law and Theology*, 117.

6) into the realm of the profane. In other words, the departure has a symbolic as well as actual reality.

I conclude that 16:7b is ambiguous. Its range of meaning is commensurate both with the supposition that the worshipers are to return to their real home territory or to some temporary dwelling in the vicinity of the shrine Yahweh has chosen. A choice between these possibilities is dependent on one's interpretation of the overall demands of the context surrounding 16:7b.

A problem with the homeward journey thesis is the demand in v. 8 for an *ʿṣrt*. But this demand takes on another light when regarded from the point of view of c.8bβ. The prohibition of work is found in connection with the *ʿṣrt* of Lev 23:36: *kl mlʾkt ʿbdh lʾ tʿśw*. A similar formula is used in combination with marking the opening and closing days of a number of sacred assemblies (*mqrʾ qdš*) in Lev 23:7, 8, 15, 21, etc. A closer formula to that of Deut 16:8bβ is that used of the Sabbath, another event on a seventh day (cf. *lʾ tʿśh kl mlʾkh* in Exod 20:10; Deut 5:12). It is possible that those who could not attend the closing ceremonies at the *mqwm* were to observe the day by work stoppage, although they would not be in a position to eat the cultic meal. In fact, this provision makes most sense for those living away from the sacred precincts, since pilgrims to the *mqwm* would obviously not be in a position to pursue their normal business.[44]

Therefore, the tension between v. 7b and v. 8 may be more apparent than real, because the instructions here seem to be capable of greater flexibility than they are often granted. Pilgrims celebrating the *psḥ* had the opportunity to "turn and go" to their tents, conceived either as temporary or permanent dwellings. In the former case, residence by the *mqwm* would allow them to participate in the closing ceremonies of the seventh day. In the latter case, they would be able to observe the seventh day by a work stoppage.

16:8a. It has been averred that the six-seven motif of 16:8 is in conflict with the command of v. 3aβ. This objection is not substantial. Various commentators (including Merendino) connect v. 8 with v. 3aβ and find the distinction unproblematic.[45] Evidence for this lies in a text such as Exod

---

[44] In this connection, one should underscore the observation made by Prof. E. Otto to the Biblical Law Group during the annual meeting of the Society of Biblical Literature in Washington, 1993. Deuteronomy mandates the centralization of sacrifice, not necessarily the centralization of worship. The possibility that prayer could legitimately take place outside the cult place is envisaged in texts such as Deut 21:7–9, and the Dtr prayer of Solomon in 1 Kgs 8 (e.g., vv. 30, 38).

[45] Merendino, *Gesetz*, 132, 145–46; Rofé, *Introduction*, 50; McConville, *Law and Theology*,

13:6, which commands seven days of *mṣwt* and singles out the seventh day as a *ḥg lyhwh*. There is no reason why the six-seven rhythm cannot be seen as a variant of this motif and not in fundamental conflict with v. 3.[46]

As a result of these considerations, one may conclude that 16:1–8 is meaningful as it stands. An initial command to observe the rites of *ḥdš h'byb* and the *psḥ* feast (v. 1a) which are connected with the Exodus event (v. 1b) is followed by the demand that a *psḥ* sacrifice of domestic animals be slaughtered at the place Yahweh chooses (v. 2). The implications of v. 7 help to explain the meaning of 16:2. Its demand that sheep and cattle are to be offered as Yahweh's *psḥ* participates in the assumption that the *psḥ* is basically another occasion for a communion or shared offering. Consequently, sheep and cattle are both legitimate sacrifices. This sacrifice is not to be eaten with leavened bread (v. 3aα); moreover, in conjunction with it, one is to eat unleavened bread for seven days (v. 3aβ). The background of the ritual is a historical memory (v. 3bα) which it is the purpose of the ritual in v. 3aβ to keep alive (v. 3bβ). Restrictions ancillary to those in 16:3a follow in 16:4 in chiastic fashion. No leaven is to be visible in the entire land (v. 4a), and there is a special restriction attached to what is apparently the inaugural sacrifice of the festival period (v. 4b). While the *psḥ* is the most prominent sacrifice during the seven-day period, there are indications that others are offered as well (v. 4b).

The demand that the *psḥ* sacrifice be celebrated at the *mqwm* is recapitulated by 16:5–7a. Not only the place, but also the timing of the sacrifice is important in 16:5–6. The concomitant rules in 16:7a underscore the character of the *psḥ* as a cultic rite. Consequently, the participants in the *psḥ* ritual are only allowed to leave the *mqwm* after the *psḥ* ceremony is completed. Thereafter, they are required to mark the closing day of the *mṣwt* week (v. 8). The ambiguity of vv. 7b–8a covers the cases of those who both dwell in temporary lodgings around the *mqwm* for the seven-day period and those who return after the inaugural sacrifice. In either case they will

---

118. Contra Halbe, "Passa-Massot," 148.

[46] Wambacq ("Les Maṣṣôt," 46) notes that the SP and LXX of Exod 13:6 has the same six-seven rhythm as the MT in Deut 16:8. He suggests that the SP and LXX witness to a parent text with a reading superior than the MT in Exod 13:6. This, in turn, would support the primitive nature of the MT reading in Deut 16:8. This judgment needs to be controlled by an examination of the textual evidence in Exodus from the point of view of translation technique. Even if secondary, the witness of the LXX and SP in Exod 13:6 suggests that variation between the seven day requirement of v. 3aβ and the six–seven rhythm of v. 8a does not substantially change the inferences of the text.

participate in the closing ceremony called an *ʿṣrt*, either by participation in the cult or by not working.

The overall effect of this clause row has been well summarized by McConville: 16:1–8 establishes a profound fusion between the events of the *mṣwt* feast and *psḥ*.[47] But given the presence of both *mṣwt* and *psḥ* traditions in this text, what is one to make of their relationship? The available evidence suggests that the presence of *psḥ* legislation is to be associated mainly—if not entirely—with Dtn composition.[48] This is clearest in vv. 2, 5–7 and also likely from the combination of *šmr* . . . *ʿśh* in v. 1a, which is a favorite Dtn formula. At the same time, the Dtn clauses show knowledge of *psḥ* traditions found elsewhere in BH. From the parallels between v. 6 and Exod 12:6, Num 9:4, 12 it is evident that there is a common tradition in the timing of the *psḥ* which is also reflected in *lylh* in v. 1b. As such, the law 16:6b is also dependent for some of its elements on a common tradition reflected in other texts.

It is often held that other *psḥ* traditions are reflected in vv. 3aα, 4b. A number of scholars believe that these verses are related to the prohibitive rows found in Exod 23:18; 34:25 which they describe as *psḥ* legislation.[49] The results of my research tend to downplay this putative relationship. The relevant parallels to v. 3aα and v. 4b are listed in Fig. 1.

First, it is to be remarked that the semantic parallels between 16:3aα and Exod 23:18; 34:25 are not compelling. The prohibition against eating the *psḥ* with leavened bread is not articulated in Exod 23:18; 34:25. The legislation in Exod 23:18; 34:25 need not mean more than that leavened meal was not to be burned on the altar; but, this is a general cultic regulation applicable to many sacrifices.[50] Prohibitions against eating *ḥmṣ* are found in conjunction with rules for the *mṣwt* week (Exod 12:15; 13:3). Other *psḥ* rules command the eating of *mṣh* with the *psḥ* meal (Exod 12:8) but not in the terms of Deut 16:3aα. It would appear that 16:3aα belongs to the tradition of *mṣwt* week rules and is a formulation only secondarily applied to the formulations of *psḥ* observance.

Secondly, the *lʾ ylyn* legislation in Exod 23:18; 34:25 is not identical. While the Exod 34:25 context is specific to *psḥ*, the Exod 23:18 passage is not. In fact, the *psḥ* is not the only sacrifice which is subject to this restriction.

---

47 McConville, *Law and Theology*, 117.

48 This is also the position of Mayes, *Deuteronomy*, 255.

49 E.g., Merendino, *Gesetz*, 129; Halbe, "Passa-Massot," 149; Cholewínski, *Heiligkeitsgesetz und Deuteronomium*, 180; Wambacq, "Origines," 306–7.

50 H. A. White, "Leaven," 90.

It is also clear that the species of shared offering called the *twdh* is governed by the same restriction (Lev 7:12–15). Further, a *psḥ* regulation of the kind found in 16:4b is not always found immediately attached to a regulation against the eating of leaven (see Exod 12:10).

These observations lead to the following conclusions. The law in 16:3aα may reflect a *psḥ* tradition but its wording is most clearly parallel to rules for the *maṣṣot* week. The law in 16:4b also reflects a *psḥ* tradition, but v. 4b suggests that the *psḥ* of 16:2 was conceived to be a species of *twdh*, an inaugural festival offering which was essentially a shared offering with special rules attached to its consumption.[51] A similar view of the *psḥ* as shared offering is strongly suggested by the language of 16:5–7. Consequently, there are no grounds for assuming that 16:3aα and 16:4b traditionally circulated together or that they are derived from the prohibitive rows of Exod 23:18; 34:25.

All the *mṣwt* regulations in 16:1–8 have substantial parallels to similar formulations in Exodus-Numbers. The regulation in v. 3aβ finds various analogues in Exod 12:15; 13:6; 23:15; 34:18. Deut 16:4a has a parallel in Exod 13:7b. The *mṣwt* instruction in v. 8 may be compared to Exod 13:6. Also, the probability is equally high that parts of v. 1 reflect non-Dtn traditions. There is a striking correspondence between the syntax of 16:1 and other texts concerning *ḥdš h'byb*. As the list in Table 1 shows, 16:1 is a member of a tradition which typically gives a command for festival observance followed by a motive clause with Exodus language.

What is to be examined is the probability that a Dtn writer may have used some of these traditions as a cohesive base in order to build his own law. In this regard, the possibility of an inner cohesion between vv. 1aα.b, 3a, 4a, 8 is suggested by the discovery of most of the same elements in a similar order in Exod 13:4–7, a fact noted both by Caloz and Halbe.[52] Caloz reached his opinion simply by removing every reference to the *psḥ* in the text of 16:1–8.[53] The result is not markedly different from Halbe's. The following correspondences are proposed by Halbe: Exod 13:4=Deut 16:1aα.b; Exod 13:6=Deut 16:3aβ*; Exod 13:7=Deut 16:4a.[54] As both Caloz and Halbe point out, the core of 16:1–4* shows a familiarity with Exod 13:4–7 but not literary

---

51 De Vaux, *Studies in Old Testament Sacrifice*, 93.

52 M. Caloz, "L'Exode, XIII, 3–16 et son rapport au Deutéronome," 56–57; Halbe, "Passa-Massot," 158–60. Merendino also points to a relationship between Exodus 13 and what he considers to be the pre-Dtn layer in 16:3–4*; see *Gesetz*, 130–32.

53 Caloz, "L'Exode, XIII, 3–16," 57.

54 Halbe, "Passa-Massot," 159.

dependence.[55] Rather, they seem to be different developments of a common tradition. Contrary to Halbe, Caloz sees the parallel between Exod 13:4–6 also in 16:8. Without v. 8, there is no commandment for a *ḥg* or its equivalent. The necessity of v. 8 in this connexion has also been noted by Merendino who reconstructs a pre–Dtn layer in 16:1–8 which originally contained only portions of vv. 3–4 and v. 8.[56] The comparison with Exod 13:6 is another argument for maintaining v. 8 as a traditional motif.

One element questionable in the reconstruction of Halbe is the equation of Deut 16:1* with a formula like Exod 13:4. Another possibility is suggested by analogy with the use of the free infinitive *šmwr* in Deut 5:12. Here, as in 16:1, *šmwr* is used of a calendar reference of sorts. But it is to be observed that the verb *šmr* belongs to a tradition behind Deut 5:12 which alternates with *zkwr* (Exod 20:8). It is noteworthy that a similar use of the free infinitive of *zkr* appears in connection with the *mṣwt* regulations of Exod 13:3:[57]

zkwr ʾt ywm hzh ʾšr yṣʾtm mmṣrym . . . wlʾ yʾkl ḥmṣ

Hence, it is possible that the original formulation on which 16:1 is based may have had a free Inf such as Exod 13:3. Other parallels suggest that the command to observe (*šmr*) the *mṣwt* pilgrimage coupled with a reference to *ḥdš hʾbyb* (Exod 12:17; 23:15; 34:18) is a traditional element of *mṣwt* regulations.

The probability that 16:1 had some traditional basis in the *mṣwt* week tradition is strengthened if one allows that 16:3aα was part of the cohesive *mṣwt* week tradition known to the Dtn writer. The text beginning in 16:3aα* (without *ʿlyw*) needs some sort of introduction. Whether the free Inf construction in the tradition behind 16:1 had originally *zkwr* or *šmwr* cannot be established.[58] The same tradition likely had most of the motive clause in 16:1b since there are a number of parallels to this thought in the biblical corpus (Exod 12:17; 13:3, 9; 23:15; 34:18).

I suggest the evidence points to a reconstruction of 16:1–8 such as the following: The Dtn writer had at his disposal a cohesive *mṣwt* feast instruc-

---

[55] Caloz, "L'Exode, XIII, 3–16," 54; Halbe,"Passa-Massot," 160.

[56] Merendino, *Gesetz*, 137.

[57] Caloz ("L'Exode, XIII, 3–16," 23) notes that *zkr* in Exod 13:3 is analogous to Exod 20:8 and approximates the use of *šmr* in Deut 5:12; 16:1.

[58] It is commonly held that *šmwr* in Deut 5:12 is a substitution for an original *zkwr*; see Caloz, "Exode XIII," 23; Mayes, *Deuteronomy*, 168. Despite this popular opinion, it should be noted that certainty is not possible. Other commentators have found reason to suggest that it is *zkwr* which is the less traditional of the two in the Decalogue's Sabbath law; see the note in N. E. A. Andreasen, *The Old Testament Sabbath*, 83.

tion and also knowledge of *psḥ* regulations and general rules of sacrifice. As the basis of his text, he used the *mṣwt* tradition now found in 16:1aα, 1b* (without *lylh*), 3aα (without *ʿlyw*), 3aβ (without *ʿlyw*), 3bα, 4a, 8. Within this framework he inserted *psḥ* regulations. His goal was to demand that all *psḥ* rites be carried out at the *mqwm*.

In 16:1 the presence of *šmwr* / *zkwr* in his base tradition led to the use of the pattern *šmr* . . . *ʿśh* in the insertion of a *psḥ* regulation in v. 1aβ. Judging from the lack of explicit parallels to *lylh* in v. 1b and the deuteronomist's own concerns for the celebration of *psḥ* in v. 6, *lylh* is probably his insertion also. Deut 16:2 is manifestly a Dtn composition. In vv. 3–4 the various tensions noted can be explained by assuming that the Dtn writer adapted existing *psḥ* (the insertion of *ʿlyw* in c.3aα) and *twdh* traditions (c.4b) to frame the *mṣwt* regulations in the tradition he used as a base. Signs of redactional work here include the somewhat awkward placement of *ʿlyw* in c.3aβ and the double motive clauses in v. 3b (the content of v. 3bβ echoes other Dtn paraenesis to remember the Exodus).[59] Following on v. 4b, the Dtn writer inserted vv. 5–7 in which he addressed specific concerns arising out of the general formulation in v. 2. This insertion also followed a chiastic pattern not unlike that in the first section.

The final regulations in the pericope (v. 8) are built on a core or base tradition (or text) which the Dtn writer adopted. The fact that the use of the term *ʿṣrt* as opposed to *ḥg* seems to be ideally suited to the Dtn writer's agenda cannot be ignored. The most conservative approach to a reconstruction of the pre-Dtn form of v. 8 is to assume that it probably was confined to cc.8a, 8bα and that its wording was close to the parallel in Exod 13:6:

> *ššt ymym tʾkl mṣwt wbywm hšbyʿy ḥg lyhwh*

The substitution of *ʿṣrt* for *ḥg* and the addition of the motif of work stoppage can be explained as part of the Dtn synthesis.

I am aware of the speculative nature of some of the positions which have been adopted. At the same time, it should be noted that my conclusions support a number of recent studies which have pointed to a common tradition between a basic layer of 16:1–8 and legislation elsewhere known in BH as related to the *ḥg hmṣwt*. Some debate may be entertained about the exact dimensions of this layer, but the broad outlines of this reconstruction are not easily challenged. Despite the fact that different methods have been

---

[59] Weinfeld, *Deuteronomy*, 327.

used, my conclusions in this regard are not far from the recent studies of Caloz, Halbe, Mayes, and Merendino.

§7.2 Deut 16:9–12

Transcription and Translation

9a	šbʿh šbʿt tspr lk	F:IVc	O V P
9b'	mhḥl ḥrmš bqmh	N:Inf	V O P
9b	tḥl	F:IVc	Pc V Pc
9b''	lspr šbʿh šbʿwt	N:Inf	V O
10	wʿśyt ḥg šbʿwt lyhwh ʾlhyk mst ndbt ydk	CoF:wqtl	V O P O
10a'	ʾšr ttn	N:Vc	V Pc
10b'	kʾšr ybrkk yhwh ʾlhyk	N:Vc	V+O S
11	wśmḥt lpny yhwh ʾlhyk ʾth wbnk wbtk wʿbdk wʾmtk whlwy ʾšr bšʿryk whgr whytwm whʾlmnh ʾšr bqrbk bmqwm	CoF:wqtl	V Pa S Pa
11b'	ʾšr ybḥr yhwh ʾlhyk	N:Vc	V S Pc
11b''	lškn šmw šm	N:Inf	V O A
12a	wzkrt	CoF:wqtl	V O
12a'	ky ʿbd hyyt bmṣrym	N:IVc	O V Pa
12bα	wšmrt	CoF:wqtl	V
12bβ	wʿśyt ʾt hḥqym hʾlh	CoF:wqtl	V Po

16:9] Seven weeks shall you count for yourself; from the time when one starts a sickle against the standing grain you shall begin to count seven weeks. [10] Then you shall observe a pilgrimage festival of weeks in honor of Yahweh your God with an appropriate personal free-will offering which you shall give according as Yahweh your God blesses you. [11] And you shall rejoice in the presence of Yahweh your God, you and your son and your daughter, your man-servant and your maid-servant, the Levite who is in your gates, and the resident alien, and the orphan, and the widow who is in your midst,[60] in the place where Yahweh your God chooses to have his name dwell. [12] And you shall remember that you were a slave in Egypt, and you shall diligently observe these statutes.

16:9. The description of the constituent structure of c.9b' is obtained by considering the noun *ḥrmš* as the object of the verbal in *mhḥl*.[61]

---

[60] The punctuation of this list and the corresponding list in 16:14 reflects the use of pausal forms in the MT.

[61] Ehrlich, *Randglossen* 2:297.

16:10. The constituent analysis follows an understanding of the syntax of v. 10 set forth by Craigie.[62] Here the verb *ʿśh* is governing a double object, a construction analogous to the use of *ʿśh* in, for example, Exod 25:18; Deut 10:3.

Although *mst* is a *hapax legomenon* in BH, an identical lexeme is well attested in Mishnaic Hebrew with the meanings "as much as, in accordance with." A cognate Aramaic form *mstʾ* means "plenty, enough" and is found regularly in the phrase *kmst* meaning "as much as" or "as many as" both in Jewish Aramaic and also in Imperial Aramaic (Bisitun 37). As well, *mst* appears in Hermopolis Papyri 2:4; 3:8 where it may be construed as connoting a "due amount."[63] According to Greenfield and Porten, *(k)mst* has the same linguistic range as BH *(k)dy*.[64] Therefore, it appears that in 16:10 *mst* may be a synonym for the well attested noun *dy* in BH meaning "sufficiency". This avenue of approach is preferable to emending the text to read *kmst* as suggested by König among others.[65] As Craigie points out, the idea of "sufficiency" in v. 10aβ is keyed to the clause in v. 10b; that is, it is related to Yahweh's provision in the harvest.[66] Hence, the translation "appropriate" to render *mst* in 16:10.[67]

Clause Row Structure

Deut 16:9 consists of two F clauses in the IVc form. The clause row is continued by *wqtl* constructions from vv. 10–12. Clauses 9a, 9b are connected through repetition of the phrase *spr šbʿh šbwʿt*. The placement of this phrase acts as a kind of inclusio around the contents of cc.9a, 9b. The vocabulary motif *šbʿwt* also appears in 16:10aα, thus aiding the cohesion of this clause with v. 9. A shift from v. 10 to v. 11 is marked by the appearance of the Sv *śmḥ*.

The inner structure of 16:9–12 has the following pattern:

---

62 NICOT, 243–44.

63 J. C. L. Gibson, *Syrian Semitic Inscriptions* 2:134.

64 J. C. Greenfield and B. Porten, *The Bisitun Inscription of Darius the Great*, 37.

65 KAT, 137.

66 NICOT, 243–44.

67 Mayes (*Deuteronomy*, 260) dismisses the translation of *mst* as "tribute" in the RSV because he finds it grounded in a questionable association with the word *ms* meaning "forced labour." But it should be noted that the plural form *missîm* in Exod 1:11 indicates that the pointing of *mst* in 16:10 would fit the assumption that it is related to the word *ms*. Therefore, the translation of the RSV cannot be dismissed out of hand on the basis of morphology. The fact that the translation of *mst* as some kind of impost has no support in the ancient Vss is the most telling against it. Consequently, the view expressed above is preferable.

9a	Prescription	F:IVc
9b	Prescription	F:IVc
10	Prescription	CoF:wqtl
11	Prescription	CoF:wqtl
12a	Prescription	CoF:wqtl
12bα	Prescription	CoF:wqtl
12bβ	Prescription	CoF:wqtl

Parallels

16:9–12. This clause row begins with two instructions in the IVc form. The second is developed by *wqtl* clauses (cf. 14:28–29).

Fig. 2. Structural Parallels between Deut 16:9–10 and Other Biblical Texts

Deut 16:9	šbʿh šbʿt	tspr	lk			
Lev 15:13		wspr	lw		šbʿt ymym	
Lev 15:28		wsprh	lh		šbʿt ymym	
Lev 23:15		wsprtm	lkm			
Lev 25:8		wsprt	lk		šbʿ šbtt šnym	
Ezek 44:26	šbʿt ymym	ysprw	lw			
Deut 16:10	wʿśyt	ḥg šbʿwt			lyhwh ʾlhyk	mst ndbt ydk
Exod 34:22		wḥg šbʿt		tʿšh lk		bkwry qṣyr ḥṭym
Exod 23:16		wḥg hqṣyr				bkwry mʿśyk ʾšr tzrʿ bśdh

16:10b–12. The following Dtn phrases occur:

v. 10b *kʾšr ybrkk yhwh ʾlhyk*[68]

v. 11 *wśmḥt lpny yhwh ʾlhyk*[69]

ʾth wbnk wbtk wʿbdk wʾmtk whlwy ʾšr bšʿryk whgr whytwm whʾlmnh[70]

hmqwm ʾšr ybḥr yhwh ʾlhyk lškn šmw šm[71]

v. 12 *wzkrt ky ʿbd hyyt bmṣrym*[72]

wšmrt wʿśyt ʾt hḥqym hʾlh[73]

---

[68] Found also in 15:10; see WA, p. 345.

[69] See note on 14:26; WA, p. 346.

[70] Found also in 12:12 (2mpl), 18; 16:14. Within this formula are two other Dtn formula which have already been discussed: "the one within your gates" (cf. the notes on 14:21, 29) and "stranger, widow, and orphan" (cf. the note on 14:29).

[71] See the note on 14:23.

[72] See note on 15:15. Deut 24:18 is exactly equivalent to 16:12; Deut 5:15, 15:15; 24:22 have *bʾrṣ mṣrym* instead of *mṣrym*.

[73] A well-attested Dtn motif; cf. especially 6:24; 17:19; 26:16. See WA, p. 336.

16:12b. With the exception of Num 30:17, the noun *ḥqym* in the Pentateuch normally participates in phrases which designate the totality of laws or ordinances given by Yahweh (see Exod 18:16, 20; Lev 10:11; 26:46 and, e.g., Deut 4:6, 40; 6:17, 24; 7:11; 26:17; 27:10.)[74] The noun phrase *hḥqym hʾlh* occurs by itself, unconnected with any other expressions for law, only in Deut 4:6; 6:24 and 16:12. In both 4:6 and 6:24 the noun phrase is closely linked with the issue of doing and keeping the covenant demands of Yahweh. Braulik suggests that an exception to this general pattern may appear in Deut 17:19 where *hḥqym hʾlh* is parallel with *kl dbry htwrh hzʾt*. He considers the phrase *hḥqym hʾlh* in 17:19 as likely a later addition to the clause row which refers specifically to the demands of the law of the king in 17:14–18.[75] But the expression *kl dbry htwrh hzʾt* occurs verbatim in Deut 27:3, 8, 26(without *kl*); 28:58; 29:28; 31:12; 32:46. In these texts it seems generally to refer to the totality of the covenant stipulations.[76] The parallelism between *hḥqym hʾlh* and *kl dbry htwrh hzʾt* suggests that the reference in 17:19 is wider than simply 17:14–18.

Literary Unity

It is Ginsberg's opinion that vv. 9–12 are altogether Dtn in origin. He regards the seven-week period in v. 9 as referring to the wheat harvest only and considers this timetable to be the result of cult centralization. According to Ginsberg, the Dtn writer has based himself on Exod 23:16, but he has no illusions about the antiquity of his legislation. The festival is called *ḥg šbʿwt* in v. 10 (as opposed to *ḥg hšbʿwt*) because the author is consciously departing from the tradition which named this festival *ḥg hqṣyr* (Exod 23:16). The festival in 16:9 is renamed to reflect its manner of calculation. Since cult centralization made it impossible to temporarily suspend harvest in order to bring the firstfruits of the wheat harvest to the local shrine, the timetable was altered to ordain an offering at the end of harvest. As a further concession to cult centralization, the Dtn writer has permitted a money gift (16:10aβ) instead of actual agricultural produce.[77]

Ginsberg is likely correct in his assumption that *ḥg šbwʿt* in 16:10 is to take place after the grain harvest has ended. An indication of this is found in the list of participants in 16:11. It is difficult to imagine that the Dtn writer could

---

[74] Braulik, "Ausdrücke für Gesetz," 51–53.

[75] Ibid., 53.

[76] Ibid., 66.

[77] Ginsberg, *Israelian Heritage*, 58–59; Nebeling (*Schichten*, 105) also sees the reference in 16:10 as the wheat harvest.

have expected the entire household, including slaves, to take part in the *ḥg* while the harvest was still underway.

Ginsberg's thesis about the origin of the seven-week timetable depends on his interpretation of *qmh* in 16:9 as a reference to the wheat harvest. Exod 23:16, however, represents the festival as a celebration of the entire grain harvest, for it ordains the offering as *bkwry mʿśyk ʾšr tzrʿ bśdh*. The term *qmh* occurs ten times in BH, mostly in contexts which cannot be restricted to the signification of wheat. Although the referent of *qmh* is wheat in Judg 15:5(twice), elsewhere *qmh* seems to refer to any kind of standing grain (Exod 22:5; Deut 23:26(twice); Isa 17:5; Hos 8:7) and even serves as a term for growing grass (2 Kgs 19:26=Isa 37:27). Consequently, without indications to the contrary, the use of *qmh* in 16:9 cannot be pushed beyond the meaning of standing grain. It cannot be shown that *qmh* in 16:9 refers to the start of the wheat harvest instead of the start of the barley harvest, the first grain to be harvested.[78] I conclude that an appeal to a text such as Exod 23:16 does not solve any of the problems involved in considering the origins of the timetable in 16:9.

Ginsberg's contention that the name *ḥg šbʿwt* is an innovation is also dubious.[79] Alternation of nouns in the festival lists cannot be taken *ipso facto* as evidence of innovation. Compare the terms *ḥg hʾsp* in Exod 23:16; 34:22 with *ḥg hskwt* in 16:13. The latter need not be considered as untraditional since it would appear that the harvest *skwt* are an old institution predating any demonstrable cult centralization in Israel.[80]

It is possible that 16:9–11 are dependent on traditional material. From a literary point of view, the language of 16:9 shows its closest affinity with expressions of calculation which otherwise occur mainly in Leviticus. The counting formula *spr l* where *lamed* resumes the subject of the verb (i.e., analogous to Latin *dativus commodi*) is found in Lev 15:13, 28; 23:15; 25:8 and Ezek 44:26. In Deut 16:9 the verse shows a chiastic pattern based on vocabulary usage:

šbʿ šbʿt spr ḥll / ḥll spr šbʿ šbʿt

---

[78] Pedersen, *Israel*, 417.

[79] It is typical to regard the name *šbwʿt* as stemming from the calculation of the festival's timing; see, e.g., Mayes, *Deuteronomy*, 260; Nebeling, *Schichten*, 105. Pedersen (*Israel*, vol 3–4, 415) has a different suggestion. He notes that harvest is the climax of the peasant's year and that the weeks of harvest are therefore the "weeks" *par excellence* (cf. Jer 5:24). In more recent times Middle-Eastern peasants have been observed to date things as so many days or weeks before or after harvest (H. N. and A. L. Moldenke, *Plants of the Bible*, 232).

[80] Rofé, *Introduction*, 52–53.

This is a well organized composition which offers no real literary-critical grounds for reduction to a shorter, more original form.[81] Deut 16:10aα contains the festival instruction which logically follows on the calendar calculation in 16:9.

A noteworthy discrepancy appears when the contents of 16:10aβ.b are compared with parallel texts referring to the same tradition. All other related legislation mentions firstfruits (*bkwrym*, cf. Exod 23:16; 34:22; Lev 23:17; Num 28:26) as the offering expected for this *ḥg*. But this well attested detail is absent in Deut 16:10. In its place one finds the requirement to celebrate the festival with a *ndbh* ("freewill offering") proportional to the harvest blessing received from Yahweh.

A number of observations suggest that the phrase *ndbt ydk* is Dtn coinage. Although 12:6, 17 differentiate offerings like *ndr*, *ndbh*, and *trwmt ydk* (= firstfruits?), these distinctions are not always carefully observed. In 23:24, which deals with vows, the offering or sacrifice which is vowed is called *ndbh*. However, from other cultic contexts it is clear that *ndr* and *nblh* are considered as distinct kinds of offerings (cf. Lev 23:38; Num 29:39; Deut 12:6, 17). A certain imprecision in the use of technical terminology is a trait of Dtn composition, which distinguishes its instructions from other books in the Pentateuch.[82] The appearance of *ndbh* for an expected reference to firstfruits would not be out of keeping for a Dtn writer, despite the fact that other texts preserve more technical distinctions.

Further support for viewing *ndbt ydk* as a Dtn coinage may be derived from a consideration of similar constructions in BH. In v. 10aβ the phrase *ndbt ydk*, although unique to this context in BH, has a similar ring to such Dtn phrases as *mʿsh ydk / ydyk* (2:7; 14:29; 16:15; 24:19; 28:12; 30:9), *mšlḥ ydk* (12:18; 15:10; 23:21; 28:8, 20) and *trwmt ydk* (12:17). The Dtn character of *ndbt ydk* becomes more apparent when incidents of the bound formation *noun* + *ydk* are examined elsewhere in BH. In fact, outside of Deuteronomy phrases of this kind are rare, and there are no cases in other books of the Pentateuch.[83] Finally, it is important that *ndbt ydk* is qualified by the clause *kʾšr ybrkk yhwh*. This clause is a recognizable Dtn motif.[84]

The evidence suggests that 16:9–10 contains a festival tradition which has been adapted by a Dtn writer in v. 10aβ.b. It is evident that 16:9–10aα refers

---

[81] Merendino, *Gesetz*, 134–135; contra Seitz, *Studien*, 198.

[82] McConville, *Law and Theology*, 55, 154. Carmichael (*Laws*, 37) has a similar opinion.

[83] Cf. *ḥrp ydk* in 2 Sam 24:16 (= 1 Chron 21:15); *mʿśh ydk* in Isa 64:7; *mtym ydk* in Ps 17:14; and *tgrt ydk* in Ps 39:11.

[84] WA, p. 345.

to a harvest festival known in the Hebrew tradition (see the parallels in Fig. 2). The counting formula in v. 9 is best attested in a non Dtn tradition. An important idiosyncrasy appears in 16:10aβ since all other related legislation gives firstfruits as the offering expected. The offering requirement in v. 10aβ.b may be regarded as a Dtn innovation which is a modification of the usual conditions for the celebration of this cultic activity. Following the modification of 16:10aβ.b, the Dtn writer continued the instruction with the *wqtl* sequence in 16:11. Note how the participants named are framed by the synonymous Dtn expressions *lpny yhwh ʾlhyk* (v. 11a) and *bmqwm ʾšr ybḥr yhwh ʾlhyk* (v. 11b).

The *wqtl* clauses in 16:12 do not appear to be well integrated into the context. Deut 16:12a functions in the context as rationale for the demand that dependent *personae miserae* are also to enjoy this harvest festival. Elsewhere in Deuteronomy the Exodus memory is used in conjunction with laws directed towards the relief of the *personae miserae* in 5:15; 15:15; 24:18, 22. But only 16:12a is found in a clause row which refers to the *mqwm*. In Deuteronomy 12–26, commands of the type in 16:12b usually appear as exhortation to obey all the laws in Deuteronomy.[85] These tensions need to be addressed with a view to the larger context that 16:9–11 may have belonged to. The integrity of 16:12 in the context will be reassessed in the next chapter.

§7.3 Deut 16:13–15

Transcription and Translation

13	ḥg hskt tʿśh lk šbʿt ymym	F:IVc	O V P A Pc
13'	bʾspk mgrnk wmyqbk	N:Inf	V P
14	wśmḥt bḥgk	CoF:wqtl	V Pa S
	ʾth wbnk wbtk wʿbdk wʾmtk		
	whlwy whgr whytwm whʾlmnh ʾšr bšʿryk		
15a	šbʿt ymym tḥg lyhwh ʾlhyk bmqwm	F:IVc	A V P Pa
15a'	ʾšr ybḥr yhwh	N:Vc	V S
15bα	ky ybrkk yhwh ʾlhyk	B:Vc	V+O S P
	bkl tbwʾtk wbkl mʿśh ydyk		
15bβ	whyyt ʾk śmḥ	CoF:wqtl	V O

[85] Within Deuteronomy 12–26 exhortation with *šmr*, or *ʿśh* or both occurs in 12:28; 13:1, 5, 19; 15:5; 16:12; 17:19; 26:16–18.

16:13] You shall celebrate the pilgrimage festival of booths for seven days after you have gathered in the harvest from your threshing floor and from your wine-press. [14] And you shall rejoice in your pilgrimage, you and your son and your daughter, your man-servant and your maid-servant, the Levite, and the resident alien, and the orphan, and the widow who is in your gates. [15] For seven days you shall hold a pilgrim festival in honor of Yahweh your God in the place which Yahweh your God chooses, so that Yahweh your God will bless you in all your harvest and in all the work of your hand.[86] And you are to be wholly rejoicing.

16:15a. The particle *ky* can mark a purpose clause.[87] This understanding of *ky* in 16:15a has been suggested by Weinfeld,[88] and previously in the commentary of Ibn Ezra. Another context in which this nuance might fit is 14:24b. It may be that travel to the chosen place was called for either as a result of Yahweh's blessing (cf. 16:10) or in order to procure it.

16:15bβ. This clause is analyzed as a V O construction because the phrase *ʾk śmḥ* is the direct complement of the verb. JPSV wishes to take v.15bβ as a continuation of the motivation clause in v.15bα, as if the joy of the harvest will serve as further stimulus to the command to hold a pilgrim festival. This is difficult to accept given the likely explanation for the particle *ʾk* in c.15bβ. Here *ʾk* has a limiting function analogous to an English expression such as "nothing but."[89] Consequently, I take v. 15bβ as a further command following on v. 15a. If the verb *śmḥ* is understood as an idiomatic expression for a certain type of religious observance (cf. Deut 12:12, 18; 16:11), then the import of the command in v. 15bβ is to enjoin festival observance as the activity exclusively permitted for this time period.

Clause Row Structure

Deut 16:13–15 begins with an F clause in the IVc form. This is followed by a *wqtl* construction in 16:14 which uses an Sv as its predicate. A new subsection appears to begin in v. 15. This is indicated by the resumption of an Av clause in c.15a and because c.15a follows c.14 asyndetically. Clause 15a is followed by a B clause (c.15bα) and then by a *wqtl* form in 16:15bβ.

The inner structure of 16:13–15 has the pattern:

---

[86] Following on the discussion of *ydk* in 15:10, the preference of this section of Deuteronomy is for the singular noun. Textual witnesses for a singular interpretation in 16:15 include both TO and the note in the *Masora Parva*. Moreover, the phrase appears in a clear case of singular usage in Deut 14:29. Hence, 16:15 is most likely an instance of a singular form in pause written with a vowel letter.

[87] F. E. König, *Historisch-Comparative Syntax der Hebräischen Sprache*, §395c.

[88] Weinfeld, *Deuteronomy*, 345.

[89] Andersen, *Sentence in Biblical Hebrew*, 175.

13	Prescription	F:IVc	Section 1
14	Prescription	CoF:wqtl	
15a	Prescription	F:IVc	Section 2
15bα	Motive clause	B:Vc	
15bβ	Prescription	CoF:wqtl	

Parallels

16:13. Deut 16:13 shows membership with the instruction pattern whereby a prescription is expanded by *wqtl* clauses.

Fig. 3. Structural Parallels between Deut 16:13 and Other Biblical Texts

Deut 16:13	ḥg hskt	tʿśh lk	šbʿt	ymym		bʾspk		mgrnk wmyqbk
Exod 34:22a	wḥg šbʿt	tʿśh lk						
Lev 23:34	ḥg hskwt		šbʿt	ymym				
Exod 23:16	wḥg hʾsp				bṣʾt hšnh	bʾspk	ʾt mʿśyk	mn hśdh
Exod 34:22b	wḥg hʾsyp				tqwpt hšnh			
Lev 23:39						bʾspkm ʾt tbwʾt hʾrṣ		
	tḥgw ʾt ḥg yhwh		šbʿt	ymym				

16:14–15. Deut 16:14–15 contain a number of Dtn phrases. Among these are the *mqwm* formula, the command *wśmḥt*,[90] the blessing formula *ky ybrkk yhwh ʾlhyk*,[91] and the combination of *brk . . . mʿśh ydyk*.[92]

Literary Unity

16:13–15. Dtn phraseology is visible in vv. 14–15. By contrast, 16:13 has a reasonable claim to belonging to a non–Dtn tradition. One indicator of this is the repetition in 16:15a of the command to celebrate the pilgrimage festival (cf. v. 13a). This doublet functions in v. 15 to demand that an action already commanded in v. 13 must take place at the *mqwm*.

It is also noteworthy that 16:13 has various parallels with instructions in Exodus and Leviticus. Exod 23:16 has a parallel to the phrase *bʾspk*, and there is a parallel in the 2mpl in Lev 23:39. Interestingly, it is Exod 23:16 which may show signs of conflation in formulation. Deut 16:13 reads *bʾspk mn*; Lev 23:39 reads *bʾspkm ʾt*; Exod 23:16 reads *bʾspk ʾt . . . mn*. Also diverging from Exod 23:16, but in common with Lev 23:39, Deut 16:13 has a time

---

90 WA, p. 346.

91 WA, p. 345. The motivational appeal to procure the blessing of Yahweh is mainly absent from the prescriptive portions of Exodus-Numbers. It is found only in Exod 20:24b; 23:25.

92 WA, p. 345.

frame of seven days. Therefore, Deut 16:13 seems to be a related but independent formula of a tradition also found elsewhere in the Pentateuch.

It is probable that the phrase *mgrnk wmyqbk* in 16:13b is Dtn in origin. The word pair *grn wyqb* is not confined to Deuteronomy. It also appears in Num 18:30; 2 Kgs 6:27; Hos 9:2. But in favor of Dtn authorship is the Dtn predilection for 2ms suffixes, as seen, e.g., on the phrase *bqrk wṣʾnk* (14:23) or the list in 16:14. When this feature of pronominalization is taken in conjunction with the fact that the closest parallels to v. 13 lack a similar qualification, it seems best to limit the non-Dtn citation in v. 13 to v. 13a.

§7.4 Deut 16:16–17

Transcription and Translation

16a	šlwš pʿmym bšnh yrʾh kl zkwrk	F:IVc	A V S O Pa Pa
	ʾt pny yhwh ʾlhyk bmqwm		
16a'	ʾšr ybḥr	N:Vc	V
	bḥg hmṣwt wbḥg hšbʿwt wbḥg hskwt		
16b	wlʾ yrʾh ʾt pny yhwh ryqm	CoF:xVc	V O Np
17	ʾyš kmtnt ydw kbrkt yhwh ʾlhyk	F:[Vc]	S [V O] P
17b'	ʾšr ntn lk	N:Vc	V P

[16] Three times in the year shall all your menfolk see the face of Yahweh your God in the place which he chooses: on the pilgrimage festival of unleavened bread, on the festival of weeks, and on the festival of booths. But no one is to see the face of Yahweh empty-handed. [17] Each [shall see the face of Yahweh] with his personal offering[93] corresponding to the blessing of Yahweh your God which he has bestowed upon you.

16:16. The reading tradition represented in the MT is a very old one, as the translation of the LXX shows. Nor does the MT represent incomprehensible Hebrew. One can construe the preposition *ʾt* in the phrase *ʾt pny yhwh* as a marker of an adverbial accusative.[94] This would yield a translation such as "to appear in the presence of Yahweh." Nevertheless, the vocalization in the MT of Deut 16:16 is probably an exegetical device to avoid an anthropomorphism.[95] Evidence for this appears in Deut 31:11 in which the phrase *lrʾt ʾt pny yhwh* is also construed as a Nifal by the reading tradition. But the *ketib* suggests the Qal.[96] Compare also Gen 33:10 and the variants listed in BHS for Ps 42:3. For this reason, the verb *yrʾh* in cc.16a, 16b is construed in

93 The idiom present here is *k . . . k.* This usage signifies the close identity between two nouns; cf. Gen 18:25; Deut 1:17; Isa 24:2 (*HALAT* 3, 433).

94 For this function of *ʾt* see Waltke and O'Connor, *Hebrew Syntax*, 181.

95 Mayes, *Deuteronomy*, 261.

96 GKC §51l.

the Qal. Consequently, the constituent analysis treats the phrase *yrʾh ʾt pny yhwh* as a V O structure and it is translated accordingly.

16:17. The word *ʾyš* is acting as a pronoun and thus refers to the subject of the verb in c.16b (which refers to *kwl zkwrk* in c.16a). For this reason, 16:17 is analyzed as a Vc construction with gapped constituents from c.16b, although it is typical for gapping to occur over clauses with more similar constituent structure.[97]

Clause Row Structure

Deut 16:16–17 consists of three F clauses. Clauses 16:16a, 16b are connected by Co and the repeated phrase *yrʾh pny yhwh.* Clause 16:17 follows asyndetically but shows cohesion with c.16b through pronominalization and ellipsis.

The inner structure of 16:16–17 has the following pattern:

16a	Prescription	F:IVc
16b	Prohibition	CoF:xVc
17	Prescription	F:[Vc]

Parallels

16:16. Deut 16:16 contains a third person prescription followed by a third person prohibition. Rows with a prescription balanced by a prohibition were noted in the discussion on 15:19 above. A case in which a prescription is followed by two prohibitions occurs in Exod 13:7.

Fig. 4. Structural Parallels between Deut 16:16 and Other Biblical Texts

Deut 16:16aα	šlwš	pʿmym bšnh yrʾh kl zkwrk	ʾt pny		yhwh ʾlhyk		
Exod 34:23	šlš	pʿmym bšnh yrʾh kl zkwrk	ʾt pny	hʾdwn	yhwh ʾlhy	yśrʾl	
Exod 23:17	šlš	pʿmym bšnh yrʾh kl zkwrk	ʾl pny	hʾdwn	yhwh		
2 Chron 8:13	šlwš	pʿmym bšnh					

Deut 16:16aβ	bḥg hmṣwt	wbḥg hšbʿwt	wbḥg hskwt
2 Chron 8:13	bḥg hmṣwt	wbḥg hsbʿwt	wbḥg hskwt
Deut 16:1–15	[ʿśh] psḥ (v. 1)	ḥg šbʿwt (v. 10)	ḥg hskt (v. 13)
Exod 34:18, 22	ḥg hmṣwt . . .	wḥg šbʿt . . .	wḥg hʾsyp
Exod 23:15–16	ḥg hmṣwt . . .	wḥg hqṣyr . . .	wḥg hʾsp
Lev 23:5–36	psḥ + ḥg hmṣwt (vv. 5–6)	[not named]	ḥg hskwt (v. 34)

97 According to O'Connor (*Verse Structure* §7.4), most lines with gapped constituents have similar constituent structures.

Deut 16:16b	wlʾ yrʾh ʾt	pny yhwh	ryqm
Exod 23:15 & Exod 34:20	wlʾ yrʾw	pny	ryqm

16:17. The phrase *kbrkt yhwh ʾlhyk ʾšr ntn lk* occurs verbatim in 12:15. Where clauses with the form *ʾyš k* appear in instruction contexts, the clause predicator is usually a verb. In the Pentateuch, the closest analogue to the syntax of 16:17 is found in Num 35:8b.

Literary Unity

16:16. Indications that 16:16 is drawing on some non-Dtn tradition rest on: a) the discrepancy between the participants named in v. 16aα and those named in 16:11, 14; and b) the parallels in Exodus 23; 34. In 16:16, notable Dtn language is confined to v. 16aβ, i.e., the *mqwm* formula.

Relationships between 16:16aα, 16:16b and Exod 23:15, 17 and 34:20, 23 are shown in Fig. 4. The differences are as follows: in neither case is the divine name identical with that in 16:16aα. The preposition in Exod 23:17 is not the same as in Exod 34:23 and Deut 16:16a (*ʾl* as opposed to *ʾt* in the latter two). In the case of 16:16b, the verb in 16:16b is in the 3ms as opposed to the plural in its Exodus parallels. In the place of the first person reference of *panay* in Exod 23:15; 34:20, Deut 16:16b reads *pny yhwh*. Finally, the legislation in Exodus links the command analogous to v. 16b to the offering of firstlings in Exod 34:20 and *ḥg hmṣwt* in Exod 23:15 and does not use it as a summarizing device. Therefore, the connection of 16:16aα.b is different than in the Exodus parallels. These are small changes, however, and the similarities are substantial enough to suggest the possibility that the writer of 16:16 borrowed from Exodus 23, Exodus 34, or both. This probability is either increased or diminished, however, depending on whether there is additional evidence that the writer of 16:16 used material from Exodus 23 or 34. This requires a conception of the text beyond the clause row level. The question will, therefore, be held in abeyance for the moment.

The wording of the *mqwm* formula in v. 16aβ is unexpected. Together with the instance in 31:11, that in 16:16 is the shortest attested in Deuteronomy.[98] Elsewhere in Deuteronomy 14–17 only 14:23 is similar in failing to provide an explicit subject for the *mqwm* formula. Probably, like

[98] Deut 31:11 shows a remarkable similarity to 16:16. Compare *bbwʾ kl yśrʾl lrʾwt ʾt pny yhwh ʾlhyk bmqwm ʾšr ybḥr* with 16:16aα.β. Deut 31:11 may show dependency on 16:16 or composition by the same hand.

14:23, 16:16 does not have the divine name because it has been mentioned in the previous clause.

A debatable point is whether the list of festival names comes from a Dtn intervenor's hand or not.[99] There is no proof that the festival list in 16:16aβ belongs to a genre of such lists. Besides Deut 16:16, the only other text which contains such a list in a single clause is 2 Chron 8:13. It cannot be established, however, that this text is independent of Dtn influence. One feature in need of explanation is the relationship of the list in 16:16 to the festivals named in Deut 16:1–15, which make no mention of *ḥg hmṣwt* (cf. vv. 1–8). Note also the variant *ḥg hšbʿwt* for *ḥg šbʿwt* in 16:10. Since this calls for an evaluation of contexts beyond the clause row, I prefer to postpone this discussion until the next chapter.

16:17. It is likely that 16:17 is a Dtn composition.[100] The phrase *kmtnt ydw* in v. 17a is unique to Deuteronomy. However, it corresponds in style to such Dtn phrases as *ndbt ydk* (16:10) etc. As well there is the variant on the Dtn bestowal formula (*ʾšr ntn lk*).[101]

There is a noteworthy repetition between 12:15 and 16:17 in the phrase *kbrkt yhwh ʾlhyk ʾšr ntn lk*. The variation in context between 12:15 and 16:17 raises the question as to whether this repetition is structurally integrated into the context or not. Here, comparison with repetitions such as 14:27b, 29aβ; 16:11, 14 is helpful. As with these repetitions, the syntactic function of the repetition in 12:15 and 16:17 is similar. I conclude that there are no grounds to suspect the presence of 16:17bβ as secondary in the context of 16:16–17.

---

99 For example, Seitz (*Studien*, 189) sees the festival list as a secondary addition to a Dtn context including 16:16a*.b, 17.

100 Nebeling, *Schichten*, 110–11. By way of contrast, Merendino (*Gesetz*, 148) thinks that v. 17a.b* belongs to the same layer as the non-Dtn material in 16:16aα.γ.b.

101 Normally this formula uses the participle. Cases using the perfect in 2ms contexts appear in 8:10; 12:1, 15, 21; 20:14; 26:11; 28:52, 53 (cf. 26:10, 15).

§8 Deut 16:18–20

Transcription and Translation

18a	šptym wštrym ttn lk bkl šʿryk	F:IVc	O V P Pa P
18a'	ʾšr yhwh ʾlhyk ntn lk lšbṭyk	N:Part	S V P
18b	wšpṭw ʾt hʿm mšpṭ ṣdq	CoF:wqtl	V Po O
19aα	lʾ tṭh mšpṭ	F:xVc	V O
19aβ	lʾ tkyr pnym	F:xVc	V O
19bα	wlʾ tqḥ šḥd	CoF:xVc	V O
19bβ	ky hšḥd yʿwr ʿyny ḥkmym	B:IVc	S V O
19bγ	wyslp dbry ṣdyqm	CoB:Vc	V O
20a	ṣdq ṣdq trdp	F:IVc	O V
20bα	lmʿn tḥyh	B:Vc	V
20bβ	wyršt ʾt hʾrṣ	CoB:wqtl	V Po
20bβ'	ʾšr yhwh ʾlhyk ntn lk	N:Part	S V P

16:18] You shall appoint judges and officials[1] for your tribes in all your gates which Yahweh your God is giving you; and they are to judge the people with just judgments. [19] You shall not pervert justice; you shall not show partiality; nor shall you accept a bribe. For a bribe blinds the eyes of discerning men and muddles the words of those who are in the right. [20] It is real justice you are to strive for so that you may live and occupy the land which Yahweh your God is giving you.

16:18a. The syntax of c.18a is difficult. Does the phrase *lšbṭyk* belong to the subordinate c.18a' or to the main clause? There is no precedent for a Dtn phrase "which Yahweh your God is giving you according to your tribes." But the bestowal formula does appear in Deuteronomy with unusual complements: *bʿbr yrdn* in 3:20; *kl hymym* in 4:40; *lšbt šm* in 13:13; *lbny yśrʾl (lʾḥzh)* in 32:49, 52. Nevertheless, modern translations typically identify *lšbṭyk* as a constituent of the main clause (e.g., NRSV, JPSV, NEB).[2] The use of *ntn* to govern a direct object and two prepositional phrases marked by *lamed* is attested elsewhere in BH (cf., for example, Gen 27:37).[3]

---

[1] The translation of *šṭrym* follows the discussion of M. Weinfeld, "Judge and Officer in Ancient Israel and the Ancient Near East," 83–38. See also Rüterswörden, *Von der politischen Gemeinschaft*, 13–14.

[2] Rüterswörden, *Von der politischen Gemeinschaft*, 14. This is also the position of Rashi and Ramban.

[3] BDB, 768.

16:18b. The verb *wšpṭw* governs two objects. The phrase *špṭ ʾt hʿm* in v. 18b has parallels in Exod 18:13, 22, 26; 1 Kgs 3:9 (= 2 Chron 1:10); 2 Kgs 15:5 (= 2 Chron 26:21); Joel 4:24; 2 Chron 1:11. Parallels to *špṭ mšpṭ* include 1 Kgs 3:28; Isa 16:5; Jer 5:28; Ezek 23:45; Zech 7:9; 8:16; Lam 3:59. Parallels to the syntax of 16:18b include, for example, Gen 42:25; 1 Sam 17:38; Mal 3:24.[4]

Clause Row Structure

Deut 16:18–20 begins with a clause in the IVc form which is continued by the *wqtl* clause in v. 18b. Clauses 19aα, 19aβ proceed asyndetically. A structural connection between c.18b and c.19aα is created by the repetition of *mšpṭ*. Co links c.19aβ and c.19bα. Following c.19bα is a B clause construction introduced by *ky* (c.19bβ) and continued by c.19bγ as indicated by Co. Deut 16:20a follows asyndetically; it governs the B clause structure of 16:20b, which consists of the *lmʿn* clause in c.20bα followed by the *wqtl* structure in c.20bβ. Clauses 18b and 20a are linked by the collocation of *mšpṭ ṣdq* and *ṣdq ṣdq*. The formulaic word pair of *ṣdq* and *mšpṭ* is well attested in BH.[5]

Deut 16:19 is framed by two complex clauses in 16:18a, 20b both of which contain the identical participial formula. All five clauses in 16:19 are simple, and four out of the five show the constituent structure V O. Because of its parallelism in clause structure, the clause group in 16:19 is organized by constituent matching. There is a match between the three F clauses and another match between the two B clauses. An additional linking device found in cc.16:19bβ, 19bγ is the formulaic word-pair *ḥkm / ṣdyq*.[6]

The inner structure of 16:18–20 has the following model:

18a	Prescription	F:IVc
18b	Prescription	CoF:wqtl
19aα	Prohibition	F:xVc
19aβ	Prohibition	F:xVc
19bα	Prohibition	CoF:xVc
19bβ	Motive clause	B:IVc
19bγ	Motive clause	CoB:Vc
20a	Prescription	F:IVc

[4] Waltke and O'Connor, *Biblical Hebrew Syntax*, §10.2.3d.

[5] W. R. Watters, *Formula Criticism and the Poetry of the Old Testament*, 192. The combination *ṣdq wmšpṭ / mšpṭ wṣdq* occurs in Hos 2:21; Pss 89:15; 97:2; 119:121; Prov 1:3; 2:9; Qoh 5:7.

[6] Avishur, *Stylistic Studies of Word Pairs*, 93.

20bα	Motive clause	B:Vc
20bβ	Motive clause	CoB:wqtl

Parallels

16:18. Deut 16:18 consists of a prescription followed by *wqtl* clause. This sequence is not continued in 16:19. The question arises as to whether 16:18b is best considered to be a prescription or a result clause given the change in subject. Similar concerns arise in 14:29; 17:5b, 9bβ. Here, an argument similar to that used with respect to 14:29 is appropriate: the clause represents the result the addresses are enjoined to obtain. Hence, it retains prescriptive value.

The following Dtn phrases occur in v. 18:

v. 18 *bkl šʿryk*[7]
v. 18 *ʾšr yhwh ʾlhyk ntn lk*[8]

16:19. Deut 16:19 distinguishes itself in its context because of its cohesion through constituent matching. It is often held that 16:19 circulated independently of its present context as a *Richterspiegel*, a model code for judges.[9] There are supposed to be three examples of this genre in the Pentateuch: Exod 23:1–3, 6–8; Lev 19:15–16; and Deut 16:19.[10]

These texts can be considered to be generically related because they are not dependent on each other. In the case of Exod 23:1–3, 6–8, the parallel between Exod 23:8 and Deut 16:19 is striking. This need not imply that Exod 23:8 is dependent on Deut 16:19 or vice versa. In particular, the presence of the word pair *ḥkm / ṣdq* in Deut 16:19 argues for a more traditional formulation than the variant with *pqḥym* in Exod 23:8.[11] Another caveat against positing the priority of the contexts in Exodus is provided by Richter's observation that it is Exod 23:6 which contains an expansionary version of a shorter and perhaps more original prohibition contained in Deut 16:19a.[12]

7 See the note on 14:28; the phrase occurs also in 12:15; 28:52(twice), 55.

8 See the note on 15:4; WA, p. 341.

9 See, e.g., K. Rabast, *Das apodiktische Recht im Deuteronomium und im Heiligkeitsgesetz*, 9; G. von Rad, *Studies in Deuteronomy*, 18; Richter, *Recht und Ethos*, 114.

10 Rabast, *Das apodiktische Recht*, 27. I accept J. Halbe's arguments that v. 9 does not participate in the structure of Exod 23:1–8 (*Das Privilegrecht Jahwes*, 434–38). Exod 23:4–5 are also generically intrusive (B. S. Childs, *Exodus*, 480). The original form of Lev 19:15–16 is likely Lev 19:15aβ–b, 16a (Gerstenberger, *Apodiktischen Rechts*, 88).

11 Richter, *Recht und Ethos*, 187.

12 Ibid., 156–57.

Recently, Cholewínski has denied that Lev 19:15–16 contain formulations independent of Exod 23:1–9 and Deut 16:18–20. In his opinion, Lev 19:15aα.b serve as an inclusio for a pair of prohibitions which are meant to supplement the Dtn concerns. A key to the Dtn connection is the use of the idiom *špṭ ṣdq* in Lev 19:15b (cf. Deut 16:18b).[13]

This connection is dubious. In the first place, the phrase *špṭ ṣdq* is not confined to Lev 19:15b and Deut 16:18b. Other references include Jer 11:20; Ps 9:5; Prov 31:9. Secondly, the only thematic link between Lev 19:15 and Deut 16:19 is in Lev 19:15aβγ and Deut 16:19aβ. There is no equivalent in Lev 19:15 to either Deut 16:19aα or 16:19bα. It is noteworthy that Lev 19:15aβγ uses different vocabulary than Deut 16:19aβ. Lev 19:15aβγ has closer relationships with Exod 23:3. The inclusio in Lev 19:15aα.b consists of a parallelism between the phrases *bṣdq* and *bmšpṭ*, whereas Deut 16:18–20 are connected by a chiasmus which uses exact repetitions of the word *ṣdq* (18b, 20a) and the Dtn donation formula (18a, 20b). In summary, the differences between Lev 19:15 and Deut 16:18b–20a are hardly close enough to prove a dependency of Lev 19:15 on the Dtn context.

Cholewínski also holds that Lev 19:16 is drawing on Exod 23:1–3, 6–9. But here again the correspondences are not compelling. His derivation of Lev 19:16aα from Exod 23:1a is to be resisted. Literal parallels to Lev 19:16aα are found elsewhere (see the list of parallels below). Similarly, his equation of Lev 19:16aβ and Exod 23:7bα fails to convince because of the difference in vocabulary.

Do the contents of Exod 23:1–3, 6–8; Lev 19:15–16; and Deut 16:19 constitute model codes for judges? Their instructions fall into two thematic categories: Exod 23:1–2 and Lev 19:16 seem to be addressed to those testifying in a legal proceeding. Exod 23:3, 6–8; Lev 19:15; and Deut 16:19 deal mainly with the act of giving judgment. A connection between these two themes is hard to make if the reader envisages a class of professional judges. But the texts in their present form lead the reader to assume that all of these verses address the same audience. The social context which lies behind these instructions has been described by Noth as the legal community "in the gate" to which every fully enfranchised Israelite belonged. In other words, these prohibitions have their unity because they arise from a cultural situation in which many of the same persons might participate in the legal sphere both as witnesses and judges depending on the situation. They are not, therefore, instructions for judges in the modern sense of the word "judge".[14]

---

[13] Cholewínski, *Heiligkeitsgesetz und Deuteronomium*, 294.

[14] M. Noth, *Leviticus*², 141; *Exodus*, 188–89.

A second piece of evidence which is relevant here is that one prohibition can be used with reference to several social situations (e.g., *lʾ tṭh mšpṭ*). The following parallels may be noted with respect to the materials in Exod 23:1–3, 6–8:

Exod	23:3	*wdl lʾ thdr brybw*
Lev	19:15aβ	*lʾ tśʾ pny dl wlʾ thdr pny gdwl*
Exod	23:6	*lʾ tṭh mšpṭ ʾbywnk brybw*
Deut	16:19aα	*lʾ tṭh mšpṭ*
	24:17	*lʾ tṭh mšpṭ gr ytwm*
	27:19	*ʾrwr mṭh mšpṭ gr ytwm wʾlmnh*
Exod	23:8	*wšḥd lʾ tqḥ*
Deut	16:19bα	*wlʾ tqḥ šḥd*
	27:25	*ʾrwr lqḥ šḥd lhkwt npš dm nqy*

Themes in Lev 19:15–16 also appear in various instructional contexts:

Lev	19:15a	*lʾ tśʾ pny dl*
Deut	16:19aβ	*lʾ tkyr pnym*
Prov	24:23	*hkr pnym bmšpṭ bl ṭwb*
	28:21	*hkr pnym lʾ ṭwb*
	18:5	*śʾt pny ršʿ lʾ ṭwb*
Lev	19:16a	*lʾ tlk rkyl bʿmyk*
Prov	20:19	*gwlh swd hwlk rkyl*
	11:13	*hwlk rkyl mglh swd*

The best model for describing the relationship of Exod 23:1–3, 6–8; Lev 19:15–16 and Deut 16:19 rests on the assumption that there was an extensive cluster of instructions on legal duties in ancient Israel. The parallels listed above show that the concerns expressed are found not only in prescriptive contexts but also in proverbial contexts and rows of curses. The typical structure for such instructions in the prohibition form seems to be the pair or triad. But it was possible for various members of such groups to be combined in more than one fashion and in more than one mode of expression.

The implication of these observations is to suggest that *Richterspiegel* is not the definitive term it appears to be. In its place, we are left with a somewhat less definable collection of "ethical norms for parties-at-law." When Exod 23:1–8; Lev 19:15–16; and Deut 16:19 are compared with themselves and other biblical parallels, what is discovered is a constellation of ethical teachings capable of various combinations and expressions. They concern various aspects of a legal context in which the listener might expect to appear in a number of roles as a party at law: plaintiff, witness, or judge. The fact that they could be combined in large and small collections points to the possibility that these ethical norms might have been promulgated in several kinds of life settings, some undoubtedly less formal than others.

16:20. Deut 16:20 consists of a prescription (v. 20a) followed by *lmʿn* motivation (v. 20b). Texts with structural similarities to 16:20 include Exod 23:12; Lev 23:42–43; Deut 5:16, 33[30]; 22:7; 25:15. The phraseology of the motive clause in 16:20 is Dtn:

lmʿn tḥyh[15]
wyršt[16]
ʾšr yhwh ʾlhyk ntn lk (see v. 18 above).

Literary Unity

The mixture of genres in 16:18–20 is unusual. Deut 16:18 consists of prescription followed by a *wqtl* form; 16:19 is a prohibition row; 16:20 is a prescription with motive clause. It was noted earlier that 16:18, 20 frame 16:19 with chiastic features. This chiastic structure seems to have been used to bring originally independent formulations into a cohesive text. While vv. 18, 20 are likely Dtn compositions, v. 19, especially v. 19a.bα, shows signs of having a different origin.

16:18. There are two literary-critical problems in v. 18. First, in v. 18a there is a redundancy with the appearance of the phrases *bkl šʿryk*, etc., and *lšbṭyk*. Secondly, the phrase *wšpṭw ʾt hʿm* is unusual in a text whose usual referent is the 2ms.[17] It is my opinion that the solution to these two difficulties is related.

Dtn rhetoric knows of the technique of redundancy; for example, *lpny yhwh ʾlhyk bmqwm ʾšr ybḥr* in 14:23; *mʾḥd šʿryk mkl yśrʾl* in 18:6; see also 15:7; 17:2; 23:17. It is also clear that a Dtn legislator would have known that his addressees had identities both as city dwellers and as tribe members (e.g., 12:14, 17; 18:5, 6). Consequently, the hypothesis that 16:18 must have

15 This motive clause occurs in the 2ms in 30:19 and in 2mpl, in 4:1; 5:33; and 8:1. Elsewhere in BH it is found only in the 2mpl: Jer 35:7; Amos 5:4; see WA, p. 345.

16 A major Dtn motif; see WA, p. 341–34. Exact equivalents of 16:20 are few and there is only one if the phrase *wyršt ʾt hʾrṣ* is sought for: 6:18. Cf. 17:14; 26:1; 30:5. In the 2mpl, cf. 4:1, 22; 8:1; 11:8, 31.

17 Rüterswörden, *Von der politischen Gemeinschaft*, 14–15.

originally appeared without either *bkl bšʿryk* [18] or *lšbṭyk* [19] can be sustained only if this redundancy is inexplicable.

The closest parallel to v. 18b occurs in Exod 18:22, 26: *wšpṭw ʾt hʿm*, which refer to the judges appointed by Moses. Further evidence that v. 18b reflects traditional legal formulation is found in the phrase *mšpṭ ṣdq*. This phrase is related to the combination *mšpṭ wṣdq*—a formulaic word pair; but the appearance of *mšpṭ ṣdq* in a bound construction is unusual. In the plural, used with reference to God, variants of the phrase *mšpṭy ṣdqk* refer to the righteous judgements of Yahweh, i.e., his covenant demands or Torah.[20] However, the phrase in 16:18b is neither plural nor definite. Parallels to it predicate the actions of a judge (usually human) or king: cf. *špṭ mšpṭ* (1 Kgs 3:28; Isa 16:5; Jer 5:28; Ezek 23:45; Zech 7:9; 8:16; Lam 3:59); or *špṭ ṣdq* (Deut 1:16; Jer 11:20; Prov 31:9).

According to the Exodus traditions of Deuteronomy (1:13–15), a tribal judiciary emerged in the conquest period, that is, before the settlement of Israel in cities. The redundancy of v. 18a and the traditional legal formulas in v. 18b might be both explained by supposing that the Dtn innovation of situating judicial authorities in cities was to replace or supplement some older tribally-based system. While controversy about the truth of the Chronicler's report of Jehoshaphat's reforms continues unabated,[21] in all likelihood some kind of judicial system, related perhaps to military organization, probably existed even in premonarchical times.[22] Since the tribal system was also the source for the Israelite militia, it follows that a military system of judges would have been mainly tribally based in the premonarchical period and into the early monarchy. It would appear that the Dtn writer is conscious that his instructions are modifying an older tradition which he chooses to acknowledge even as its terms of reference are changed.

16:19. The collocation of *hṭh mšpṭ*,[23] *hkyr pnym*, and *lqḥ šḥd*[24] is unique to 16:19 in BH. It has been suggested that originally only vv. 19aα.bα were

---

[18] For example, Merendino, *Gesetz*, 153.

[19] For example, Rüterswörden, *Von der politischen Gemeinschaft*, 14.

[20] Ps 119:7, 62, 106, 164. Once in the singular as *kl mšpṭ ṣdqk* in Ps 119:160; once in the indefinite plural as *mṣpṭy ṣdq* in Isa 58:2; cf. Yahweh's Torah as *mšpṭym ṣdyqym* in Deut 4:8.

[21] For example, Rüterswörden's recent analysis of 2 Chronicles 19 vindicates the view of Wellhausen that the tale is based on the etymology of the name of Jehoshaphat (*Von der politischen Gemeinschaft*, 15–19).

[22] Weinfeld, "Judge and Officer," 86–88.

[23] Found elsewhere in Exod 23:6; Deut 24:17; 27:19; 1 Sam 8:3; Prov 17:23; 18:5; Lam 3:35.

[24] Found elsewhere in Exod 23:8; Deut 10:17; 27:25; 1 Sam 8:3; Ezek 22:12; Ps 15:5; Prov

connected and that v. 19aβ is a secondary insertion.[25] A compelling argument for this position is that various parallels to the prohibitions of 16:19 usually involve pairs of instructions, never triads.[26]

Nevertheless, it is difficult to determine if the pairing of cc.19aα, 19aβ is more likely original than a combination of cc.19aβ.bα. The equivalents of the three prohibitions in 16:19 are not directly associated in Exodus 23. A thematic equivalent to Deut 16:19aβ may be found in Exod 23:2–3.[27] Deut 16:19aα=Exod 23:6 and 16:19bα=Exod 23:8. It is arguable that 16:19bα shows a thematic linkage with 16:19aα and follows logically on that context. The combination of *hṭh mšpṭ* and *lqḥ šḥd* occurs in 1 Sam 8:3 and Prov 17:23. On the other hand, an explicit connection between preferential treatment (c.19aβ) and the act of bribe-taking (c.19bα) is made in Deut 10:17 and 2 Chron 19:7 by the phrase *nś᾽ pnym* which acts as a synonym of *hkyr pnym*[28] in these contexts (cf. Prov 6:35; Job 34:19).[29] However, *nśh pnym* is coupled with the phrase *hṭh mšpṭ* in Prov 18:5.

In the case of Deut 16:19, formal analysis shows the possibility of a cohesive triad of instructions for participation-at-law. However, 16:19 is composed of elements which also circulated independently. What is most certain is that all three prohibitions have parallels which demonstrate their non-Dtn origins. Lack of content parallels to the present triadic structure suggests that 16:19 represents some sort of secondary combination. But it is a matter of speculation whether the current text was discovered by the Dtn writer in its present form or is a Dtn conflation of more than one preexisting tradition.

16:20. In v. 18b the combination of *mšpṭ ṣdq* yields an emphatic notion such as, "totally correct judgment." The phrase shows structural cohesion with 16:20 through repetition by collocation: the phrase *ṣdq ṣdq* is also an emphatic construction. The wording and thought of v. 20, "seek *ṣdq* that you may live," is suggestive of Prov 21:21. This sentiment is broader than ethical counsel for legal disputation, as are the other contexts which link *ṣdq* and life

---

17:23; 2 Chron 19:7.

[25] Merendino, *Gesetz*, 154; Mayes, *Deuteronomy*, 264.

[26] Rüterswörden, *Von der politischen Gemeinschaft*, 20.

[27] Richter, *Recht und Ethos*, 133.

[28] It has been pointed out that the phrase *hkyr pnym* is unique to proverbial contexts (Prov 24:23; 28:21) outside Deut 1:17; 16:19 (Weinfeld, *Deuteronomy*, 273; Mayes, *Deuteronomy*, 264). But *hkyr* also appears in two other contexts with juridical overtones (Deut 21:17; Job 34:19).

[29] BDB (p. 670) lists the following contexts in which *nśh pnym* means "to show partiality": Lev 19:15; Deut 10:17; Mal 2:9; Ps 82:2; Prov 6:35; 18:5; Job 13:8, 10; 34:19.

in Proverbs.[30] This observation raises the question of the match in genre between 16:18–19 (which are addressed to participants in legal process) and v. 20.

A similar concern arises from consideration of the motive clauses in v. 20b. The motive clause *lmʿn tḥyh* has its best parallels in Deuteronomy. Three are found in the 2mpl (4:1; 5:33[30]; 8:1) and one in the 2ms (30:19). The closest 2ms context to c.20bβ is 6:18 where alone in Deuteronomy the exact parallel *wyršt ʾt hʾrṣ* occurs. Here it is a question of doing what is upright (*yšr*) and good *lmʿn yyṭb lk wbʾt wyršt ʾt hʾrṣ hṭwbh ʾšr nšbʿ yhwh lʾbtyk*. The motif of land occupation also occurs in the context of parallels to *lmʿn tḥyw(n)*. Elsewhere in Deuteronomy this clause is not followed directly by a clause predicated by *yrš* but with the combination *bwʾ . . . yrš* (4:1, 2mpl), or a longer variant of this common sequence in Deuteronomy (8:1, 2mpl).[31] The same thing is also true of 30:19, although not as explicitly (cf. 30:18 where the combination *bwʾ . . . yrš* occurs). All of the parallels to v. 20b, therefore, show that the motifs of having life and inheriting the land are closely connected with conquest, not simply enjoyment of the land. This seems to be inconsistent with the implication of v. 18 in which possession of cities is presupposed (i.e., conquest).[32] This observation has led to the view that 16:18b and 16:20 cannot belong to the same layer of composition.[33]

The proverbial association between the pursuit of *ṣdq* and life make it likely that v. 20a.bα is a Dtn formulation of this wisdom motif. If v. 20b is unacceptable in the composition of 16:18, then so is v. 20a. Parallels to v. 20b point to speeches of the covenant mediator in which the motif of conquest is explicit. It is possible that the motif may be present elsewhere in the clause row sequence to which 16:18 belongs, although it does not appear to be present in v. 18. A final decision on the composition of v. 20 vis à vis 16:18–19 will be reserved until the discussion of clause row sequences.

---

30 Weinfeld (*Deuteronomy*, 273) notes that the relationship posited between acquiring *ṣdq* and life is a wisdom motif, e.g. Prov 11:19; 12:28; 16:31.

31 In Deuteronomy 12–26 the combination *bwʾ . . . yrš* is found in 12:29; 23:21; 26:1; see WA, p. 342.

32 Rüterswörden, *Von der politischen Gemeinschaft*, 23. Contra Weinfeld, *Deuteronomy*, 313. 315.

33 E.g., Merendino, *Gesetz*, 169–170; Rüterswörden, *Von der politischen Gemeinschaft*, 23.

§9 Deut 16:21–22

The Set tradition distinguishes 16:21 and 16:22. But there is a contradiction in the disposition of the text. While the Set divisions distinguish the two verses on the basis of content, syntax draws them together because 16:22 is coordinated with 16:21. Following the method used in this study priority is given to the feature marking syntactic cohesion.

Transcription and Translation

21	lʾ tṭʿ lk ʾšrh kl ʿṣ ʾṣl mzbḥ yhwh ʾlhyk	F:xVc	V P O Pa
21'	ʾšr tʿśh lk	N:Vc	V P
22	wlʾ tqym lk mṣbh	CoF:xVc	V P O
22'	ʾšr śnʾ yhwh ʾlhyk	N:Vc	V S

16:21] You shall not plant any wooden object as an *ʾšrh*[1] beside the altar of Yahweh your God which you make for yourself. [22] Nor shall you erect a *mṣbh* which Yahweh your God hates.

Clause Row Structure

The clause row begins with a clause in the xVc form (c.16:21) to which is connected another xVc clause in v. 22 by Co. Clauses 21, 22 are linked by the breakup of a stereotyped word pair. It appears from the contexts in which they are associated (Exod 34:13; 1 Kgs 14:23; 2 Kgs 17:10; Mic 5:12–13; 2 Chron 14:2; 31:1) that the coordination of *mṣbwt wʾšrym* was a traditional collocation on the model of other pairs of cultic terms, such as the *ʾwrym wtmym*.[2] There is no evidence in BH for a formulaic word pair *ʾšrh wmṣbh* as attested in 16:21, 22. But this is no barrier to the observation of a word pair between cc.16:21, 22 since reversed word pairs are known to be common in BH as opposed to Ugaritic, for example, where they are much rarer.[3]

The inner structure of 16:21–22 has the following model:

21	Prohibition	F:xVc
22	Prohibition	CoF:xVc

---

[1] Neither the shape or function of the *ʾšrh* and *mṣbh* can be determined from the words themselves, so it is best to leave them untranslated. The word *ʾšrh* can refer to either the goddess or her cult object in BH (J. Day, "Asherah in the Hebrew Bible and Northwest Semitic Literature," 401). Here, it is evidently the cult object which is being referred to. The translation follows that suggested by Day (ibid., 402).

[2] O'Connor, *Verse Structure*, §5.2.1. Avishur (*Stylistic Studies of Word-Pairs*, 91) calls such word pairs "syndetic parataxis."

[3] W. G. E. Watson, "Reversed Word-Pairs in Ugaritic Poetry," 189, 192.

Parallels

This clause row belongs to the prohibition row genre. The *ʾšr* clause in 16:22b may be interpreted as an internal motive clause.[4] Its motive element can be established because of its parallelism with the motif of 17:1b, as witnessed in other BH texts (Deut 12:31; Jer 44:4; Prov 6:16). The motive clauses in 16:22b and 17:1a, therefore, express related ideas in different vocabulary. Cases of parallel instructions possessing motive clauses using the same vocabulary are not uncommon; cf. Lev 17:11, 14; 19:3b, 4b; Deut 14:7b, 8a; 24:18, 22. Cases in which two motive clauses express the same idea in different vocabulary occur in Lev 18:22b, 23b; 20:12b, 13aβ.

Literary Unity

Richter suggests that the original form of 16:21–22 was *lʾ tṭʿ lk ʾšrh lʾ tqym lk mṣbh*.[5] But the grounds for this seem somewhat arbitrary. The phrase *ʾṣl mzbḥ yhwh* is not necessarily secondary to v. 21a. Richter himself observed a connection in sound between the mention of *mzbḥ* in 16:21b and *mṣbh* in 16:22. This association could argue for an original connection between v. 21bα and v. 22a because of alliteration. In fact, there is no literary-critical reason to suppose that the original form of v. 21 would not have included v. 21bα.[6]

The most problematic portion of v. 21 is the redundancy created by the *ʾšr* clause in v. 21bβ. Especially to be noted is *lk*, which recapitulates the subject of the verb in both the main clause and the *ʾšr* clause. In this, it resembles the kind of rhetorical redundancy found in passages such as Deut 14:29b; 15:8b. A second feature to be considered is the communication value of the *ʾšr* clause. The clause highlights the tension between erecting a forbidden cult object *lk* and the altar of Yahweh *lk*. As such, it appears to belong to the concerns of vv. 22b; 17:1b which expose the incompatibility of such practices with the worship of Yahweh. Therefore, it is likely that the *ʾšr* clauses in cc.21' and 22' are a Dtn addition to this prohibiton row.

What was the source of 16:21*–22a? It is my view that 16:21a.bα, 22a were a prohibitive row which was adapted by a Dtn writer by the addition of cc.21', 22'. It is necessary to point out that the cultic interests involved in 16:21a, 22a are close to the heart of Dtn theology (cf. 7:5 and 12:3). The relationship between 7:5; 12:3 and Exod 34:13 has been examined in detail by Halbe. It is his view that the commands in Exod 34:13 appear in a text

---

[4] Doron, "Motive Clauses," 70; Sonsino, *Motive Clauses*, 72, 251. Doron assumes that c.22' is related to both 16:21a and 22a.

[5] Richter, *Recht und Ethos*, 109.

[6] See, e.g., von Rad, *Studies in Deuteronomy*, 18.

which is pre-Dtn in origin.[7] On that basis, it can be assumed that the concept behind the prohibitive row in cc.21–22 is attested independently of the book of Deuteronomy.

Further support for an independence of these prohibitions from their current Dtn context appears in Lev 26:1: *wpsl wmṣbh lʾ tqymw lkm*. It has been claimed that this clause may be dependent on Deut 16:22 since all of Lev 26:1 has a Dtn ring to it.[8] But, if so, why is there no corresponding law for the *ʾšrh*? The command *mṣbh lʾ tqymw lkm* belongs to a tripartite prohibitive row banning various sorts of idolatrous fixtures, including *ʾlylm*, *psl*, and *ʾbn mśkyt*. Such parallelism suggests that the command not to raise a *mṣbh* could have circulated in Dtn circles independently of the prohibition of the *ʾšrh*. Therefore, one cannot identify the origin of the prohibition in 16:22 with its present context.

---

7 Halbe, *Privilegrecht Jahwes*, 119.

8 Cholewínski, *Heiligkeitsgesetz und Deuteronomium*, 267–68.

§10 Deut 17:1

Transcription and Translation

1a	lʾ tzbḥ lyhwh ʾlhyk šwr wśh	F:xVc	V P O
1a'	ʾšr yhyh bw mwm kl dbr rʿ	N:Vc	V P S
1b	ky twʿbt yhwh ʾlhyk hwʾ	B:Nc	Pred S

17:1] You shall not sacrifice in honor of Yahweh your God a cattle-beast or sheep on which there is a blemish, any wrong thing, for that is loathsome to Yahweh your God.

Clause Row Structure

Deut 17:1b is connected to c.17a by the subordinating particle *ky* and the pronominal reference *hwʾ*. The inner form of 17:1 has the following model:

1a	Prohibition	F:xVc
1b	Motive clause	B:Nc

Parallels

Deut 17:1 belongs to the genre of prohibition modified by a motive clause. The motive clause *ky twʿbt yhwh* occurs six times in Deuteronomy, five times with the divine name *yhwh ʾlhyk* (7:25; 17:1; 22:5; 23:19; 25:16), and once with *yhwh* (18:12).

Literary Unity

Any evaluation of 17:1 must deal with the similarities between 17:1a and 15:21a. Deut 15:21a and 17:1a are compared above with reference to 15:19–23. It has been established that although there are many similarities between these texts, 15:21 is not likely dependent on 17:1. It remains possible that 17:1a is dependent on 15:21 or that both 15:21 and 17:1a are mutually dependent on an older tradition.

There is one element in 17:1a which is not attested in 15:21a: the combination *šwr wśh*. This does not preclude the possibility of Dtn authorship of 17:1a since this is a common word pair and it cannot be ascribed to the province of one style.[1] Other details suggest that both 15:21a and 17:1a may be dependent on a common tradition which both have adapted to their purposes (cf. Lev 22:23). On the one hand, the imperfections mentioned in 15:21a seem particularly adapted to the interests of 15:19–23 since they name defects which would prevent the animals from being driven to the cult place. On the other hand, the phrase *kl dbr rʿ* is suspicious in the context of 17:1a.

[1] For example, Exod 34:19; Lev 22:28; 27:26; Deut 14:4; 18:3; 1 Sam 14:34; Isa 7:25. Note that the phrase *šwr wśh* is common both to Lev 22:23 and Deut 17:1.

It has been suggested in the discussion of 15:21 that *kl mwm rʿ* in 15:21a is a more authentic reflection of the mutual tradition and that *kl dbr rʿ* has been deliberately coined for a particular purpose. There it is pointed out that out of 13 occurrences of variants of the phrase *dbr rʿ* in BH, five of them occur in Deuteronomy (13:12; 17:1, 5; 19:20; 23:10).[2] Outside 17:1, three of these occur in a context dealing with cultic apostasy: 13:12; 17:5; 19:20. The context of cultic apostasy surrounds 17:1 (cf. 16:21–22; 17:2–7). It is likely that *kl dbr rʿ* appears due to similar concerns. Since the relationship between 17:1 and 15:21 involves a possible dependency between clause rows, a final decision on its meaning will be reserved for the next chapter.

Merendino believes that the phrase *ky twʿbt yhwh ʾlhyk* in 17:1b had as its original form *ky twʿbt yhwh*. In his opinion the application of this motivation to 17:1a is pre-Dtn.[3] It must be admitted that this is possible. In fact, it can be shown that this motivation is not even uniquely Israelite. A good parallel occurs in the *Tabnit* inscription in Phoenician.[4]

But a comparison with the situation in Proverbs is instructive. In Proverbs the bound construction *tʿbt yhwh* occurs eleven times (3:32; 11:1, 20; 12:22; 15:8, 9, 26; 16:5; 17:15; 20:10, 23), never with the apposition *ʾlhyk* and only once in the form *ky tʿbt yhwh* (3:32). In Deuteronomy the situation is different. The motive clause occurs six times, five times with the divine name *yhwh ʾlhyk* (see above on parallels). By contrast, the phrase *tʿbt yhwh* occurs twice, both times without the apposition *ʾlhyk* (12:31; 27:15). The evidence points to the conclusion that the motive clause *ky tʿbt yhwh ʾlhyk* is a characteristic Dtn expression. It cannot be maintained with certainty that every instance of the motive clause *ky tʿbt yhwh ʾlhyk* is an expansion from a putatively original form without *ʾlhyk*.

Evidence for the view that *ky tʿbt yhwh ʾlhyk* in 17:1b is due to Dtn composition is found in the presence of the motivation *ʾšr śnʾ yhwh ʾlhyk* in 16:22b. The combination of *twʿbh* with "that which Yahweh hates" is found in four texts in BH: Deut 12:31; 17:1; Jer 44:4; and Prov 6:16. In Deut 12:31 and Jer 44:4 the contexts contain an anti-Canaanite polemic using variants of the formula *ʿśh tʿbh ʾšr (yhwh) śnʾ*. In 16:22, therefore, *ʾšr śnʾ yhwh ʾlhyk* is parallel to the phrase *ky twʿbt yhwh ʾlhyk hwʾ*. The variation in the formula between

---

[2] Found also in Exod 33:4; Jos 23:15; 2 Kgs 4:41; Pss 64:6; 141:4; Qoh 8:3, 5; Neh 13:17.

[3] Merendino, *Gesetz*, 156–57.

[4] *Tabnit* 6, *k tʿbt ʿštrt hdbr hʾ*. According to the inscription, opening the sarcophagus and disturbing the body (*hdbr hʾ*) is an abomination to Astarte. The inscription is dated by J. C. L Gibson to the first quarter of the fifth-century BCE (*Syrian Semitic Inscriptions* 3:102).

Prov 6:16 and the Dtn examples suggests that the clauses in 16:22b; 17:1b have their closest correspondences with Dtn material.

The construction in 12:31 makes it difficult to argue for literary dependency between 12:31 and 17:1b either way. What is apparent is that the combination was current in Dtn thought. The evidence supports the conclusion that Dtn intervention is responsible for both the application of *ʾšr śnʾ yhwh ʾlhyk* to 16:22a and 17:1b to 17:1a.[5]

---

[5] Richter, *Recht und Ethos*, 109–10.

§11 Deut 17:2–7

Transcription and Translation

2	ky ymṣʾ bqrbk bʾḥd šʿryk	B:Vc	V P Pa S
2a'	ʾšr yhwh ʾlhyk ntn lk	N:Part	S V P
	ʾyš ʾw ʾšh		
2b'	ʾšr yʿśh ʾt hrʿ bʿyny yhwh ʾlhyk	N:Vc	V Po Pc
2b''	lʿbr brytw	N:Inf	V O
3aα'	wylk	CoN:wyqtl	V
3aβ'	wyʿbd ʾlhym ʾḥrym	CoN:wyqtl	V O
3aγ'	wyštḥw lhm	CoN:wyqtl	V P
	wlšmš ʾw lyrḥ ʾw lkl ṣbʾ hšmym		
3b'	ʾšr lʾ ṣwyty	N:Vc	V
4aα	whgd lk	CoB:wqtl	V P
4aβ	wšmʿt	CoB:wqtl	V
4bα	wdršt hyṭb	CoB:wqtl	V Np
4bβ	whnh ʾmt nkwn hdbr	CoB:Part	Np V S
4bβ'	nʿśth htwʿbh hzʾt byśrʾl	N:Vc	V S P
5a	whwṣʾt ʾt hʾyš hhwʾ	CoF:wqtl	V Po Pa
	ʾw ʾt hʾšh hhwʾ		
	ʾšr ʿśw ʾt hdbr hrʿ hzh	N:Vc	V Po
	ʾl šʿryk [ET]		
5bα	wsqltm bʾbnym	CoF:wqtl	V+O P
5bβ	wmtw	CoF:wqtl	V
6a	ʿl py šnym ʿdym ʾw šlšh ʿdym	F:IVc	P V S
	ywmt hmt		
6b	lʾ ywmt ʿl py ʿd ʾḥd	F:xVc	V P
7a	yd hʿdym thyh bw brʾšnh	F:IVc	S V P Pa Pc
7a'	lhmytw	N:Inf	V+O
7bα	wyd kl hʿm bʾḥrnh	CoF:[IVc]	S [V P] Pa
7bβ	wbʿrt hrʿ mqrbk	CoF:wqtl	V O P

[2] If there is discovered[1] in your midst, in one of your gates which Yahweh your God is giving you, a man or a woman who does what is evil in the eyes of the Yahweh your God by transgressing his covenant—[3] that is, he went and served other gods and bowed down to them, namely to the sun, or the moon, or any of the heavenly host which I prohibited—[4] and it is told to you or you hear of it,[2] you investigate thoroughly and the report that this abominable deed has been done in Israel is proven true, [5] then you shall bring out that man or that woman who did this evil deed to your gates and stone them with stones so they die.[6] The one who deserves death shall be executed on the testimony of two or three witnesses. He shall not be executed on the testimony of one witness. [7] The hands of the witnesses shall be against him first to put him to death, then the

---

[1] The principal idea of the *ky ymṣʾ* formula is the discovery of criminal activity, either through an eyewitness or some other means. See S. Dempster, "The Deuteronomic Formula KÎ YIMMĀṢĒʾ in the Light of Biblical and Ancient Near Eastern Law," 207.

[2] See NRSV, JPSV, NEB.

hands of all the people [shall be against him] afterwards. So you shall remove the evil one from your midst.

17:3. The string of *wyqtl* clauses explains the clause *lʿbr brytw*.[3] A similar construction can be found in 1 Kgs 18:18: *bʿzbkm ʾt mṣwty wtlk ʾḥry hbʿlym*. See also Isa 38:9.[4]

17:4bβ'. The clause analysis assumes that c.4bβ' is a noun equivalent standing in apposition to the substantive *hdbr*.[5]

17:5a. *ʾšr ʿśw ʾt hdbr hrʿ hzh ʾl šʿryk ʾt hʾyš ʾw ʾt hʾšh* MT, LXX (O, 106, t)
> LXX
qui rem sceleratissimam perpetrarunt ad portas civitatis tuae Vg, cf. LXX (–O, 106, t)

The LXX reflects a Hebrew text in which all of v. 5aβ was absent. The LXX apparently used a manuscript in which the Hebrew text had a scribal error due to homoioteleuton (*hʾšh* 1° —> *hʾšh* 2°). There is a divergence in the subsequent transmission of the LXX. Most LXX witnesses contain a restored reading which follows the manuscript tradition attested in the Vg, in which there is no equivalent for the phrase *ʾt hʾyš ʾw ʾt hʾšh*. But hexaplaric MSS show a text equivalent to the MT. It seems, therefore, that there were three Hebrew manuscript traditions for v. 5a. The original LXX is based on tradition with a scribal error. Of the two other traditions, the longer text of the MT is best explained as containing a later gloss which the manuscript tradition of most of the LXX tradition and the Vg does not reflect.

17:7bβ. The LXX, the Targums, and Syr all construe *hrʿ* as a concrete reference to the evildoer rather than as a abstract noun. Modern translations prefer the abstract (e.g., JPSV, NRSV, NICOT). There is some ancient evidence for the abstract translation also. Some LXX minuscules read τὸ πονηρόν (there is a typographical error in BHS note 7a; read 𝔊min) and Syr attests an abstract translation in 13:6. The situation can be clarified with reference to the phrase "to do what is evil" as found in 4:25; 9:18; 17:2. Here the abstract noun is pointed with a *pataḥ* (the apparent exception in 31:29 is a pausal form). But the object *hrʿ* in the *bʿrt* formula always has the nominal pointed with *qamɛṣ*, the pointing given in Deuteronomy to the adjective. So *hrʿ* in 17:7 must refer to either "the evil

---

[3] Rüterswörden, *Von der politischen Gemeinschaft*, 32.

[4] Joüon, *Grammaire*, §124q.

[5] Williams, *Syntax*, §485.

thing" or "the evil person." Context demands that the reference be to the person

Clause Row Structure

The formula *ky ymṣʾ* introduces a protasis in which the general terms of the crime are elaborated by a string of *wyqtl* clauses in v. 3 which modify the Inf clause in c.2b". The protasis introduced in c.2 is extended by a series of *wqtl* constructions in v. 4 ending with the Part construction in c.4bβ. The end of the protasis is marked by the deictic particle *hnh* and the shift in clause predication. This creates a disjunction which acts to distinguish the coordinated construction in v. 4 from the *wqtl* clauses beginning in v. 5. The *waw* in c.5a may be interpreted, therefore, as the *waw* of apodosis.

Procedural regulations affecting the disposal of the criminal matter are attached in vv. 6–7. These are distinguished by the form of cc.6a, 6b which interrupt the string of *wqtl* clauses in v. 5, and by their lexical cohesion through repetitions of *ywmt* and *ʿd*. The article in the phrase *hmt* of c. 6a is not an anaphoric but rather an exophoric marker. The indefinite subject is often expressed by the third person and the participle (e.g., Deut 22:8b; 2 Sam 17:9b; Isa 16:10).[6] In such cases, the article refers to an individual or subclass identifiable in the specific situation.[7] Pronominal reference connects c.7a with cc.6a, 6b. Clause 7bα is connected to c.7a by the ellipsis of *thyh bw* and the phrase *bʾḥrnh*, a case of lexical cohesion by collocation (cf. *brʾšnh* in c.7a). The article of the object *hrʿ* is taken as an anaphoric reference to the prepositional phrase *bw* in c.7aα.

The evidence suggests the following model of inner structure:

2	Conditional	B:Vc	Protasis (vv. 2–4)
4aα	Statement	CoB:wqtl	
4aβ	Statement	CoB:wqtl	
4bα	Statement	CoB:wqtl	
4bβ	Statement	CoB:Part	
5a	Prescription	CoF:wqtl	Apodosis (v. 5)
5bα	Prescription	CoF:wqtl	
5bβ	Prescription	CoF:wqtl	
6a	Prescription	F:IVc	Procedural instructions
6b	Prohibition	F:xVc	(vv. 6–7)
7a	Prescription	F:IVc	
7bα	Prescription	CoF:(IVc)	
7bβ	Prescription	CoF:wqtl	

---

6 König, *Hebräischen Sprache*, §324 l.

7 See Halliday and Hasan, *Cohesion in English*, 71.

Parallels

17:2–5. The four Dtn laws which begin with the phrase *ky ymṣʾ* (17:2–7; 21:1–9; 22:22; 24:7) demonstrate a common bond which links them with other legislation in the Hebrew Bible outside Deuteronomy. There is ample evidence that the verb *mṣʾ*, particularly in the N-stem, was a term with a technical function in the province of law. This function involves the use of evidence which was usually provided by eyewitnesses but not exclusively so.[8]

17:2. The following Dtn phraseology occurs:

bʾḥd šʿryk	15:7; 16:5; 23:17.
ʾšr yhwh ʾlhyk ntn lk	See the discussion on 16:18; modifies *bʾḥt ʿryk* in 13:13, *bkl šʿryk* in 16:18a.
ʿśh ʾt hrʿ bʿyny yhwh ʾlhyk	4:25; 9:18; 31:29.[9]

17:3. The following Dtn phraseology occurs:

ʾbd ʾlhym ʾḥrym	7:4; 11:16 (*whštḥwh lhm*); 28:36, 64.
hlk . . . ʿbd ʾlhym ʾḥrym	13:7, 14.
hlk . . . ʿbd ʾlhym ʾḥrym . . . hštḥwh lhm	29:25.
hlk ʾḥry ʾlhym ʾḥrym . . . ʿbd . . . hštḥwh lhm	8:19.

17:4. The following Dtn phraseology occurs:

wdrst hyṭyb	13:15 *wdrst wḥqrt wšʾlt hyṭb.*
	19:18 *wdršw hšpṭym hyṭb.*
whnh ʾmt nkwn hdbr	13:15.
nʿśth htwʿbh hzʾt byśrʾl	13:15. Cf. 12:31; 18:9; 20:18 in which *twʾbh* is that which the nations do (*ʿśh*).[10]

17:5. Capital punishment prescribed as *sql bʾbnym wmt/w/h* is found in Deut 13:11; 22:21, 24; 1 Kgs 21:10, 13.

17:6. A content parallel to this verse occurs in Num 35:30. The phrase *ʿl py šnym ʿdym ʾw šlšh ʾdym* occurs in Deut 19:16b with slight variation: *ʿl py šny ʿdym ʾw ʿl py šlšh ʾdym.*

17:7. The following Dtn phraseology occurs:

yd hʿdym (cf. *ydk* in 13:10) *thyh bw brʾšnh lhmytw wyd kl hʿm bʾḥrnh* 13:10.
wbʿrt hrʿ mqrbk/myśrʾl 13:6; 17:12; 19:19; 21:21; 22:21, 22, 24; 24:7.

---

[8] Dempster, "KÎ YIMMĀṢĒʾ," 202, 211. Cf. Gen 44:9. 10; Exod 21:16, 22:1, 3, 6, 7.

[9] WA, p. 339. This phrase is common in Dtr style (over 40 times).

[10] WA, p. 323.

Literary Unity

Literary-critical questions about 17:2–7 concern its original form, the probability that its core contains a pre- or non-Dtn formulation, and its relationship to Deuteronomy 13. The presence of the *bʿrt* formula in a number of Dtn laws dealing with criminal matters has lead many scholars to propose the existence of a pre-Dtn collection of criminal law marked by this cliché. But recent study has seen this opinion become increasingly unsupportable.[11] It now appears that the phrase had its origins in royal ideology in which the expulsion of evil was part of the iconography of kingship (cf. 2 Sam 4:11). This motif was taken up by the Dtn school and added to various laws, especially those sanctioned by capital punishment. The presence of the *bʿrt* formula in 17:7 is, in fact, an indicator Dtn composition.[12]

The parallels listed above provide ample evidence that 17:2–7 shows thoroughgoing marks of Dtn composition. In particular, it is related in both its contents and its phraseology to Deuteronomy 13.[13] At question is the meaning of this relationship and whether it is possible to detect an earlier form of the text. My opinion is that 17:2–7 has a cohesive literary unity and that there are no literary-critical grounds for establishing a shorter, more original form.

Rüterswörden has stressed the generalizing tendency of this text in relationship to Deuteronomy 13.[14] Relevant factors include:

1. The use of the general terms "man or woman" instead of named persons (e.g., "a prophet or dreamer of dreams" 13:2; "your kinsman, or your wife, or your neighbour" 13:7);
2. The replacement of the invitation to serve other gods in direct speech (13:3, 7, 14) with an indirect report (17:4);
3. The introduction of the theme of transgressing the covenant (17:2b");
4. The supplementary nature of 17:6–7.

Such observations suggest that 17:2–7 is intended to be a comprehensive and abstract commentary on judicial procedure appropriate for the cases of Deuteronomy 13. Several features in addition to those noted by Rüterswörden bear this out. First, this is suggested by the collocation of several phrases and motifs spread throughout Deuteronomy 13: 17:2 reflects 13:2 (*bqrbk*) and 13 (*bʾḥt ʿryk*); 17:4 reflects 13:10 and 15 by combining the

---

11 Preuss, *Deuteronomium*, 120.

12 See P. E. Dion, "Tu feras disparaître le mal du milieu du toi," 326, 346.

13 Weinfeld, *Deuteronomy*, 92.

14 Rüterswörden, *Von der politischen Gemeinschaft*, 38; cf. Seitz, *Studien*, 153–54.

concepts of becoming informed and diligent inquiry of what has been heard.[15]

Second, the text contains rhetorical formulas not derived only from Deuteronomy 13. Dtn formulas used include the clichés of "doing what is evil in the sight of Yahweh your God" and "doing a *tw'bh.*" Examples of Dtr formulas include 17:2b'', which is otherwise attested in the Dtr texts Josh 23:16; Judg 2:20 and 2 Kgs 18:12 (also with a 3ms suffix),[16] and 17:3b' which is attested in Jer 7:31; 19:5; 32:35.[17] This concentration of the rhetoric of malfeasance casts light on the unusually full description of the act of apostasy in v. 3. Rüterswörden is of the opinion that the expansion of the phrase *lhm* in c.3aγ' by the mention of heavenly powers is an addition to the text since there is no biblical evidence that the verb sequence "to serve" and "to bow down" otherwise refers to worship of the heavenly bodies.[18] But the same portion of text (vv. 2–4) is a virtual compendium of the Dtn and Dtr rhetoric of apostasy. The mention of the heavenly bodies is hardly out of place in a text which is so obviously striving for an encyclopedic description of the crime of idolatry. Here the theme of illegitimate worship has been once again (cf. 17:2'') supplemented with a motif which best attested in Dtr texts (2 Kgs 17:16; 21:3; Jer 8:2; 19:13).[19] Clause 3b' can be accepted as part of the original composition due to the same comprehensive interests, despite the fact that the first person reference appears to be a breach of style.[20]

Finally, certain details point to a desire for legal precision. These include:

a) The use of the introduction *ky ymṣ'*. This draws attention to the instructions that follow as a matter of criminal procedure involving the assessment of (eyewitness) evidence;

b) Explicit acknowledgment that the charge might be a result of either third-party information or personal apprehension (cc.4aα, 4aβ);

c) The description of careful inquiry (c.4bα) which characterizes judicial investigation (cf. 13:15; 19:18);

d) The procedural supplement in vv. 6a–7bα. The formula in 17:6 seems to be dependent on a pre-Dtn legal tradition but the available evidence cannot determine if 17:6 is a pre-Dtn statement of that tradition. An implied

---

15 Reading *hrg thrgnw* as *hgd tgydnw* on the basis of the LXX. See Weinfeld, *Deuteronomy*, 94–95.

16 WA, p. 340.

17 Mayes, *Deuteronomy*, 266.

18 Rüterswörden, *Von der politischen Gemeinde*, 35.

19 WA, p. 321.

20 Contra von Rad, ATD, 84.

insistence on at least two witnesses for capital crimes is found in the non-Dtn contexts of Num 35:30 and 1 Kgs 21:10, 13. Deut 19:15–16 does not shed additional light on the matter. In that context the exclusion of the single witness applies to all crimes, not simply to capital crimes. Moreover, 17:6 does not appear to be dependent on 19:16.[21] But however it was derived, 17:6 stands in its context as a statement of a legal tradition which is meant to qualify the procedures of Deuteronomy 13.

Another qualification is to be observed in the change of *ydk* in 13:10 to *yd hʿdym* in 17:7a. This change suggests a deliberate effort to conform a text which might suggest summary execution to the customary rules of evidence.[22] Therefore, it belongs to the same interests which added the rules of evidence in 17:6;

e) The *bʿrt* formula also points to a concern for matters of criminal procedure. Relevant here is the fact that 17:2–7 is bracketed with formulas having this concern. The association of the *ky ymṣʾ* formula and the *bʿrt* formula is also to be found in 22:22 and 24:7 in connection with capital crimes associated with kidnapping and adultery. In both cases, the suspects are apprehended in flagrante delicto. The relevance of eyewitness evidence in these situations is germane to the concerns of the compiler of 17:2–7. The serious charge of apostasy demands similar certain proof.

In summary, this clause row displays many signs of deliberate compilation of expressions of Dtn and Dtr rhetoric related to the crime of apostasy. Concern for exactitude, precision, and comprehensiveness mark this composition throughout. There are no internal literary inconsistencies, and the collocation of various expressions found elsewhere in distinct contexts is characteristic of this text. Therefore, there is no evidence for reducing it to a shorter, more original form. The overall effect and intention of this composition has been ably described by Dempster. This long and complex legal description has a purpose:

> [The] pedantic legal precision which occurs throughout [17:2–7] is not a coincidence: Since the law draws from elements found in each of the laws treating idolatry in chapter 13, it is a judicial paradigm for dealing with this crime.[23]

Another literary problem associated with 17:2–7 concerns its present placement in Deuteronomy. It has been suggested that this text has been mis-

---

21 If there is dependency between 17:6 and 19:15, the influence may be on 19:15 from 17:6. See Mayes, *Deuteronomy*, 266.

22 Levinson, *The Hermeneutics of Innovation*, 381–83.

23 Dempster, "KÎ YIMMĀṢĒʾ," 210.

placed and belongs better in Deuteronomy 13, which shows similar rhetoric and content.[24] Since this discussion cannot be addressed without reference to evidence above the clause row level, it will be deferred to the chapters on clause row analysis and organization.

---

[24] Preuss, *Deuteronomium*, 134.

§12 Deut 17:8–13

Translation and Transcription

8a	ky ypl᾽ mmk dbr lmšpṭ	B:Vc	V P S
	byn dm ldm byn dyn ldyn		
	wbyn ngʿ lngʿ dbry rybt bšʿryk		
8bα	wqmt	CoF:wqtl	V
8bβ	wʿlyt ᾽l hmqwm	CoF:wqtl	V Pa
8bβ'	᾽šr ybḥr yhwh ᾽lhyk bw	N:Vc	V S Po
9a	wb᾽t ᾽l hkhnym hlwym w᾽l hšpṭ	CoF:wqtl	V P
9a'	᾽šr yhyh bymym hhm	N:Vc	V Pa
9bα	wdršt	CoF:wqtl	V
9bβ	whgydw lk ᾽t dbr hmšpṭ	CoF:wqtl	V P Po
10a	wʿśyt ʿl py hdbr	CoF:wqtl	V P
10a'	᾽šr ygydw lk mn hmqwm hhw᾽	N:Vc	V P Pa
10a''	᾽šr ybḥr yhwh	N:Vc	V S
10b	wšmrt	CoF:wqtl	V Pc
10b'	lʿśwt kkl	N:Inf	V P
10b''	᾽šr ywrwk	N:Vc	V+O
11a	ʿl py htwrh	F:IVc	P V
11a'	᾽šr ywrwk	N:Vc	V+O
	wʿl hmšpṭ		
11a''	᾽šr y᾽mrw lk	N:Vc	V P
	tʿśh		
11b	l᾽ tswr mn hdbr	F:xVc	V P A
11b'	᾽šr ygydw lk	N:Vc	V P
	ymyn wśm᾽l		
12a	wh᾽yš	CoF:[Vc]	[V] S
	᾽šr yʿśh bzdwn	N:Vc	V Pc
12a''	lblty šmʿ ᾽l hkhn	N:xInf	V P
12a'''	hʿmd	N:Part	V Pc
12a''''	lšrt šm ᾽t yhwh ᾽lhyk	N:Inf	V A Po
	᾽w ᾽l hšpṭ		
12bα	wmt h᾽yš hhw᾽	CoF:wqtl	V S
12bβ	wbʿrt hrʿ myśr᾽l	CoF:wqtl	V O P
13aα	wkl hʿm yšmʿw	CoF:IVc	S V
13aβ	wyr᾽w	CoF:wqtl	V
13b	wl᾽ yzydwn ʿwd	CoF:xVc	V Np

[8] If a decision requiring a judgment between different types of homicide, civil suits, or assaults which become contentious cases in your gates becomes too difficult for you, then you shall promptly go up to the place which Yahweh your God chooses, [9] go to the levitical priests and the judge who will be there in those days, make inquiry and they will give you the decision. [10] Then you must act according to the decision that they give you from that place which Yahweh chooses and you shall diligently observe everything which they instruct you. [11] You shall act according to the instruction they give you and according to the judgment they deliver to you. You shall not turn from the decision they give you either to the right or to the left. [12] Moreover, if there is someone who acts obstinately by not obeying the priest who has the office to serve Yahweh your God there, or the judge, then he shall die. So you shall remove the evil one from Israel. [13] Then all the people will hear of it, become afraid, and no longer act obstinately.

17:8a. The phrase *lmšpṭ* is a modifier of the clause constituent *dbr*. The syntactic analysis takes v. 8aβ beginning with *byn dm ldm* as a modifier of the phrase *lmšpṭ*, which is also below the clause constituent level. The idiom *špṭ byn* . . . is well attested in BH (e.g., Gen 16:5; Judg 11:27; Ezek 34:17, 22). A parallel to the phrase *mšpṭ byn* occurs in Jer 7:5.

Ramban allows for both a midrashic and a plain interpretation of the text. According to the midrashic tradition, *byn dm ldm* refers to types of ritual uncleanness related to bleeding; *dyn ldyn* refers to verdicts in capital and civil cases; and *ngᶜ lngᶜ* to various categories of leprosy. Ramban extends this line of thought by suggesting that *dbry rybt* refers to other matters of controversy such as the purification of the *śoṭâ* in Numbers 5 and the ritual of the red heifer. But there is also a plain interpretation of the text in which *dm* refers to homicide, *dyn* to civil cases, and *ngᶜ* to bodily injury. All three categories are topics in which disagreements (*dbry rybt*) are likely to arise. Among other medieval commentators, Ibn Ezra follows the plain sense interpretation whereas Rashi favors the midrashic approach. Other authorities have a mixed approach such as TO which lists the matters requiring judgment as homicide, civil law, and leprosy.[1] The translation adopted here follows the tradition of Ibn Ezra.

17:8b. The identification of the beginning of the apodosis of the conditional marked by c.8a is disputed. Rüterswörden has suggested that the apodosis begins in c.10a. He holds that the repetition of the phrase *hdbr ʾšr ygydw lk* in v. 10 following *whgydw lk ʾt dbr hmšpṭ* in c.9bβ is a stylistic signal that the apodosis begins with *wᶜśyt*.[2]

Most of the ancient versions are too literal at this point to be of help. But Syr marks the apodosis at c.8bα as do modern translations such as JPSV,

---

1 See M. and S. Sprecher, *The Torah Anthology*, 17:217–18.

2 Rüterswörden, *Von der politischen Gemeinschaft*, 46.

NRSV, NICOT, NEB, and JB. This is the tradition that has been followed in the translation above. It is supported by the observation of a shift in the class of verb used in cc.8a and 8b. The situation described in the conditional of c.8a is predicated by an Sv construction; a sequence of Av constructions follow in vv. 8b–9. This creates a kind of cause and effect relationship which is typical of the relationship between conditional protases and apodoses.[3] A similar relationship can be seen in the conditional constructions of 14:24–25a; 15:21a–21b. Another lexical clue for a shift between the functions of v. 8a and v. 8b is found in the combination *wqmt wʿlyt*. This combination often indicates the initiation of some new action in BH: Gen 35:1, 3; Jos 8:1, 3; Judg 18:9; 20:18; 2 Kgs 1:3. Hence the translation "promptly" (following JPSV) above.

17:12a. The translation treats c.12a as an unmarked conditional. The *casus pendens* construction of 17:12a has the status of a clause by virtue of its continuation in 17:12bα in the *wqtl* structure *wmt*. A construction identical to 17:12a occurs in 18:20. Elsewhere in Deuteronomy, the phrase *wmt(w)* marks the apodosis of a marked conditional (*ky ymṣʾ*; see 22:22, 25; 24:7). All of these texts are related in that they treat capital crimes. Unlike 22:22, 25, and 24:7, 17:12a is not well-formed. But the structure of 17:12a can be taken as a transformation of the *ky ymṣʾ* construction used by these parallel structures.

Clause Row Structure

The text proceeds as a series of *wqtl* statements in the apodosis (cc. 8b–9bβ) of a conditional protasis in c.8a. The apodosis is best regarded as ending in c.9bβ. This is due to the similarity in form and function between the clauses in v. 10 and v. 11. Clauses 11a and 11b consist of a balanced IVc prescription (c.11a) and xVc Prohibition (c.11b) which breaks the string of *wqtl* clauses in v. 10. They are connected by the lexical collocation of *hmšpṭ ʾšr yʾmrw lk* (c.11a) and *hdbr ʾšr ygydw lk* (c.11b). The shift in subject between c.9b and 10a and repeated elements between v. 10 and v. 11 combine to suggest a similarity in function with v. 11. Despite its *wqtl* form, therefore, v. 10 does not appear to extend the apodosis of the condition but acts as a type of exhortation or paraenesis similar to v. 11.

The coordinated conditional construction in v. 12a.bα contains negative sanctions which repeat motifs of acting (see c.10a and c.11) in accordance with the priest and judge (cf. c.9a). The text ends with several coordinated clauses in v. 13 which suggest the results of the action described in v. 12bβ.

The following inner structure seems indicated for 17:8–13:

---

[3] See Halliday and Hasan, *Cohesion in English*, 258.

8a	Conditional	B:Vc	Protasis
8bα	Prescription	CoF:wqtl	Apodosis vv. 8b–9
8bβ	Prescription	CoF:wqtl	
9a	Prescription	CoF:wqtl	
9bα	Prescription	CoF:wqtl	
9bβ	Prescription	CoF:wqtl	
10a	Prescription	CoF:wqtl	Exhortation 1
10b	Prescription	CoF:wqtl	
11a	Prescription	F:IVc	Exhortation 2
11b	Prohibition	F:xVc	
12a	Unmarked conditional	CoF:[Vc]	Negative Sanctions
12bα	Prescription	CoF:wqtl	
12bβ	Prescription	CoF:wqtl	
13aα	Result Clause	CoF:IVc	Motivation for v. 12
13aβ	Result Clause	CoF:wqtl	
13b	Result Clause	CoF:xVc	

Parallels

The conditional construction in 17:8–9 is an If-You formulation. It has parallels in construction to the conditionals in 14:24–26bα; 15:21. In all three cases the protasis is predicated by an Sv and the apodosis is marked by a *wqtl* construction using an Av.

The following Dtn phrases are found in 17:8–13:

17:8 *bšʿryk* See the discussion on 14:21aβ.

17:8, 10 *hmqwm ʾšr ybḥr yhwh.*[4]

17:11 *swr ymym wśmʾl* 5:32[29](2mpl); 17:20; 28:14.[5]

17:12 *wbʿrt hrʿ myśrʾl* See the discussion on 17:7.

17:13 (*kl hʿm*) *yšmʿw wyrʾw* 13:12; 19:20; 21:21.

Literary Unity

There are two important literary-critical problems in 17:8–13. The first concerns the nature of the central authority in 17:9. Did the text at one time lack the coordination of priests and judge? Second, the question of possible supplements to the text in 17:10–13 needs to be addressed.

17:8–9. A case exists for stating that judge and priest did not originally cooperate together in the administration of justice in ancient Israel. In its present form, however, Deuteronomy seems to envisage these two functionaries as combined in a common task. The priest, for example, administers not only sacral but also civil law according to texts such as 19:17 and 21:5. It

[4] WA, p. 324.

[5] WA, p. 339.

is likely that the combination of these two functionaries into a common judiciary is the work of the writers of Deuteronomy.[6]

The question arises as to whether it is possible to uncover an earlier version of 17:8–9 in which this combination did not appear.[7] It is unlikely, however, that any simple literary-critical operation will be successful with respect to v. 9, for there are no pressing indications of secondary additions to this verse.[8] The fact that this text partakes of the typical Dtn contrast between *šʿryk* and the *mqwm* identifies it as a Dtn composition quite a part from the form of the judiciary in v. 9. Removal of either the priests or the judge of v. 9 does not yield evidence which can contest the integrity of 17:8–9 as a literary unit. It remains identifiable as a Dtn composition. If the combination of priests and judge is a Dtn innovation, then this is to be expected in a text such as 17:8–9. Below it will be argued that v. 12 is secondary to the composition of vv. 8–9. But v. 12 may be taken as an ancient commentary which assumes the presence of both judge and priest in v. 9.[9]

17:10–13. Rüterswörden points to shifts in vocabulary as reason for viewing 17:11 as a supplement to v. 10. First, the terms *twrh* and *mšpṭ* are used instead of *dbr* or *dbr hmšpṭ / dbr lmšpṭ*. Secondly, the judgment words are the object of the verb *ʾmr* instead of *ngd*. Here, I support Rüttersworden, but I also regard vv. 12–13 as additions to the text which stem from the same hand which added v. 11 to vv. 8–10.[10]

Seitz has argued that c.10b and v. 11 are superfluous after vv. 9b, 10a.[11] In this regard, the function of the *wšmrt* in c.10b requires particular scrutiny

---

[6] Weinfeld, *Deuteronomy*, 235.

[7] E.g., von Rad (ATD, 84) and A. Rofé ("The Law about the Organization of Justice in Deuteronomy," 318) believe that the presence of priests in v. 9 is a later addition. Seitz (*Studien*, 202) views the judge as a secondary addition to v. 9.

[8] Mayes, *Deuteronomy*, 268.

[9] Weinfeld (*Deuteronomy*, 235) argues that evidence for the combination of judge and priest in v. 9 is also to be found in the phraseology of v. 11: *hdbr ʾšr ywrwk* is to be derived from priestly practice and *hmšpṭ ʾšr yʾmrw lk* from judicial practice. This is unlikely, however. In the first place, when *mšpṭ* is the object of a verb of speaking, the verb *dbr* is more common (e.g., 2 Kgs 25:6; Isa 32:7; Jer 1:16; Ps 37:30). Secondly, the phrases *ywrwk* and *ʾmrw lk* occur juxtaposed in Job 8:10. Both are predicated of the same referent: the ancestors in Job 8:8. Thirdly, the nouns *twrh* and *mšpṭ* can be considered a formulaic word pair; see Isa 42:4; 51:4 (Watters, *Formula Criticism*, 175). For these reasons, it is not clear that the phrase *ʾmr mšpṭ* comes from a different cultural setting than *hwrh twrh*.

[10] Rüterswörden (*Von der politischen Gemeinschaft*, 47) considers v. 11 as interrupting an original connection between v. 10 and vv. 12–13. Seitz (*Studien*, 203) and Merendino (*Gesetz*, 177) are examples of scholars who consider vv. 12–13 as later additions to v. 11.

[11] Seitz, *Studien*, 202.

since *wšmrt* clauses are usually found in speeches of the covenant mediator and demand obedience to all the Dtn laws (see 4:40; 6:3; 7:11; 8:6; 11:1; 16:12; 26:16). But the *wšmrt* clause in v. 10b does not participate in the pattern of general exhortation. First, it enjoins the reader to follow priestly teaching *kkl ʾšr ywrk*. This formula is also used in Deut 24:8 to demand obedience to a specific *twrh*. Secondly, the beginning of v. 10b involves a violation of a well established Dtn idiom. Here alone in Deuteronomy one encounters the combination *wʿśyt . . . wšmrt*, the reverse of the well established cliché "to guard and to do" which is associated with general paraenesis in speeches of the covenant mediator (cf., e.g., 15:5). In summary, the lack of evidence for its general paraenetic value, and the violation of a well-established Dtn cliché suggest that Seitz is not correct to view v. 10b as a secondary supplement to v. 10a.

Secondary supplementation appears to begin in v. 11. Two kinds of evidence support this claim, in addition to the shift in vocabulary noted by Rüttersworden. First, v. 11 is a repetition of the terms of v. 10. But this repetition has no evident structural value. Instead (and this is the second kind of evidence), it introduces a span of discourse which uses expressions which do promote adherence to all Dtn instructions. For example, the motif of "not turning to the right or the left" in v. 11 occurs in general paraenetic contexts having to do with the obedience to all *twrh* (cf. 5:32[29]; 28:14). Hence, there is a breach in focus between the exhortations of v. 10 and v. 11.

The question of the continuity of v. 11 in v. 12 is best considered after the relationship between v. 12 and v. 13 has been established. Deut 18:22 is the only other text in Deuteronomy which uses the noun *zdwn*. It follows a verse (18:20) which is the closest structural parallel to 17:12a.bα in Deuteronomy. The context of 18:20, 22 has to do with speaking a *dbr* which Yahweh has not spoken. This is a form of apostasy and it carries the death penalty. There is also a thematic correspondence with the refusal of ordinary human beings to listen to the central authorities who represent Yahweh in 17:9. Therefore, it is understandable why the death penalty is imposed in 17:12 and, as a form of apostasy, why the *bʿrt* formula also appears (cf. 17:7).

The verb *zwd* appears in v. 13 (cf. 18:20). Deut 1:43; 17:13; and 18:20 are the only Dtn contexts attesting this verb. There are grounds for positing that the *bʿrt* formula in v. 12 and the dissuasion formula in v. 13 belong to different streams of Dtn composition because their rationales for capital punishment are different. The *bʿrt* formula considers it to be justified on the basis that evil is removed from the body politic. The dissuasion formula in v.

13 justifies the punishment as a deterrent.[12] Nevertheless, that does not mean that the combination in 17:12–13 is evidence of secondary addition in v. 13. Like v. 12, v. 13 also recalls 18:20–22 through the use of a form of *zwd*. The fact that vv. 12–13 share common parallels with 18:20–22 which are otherwise unique in Dtn instructions argues for an original cohesion in composition. Compare also the use of both formulas in parallel positions in the capital cases of 13:6, 12. The parallels with Deuteronomy 13 underscore the common concern of 17:12–13 as one of apostasy, as do the parallels with Deuteronomy 18.

The immediate signal for reading the concept of apostasy into 17:8–10 is to be found in the *l' tswr* clause of 17:11b. What one turns aside from in v. 11 is the *dbr* (cf. 18:20, 22) which the addressee is given by the central authorities. Consequently, vv. 12–13 proceed logically from v. 11 and develop a theme which vv. 12–13 possess in common with 18:22, where obstinacy with respect to Yahweh's *dbr* also meets the death penalty.

In summary, 17:8–10 is a unit displaying no signs of literary compositeness. It has been supplemented with material beginning in v. 11. This supplement has signs of cohesion which suggest that vv. 11–13 were added to the original composition of 17:8–10 at one time.

---

12 Dion, "Tu feras disparaître," 330.

Chapter Five

CLAUSE ROW SEQUENCES IN DEUTERONOMY 14:1–17:13

The purpose of this chapter is to identify sequences of clause rows which show signs of an original literary unity. The chapter will be begin by identifying the most obvious clause row sequence in Deut 14:1–17:13: the *mqwm* sequence in 14:22–16:17. The characteristics of this clause row sequence will be used along with other criteria noted in the discussions of literary unity above to determine other unified clause row sequences in the text. Finally, the identification of these longer spans of text will provide a context for the resolution of a number of literary-critical tensions which were left unresolved in the previous chapter.

The mqwm Sequence in 14:22–29; 15:19–16:17

Those clause rows between 14:22–16:17 which use the *mqwm* formula or play on the distinction between *bmqwm* and *bšʿryk* show a number of signs of an original literary unity. The clause rows in question are 14:22–27*, 28–29; 15:19–23; 16:1–8, 9–12, 13–15, 16–17. This group of clauses will be referred to below as the *mqwm* sequence. This sequence is indicated by common structural properties as well as common content.

These clause rows are linked by a number of repetitions on the clause constituent level:

wʾklt	14:23a, 26bα; 16:7aβ. Cf. also 14:29aβ (*wʾklw*); 15:20, 22 (*tʾklnw*).
twkl	14:24aβ; 16:5
whlkt	14:25bβ; 16:7bβ
wśmḥt	14:26bβ–27a*; 16:11, 14
ky ʾyn lw ḥlq *wnḥlh ʿmk*	14:27b, 29aα'
ʾth wbytk	14:26bβ–27a*; 15:20. Cf. 16:11, 14 (*ʾth wbnk wbtk ʿbdk wʾmtk*)
hlwy whgr *whywtm whʾlmnh*	14:29aα; 16:11, 14
lpny yhwh ʾlhyk	14:23, 26: 15:20; 16:2

bmqwm	14:23a; 15:20; 16:2, 7, 11, 15, 16
ʾl hmqwm	14:25; 16:6
bšʿryk	14:28; 15:22; 16:5
ʾšr bšʿryk	14:27; 29aα; 16:11, 14

A prominent feature found in the *mqwm* sequence is the development of a row of prescriptions using *wqtl* forms following a prescription in the IVc word order (cf. 14:22–23; 16:9–11; 16:13–14). Deut 14:22–27* and 15:19–23 share a more unusual structure: both contain a general instruction (14:22–23; 15:19–20) followed by an If-You construction (14:24–27*; 15:21–23).

There are also parallels to phraseology found in 12:13–19. The parallels to 12:17–18 are particularly rich:

lʾ twkl . . . ky ʾm	12:17–18; cf. 16:5–6
bšʿryk . . . bmqwm	12:17–18; cf. 16:5–6 (*ʾl hmqwm*); 15:20, 22 (*bmqwm . . . bšʿryk*)
mʿśr dgnk, etc.	12:18; cf. 14:23a
lpny yhwh ʾlhyk tʾklnw	12:18; cf. 15:20
ʾth wbnk wbtk ʿbdk wʾmtk whlwy ʾšr bšʿryk	12:18; cf. 16:11, 14
wśmḥt	12:18; cf. 14:26bβ–27a*; 16:11, 14

The discovery of an intertextual connection between the *mqwm* sequence and 12:13–19 helps to identify 16:16–17 with the *mqwm* sequence. The repetition of the phrase *kbrkt yhwh ʾlhyk ʾšr ntn lk* in 12:15 and 16:17b has structural value. The immediate concern of 12:15 is with the issue of profane slaughter. But the phrase occurs within a clause row in which concerns about the presentation of offerings at the *mqwm* are preeminent. Deut 16:17 is also concerned with the presentation of offerings at the *mqwm*. The language of blessing in 16:17 (*kbrkt yhwh ʾlhyk*) also approaches that found in 16:10b (*kʾšr ybrkk yhwh ʾlhyk*).

Do the intertextual references of the *mqwm* sequence imply a primary cohesion with a larger span of text in Deuteronomy 12 than 12:13–19? The possibility of relationships between the *mqwm* sequence and 12:20–24 must also be discussed. The phrase *tʾwh npšk* is found in 12:20a and 14:26a. There are also repetitions between 12:22–23 and 15:22–23.

The repetition of *tʿwh npšk* in 12:20a and 14:26 does not indicate a relationship on the level of clause row sequence. The phrase occurs in twice 14:26a in the form *bkl ʾšr tʾwh npšk*. The idiom occurs in the form *ky tʾwh npšk* in 12:20a. Deut 12:20–24 employ the phrase *bkl ʾwt npšk* in 12:20b, 22.

But the phrase *bkl ʾwt npšk* also appears in 12:15. The evidence falls short of requiring the opinion that 12:20–24 belong to the intertextual references of 14:22–27. The syntax of 14:26a is not an exact recapitulation of the terms of 12:20–24 and the idea of appetitive desire occurs in a text with clear intertextual references to 14:22–27*.

Deut 15:22–23 also shares phraseology with 12:20–24. The phrase *hṭmʾ whṭhwr yḥd* is found in both 15:22 and 12:23. But, except for the word *yḥd*, 15:22–23 more closely resembles 12:15–16 in syntax and vocabulary than 12:22–23.[1] Another substantial clue that the intertextual context of 15:20–23 is to be located in 12:15–18 is found in the fact that 15:20a is almost an exact repetition of 12:18aα. Coupled with the repetition of 12:15b in 15:22bβ and the close proximity of 15:23 and 12:16, the evidence suggests that the intertextual reference of 15:20–23 need not go beyond 12:15–18.

It is my conclusion, therefore, that intertextual references in the *mqwm* sequence do not imply a primary literary unity with a larger span of text in Deuteronomy 12 than 12:13–19. In the arguments which follow, Seitz's analysis of 12:13–19 will be assumed as basically correct. The results of this study give added support to Seitz in his analysis of 12:13–19 as the basic and original clause row in Deuteronomy 12.[2] It may be assumed that the basic Dtn layer in 12:13–19 belongs to the span of text identified in Deuteronomy 14–16 as the *mqwm* sequence.

Deut 14:1–21 and the mqwm Sequence

The repetition of the motive clause *ky ʿm qdwš ʾth lyhwh ʾlhyk* suggests that 14:1–21a represents a cohesive span of text.[3] The motive clauses in 14:2a, 21aϵ show structural similarity, each ending a set of second person instructions. It is likely that the Dtn writer implicated in 14:21aβ–e is responsible for the composition of 14:2. The same hand is also implicated in 14:3. The juxtaposition of 14:3 to 14:2 shows that it belongs to the constellation of Dtn concerns for cult purity and election identified by Humbert.[4] What the text of 14:4–20* brands as *ṭmʾ*, the Dtn writer calls *twʿbh*.

---

[1] This case is made difficult by the fact that 12:16a occurs in the 2mpl whereas the parallel in 12:23 is singular. But the 2mpl in 12:16a is probably due to corruption in the transmission of the text (cf. the 2ms in Sam). See Seitz, *Studien*, 211.

[2] Seitz, *Studien*, 206–12 (Seitz excludes v. 14b). This is also the conclusion of the recent study by Reuter (*Kultzentralisation*, 105–106), although she limits the original text to Deut 12:13–14a, 15–18.

[3] Bettenzoli, "Deuteronomium und Heiligkeitsgesetz," 388; J. R. Lundbom, "Poetic Structure and Prophetic Rhetoric in Hosea", 301.

[4] P. Humbert, "Le substantif *toʿēbā* et le verbe *tʿb* dans l'Ancien Testament," 223–26.

It seems sufficient merely to repeat the injunctions of the non-Dtn text until the question of the *nblh* appears.

Deut 14:3, 21aβ–ϵ is further evidence for the Dtn composer's preference for the 2ms in 14:1–21. There is no hint of Dtn composition within the 2mpl sections of 14:4–21aα. These observations help to clarify the origins of 14:1, which is written in the 2mpl and qualified by Dtn clauses written in the 2ms (v. 2). Comparison with the composition of 14:3–21a makes it probable that the 2mpl composition in 14:1 is a citation from a non-Dtn source.

The establishment of the clause row sequence of 14:1–21a allows judgments about the function of 14:21b in the discourse. Despite its lack of endophoric reference, 14:21b probably has points of contact with the exophoric context of 14:1–21 (i.e., holiness and ethnic purity).[5] The placement of this text, however, is problematic. It stands outside the inclusio created by 14:2, 21aϵ. In comparison with other non- and pre-Dtn material identified in 14:1–17:13, 14:21b appears without Dtn framing or development (cf. 14:22; 15:2aβ.b, 19*, 16:9–10a, 13, 16*, 19, 21*, 22*, 17:1).

But there is another text in 14:1–17:13 which ends with a non-Dtn formulation: 16:8bβ, a traditional injunction for work stoppage. The relationship of 16:8bβ with its context also does not depend on formal endophoric reference. In the case of 14:1–21, the text in its present form both begins and ends with a non-Dtn instruction. Identifiable Dtn motifs occur inside. The structure of 16:1–8 is comparable. Deut 16:1 begins with a non-Dtn element which is subsequently developed with Dtn terms; the text also ends with non-Dtn material in 16:8. Therefore, a text like 14:1–21 has an analogue of sorts in Dtn composition (cf. 16:1–8). This means that the fact that 14:21b stands outside the inclusio created by 14:2, 21aϵ may not be of literary-critical significance.

Deut 14:21b was obviously understood as a food taboo at the time of its placement in 14:21b. It also belonged to the polemic against non-Israelite culture.[6] In the light of the literary ambiguities which surround the meaning and placement of 14:21b in this context, it is best to regard the clause as an original part of the composition of 14:1–21.

The clause row of 14:1–21 does not belong to the *mqwm* sequence. The most telling sign of this is the point of intertextual reference. The Dtn repetitions in 14:2, 21a refer to 7:6 not to 12:13–19. This association can be coupled with the observation that 14:1–21 does not specifically address the question of activities *bmqwm* as opposed to *bšʿryk*. Rather, 14:1–21 is occupied

[5] See Fishbane, *Biblical Interpretation*, 228–30.

[6] Axel, "Zur Herkunft und Sozialgeschichte Israels. 'Das Böckchen in der Milch seiner Mutter,'" 167.

with the question of ethnic distinctions, as is 7:1–6 with its prohibitions against idolatry and intermarriage.

The relationship between 14:1–21 and 7:1–6 is difficult to determine. Deut 7:1–6 has its own literary history.[7] The text in 14:1–21a shows a structural relationship through the repetition of 7:6. It shows similarity in content with its concern to distinguish Israel from the surrounding nations. Recently, Achenbach has restated the case for a dependency of 14:2, 21aε on 7:6. He finds the *Numeruswechsel* in 14:1–21 as evidence of this.[8] The shift between 2ms and 2mpl texts in 14:1–21 acquires its significance from the probability that the original form of 7:1–6 used only the 2ms. The 2mpl (*Numeruswechsel*) elements in 7:1–6 are likely secondary.[9] By implication, the text of 14:1–21 which shows an original mixture of 2ms and 2mpl contexts is also a secondary development of the (originally singular) text of 7:1–6.

Deut 15:1–18 and the mqwm Sequence

It is best to consider 15:1–3 as originally belonging to the *mqwm* sequence. Evidently, 15:1–3 was expanded at some point in the transmission of the text by the addition of 15:7–18. The context of 15:1–3, 7–18 was subsequently altered by the insertion of 15:4–6.

15:7–18. A comparison between the structure and contents of 15:7–11, 12–18 and the *mqwm* sequence suggests that 15:7–18 does not belong to the *mqwm* sequence in 14:22–16:17. The clause rows of 15:7–11, 12–18 show signs of a primary cohesion with each other, but not with clause rows found in the *mqwm* sequence.

First, 15:7–11, 12–18 share a unique genre membership among the clause rows in 14:22–16:17. They belong to the subset of If-You laws known as casuistic laws governing primary rights and duties. Unlike those in the *mqwm* sequence, these conditional structures do not introduce special cases to preceding general instructions (cf. 14:24–26; 15:21–23).

Secondly, both 15:7–11 and 15:12–18 also use a number of unique constructions. None of these characteristics can be found in the *mqwm* sequence.

a) Chief among these is the method used for ending their clause rows. Deut 15:11b and 15:18a recapitulate the first portion of their clause rows. In both cases these resumptive clauses are not necessary to complete the sense of the clauses which immediately precede them (cf. 15:10, 16–17).

---

[7] F. García López, "'Un peuple consacré': Analyse critique de Deutéronome VII," 451.

[8] R. Achenbach, *Israel zwischen Verheissung und Gebot*, 301–2.

[9] López, "Un peuple consacré," 439–44.

b) Another structural idiosyncracy is exemplified in the use of direct speech in 15:9, 16. According to Richter, the presence or absence of direct speech is an important formal characteristic.[10] While the presence of speech in 15:16 might be explained by appealing to an earlier tradition on which it is based (cf. Exod 21:5–6), the presence of speech in 15:9aα cannot.

c) Deut 15:7–11 and 15:12–18 also stand out from the *mqwm sequence* in their use of *hyh* clauses to frame sections of discourse. This occurs in 15:9aβ–9bβ and 15:16aα–17aγ.

Thirdly, homiletic style and the way references to their exophoric context are made by 15:7–18 can also be considered:

a) The promulgation formulas in 15:11b, 15b which use the phrase *hywm* distinguish 15:7–18 from the clause rows in the *mqwm* sequence.(cf. 12:14b). Dtn promulgation formulas use *hywm* to draw attention to the exophoric context of the accompanying instructions as a speech of the covenant mediator.[11] The form with the phrase *hywm hzh* in 15:15 is even more emphatic than that with *hywm*.[12]

b) The repeated *ʿl kn* motive clauses in the first person in 15:11, 15 also highlight the contents of 15:7–18 as delivered speech.

c) Another indicator of the emphasis on an exophoric context which reports the oral delivery of the Dtn laws is the presence of multiple constructions using the free Inf. This has been identified as a distinctive feature of direct discourse in BH.[13]

d) Similarly, the use of the particle *ʾšr* (15:14b) as a causal conjunction is also a feature of direct speech.[14]

None of these characteristics can be found in the *mqwm* sequence. In general, the character of clause rows in the *mqwm* sequence as spoken address is not as emphasized as it is in 15:7–11, 12–18.

15:4–6. Deut 15:4–6 has a number of structural features in common with 15:7–11. The majority of clauses in 15:4–6 have their parallels in speeches of the covenant mediator which occur either as the prologue or epilogue to the promulgation of a set of laws. Therefore, like 15:7–11, 15:4–6 also emphasizes the exophoric context of the speech of the covenant mediator. There are also vocabulary links between 15:4–6 and 15:7–11. Cf. the clause

---

10 Richter, *Exegese*, 92.

11 Braulik, "Ausdrücke für 'Gesetz,'" 42.

12 De Vries, "The Development of the Deuteronomic Promulgation Formula," 301.

13 Macdonald, "Some Distinctive Characteristics of Israelite Spoken Hebrew," 168–69.

14 Ibid., 167. In making this observation I am opposing Macdonald's statement that no instance of the causal *ʾšr* occurs in Deuteronomy. Cf. also the use of *ʾšr* in 16:22.

elements *yhyh ʾbywn bk* in 15:4a, 7a; the root *ʿbṭ* (15:6, 8) and the prominence of emphatic expressions using the free Inf (cf. 15:4b, 5, 8, 10a).

But there is a significant tension in content between 15:4–6 and 15:7–11. Deut 15:11 insists that the poor will never be absent from the land, whereas 15:4a states that none of the addressees should be poor. Some commentators have attempted to relieve this tension by treating 15:4a as the apodosis of a conditional construction with the protasis in 15:5, leaving Deut 15:4b to be regarded as a parenthetical remark. The notes to the translation have dealt with this interpretation and dismissed it. Deut 15:4a is not a member of a conditional construction. It is an instruction, and its unconditional nature makes the tension between 15:4–6 and 15:7–11 acute. Therefore, content would indicate that 15:4–6 and 15:7–11 were not originally cohesive.

Another indication of the secondary nature of 15:4–6 to 15:7–11 appears in v. 6. Deut 15:6b shows a marked affinity to 28:12 where the motif of blessing (*lbrk ʾt kl mʿśh ydk*) is found immediately preceding the clause *whlwyt gwym rbym wʾth lʾ tlwh*. In 15:6, the unusual root *ʿbṭ* appears instead of *lwh*, a common word for lending in BH.[15] This can be explained by assuming that 15:6 took its language from 28:12 but changed the verbs involved under the influence of the use of the root *ʿbṭ* already present in 15:8.

It is evident, therefore, that 15:4–6 is secondary to the context of 15:1–3, 7–11.[16] The flow of content from 15:1–3 to 15:7–11 also favors this opinion. Deut 15:7–11 looks over 15:4–6 to comment on the *šmṭh* instructions in 15:1–3. Previously it was noted that the cohesion between 15:1–3 and vv. 4–6 is rather loose and that 15:4–6 seems to have a polemical posture towards the assumption of poverty implicit in the debt release regulations of 15:1–3. This lack of cohesion can also be explained by assuming that 15:4–6 interrupts a text which at one time went directly from 15:1–3 to 15:7–11.

15:1–3. A case can be made either for or against an original cohesion of 15:1–3 and 15:7–11. The case for the common authorship of 15:1–3 and 15:7–11 has been made by Seitz, who is particularly impressed by signs of chiastic arrangement present in both 15:1–3 and 15:7–11.[17] Nevertheless, an argument can be made for the membership of 15:1–3 in the *mqwm* sequence.

Seitz's perception of chiastic construction in 15:7–11; 12–18 needs to be qualified. Chiastic arrangement is not as salient a feature of the composition

---

[15] *ʿbṭ* in BH found in Deut 15:6,8; 24:10. *lwh* in BH found in Exod 22:24; Deut 28:12, 44; Isa 24:2; Pss 37:21, 26; 112:5; Prov 19:17; 22:7; Neh 5:4.

[16] Mayes, *Deuteronomy*, 246; Merendino, *Gesetz*, 110–11; Nebeling, *Schichten*, 84; Seitz, *Studien*, 169.

[17] Seitz, *Studien*, 167–69; 174.

of this clause row as he represents it. There is not a strong case for viewing 15:12–18 as organized by chiastic structure. The overarching construction in 15:7–10 is best described as a ring composition in which the chiastically arranged elements (vv. 7b, 8; 10aα, 10aβ) frame a central portion (v. 9). But chiastic arrangements of content can also be found in 14:22–26; 16:3–4; and 16:6–7. Therefore, chiastic arrangment is used by the author of the *mqwm* sequence as well as the writer of 15:7–11, 12–18.

Deut 15:1–3 lacks explicit reference to either the *mqwm* or its opposite, *šʿryk*. This objection is substantial. But in favor of its inclusion in the *mqwm* sequence are two structural characteristics. First, 15:3 consists of a prohibition in 15:3a which is balanced by a prescription in 15:3b. But unlike the balanced prescriptions in 15:8, 10, 14, 15:3b is not an emphatic Vc construction. Therefore, the structure of the instructions in 15:3 is a departure from the style of 15:7–11, 12–18. Secondly, the closest parallel to 15:1 is found in 14:28. The parallelism has a formal feature (both are IVc constructions at the head of a row of discourse) and one of content: both contain time phrases using the P *mqṣ(h)*. On balance, therefore, 15:1–3 shares more structural features with clause rows in the *mqwm* sequence than 15:7–18. For that reason, it is best to consider 15:1–3 as originally belonging to the *mqwm* sequence.

Deut 16:18–17:13 and the mqwm Sequence

Deut 16:18–20 + 17:8–10 belong to the *mqwm* sequence. Their unity has been interupted by the insertion of the clause row sequence 16:21–17:7.

16:21–17:7. The extensive addition to 17:8–10 in vv. 11–13 finds structural and content parallels with 17:2–7. Both sanction an act of apostasy with the death penalty using the *bʿrt* formula. Both tend to conflate phraseology which is found elsewhere in distinct contexts in Deuteronomy. Both texts arrest a string of *wqtl* clauses with an IVc construction beginning with the preposition *ʿl py* which is followed by an xIVc (17:6, 11).

The context of apostasy also appears in the clause row of 16:21–17:1. Both vv. 21 and 22 are explicitly concerned with avoiding the contamination of Yahweh worship by illegitimate cult objects. The connection with 17:1 occurs implicitly in the idea of mixing the clean and the unclean, and explicitly with the association between "that which Yahweh hates" (v. 22) and *twʿbt yhwh* (v. 1). Also the qualification of the unacceptable blemish as *kl dbr rʿ* recalls the rhetoric of apostasy found elsewhere in Deuteronomy, including 17:5. In effect, 16:21–17:1 seems to act as a secondary ethical code for judicial authorities, but one which focuses on cultic orthodoxy. Deut 16:21 follows 16:19 on the basis of paranomasia (*lʾ tṭh* v. 19aα; *lʾ tṭʿ* v. 21a).

As an address to the judges, it states a general principle about the unacceptability of compromising the worship of Yahweh, which leads to the discussion of legal process in the case of apostasy in 17:2–7. Vocabulary links with the theme of apostasy appear in the motive clauses of 16:22; 17:1 (cf. 17:4) as well as between 17:1a and 17:5.

The movement from 16:21–17:1 to 17:2–7 shows breaches in the style of composition of the *mqwm* sequence. In particular, the function of the prohibition in 17:1 stands out. The clause row in 16:21–17:1 had no unity in pre-Dtn tradition. Thus, the addition of 17:1a may be partly explained as imitation of the form of the threefold prohibitions in 16:19.[18] The texts most closely parallel to 17:1a (Lev 22:20; Deut 15:21) do not show concerns such as those registered in 16:21, 22.

There is no need to discover a source for 17:1a other than in Dtn literature. Most of the vocabulary is found in 15:21b. The other elements may be found in 13:12; 17:5 (*dbr rᶜ*) and 18:3 (*zbḥ . . . šwr . . . śh*). A Dtn origin for 17:1a is also indicated by the structure of 16:21–17:1. The motivations used in 16:22b and in 17:1b have parallels outside Deuteronomy. But they are most closely related to the motive clauses in Deut 12:31. These uses of *twᶜbh* show community with the Dtn concern for cultic purity and the election of Israel identified by Humbert.[19]

As noted in the previous chapter, the phrase *kl dbr rᶜ* in 17:1 is more likely secondary to the formula *kl mwm rᶜ* than vice versa. Such a reappropriation of previously appearing material is alien to the way in which repetition is used in the *mqwm* sequence. Repetition of instructions is used for explicative purposes in similar contexts (cf. 12:17–18 and 14:23; 15:20 and 16:5–6; cf. 12:15–16 and 15:22–23) to create rhetorical unity. Neither purpose is served by the repetition of 15:21 in 17:1. Instead the prohibition has been appropriated for a different application than that addressed by the context of 15:21. The substitution of *dbr rᶜ* and the presence of the motive element *twᶜbh* in 17:1 both pave the way for 17:2–7 (cf. *hdbr hrᶜ* in 17:5 and *twᶜbh* in 17:4). Thus, the construction of 17:1 reveals 16:21–17:1 to be an introduction to the rules of evidence related to the prosecution of cases involving apostasy *bšᶜryk* (17:2–7). Evidently, Deut 16:21–17:1 possesses cataphoric rather than anaphoric references to the context. Therefore, unlike clause rows in the *mqwm* sequence, the intertextual point of reference is distinct from 12:13–19.

In summary, the following features argue against an original association between 16:21–17:1 and the *mqwm* sequence:

---

[18] Rofé, "Order of the Laws in Deuteronomy," 222.

[19] Humbert, "Le substantif *toᶜēbā*," 223–24.

The analysis above suggests that the composition of 16:21–17:1 and 17:2–27 is related. The following reasons support this postulate: both 16:21–22 and 17:3 proscribe non-standard cult practices. There are cataphoric references to 17:4, 5 in 17:1. The motive clauses of 16:22; 17:1 are related to contexts opposing apostasy to which language used by 17:2–7 is also related (cf. 17:4bβ' and 12:31).

The postulate of 16:21–17:7 as an original clause row sequence points to another breach with the style of clause rows in the *mqwm* sequence. In the two cases in which the pre-Dtn material begins a clause row and is qualified by an If–You construction (14:22–27*; 15:19–23), the If-You clauses introduce an exception to the general rule. This is not true of the relationship between 16:21–17:1 and 17:2–7.

16:18–20 + 17:8–10. The secondary adhesion of the theme of apostasy and the death penalty in 17:11–13 suggests that the theme of apostasy was not original in the context of 17:8–10. If the materials dealing with apostasy in 16:21–17:7 are also considered to be secondary because of thematic and structural links with 17:11–13 and stylistic variance with the *mqwm* sequence, then a primary relationship between 16:18–20 and 17:8–10 suggests itself.

The clause row sequence 16:18–20 + 17:8–10 appears to be of a piece. Parallels to the instructions for parties-at-law in v. 19 do not suggest that religious apostasy was a typical concern of their addressees. Echoes of legal concerns appropriate to the genre of instruction found in 16:19 occur in 17:8a, in which categories of homicide, civil restitution, and assault are indicated.

This evidence strengthens the thesis that the original complement of 16:18 appears in 17:8–10, where a distinction is made between the competence of the judges *bšʿryk* and those in the *mqwm*. The phrase *bšʿryk* linked with the appointment of judicial figures who are responsible for *mšpṭ* has its substantial echoes after 16:18 only in 17:8–9, where again *mšpṭ*, *bšʿryk* and the figure of legal authorities appear.[20]

Various details of composition implicate 16:18–20; 17:8–10 in the *mqwm* sequence. Deut 16:18a is an IVc prescription clause followed by a *wqtl* clause (cf. 14:28–29a; 16:13–14). Deut 16:18 makes a general statement to which 17:8–10 adds a proviso in the case of a difficult legal matter. This is a pattern which has appeared in previous *mqwm* legislation (cf. 14:23, 24–26bα; 15:20, 21–23).[21] The dichotomy between the *mqwm* and *bšʿryk* is found also in 14:22–29; 15:19–23 and in 16:5–6. Despite the shift in subject matter, there is

---

[20] Seitz, *Studien*, 200–1.

[21] Ibid., 201.

no compelling reason to divorce 16:18–20 from the same layer as 14:22–27*, 28–29 etc.

As in other clause rows in the *mqwm* sequence, there are connections between 16:18 and 12:13–19. Cf. *bkl šʿryk* in 12:15 and 16:18a. Deut 16:18 contains the first instance of the modification of *šʿryk* with *kl* since 12:15. Cf. *šbṭyk* in 12:14 and *lšbṭyk* in 16:18a. Deut 16:18a contains the first mention of the noun *šbṭ* since 12:14.

Clause-Level Accretions in the mqwm Sequence

The clause rows of the *mqwm* sequence include 14:22–15:3; 15:19–16:20; 17:8–10. It is likely that some secondary accretions appear within it. Those already identified include 14:24aγ and 14:27aβ. Questions have also been raised about the integrity of the object in 14:23a; the motivational elements in 14:23b; 16:12, 20; and the festival list in 16:16.

14:23a. The best argument for preservation of the mention of firstlings in 14:23a is the matter of compensation. If the firstling reference is excised from 14:23, then there is no indication in the *mqwm* sequence of how the cult is to be compensated for the firstlings it will lose because of the instructions of 15:21–23. For this reason the mention of firstlings in 14:23 is appropriate and likely original.

If the mention of firstlings is original to 14:23, there is a still a significant doublet between 14:23 and 15:20 which requires an explanation. Both passages command the same action: the consumption of the firstling at the *mqwm*. Even given Carmichael's perception that the laws of 14:22–23 and 15:19–20 are deliberately repetitious since they act as subsections of 12:17–18,[22] a third demand to eat the same thing at the *mqwm* is unusual. One must ponder why the demand to eat at the *mqwm* occurs a third time with respect to the firstlings.

The repetition of the command to eat the firstling in 15:20 is redundant after essentially the same command occurs in 12:18 and 14:23. Such a repetition would be acceptable, however, if it were necessary to incorporate traditional material in 15:19 into a Dtn composition. This has been established in the previous chapter.

14:23b. Deut 14:23b is problematic because of the context in which it appears. The idea of the "fear of Yahweh" is common in Deuteronomy, but the concept of "learning to fear Yahweh" is confined to 4:10 (3mpl); 14:23 (2ms); 17:19 (3ms); 31:12–13 (3mpl). Both Merendino and Mayes point out

---

[22] Carmichael, *Laws*, 88–89.

that the context of 31:12–13 is that of the harvest festival.[23] More important, however, is the didactic motif which the idea of learning to fear represents. The concept appears in texts concerned with hearing the words of *twrh* (4:10; 17:19) or reports of the Exodus (Jos 4:24). Such an explicit didactic concept is missing in 14:23.

Deut 14:23b can also be compared to other motive clauses assumed to be original in the *mqwm* sequence: 14:24b, 27a (cf. v. 29aα'); 16:3bβ, 15bα. In the case of 14:27b; 16:3bβ there are explicit content relationships between the motivation and the related instruction: the condition of the Levite (cf. 14:27bα) and Exodus memorial (cf.16:2–3a). Less explicit relationships employ the vocabulary of Yahweh's blessing (14:24a; 16:15a). The presence of 14:23b cannot be accounted for by either of these patterns.

Another observation concerns the relationship between the motif of "learning to fear" and keeping a treaty or covenant which is explicit in the parallels, but not in 14:23. Weinfeld points out that both the motifs of "fear" and of "learning to fear" have parallels with the vocabulary of Akkadian treaty making. Instructional texts in Deuteronomy 12–26 which have important parallels in this regard are found in Deuteronomy 13.[24] The *mqwm* sequence bears no intertextual references to this text.

The various tensions between the typical contexts of the motif of "learning to fear" and its application to 14:23a as well as the patterns of motive clause usage in the *mqwm* sequence suggest that 14:23b is anomolous. It is likely the result of a secondary addition, probably to connect the cultic instructions in 14:23 with the general rhetoric of *twrh* observance. The connection between this motif and the harvest festival as the time for hearing *twrh* (31:12–13) may have prompted its insertion in 14:23.

16:12. The genre of the *wzkrt* clause in 16:12a is related to that of the *wśmḥt* clauses. Both function as paraenetic elements in their instruction rows. But 16:12a is the only example of the *wzkrt* type of parenesis in the *mqwm* sequence, which clearly prefers exhortation of the *wśmḥt* type; see 12:18b; 14:26b; 16:11, 14 (cf. 16:15). Literal repetitions of 16:12a are found in 5:15; 15:15; and 24:22. The clause row containing 15:15 has been shown not to belong to the *mqwm* sequence. Therefore, there are significant literary tensions with respect to the presence of 16:12a. The *wzkrt* clause is connected to the motif of care for the *personae miserae*, which is a concern of the instructions of Sabbath observance, *šmṭh* observance, and bans on gleaning. Its presence in 16:12a is likely a secondary addition under the influence of 15:15 or 24:22.

---

23 Mayes, *Deuteronomy*, 245; Merendino, *Gesetz*, 98.

24 WA, p. 332.

The position of v. 12b is the best argument for its secondary placement in the clause row. Deut 16:12b is coordinated with and follows c.12a, which seems to be an addition to the clause row. Elsewhere in Deuteronomy the exact combination of *wšmrt wʿśyt* only occurs in 26:26, where the pronominal object resumes the object *ʾt kl hḥqym hʾlh wʾt hmšpṭym*. This proximity to 26:16 suggests that the referent of the phrase *kl hḥqym hʾlh* in 16:12b is to all of the Dtn instructions and is not limited to 16:9–11.[25] This is a tension to be considered along with the clause's coordination with v. 12a. Deut 16:12b was likely derived from 26:16 and attached secondarily to v. 12a. It may have been considered appropriate since the festival of weeks was traditionally associated with the giving of the *twrh* at Sinai.[26]

16:16. The question of the origin of the list in 16:16 can be considered in the light of the established context of 16:1–17. This context includes knowledge of pre-Dtn instructions in 16:3–4, 8 which imply knowledge of the traditions of *ḥg hmṣwt*, as well as 16:9–10a, 13 and the tripartite festival tradition found in 16:16aα, 16b. Although there is no mention of *ḥg hmṣwt* in 16:1–8 and the festival called *ḥg hšbʿwt* in 16:16 is *ḥg šbʿwt* in 16:10 (the modification of *ḥg šbʿwt* by *lyhwh* makes the article unnecessary),[27] it is clear that the list in 16:16aβ reflects the tradition implied in the pre-Dtn materials at the writer's disposal in 16:1–15. Consequently, it is likely that the list in 16:16aβ is a non-Dtn tradition known to the composer of 16:1–16. But, it may not have circulated with 16:16aα. Parallels to 16:16aα.b suggest a correspondence in clause length which the festival list interrupts. It is evident that a Dtn writer expanded the text by adding the *mqwm* formula to 16:16aα. The same writer probably also added the festival list in 16:16aγ.

16:20. In all instructional texts of the *mqwm* sequence the motif of conquest is inconspicuous. This enforces the perception of some sort of generic tension between 16:20 and 16:18. However, this tension is diminished if it is assumed that the phrase *lšbṭyk* is considered as original to the text and if the text can be implicated in a span of discourse which was introduced by the words of a covenant mediator. The concept of tribal occupation is also implied in 12:14 as is the implication that the instructions are being delivered through a covenant mediator (12:14b). Promulgation formulas which use the participle of *ṣwh* refer to the covenant on the plain of

---

[25] Contra Braulik, "Ausdrücke für 'Gesetz,'" 52. Cf. 4:6; 6:24.

[26] S. Lachs, "Two Related Arameans: A Difficult Reading in the Passover Haggadah," 67.

[27] Joüon notes that the use of the *lamed* instead of a bound construction is sometimes not far from the use of the *lamed* to indicate for whom an action is to be performed (*Grammaire*, §130g).

Moab as the context for their delivery.[28] Consequently, 16:20 can be implicated in a span of text which has a clause row referring to the speech of a covenant mediator (12:14b). Therefore, a significant literary-critical tension between 16:18 and 16:20 may not exist. In the discusssion which follows, 16:20 will be retained as an original part of the clause row in 16:18–20; 17:8–10.

---

[28] Braulik, "Ausdrücke für 'Gesetz,'" 42.

Chapter Six

LAYERS OF COMPOSITION IN DEUTERONOMY 14:1–17:13

The results obtained in the last chapter yield sufficient evidence to reach the following literary-critical conclusion: the primary literary layer of Deut 14:1–17:13 is found in the *mqwm* sequence. This sequence of clause rows consists of 14:22–24aβ, 24b–27aα, 27b–29; 15:1–3, 19–23; 16:1–20; 17:8–10. This layer is principally concerned to state the cultic and social implications of the selection of the *mqwm ʾšr ybḥr yhwh ʾlhyk* as the sole legitimate cult site, and was written as a commentary on 12:13–19.

Other clause row sequences have been identified which do not give evidence of belonging to the *mqwm* sequence. These include: 14:1–21; 15:7–18; 16:21–17:7. Among major distinctions between the literary characteristics of the *mqwm* sequence and these other clause row sequences are the following:

Deut 14:1–21 differs from the *mqwm* sequence in having as its principle reference 7:1–6. It shows familiarity with the composition technique of *Numeruswechsel*, unlike the *mqwm* sequence.[1] Finally, it participates in an extensive span of text which separates 14:22–27 from its primary reference point in 12:18–19.

Deut 15:7–11, 12–18 show a unique style of composition in which the last clauses form an inclusio with the beginning of the clause row. Their phraseology makes a marked appeal to the exophoric context of oral delivery by the covenant mediator which is not typical of the *mqwm* sequence. The genre membership of 15:17–11, 12–18 is also at odds with conditionally introduced instructions in the *mqwm* sequence.

Deut 16:21–17:7 interrupt a more primary relationship between 16:18–20 and 17:8–10. The prohibition row in 16:21–17:1 was written in imitation of 16:19 and shows a secondary use of the formula in 15:21 in order to introduce 17:2–7, which is a legal commentary derived from formulas found

[1] An apparent exception to this statement might be indicated in 12:16a by the form *tʾklw*. But this isolated 2mpl reference seems to be the result of some secondary influence on the transmission of the text;. see, e.g., Mayes, *Deuteronomy*, 228; or Seitz, *Studien*, 211.

in Deuteronomy 13. The points of intertextual reference of 16:21–17:7 are with texts dealing with religious apostasy in 12:31 and 13:2–18, not 12:13–19.

In addition, there is evidence that certain clause rows have been secondarily expanded. Additions involving rows of clauses can be observed in 15:4–6; 16:12; and 17:11–13. Those consisting of a single clause occur in 14:24aγ and 14:27aβ. Phrase level expansions occur in 14:7a; 14:13; the bird names modified by *ʾt* in 14:12–18; and 17:5aγ.

The purpose of this chapter is twofold. First, an attempt will be made to sketch the major organizational principles used to compose the *mqwm* sequence in Deuteronomy 14–17. A special interest is to disprove suggestions that the present disposition of the *mqwm* sequence in 14:22–17:10 is dependent on a single pre–Dtn text belonging to the *Privilegrecht* tradition. Secondly, an effort will be made to place the various indicators of redaction through time into some sort of relative framework. Although description of organizational features is inevitable in describing features of the redactional layers of 14:1–17:13, this chapter will not present its findings in the detail found in Chapter Two.

Organizational Principles of the mqwm Sequence

The mqwm Sequence and Privilegrecht Traditions

14:22–16:17. Various scholars have suggested that the order of the clause rows in 14:22–16:17 is dependent on a pre-Dtn row of festival regulations which can be isolated in the present text. Such a series is sometimes referred to in German as a *Privilegrecht Jahwes*. A *Privilegrecht* is a series of prescriptions and prohibitions which are given to the people in direct address either by Yahweh or his representative.

Some previous attempts to identify a *Privilegrecht* tradition underlying 14:22–16:17 have yielded the following results:

Horst	14:22; 15:1, 19, 16:1a, 3aα, 4b, 16*
Nebeling	14:22*; 15:1, 19b, 16:1–8*, 10aα*, 13*, 16aα.b
Seitz	14:22, 28; 15:19*; 16:1a, 9*, 10aα*, 13

Another model for the *Privilegrecht* arrangement is the unitary theory of Kaufman. He suggests an arrangement by reference to a *Privilegrecht* tradition which lies outside the corpus of 14:22–16:17 (i.e., the Ten Commandments).[2]

[2] Horst, *Privilegrecht*, 152; Nebeling, *Schichten*, 263–64; Seitz, *Studien*, 200; Kaufman, "Structure," 108–9. The reconstructions of Horst and Nebeling belong to larger contexts of pre–Dtn prescriptive series. Rofé (*Introduction to Deuteronomy*, 75) also posits a series of commands as the pre-Dtn core in Deut 14–16; however, his reconstruction is more

A more complex scheme is proposed by Merendino, who posits the existence of two independent compilations:

a) 14:22, 28, 29a*.b, 15:1–2a, 3, 12a.b, 13a, 14a
b) 16:3a*, 4a, 8, 9, 10*, 13, 14

These two instruction rows were brought together at a secondary stage in the history of the composition of the text.[3] In other words, Merendino disputes the thesis that there is a cohesive pre-Dtn tradition which extends throughout 14:22–16:17.

In order to assess these theories, one must first identify where pre-Dtn materials are present in the text. By pre-Dtn materials are meant prescriptions or prohibitions which the Dtn writer seems to have used as a basis for his own laws.

14:22. Deut 14:22 stands out from its context because of the species of tithe identified in v. 22 as opposed to v. 23. Deut 14:23–27* contains a cohesive Dtn composition dealing with the disposal of tithes from the field, vineyard, and orchard. Field crops alone are mentioned in v. 22. The general conclusion by critical scholars, that the Dtn writer is basing his clause row on an older prescription,[4] is the simplest way of accounting for the present text.

15:2aβ.b. The introductory formula in 15:2aα shows that the Dtn writer is citing material which he has not composed but taken from some other source. In its current position, 15:2aβ.b stands as an explication of the prescription found in 15:1. There is no indication, however, that 15:1–3 owes its present position in the text to the pre-Dtn material in 15:2aβ.b. It is a Dtn composition following on 14:28–29 (cf. 14:28a; 15:1) and designed for an identical motive: the relief of the socially disadvantaged.

15:19. Deut 15:19 is at variance with its context because the automatic sanctity implicit in 15:19a conflicts with the provisions of the If-You instruction in vv. 21–23. Efforts to defend the unity of 15:19–23 as a thoroughly Dtn composition founder because of this. On the one hand, they do not deal adequately with the automatic sanctity issue implicit in 15:19a. On the other hand, they ignore the fact that 15:19a has close parallels with Exod 13:1, 12, 15 in which there is no provision for the secular use of unblemished firstlings.

---

tentative.

[3] Merendino, *Gesetz*, 159–65.

[4] See, e.g., Mayes, *Deuteronomy*, 245.

Parallelism by itself may indicate either reliance on a common tradition or dependency of one text on the other. The stem and mood of the verb in Deut 15:19 argue against dependency on Exod 13:2. Moreover, Deut 15:19a does not show the use of *pṭr* found in Exod 13:2, 12, 15 or the apposition of the plural form *zkrym*. It is evident, therefore, that 15:19 is a citation from a non-Dtn tradition similar to, but not identical with, material in Exodus 13.

It is difficult to determine the pre-Dtn form of v. 19; but it is probable that the *ʾšr* clause in 15:19a' is a Dtn insertion because of its characteristic Dtn vocabulary. The phrase *bqrk wṣʾnk* is found in Deut 8:13; 12:6(2mpl), 17, 21; 15:19. Outside Deuteronomy, the modification of the phrase "cattle and sheep" by the 2ms suffix is not attested. The removal of 15:19a' yields an inclusive command involving human firstlings as well as animals. This agrees with the parallel tradition in Exod 13:2.

A second question in 15:19 concerns the original connection of 15:19a*, 19bα, 19bβ. It is likely that 15:19b is a Dtn addition to v. 19a*. The provisions of 15:19b are ideally suited to a milieu which could not sacrifice firstlings in short order (cf. Exod 22:29) but had to drive them to the cult place annually as the Dtn writer seems to contemplate (cf. v. 20 *šnh šnh*). Therefore, a reconstruction of pre-Dtn material must be limited to 15:19a*.

16:1aα.b, 3aβ*.bα, 4a, 8a.bα**. Deut 16:1–8 is based on a core which is similar to the *mṣwt* instructions in Exod 13:4–7. This core is found in 16:1aα, 1b*(without *lylh*), 3aβ*(without *ʿlyw*), 3bα, 4a, 8a, and 8bα* (assuming an original *ḥg* instead of *ʿṣrt*). There are also pre-Dtn *psḥ* traditions in vv. 3aα, 4b. But investigation of the formal relationships of 16:3aα, 4b does not suggest that they possessed a traditional cohesion with the *mṣwt* instructions. Chiastic constructions present in both 16:3–4 and 16:5–7 show a common technique of composition. The presence of isolated *psḥ* traditions in 16:3a, 4b is probably due to Dtn activity.

The *mṣwt* tradition in 16:1aα, 1b*, 3aβ*, 3bα, 4a, 8a, and 8bα* does not appear to be dependent on the parallel in Exodus 13. For example, motifs found together in Exod 13:6 occur separately in 16:3 (cf. Exod 13:6a) and 16:8* (cf. Exod 13:6b). Also, the initial call to festival observance in 16:1* is not closely paralleled in Exodus 13. By the same token, I follow Caloz in his conclusion that the *mṣwt* traditions in Exodus 13 are independent of the Dtn material.[5]

16:9–10aα. Deut 16:9–11 alludes to a festival which celebrated the grain harvest by a presentation of firstfruit offerings. The appearance of freewill offerings (16:10aβ) instead of the firstfruits traditional for this festival seems

---

[5] Caloz, "L'Exode XIII," 62.

to be an innovation by the Dtn writer. But the counting formula *spr l* attested in 16:9 is common in language usually associated with Leviticus. Deut 16:9–11 and 16:13–15 show a similar mode of composition: timing of the festival is established (16:9–10a, 13) followed by Dtn paraenesis calling for celebrations which include *personae miserae* (16:11, 14). The literary critical distinction which can be made between 16:13 and 14 helps to illuminate the structure of 16:9–11. I conclude that the details of 16:9 are derived from a pre-Dtn tradition which probably contained 16:10aα as well. The name *ḥg šbʿwt* in v. 10a follows logically from the time frame in v. 9.

16:13. The position of 16:13 in its context is telling. Not only is the command to celebrate the *ḥg* for seven days repeated, but 16:14–15 evidences an envelope structure in which 16:13 plays no part. I conclude that Deut 16:13 is a citation from a pre-Dtn tradition.

16:16aα.b. The specification of "your menfolk" is at variance with the lists of participants in 16:11, 14. Parallels to 16:16aα.b establish these clauses as non-Dtn in origin. The fact that the other pre–Dtn materials in 16:1–15 are not derived from Exodus 23 and 34 is the best argument for suggesting that the tradition at the base of 16:16 is not derived from the parallels Exodus texts either. Variations in syntax and placement also make it unlikely that 16:16aα.b are dependent on the Exodus parallels. A case for an traditional cohesion between 16:16aα.b can made on the basis of their connection by repetition.

From this survey, it will appear that the materials which exist for the reconstruction of an original *Privilegrecht* in 14:22–16:17 are the following: 14:22; 15:19a*; 16:1aα.b*, 3aβ*.bα, 4a, 8*, 9–10aα, 13, 16aα.b. They are set out in Fig. 5.

Fig. 5. Texts for a Reconstruction of a *Privilegrecht* Tradition in Deut 14:22–16:17

14:22	ʿśr tʿśr ʾt kl tbwʾtk zrʿk hyṣʾ hśdh šnh šnh
15:19a*	kl hbkwr hzkr tqdyš lyhwh [ʾlhyk]
16:1aα	šmwr ʾt ḥdš hʾbyb
1b*	ky bḥdš hʾbyb hwṣyʾk yhwh [ʾlhyk] mmṣrym
3aβ*	šbʿt ymym tʾkl mṣwt lḥm ʿny
3bα	ky bḥpzwn yṣʾt mʾrṣ mṣrym
4a	wlʾ yrʾh lk śʾr bkl gblk šbʿt ymym
8a	ššt ymym tʾkl mṣwt
8bα*	wbywm hšbyʿy ḥg lyhwh [ʾlhyk]
9a	šbʿh šbʿt tspr lk
9b	mhḥl ḥrmš bqmh tḥl lspr šbʿh šbʿwt
10aα	wʿśyt ḥg šbʿwt lyhwh [ʾlhyk]
13	ḥg hskt tʿśh lk šbʿt ymym bʾspk mgrnk wmyqbk

16aα šlwš pʿmym bšnh yrʾh kl zkwrk ʾt pny yhwh [ʾlhyk]
16b wlʾ yrʾh ʾt pny yhwh ryqm

N.B. The modification of *yhwh* by *ʾlhyk* is characteristic of Deuteronomy. In the legal portions of the Pentateuch, *yhwh ʾlhyk* is found only in Exod 20:2, 5, 7, 10, 12; 23:19; 34:24, 26. It is probable that many, if not all, of the instances of *yhwh ʾlhyk* listed in Fig. 5 are due to Dtn influence.

What is disturbing about the postulate of a single pre-Dtn festival code implicated in Fig. 5 is the eclectic nature of the pre-Dtn materials identified. A major difficulty involves the cohesion of 14:22 and the pre-Dtn material in 16:1–16*. Deut 16:13 assumes a different and richer agricultural context than 14:22. In fact, it assumes the conditions also reflected by the tithe laws of 14:23a. Deut 14:22 ordains a yearly tithe of cereal crops. But 14:23 mentions tithes of orchard and vine crops as well as grains. Deut 14:22 must stem from a geographical location or historical era in which the variety of foodstuffs mentioned in 14:23aβ and assumed by 16:13 was not produced. By the principles of literary-criticism, the unity of 14:22 and 16:13 is an editorial creation.

Who created it? Was it the Dtn writer who composed the *mqwm* sequence; or was 14:22 already joined to the rest of the material isolated in Fig. 5 in some pre-Dtn tradition? These difficulties can be illuminated by examining the relationship between the tithe law of 14:22 and the firstling instruction in 15:19*.

The tithe law of 14:22 is unique in BH literature. There is little evidence for a tradition which associates tithes and firstlings in that order outside the Dtn list of offerings in 12:17 and its Dtn parallels. Where the tithe is mentioned in a parallel context with other cultic imposts, a close connection with firstlings is not generally apparent. The tithe is connected with *trwmh* in Mal 3:8. Tithes are parallel with sacrifices (*zbḥym*) in Amos 4:4. The tithe is found in lists of cultic imposts in Neh 10:36–38; but it is not immediately juxtaposed to the mention of firstling animals. In Neh 13:5 and 2 Chron 31:5, 12 the tithe appears in lists of cultic imposts where the firstling is not mentioned. Tithes are mentioned in a context which also mentions firstlings in Leviticus 27 and Numbers 18. In both cases, however, the mention of tithes (Lev 27:30–33; Num 18:21–24) does not immediately precede the firstling context (Lev 27:26–29; Num 18:15–18) but only appears after it. In the case of Numbers 18, there is intervening material concerning the *trwmh* in Num 18:19.

Parallel contexts show, therefore, that tithes and firstlings are juxtaposed in that order in Dtn compositions but not elsewhere. There are no literary grounds for assuming a pre-Dtn association of tithes and firstlings.

Therefore, the juxtaposition of tithes and firstlings is probably Dtn in origin. Consequently, the citation of 14:22 was made by the Dtn writer independently of any pre-Dtn context which contained 15:19*.

An association of the festival of *mṣwt* and firstling offerings is made in some pre-Dtn traditions (cf. Exod 13:2–16; 34:18–20), though not all (cf. Exod 22:28–29).[6] Associations between *ḥg hmṣwt* and firstling sacrifice have their own history of development. For example, the presence of Exod 13:2 in its present context is suspicious. Firstling legislation in Exodus 13 only reappears in Exod 13:11–13. Vocabulary shows that the tradition found in Exod 13:3–13 could have been transmitted without the elements of Exod 13:2. Note, for example, that the offering vocabulary used in Exod 13:11 does not repeat the verb *qdš* in Exod 13:2. It is likely that Exodus 13 possesses its own history of growth and development.[7] It is not necessary to hold that Exod 13:2 belongs to the same tradition as Exod 13:11–16.[8]

The timing of the firstling requirement in 15:19* is an important consideration in the light of biblical parallels. Evidently, those contexts in which firstling requirements envelop (Exod 13:2–16) or follow regulations for *ḥg hmṣwt* (34:18–20) imply that the firstlings are to be offered then. But the tradition of Exod 22:29 points to a different timing for the sacrifice of firstlings: an eight day limitation which is not regulated by the timetable for pilgrimage festivals. Therefore, firstling sacrifice was not always associated with the festival of *ḥg hmṣwt*.

The position of 15:19* and the Dtn time indicator contend against an original connection with 16:1–8*, despite the fact that both 15:19* and 16:1–8* have mutual parallels with Exodus 13. Since 15:19 precedes regulations

---

6 Critics are divided as to whether Exod 23:10–12a, 14–19 and Exod 34:17–26 represent independent versions of a common tradition. Recently, several scholars have suggested that Exod 34:10–26 is a literary imitation of the text which is found in Exod 23:10–19 and not independent of it; see, e.g., H. Brichto, "The Golden Calf Episode in Exod 32–34," 31–34; Fishbane, *Biblical Interpretation*, 195; J. van Seters, "The Place of the Yahwist in the History of Passover and Massot," 179. Ginsberg (*Israelian Heritage of Judaism*, 63–65) thinks that Exod 34:10–26 shows a dependency on Exodus 13; 23:10–33 and Deuteronomy 7 and 16. It is my opinion, however, that the arguments of Halbe for the independence of the *Privilegrecht* tradition in Exodus 34 from Exodus 23 have yet to be answered; see Halbe, *Privilegrecht*, 449. For example, no theory of a dependence of Exod 34:18–26 on Exod 23:10–19 will explain the placement of the Sabbath law in Exod 34:21. For an account of the Sabbath law in Exod 34:21, see Halbe, *Privilegrecht*, 212–20. But the following discussion is not materially affected by the view that Exodus 34 is a recension of Exodus 23. In either case, it is clear that these texts attest to a tradition which is non-Dtn in background.

7 Noth, *Exodus*, 101.

8 Childs, *Exodus*, 203.

for the festival of unleavened bread, the position of 15:19* suggests it is not determined by the chronology of 16:1–8*. More proof for this contention appears in the fact that it is the Dtn writer who is responsible for making the offering of firstlings a yearly requirement (*šnh šnh* in 15:20) in parallel with the tithe law (cf. *šnh šnh* in 14:22). Evidently the formula of 15:19* was undetermined with respect to time before the Dtn writer adapted it. Therefore, 15:19* did not circulate with the festival traditions at the base of 16:1–16*. It is a citation from an independent tradition.

The independence of the parallel in Exod 13:3–7 might imply that 16:1–8* also circulated unconnected to the row of festival instructions now found in 16:1–16*. However, it is clear that this common tradition has had its own complex history of elaboration in Exodus 13. Moreover, the cohesion of Deut 16:1–8* with what follows is not inappropriate. Firstly, 16:16 supposes a tripartite pilgrimage calendar. Secondly, the reconstructed pre-Dtn festival instructions underlying 16:1–15 use the number seven consistently with reference to all three pilgrimages. Thirdly, as in the case of the parallels in Exodus 23 and 34, more space is given over to the details of the festival of unleavened bread than the other two in 16:1–16. Therefore, a unity between the tradition underlying 16:1–8 and those at the base of 16:9–15 can be defended.[9]

It is a common assumption of scholars that festival laws were often transmitted in a *Privilegrecht* tradition. It is not a question whether such a tradition exists, but how the *mqwm* sequence in Deut 14:22–16:17 is related to it. One suggestion, which appears in various forms in the reconstructions of Horst, Nebeling, Seitz *et al.* is that one, cohesive pre-Dtn *Privilegrecht* tradition can be isolated in Deuteronomy 14–16. My research suggests that such a view needs to be modified. The series of cultic requirements in Deut 14:22; 15:19*; 16:1aα.b*, 3aβ*.bα, 4a, 8*, 9f., 13, 16a*.b are best considered to be an eclectic assemblage based on at least three independently circulating traditions: 14:22; 15:19*; 16:1–16*. The compiler of these pre-Dtn traditions is the Dtn writer of the *mqwm* sequence. Why the writer chose to cite commands which are not in harmony with his own cultural and religious perspective, e.g., 14:22; 15:19*; 16:16aα will be addressed further below.

16:18–20 + 17:8–10. The present position of 16:18–20; 17:8–10 needs to be accounted for. In structure and phraseology these verses belong to the Dtn layer implicated in the texts with the *mqwm* formula in 14:22–16:17. According to A. C. Welch, "An arrangement of the material which involves the separation of the laws about priests (18:1–8) from those which regulate

[9] Halbe, "Passa-Massot," 162.

the cult (16:1–17), it must be frankly acknowledged, is illogical and arbitrary." Welch offers no insight into this situation other than concluding that the laws about officials (i.e., 16:18–20, 17:8–18:22) "seem to be thrown together rather than arranged."[10]

A polemical appeal to 18:1–8, however, does not solve the problems of order associated with 16:18–20. There are signs which show that 18:1–8 can be associated with the themes of 17:8–10. The law of the priests and Levites in 18:1–8 is devoted to a statement about their rights, *mšpṭ* (18:3). This is appropriate in the context because the administration of *mšpṭ* (16:18; 17:8, 9) has been previously mentioned.[11] Deut 17:9 also mentions *hkhnym hlwym* (cf. 18:1) who are involved in the dispensation of *twrh* (17:10). Therefore, a law proclaiming the *mšpṭ* of the transmitters of *twrh* is not out of place in 18:1ff.[12]

Kaufman has attempted to account for the current arrangement of 16:18–20 on the assumption that the Dtn law is arranged in correspondence to the disposition of the Ten Commandments in Deuteronomy 5. Beginning with 16:18, the Dtn writer is supposed to explicate the commandment of 5:16, "Honor your father and your mother, etc." Proof of this thesis is supposedly found in the proximity of the motive clauses in 16:20 and 17:20 to those of Deut 5:16.[13] It must be noted, however, that 17:20 is much closer to 5:16 than to 16:20, which has its best parallels with 8:1; 30:19. Moreover, why is the order of 16:18–18:22 necessarily judges, king, priests, and prophets, if it is based on 5:16? The hypothesis that Deut 16:18–20 is conditioned by the Fifth Commandment does not in itself explain the current disposition of the text. A greater difficulty with Kaufman's thesis is found in the prescription preceding the motive clause in 16:20a. The issue involved is not the obedience of the Israelites to their God-given authorities: it is "seek justice and you shall live". In summary, 16:18–20 do not show clear enough relationships with 5:16 to make Kaufman's theory plausible.[14]

The question remains, why does the Dtn writer switch from being dominated by concerns of cultic practise (14:22–16:17) to concerns for the administration of justice? Traditional answers to this question have pointed

---

[10] Welch, *The Code of Deuteronomy*, 87.

[11] G. Hölscher, "Komposition und Ursprung des Deuteronomiums," 199; Horst, *Privilegrecht*, 142.

[12] See also Braulik, "Zur Abfolge der Gesetze in Deuteronomium 16,18–21,23," 79–80.

[13] Kaufman, "Structure," 133–34.

[14] Braulik ("Die Abfolge der Gesetze in Deuteronomium 12–26," 264) has examined Kaufman's thesis at length. His conclusion is that the order of Deuteronomy 12–16 has no original connection with the Decalogue.

to the function of the *byt dyn* as police and determiners of festival times.[15] Even so, why command the establishment of this legal institution after the practises it is supposed to regulate have been proclaimed?

One might answer this question by pointing to an analogy with *Privilegrecht* traditions in which cultic and social injunctions often appear combined (e.g., The Ten Commandments; Exod 22:20–23:19). The provisions of 16:18–20 may be explained as a Dtn frame (16:18, 20) around a pre-Dtn centre in 16:19. In terms of genre, 16:19 belongs to a constellation of instructions about duties in judicial processes which do not appear to be confined to professional judges. Instructions similar to v. 19 appear in contexts which also address cultic concerns (cf. Exod 23:1–13; Leviticus 19).

But it is unlikely that 16:19 circulated with the pre-Dtn materials found in 16:9–10α, 13, 16aα.b. A structural distinction can be made between these clauses and 16:19. Unlike 16:19, they stand at the beginning of the clause row. A comparison with the structure of 15:1–3 and 16:18–20 is helpful. In 15:1–3 a chiastic device (based on repetition of roots) is used in order to integrate 15:2aβ.b into the context. So, in 16:18–20 one may observe that a chiastic structure in 16:18, 20 envelops 16:19. Also, both 15:1–3 and 16:18–20 introduce their pre-Dtn elements by a third person coordinated clause (15:2aα; 16:18b). In other words, from the point of view of structure, the Dtn writer accords 16:19 the same status as the isolated citation of 15:2.

Parallels between 16:19 and *Privilegrecht* traditions show that there is no intrinsic relationship between the position of the justice concerns in 16:19 and festival laws in 16:1–17. The justice provisions in Exod 23:1–8 come before social and religious provisions related to the Sabbath etc. The festival laws in Exodus 34 and Leviticus 23 which parallel those in Deut 16:1–17 are not closely associated with instructions possessing legal and social associations. This is further evidence against the opinion that 16:19 circulated with the pre-Dtn materials in 16:1–11; 13–17. There is no reason to assume, therefore, that the position of 16:18–20 is dictated by a particular pre-Dtn tradition taken over by the writer of the *mqwm* layer.

Recently Lohfink has restated an older opinion that a connection must exist between the present form of Deuteronomy 12–26 and Exod 20:22–23:33; 34:10–26. His analysis leads him to posit a topical arrangement of Deuteronomy 12–26:

I.	12:2–16:17	Privilegrecht Jahwes
II.	16:18–18:22	*Ämtergesetze*
III.	19:1–25:19	Straf- und Zivilrecht

---

[15] Sprecher, *The Torah Anthology* 17:191–92.

IV. 26:1–15 Liturgischer Anhang [16]

It is possible that this scheme may help to explain the final form of Deuteronomy 12–26. But neither this topical arrangement or any other can explain the original disposition of the *mqwm* sequence. These texts exist to draw out the implications of the *mqwm* law in 12:13–19. Most are related to *Privilegrecht* traditions in some way, including 16:18–20 + 17:8–10 But it should also be noted that there is no evidence in the *mqwm* sequence for direct dependence upon texts in Exod 23:14–19 or Exod 34:18–26. In fact, the writer of the *mqwm* sequence has not used any pre-Dtn materials which can be convincingly derived from other existing biblical texts. It must be assumed that he knew a number of traditions common to other biblical texts but not transmitted in canonical forms.

The Literary Logic of the mqwm Sequence

My account of the literary logic of the *mqwm* sequence begins with the observation that 16:18–20+17:8–13 represents a juncture from preceding instructions in terms of those who are addressed as well as in subject matter. This is indicated by the switch between second person and third person references in 16:18–20. The situation is different, however, from the case of the socially disadvantaged who are also described in the third person (cf. 14:27b, 14:29a). *Personae miserae* such as the Levite, the widow, the orphan, and the *gr* do not belong to the same stratum of society as the 2ms addressees of the *mqwm* sequence because they not control tribal patrimony. Hence, they are often listed along with other dependents of the 2ms addressees (cf. 16:11, 14). But the fact that the judges and officers are subsequently addressed in 2ms formulas in 16:19–20 indicates some kind of continuity with the group of 2ms addresses in the *mqwm* sequence, even if the third person references indicate a distinction. Evidently, it is expected that some of the 2ms addressees of the *mqwm* sequence will be apppointed as judges and officers, but not all.[17]

This line of reasoning can be extended by noting the mediating position that 16:18–20 + 17:8–10 occupies between previous *mqwm* instructions and

---

[16] Lohfink, "Zur deuteronomischen Zentralisationsformel," 324–26.

[17] Rüterswörden (*Von der politischen Gemeinschaft*, 94–95) follows H. Cazelles ("Droit publique dans le Deutéronome," 101–102) in supposing that there is a complete overlap between the 2ms addressees of Deut 16:1–17 and those designated as judges in 16:18. My opinion is that 16:18 requires the appointment of a class of judges and court officials out of those addressees. Deut 1:15 identifies these people as leaders and outstanding individuals among the tribes of Israel. See also Weinfeld, "Judge and Officer in Ancient Israel and in the Ancient Near East."

that found in 18:1–8. In fact, 18:1–8 can be plausibly regarded as another clause row in the *mqwm* sequence. Its present form (including the conditional beginning in v. 6) shows features typical of clause rows in the *mqwm* sequence. There is a structure in which a general instruction (vv. 1–5) is followed by a special case (vv. 6–8), a citation of an archaic tradition (v. 3), the use of the *mqwm* formula (v. 6), the designation of foodstuffs in standard Dtn terms (v. 4, cf. 12:17; 14:23), solicitation for the welfare of the Levite, and a reference to the tribal divisons of Israel (vv. 1–2, cf. 12:14; 16:18).[18]

In the discussion which follows, it will be assumed that 18:1–8, in more or less its present form, belongs to the *mqwm* sequence. This assumption will not be made about the intervening clause row of 17:14–20, however, due to a lack of structural parallels. The king also belongs to the land-holding tribes of Israel. Therefore, it is understandable why 17:14–20 appears before 18:1–18. Deut 17:14–20 follows 17:8–10 as a sort of special case since the office of king is much less common than the office of judge. The organizational structure remains clear whether 17:14–20 is original to the *mqwm* sequence or is the result of secondary composition. In either case, the *mqwm* sequence acts as a kind of backbone to which other material is appended both primarily (e.g., 15:1–3) or secondarily (e.g., 15:7–11, 12–18).

A reasonable solution to the present disposition of the *mqwm* sequence can be made on the observation that the instructions of the *mqwm* sequence are addressed to three classes which can be divided according to social membership:

a) 2ms instructions which *all* of those addressed by the *mqwm* sequence are required to observe (14:22–15:3, 19–23; 16:1–17);

b) 2ms instructions which *some* of those addressed by the *mqwm* sequence must observe (16:18–20, 17:8–10), namely those who are appointed as judges and court officials;

c) 3ms instructions for a group to which *none* of the second person addressees of the *mqwm* sequence belong (18:1–8), namely members of the priestly tribe.

---

[18] Other scholars also agree that some form of 18:1–8 belonged to the same literary layer which contained the law on judges now found in 16:18–20, although they may disagree about the original form of 18:1–8, or the way in which the complex of laws about judges and priests relate to the layer of cultic instructions in 14:22–16:17. See, e.g., Seitz, *Studien*, 204–6; Mayes, *Deuteronomy*, 274–75; Rüterswörden, *Von der politische Gemeinschaft*, 89–90. For a discussion of the relationship between the Levite mentioned in 18:6–8 and priestly privilege see R. K. Duke, "The Portion of the Levite: Another Reading of Deuteronomy 18:6–8."

In other words, the primary principle which governs the organization of the *mqwm* sequence is that of "all, some, and none," based upon membership in social groups in Israel. This inner logic is used by the various clause rows of the *mqwm* sequence in 14:22–18:8 as they develop the primary command to centralize sacrifice at the place Yahweh will choose in 12:13–19.

The writer of the *mqwm* sequence recognized two tribal divisions in Israel: those who traditionally received a patrimony of land during the conquest, and the priestly tribe which did not. Throughout the 2ms instructions, it is clear that the writer does not consider members of the priestly tribe to belong to the group of 2ms addressees. By the same token, the clause row which addresses the rights of the priests and Levites in 18:1–8 is the only one in the *mqwm* sequence in which the majority of instructions are predicated in the third person (except for the 2ms instruction to the offerer in v. 4). Some of those from the land-holding tribes, however, hold a special office which will bring them into occasional contact with the legitimate cult center other than during regular pilgrimages. They are those appointed from the group of 2ms addressees as judges and officers. Hence the logic of arrangement by social location: instructions relevant to all the 2ms addressees precede instructions addressed to some from this group. Then follow instructions to that part of Israel which has least affinity with the land-owning tribes of Israel: the priestly tribe. Since I describe at length in the second chapter of this book the techniques by which the *mqwm* sequence is organized, I will not deal with questions of the inner logic of the organization of the *mqwm* sequence in 14:1–17:13 beyond articulating this basic principle.

It is within the literary framework of the "all, some, none" model and the development of the *mqwm* sequence as an exposition of 12:13–19 that one must fit an explanation for the citation of *Privilegrecht* traditions. One can only speculate as to why the Dtn writer chose to use a selection of independent *Privilegrecht* traditions in his work. The tensions between 14:22 and 16:13 point to the probability that he did not have one cohesive pre-Dtn text which touched on all of the issues he wanted to address. It is difficult to be sure how the texts of 14:22; 15:19*; 16:1aα.b*, 3aα, 3aβ*.b, 4a, 4b, 8*, 9–10aα, 13, 16aα.b were transmitted to the Dtn writer. All that can be determined with certainty is that the Dtn writer had a great concern to integrate his own laws with older material. This is apparent not only in 14:22; 15:19*; 16:1–8* but also from the texts of 15:2 and 16:19.

The writer of the *mqwm* sequence did not take many pains to smooth over inconsistencies between his own formulations and the traditions he used. It would appear that he was conscious that he was citing such material (cf. 15:2; 16:19) and that he viewed his own program as one in continuity with their interests. The large number of citations suggest that the Dtn writer wanted his readers to identify his work as one in continuity with previous venerable institutions. A related explanation for the citation of pre-Dtn materials can be also advanced: The Dtn writer may be striving for an archaic effect, since *Privilegrecht* traditions typically relate their contents to the time of Moses. It would be important for a cultic innovator to show continuity with older traditions as well as to indicate how his program demands a new perspective for traditional practices.

The Redaction History of Deut 14:1–17:13

The evidence above suggests that a number of additions have been made in the history of the transmission of Deuteronomy to an original layer of the text identified as the *mqwm* sequence. The span of text identified consists of 12:13–19 (more or less in its present form); 14:22–23a, 24aα.aβ.b, 25–27aα.b, 28–29; 15:1–3; 15:19–23; 16:1–11, 13–20; 17:8–10; and 18:1–8 (more or less in its present form). The close relationships between the *mqwm* sequence in 14:22–27 and 12:13–19 are now disturbed because of the amount of material between 12:19 and 14:22. Nevertheless, the fact that 14:22–27 goes back to 12:13–19 seems certain because of the correspondences in language and theme which have been adduced above. It is probable that the *mqwm* sequence in 14:22–27 followed 12:13–19 much more closely in an earlier form of Deuteronmy 12–18.

A difficulty in proposing a redaction history of 14:1–17:13 lies in identifying plausible redactional layers of the book of Deuteronomy to which the various clause row sequences and their expansions belong. This study will base itself on the categories used by Dion to identify four main stages in the formation of Deuteronomy:[19]

1) Pre-deuteronomic sources
2) The contribution of those Dtn writers who put together the book of the law found in 622
3) A pre-exilic Dtr layer to be assigned to the time of Josiah
4) Exilic Dtr additions

It will also follow Dion's conclusion that it is best to associate the composition of Deuteronomy 13 with the time of the Josianic reforms.[20]

In general, the following conclusions can be made based on the four stage scheme sketched above: the *mqwm* sequence appears to belong to the

[19] P. E. Dion, "Deuteronomy and the Gentile World: A Study in Biblical Theology," 201–2.

[20] Dion, "Deuteronomy 13," 196.

strata of Dtn activity responsible for the form of Deuteronomy discovered and redacted in Josianic times (# 2). This layer shows knowledge of many pre-Dtn (# 1) traditions, although the arrangement of the *mqwm* sequence was not determined by any one pre-Dtn tradition. It is written as a commentary on 12:13–19 and has no intertextual references to intervening material. Since, the *mqwm* sequence does not show any knowledge of Deuteronomy 13 or its attendent rhetoric of apostasy, it was likely prior to the composition of Deuteronomy 13. It is possible that all literary activity subsequent to the composition of the *mqwm* sequence belongs to the fourth category: Dtr additions to the book of Deuteronomy from the time of the exile and later. In other words, evidence of redactional activity at stage # 3, the Josianic redaction, does not appear very clearly in the disposition of 14:1–17:13.

The most obvious exilic addition to the *mqwm* sequence occurs in 16:21–17:7. Dion suggests that 17:2–7 was composed by a late redactor who imitated Deuteronomy 13 and who was also inspired by criminal laws already present in the book. He concludes that the phraseology and concern about astral cults bring the writer of 17:2–7 very close to the author of Deuteronomy 4.[21] In all likelihood, therefore, 16:21–17:7 is later than the redactional activity responsible for the insertion of the law of the king and the prophet which Lohfink identifies as early exilic compositions.[22]

My study has concluded that 16:21–17:1 belongs to the same literary layer as 17:2–7. A related piece occurs in 17:11–13, which shows affinities with the composition of 16:21–17:7 in terms of both structure and content. The association of 17:11–13 with 16:21–17:7 tends to confirm the supposition that 16:21–17:7 is later than the composition of the law on the prophets because of its apparent reliance on the vocabulary of 18:20–22.

Another diachronic indicator is evidenced through association with a redaction which reread the instructions of Deuteronomy 12–26 in the light of the Ten Commandments (Deut 5:6–21[18]). The parallel between 15:15a and 5:15 shows that 15:7–18 (and presumably 16:12a) have the most identifiable formal relationships with the Ten Commandment paradigm among clause rows in 14:1–17:13.[23] According to Braulik, this *relecture* is best assigned to the exilic or post-exilic period, however, in my view, this

---

[21] Ibid., 162.

[22] N. Lohfink, "Distribution of the Functions of Power: The Laws Concerning Public Offices in Deuteronomy 16:18–18:22," 345–46. See also Dion, "Deuteronomy and the Gentile World," 220.

[23] Hamilton, (*Social Justice and Deuteronomy*, 106–7) has recently restated the case for reading 15:7–18 in the light of 5:15. In this regard, he approves of the earlier work of Braulik and Kaufman.

opinion is subject to verification and/or change depending on the possibility of assigning such a *relecture* to Josianic times.[24]

Positionally, 14:1–21 seems to assume a context in which 14:22–27 followed Deuteronomy 13. This provides an explanation as to why death rules (14:1–2) precede food rules in these holiness instructions. The use of *Numeruswechsel* identifies the text with Dtr composition.[25] Braulik has suggested a possible connection between the terms of 14:1–21 and the misuse of the divine name in the Ten Commandments.[26] But the intertextual references of 14:1–21 are to 7:6. Therefore, an association with a redaction using the Ten Commandments paradigm seems unprovable with respect to the placement of 14:1–21. Nevertheless, the text may be regarded as a stage-four composition which has in common with texts such 15:7–11; 16:21–17:7, and 17:11–13 the technique of using intertextual references to prior Dtn contexts as well as extending commentary on pre-existing contexts.

Deut 14:23b; 16:12b appear to have a common concern to relate festival observance with Torah observance. But 16:12a repeats phraseology belonging to the layer of 15:15. It would follow then that 14:23b and 16:12 are related to the editorial activity that is responsible for 15:7–18. However, hortatory material later than the redaction responsible for 15:7–18 occurs in 15:4–6, which also has some linguistic echoes of 15:7–11. I see no objective way, therefore, of determining if 14:23b, 16:12 are best related to redactional activity associated with the Ten Commandments (or even if such a *relecture* occurred only once in the history of the composition of Deuteronomy).

The evidence suggests, therefore, that all additions to the *mqwm* sequence in 14:22–17:10 may stem from exilic times and later. The secondary clause row sequences were not likely added at one time. Although there is evidence that one redaction was motivated by a concern to reread the instructions of Deuteronomy 12–26 in the light of the Ten Commandments, it is not evident whether the additions of 14:1–21 and 16:21–17:7, 11–13 were prior to, later than such a redaction, or associated with it.

One general distinction can be maintained between the compositional activity that created the *mqwm* sequence and subsequent redactional activity in 14:1–17:13: whereas the *mqwm* sequence is interested principally in defining the relationship between its addressees and the *mqwm*, later additions are mainly concerned with circumscribing the nature of the group

---

[24] Braulik, "Die Abfolge der Gesetze in Deuteronomium 12–26," 271.

[25] Mayes, *Deuteronomy*, 237.

[26] Braulik, "Die Abfolge der Gesetze in Deuteronomium 12–26," 264.

which relates to the *mqwm*. A concern to identify social responsibilities of the people is found in the *mqwm* sequence (cf. 14:28–15:3; 16:11, 14). But secondary redactional activity is concerned to enhance the ethnic distinctiveness of the holy people (14:1–21; 16:21–17:7) while promoting a solidarity within Israel which seeks to ameliorate distinctions between rich and poor in the community (15:7–18).

A redaction history of Deut 14:1–17:13 can only be indicated in general terms based on the study above. The reason for this is that the evidence uncovered in this study is not sufficient to determine the diachronic relationships between all of the materials which are secondary to the *mqwm* sequence. The following broad stages suggest themselves:

a) Primary layer (the *mqwm* sequence): The span of text identified consists of 14:22–23a, 24aα.aβ.b, 25–27aα.b, 28–29; 15:1–3, 19–23; 16:1–11, 13–20; 17:8–10. It probably stems from a time prior to the Josianic reforms. The basic Dtn forms of 12:13–19 and 18:1–8 also belong to this layer.

This description raises the question of continuity in Deuteronomy 19–26. A text which shows a number of formal affinities with those of the *mqwm* sequence is found in 26:1–11. Deut 26:1–11 provides a fitting conclusion to the *mqwm* sequence by bringing together the categories described above by the terms "all" and "none." The worshipers, addressed by 2ms instructions, and the priests, addressed by 3ms instructions (v. 4), are brought together in a text which obligates both to certain liturgical actions connected to the offering of basic agricultural imposts. Here one finds the next explicit citation of the *mqwm* formula after 18:1–8 (26:2). The text also seems to contain a citation of an archaic formula (vv. 5b–10),[27] and a concluding *wśmḥt* instruction, which mentions the socially disadvantaged. Nevertheless, Deut 26:1–11 is not without its literary-critical difficulties.[28]

Given the terms of this study, it remains unclear whether 26:1–11 belongs to the *mqwm* sequence or not. But the fact that the next text with obvious triats of *mqwm* legislation occurs in Deuteronomy 26 emphasizes the apparent lack of continuity from the *mqwm* sequence into chapters 19–25. In addition, material beginning in Deuteronomy 19 also seems to break with the "all, some, and none" pattern described as an organizing feature of the *mqwm* sequence in Deuteronomy 12–18. Such literary tensions can be explained on the model of Braulik's suggestion that Deuteronomy 19–25 has been organized by a *relecture* of Dtn law using the Ten Commandments

---

[27] Seitz, *Studien*, 245–47.

[28] Mayes, Deuteronomy, 332–333.

which did not affect the organization of Deuteronomy 12–18 to the same degree.[29]

Relationships between the *mqwm* sequence and speeches of the covenant mediator in Deuteronomy 5–11, 29–31 also remain unclear. But allusions to the exophoric context of covenant mediation and conquest occur in 12:14b and 16:20. This suggests there the composition of the *mqwm* sequence may have originally contained some sort of introduction and/or conclusion to its instructions.

b) Secondary redactions: As a rule, these texts are interested in describing the nature of the society that organizes itself around the *mqwm*. They are particularly interested in promoting cultural solidarity and distinctiveness. Diachronic discriminations within this group are difficult, though all may come from exilic times or later. This group includes, 14:1–21; 14:23b; 15:4–6 (which is definitely later than 15:7–18); 15:7–11, 12–18; 16:12; 16:21–17:7, 11–13. At least some of this material (especially 15:7–18, 16:12) probably stems from a systematic effort to reread the Dtn laws in terms of the Ten Commandments

c) Copyists' additions: There are a number of small expansions which likely come from the later transmission tradition. Some of these are identifiable by text-critical methods. Here one might include *hšswʿh* in 14:7a; *whdyh* in 14:13; the bird names with *ʾt* in 14:12–18; 14:24aγ; 14:27aβ; 17:5aγ.

---

29 Braulik, "Die Abfolge der Gesetze in Deuteronomium 12–26," 271–272.

APPENDIX

Structural Ties in the Clause Rows of Deut 14:1–17:13

Cl.	Ties	Cohesive item	Type	Dist	Presupposed item
§ 1		**14:1–2**			
1bα	1	*ttgddw*	Pr.1	M.1	*ʾtm*
1bβ	2	*wlʾ*	C.1	1	c.1bα
		tśymw	Pr.1	M.2	*ttgddw* → c.1a
2a	2	*ky*	C.2	1	c.1bβ
		lyhwh ʾlhyk	L	N.3	*lyhwh ʾlhykm* c.1a
2b	2	*wbk*	C.1	1	c.2a
			Pr.2	1	*ʾth*
§2.1		**14:3–8**			
4–6a	1	*tʾklw*	L	1	1° *tʾkl*
6b	3	*ʾth*	Pr.2	1	*wkl bhmh*
		tʾklw	Pr.1	1	*tʾklw* c.4a'
			L	1	2° → cc.4a', 3
7a*	7	*ʾk*	C.1	1	c.6b
		ʾt zh	K	1	*ʾt hgml* etc. c.7bα
				4	*wʾt hḥzyr* c.8aα
		tʾklw	Pr.1	M.1	*tʾklw*
			L	1	3° → cc.6b, 4a', 3
		hgrh	D	N.2	*grh* c.6a'''
		hprsh	D	N.2	*prsh* c.6a'
7bα	1	*ʾt hgml* etc.	E	1	[*lʾ tʾklw*] ← c.7a*
7bβ	3	*ky*	C.2	1	c.7bα
		mʿlh grh	L	N.4	1° *mʿlt grh* c.6a'''
		hmh	Pr.1	1	*ʾt hgml* etc.
7bγ	3	*wprsh hprysw*	C.1	1	c.7bβ
			Pr.1	M.1	*hmh*
			L	N.5	1° *mprst prsh* c.6a'
7bδ	2	*hm*	Pr.1	M.2	*hprysw* → c.7bβ
		lkm	Pr.2	N.4	*tʾklw* c.7a*
8aα	2	*wʾt hḥzyr*	C.1	N.4	c.7bα
			E	N.5	[*lʾ tʾklw*] ← c.7a*
8aβ	3	*ky*	C.2	1	c.8aα
		mprys prsh	L	N.3	2° → cc.7bγ, 6a'
		hwʾ	Pr.1	1	*hḥzyr*
8aγ	3	*wlʾ*	C.1	1	c.8aβ
		grh	E	N.5	[*mʿlh*] ← c.7bβ
			L	N.5	2° → cc.7bβ, 6a'''
8aδ	3	*ṭmʾ*	L	N.4	*ṭmʾym* c.7bδ
		hwʾ	Pr.1	N.1	*hwʾ* c.8aβ
		lkm	Pr.2	N.4	*lkm* c.7bδ

8bα	4	*mbśrm*	Pr.2	N.1	c.8aδ
				N.5	c.7bδ
		lʾ tʾklw	Pr.1	1	*lkm*
			L	N.9	4° → cc.7a*, 6b, 4a', 3
8bβ	4	*wbnbltm*	C.1	1	c.8bα
			Pr.2	1	*mbśrm*
		tgʿw	Pr.1	1	*tʾklw*
			Ma	1	Po V
§2.2		**14:9–10**			
9a	1	*ʾt zh*	K	1	c.9b
9b	2	*tʾklw*	Pr.1	M.1	*tʾklw*
			L	1	1°
10a	5	*wkl*	C.1	1	c.9b
		snpyr wqśqśt	L	1	
		tʾklw	Pr.1	M.2	*tʾklw* → c.9a
			L	1	2° → cc.9b, 9a
			Ma	1	O V
10b	2	*hwʾ*	Pr.1	1	*kl*
		lkm	Pr.2	1	*tʾklw*
§2.3		**14:11–20**			
12–18*	3	*wzh*	C.1	1	c.11
		tʾklw	Pr.1	1	*tʾklw*
			L	1	1°
19a	2	*wkl*	C.1	1	c.12–18*
		lkm	Pr.2	1	*tʾklw*
19b	1	*yʾklw*	Pr.1	1	*kl šrṣ hʿp*
20	3	*ʿwp ṭhwr*	L	N.4	*ṣpwr ṭhwrh* c.11
		tʾklw	Pr.1	N.2	*lkm*
			L	N.3	2° → cc.12–18*, 11
§2.4		**14:21a**			
21aβ	1	*ttnnh*	Pr.2	M.1	*nblh*
21aγ	4	*wʾklh*	C.1	1	c.21aβ
			Pr.1	1	*lgr*
			Pr.2	M.2	*ttnnh* → *nblh* c.21aβ
			L	N.2	*tʾklw* → c.21aα
21aδ	3	*ʾw*	C.1	N.2	c.21aβ
		mkr	E	1	[*nblh*] ← *wʾklh* c.21aγ
		lnkry	L	N.2	*lgr* c.21aβ
21aϵ	2	*ky*	C.2	1	c.21aδ
		ʾth	Pr.1	N.3	*ttnnh* c.21aβ
§3.1		**14:22–27**			
23a	2	*wʾklt*	C.1	1	c.22
			Pr.1	M.1	*tʿśr*
23b	2	*lmʿn*	C.2	1	c.23a
		tlmd	Pr.1	M.2	*wʾklt* → c.22

24aα	3	*wky*	C.1	N.2	c.23a
			C.2	N.4	c.25a
		mmk	Pr.2	1	*tlmd*
24aβ	3	*ky*	C.2	1	c.24aα
		twkl	Pr.1	1	*mmk*
		ś'tw	Pr.2	N.3	*mʿśr* etc. c.23a
24aγ	3	*ky*	C.2	N.2	c.25a
		mmk	Pr.2	1	*twkl*
		'šr ybḥr . . . šmw šm	L	N.4	1° *'šr ybḥr . . . šmw šm* c.23a'
24b	3	*ky*	C.2	1	c.24aγ
		ybrkk	Pr.2	1	*mmk*
		yhwh 'lhyk	L	1	1° c.24aγ'
25a	3	*wntth*	C.1	N.4	c.24aα
			Pr.1	1	*ybrkk*
			E	N.3	[*mʿśr* etc.] ← *ś'tw* c.24aβ
25bα	3	*wṣrt*	C.1	1	c.25aα
			Pr.1	M.1	*wntth*
		hksp	D	1	*bksp*
25bβ	4	*whlkt*	C.1	1	c.25bα
			Pr.1	M.2	*wṣrt* → c.25a
		'šr ybḥr etc.	L	N.4	2° → cc. 24aγ', 23a'
		yhwh 'lhyk	L	N.3	2° → cc. 24b, 24aγ'
26a	4	*wntth*	C.1	1	c.25bβ
			Pr.1	M.3	*whlkt* → c.25a
			L	N.3	c.25a
		hksp	L	N.2	c.25bα
26bα	5	*w'klt*	C.1	1	c.26a
			Pr.1	M.4	*wntth* → c.25a
			L	N.10	*w'klt* c.23
		šm	Sub	N.10	*bmqwm* c.23a
		lpny yhwh 'lhyk	L	N.10	c.23a
26bβ–27a*	2	*wśmḥt*	C.1	1	c.26bα
			Pr.1	M.5	*w'klt* → c.25a
27b	3	*ky*	C.2	1	c.26bβ–27a*
		lw	Pr.2	1	*hlwy*
		ʿmk	Pr.2	1	*wśmḥt*
§3.2		**14:28–29**			
28b	3	*whnḥt*	C.1	1	c.28a
			Pr.1	M.1	*twṣy'*
			E	1	[*'t kl mʿśr . . .*] ←c.28a
29aα	2	*wb'*	C.1	1	c.28b
		ʿmk	Pr.2	1	*whnḥt*
29aβ	2	*w'klw*	C.1	1	c.29aα
			Pr.1	M.1	*hlwy* etc.
29aγ	2	*wśbʿw*	C.1	1	c.29aγ
			Pr.1	M.2	*w'klw*

29b	2	*lmʿn*	C.2	1	c.29aγ
		ybrkk	Pr.2	N.3	*bšʿryk* c.29aα
§4.1		**15:1–6**			
2aα	3	*wzh*	C.1	1	c.1
			K	1	c.2aβ
		hšmṭh	D	1	*šmṭh*
2bα	1	*ygś*	Pr.1	1	*kl bʿl*
2bβ	2	*ky*	C.2	1	c.2bα
		šmṭh	L	N.4	*šmṭh* c.1
3a	2	*tgś*	Pr.1	N.5	*tʿśh* c.1
			L	N.2	*ygś* c.2bα
3b	2	*wʾšr*	C.1	1	c.3a
		tšmṭ	Pr.1	M.1	*tgś*
4a	3	*ʾps ky*	C.2	1	c.3b
		yhyh	L	1	c.3b'
		bk	Pr.2	1	*tšmṭ*
4b	2	*ky*	C.2	1	c.4a
		ybrkk	Pr.2	1	*bk*
5	2	*rq ʾm*	C.2	1	c.4b
		tšmʿ	Pr.1	1	*ybrkk*
6a	3	*ky*	C.2	1	c.6bα
		yhwh ʾlhyk brkk	Pr.2	1	*tšmʿ*
			L	N.2	*ybrkk yhwh* c.4b
6bα	2	*whʿbṭt*	C.1	1	c.6a
			Pr.1	1	*brkk*
6bβ	2	*wʾth*	C.1	1	c.6bα
			Pr.1	1	*whʿbṭt*
6bγ	3	*wmšlt*	C.1	M.1	c.6bβ
			Pr.1	M.2	*tʿbṭ*
		bgym rbym (Po)	L	N.2	*gym rbym* (O) c.6bα
6bδ	5	*wbk*	C.1	1	c.6bγ
			Pr.2	1	*wmšlt*
		ymšlw	Pr.1	1	*gwym rbym*
			L	1	*wmšlt*
			Ma	1	Po V / V Po
§4.2		**15:7–11**			
7a	1	*ky*	C.2	1	c.7bα
7bα	1	*tʾmṣ*	Pr.1	1	*bk*
7bβ	3	*wlʾ*	C.1	1	c.7bα
		tqpṣ	Pr.1	M.1	*tʾmṣ*
		ʾt ydk	L	M.1	1° *ʾt lbbk*
8a	4	*tptḥ*	Pr.1	M.2	*tqpṣ* → c.7bα
		ʾt ydk	L	M.2	2° → c.7bβ, c.7bα
		lw	Pr.2	1	*ʾḥyk hʾbywn*
			Ma	1	V Po P / V Po P
8b	3	*whʿbṭ*	C.1	1	c.8a
		tʿbyṭnw	Pr.1	M.3	*tptḥ* → c.7bα
			Pr.2	1	*lw*

9aα	1	*lk*	Pr.2	1	*tʿbyṭnw*
9aβ	3	*pn*	C.2	1	c.9aα
		yhyh	L	N.6	1° *yhyh* c.7a
		lbbk	Pr.2	1	*lk*
9aγ	2	*wrʿh*	C.1	1	9aβ
		ʿynk	Pr.2	1	*lbbk*
9aδ	4	*wlʾ*	C.1	1	c.9aγ
		ttn l	Pr.1	1	*ʿynk*
			L	N.8	1 ° *ntn l* c.7a'
		lw	Pr.2	1	*bʾḥyk hʾbywn*
9bα	3	*wqrʾ*	C.1	1	c.9aδ
			Pr.1	1	*lw*
		ʿlyk	Pr.2	1	*ttn*
9bβ	3	*whyh*	C.1	1	c.9bα
			L	N.4	2° → cc.9aβ, 7a
		bk	Pr.2	1	*ʿlyk*
10aα	3	*ttn lw*	Pr.1	1	*bk*
			Pr.2	N.2	*wqrʾ*
			L	N.3	2° → cc.9aδ, 7a'
10aβ	4	*wlʾ*	C.1	1	c.10aα
		yrʿ lbbk	Pr.2	1	*ttn*
			L	N.5	*wrʿh ʿynk* c.9aγ
		bttk lw	L	1	3° → cc.10aα, 9aδ, 7a'
10b	3	*ky*	C.2	1	c.10aβ
		ybrkk	Pr.2	1	*lbbk*
		yhwh ʾlhyk	L	N.13	*yhwh ʾlhyk* c.7a'
11a	2	*ky*	C.2	N.2	c.10aβ
		ʾbywn	L	N.14	*ʾbywn* c.7a
11b	4	*ʿl kn*	C.1	1	c.11a
		mṣwk	Pr.2	N.2	*ybrkk*
		ptḥ tptḥ ʾt ydk	L	N.13	*ptḥ tptḥ ʾt ydk* c.8a
		bʾrṣk	L	N.15	c.7a
§5		**15:12–18**			
12aα	1	*ky*	C.2	1	c.12b
12aβ	3	*wʿbdk*	C.1	1	c.12aα
			Pr.1	1	*ʾḥyk*
			Pr.2	1	*lk*
12b	4	*wb(h)šnh*	C.1	N.2	c.12aα
			D	1	*šnym*
		tšlḥnw	Pr.1	1	*wʿbdk*
			Pr.2	1	
13a	5	*wky*	C.1	1	c.12b
			C.2	1	c.13b
		tšlḥnw ḥpšy mʿmk	Pr.1	M.1	*tšlḥnw*
			Pr.2	M.1	
			L	1	*tšlḥnw ḥpšy mʿmk*
13b	3	*tšlḥnw*	Pr.1	M.2	*tšlḥnw* → c.12b
			Pr.2	M.2	

			L	1	2° → cc.13a, 12b
14a	2	*tʿnyq*	Pr.1	M.3	*tšlḥnw* → c.12b
		lw	Pr.2	1	*tšlḥnw*
14bα	2	*ʾšr*	C.2	1	c.14bβ
		brkk	Pr.2	1	*tʿnyq*
14b	2	*ttn*	Pr.1	1	*brkk*
		lw	Pr.2	N.2	*lw* c.14a
15a	2	*wzkrt*	C.1	M.1	*ttn*
		yhwh ʾlhyk	L	N.2	c.14bα
15b	2	*ʿl kn*	C.1	1	c.15a
		mṣwk	Pr.2	1	*wzkrt*
16aα	2	*whyh*	C.1	1	c.15b
			L	N.2	*hyyt* c.15a'
16aβ	3	*ky*	C.2	1	c.17aα
		yʾmr	Pr.1	N.4	*lw* c.14b
		ʾlyk	Pr.2	N.2	*mṣwk* c.15b
16bα	3	*ky*	C.2	1	c.16aβ
		ʾhbk	Pr.1	M.1	*yʾmr*
			Pr.2	1	*ʾlyk*
16bβ 3		*ky*	C.2	1	c.16bα
		lw	Pr.2	1	*ʾhbk*
		ʿmk	Pr.2	1	*ʾhbk*
17aα 2		*wlqḥt*	C.1	N.3	c.16aβ
			Pr.1	1	*ʿmk*
17aβ 5		*wntth*	C.1	1	c.17aα
			Pr.1	M.1	*wlqḥt*
			L	N.10	*ttn* c.14b
			E	1	[*ʾt hmrṣʿ*] ← c.17aα
		bʾznw	Pr.2	N.2	*lw* c.16bβ
17aγ 5		*whyh*	C.1	1	c.17aβ
			Pr.1	1	*bʾznw*
			L	N.6	2° → cc.16aα, 15a'
		lk	Pr.2	1	*wntth*
		ʿbd	L	N.8	*ʿbd* c.15a'
17b	3	*wʾp*	C.1	1	c.17aγ
		tʿśh	Pr.1	1	*lk*
		kn	Sub	N.1–3	cc.17aα–17aγ
18aα	3	*bʿnyk*	Pr.2	1	*tʿśh*
		bšlḥk ʾtw ḥpšy mʿmk	Pr.2	N.2	*whyh*
			L	N.15	2° → cc.13a, 12b
18aβ	4	*ky*	C.2	1	c.18aα
		ʿbdk šš šnym	L	N.18	c.12aβ
			Pr.1	1	*ʾtw*
			Pr.2	1	*bʿnyk*
18b	4	*wbrkk yhwh*	C.1	1	c.18aβ
		ʾlhyk	Pr.2	1	*ʿbdk*
			L	N.14	c.14b
		tʿśh	L	N.3	c.17b

§ 6		**15:19–23**			
19bα	1	*tʿbd*	Pr.1	M.1	*tqdyš*
19bβ	3	*wlʾ*	C.1	1	c.19bα
		tgz	Pr.1	M.2	*tʿbd* → c.19aα
		ṣʾnk	L	1	*šwrk*
20	2	*tʾklnw*	Pr.1	M.3	*tgz* → c.19aα
			Pr.2	N.3	*hbkr* c.19a
21a	3	*wky*	C.1	1	c.20
			C.2	1	c.21b
		bw	Pr.2	1	*tʾklnw*
21b	3	*tzbḥnw*	Pr.1	N.2	*tʾklnw* c.20
			Pr.2	1	*bw*
		lyhwh ʾlhyk	L	N.5	*lyhwh ʾlhyk* c.19aα
22	4	*tʾklnw*	Pr.1	M.1	*tzbḥnw*
			Pr.2	M.1	
			L	N.3	1° *tʾklnw* c.20
		bšʿryk	L	N.3	*bmqwm* c.20
23a	3	*dmw*	Pr.2	1	*tʾklnw*
		tʾkl	Pr.1	M.2	*tʾklnw* → c.21b
			L	1	2° → cc.22, 20
23b	2	*tšpknw*	Pr.1	M.3	*tʾkl* → c.21b
			Pr.2	1	*dmw*
§ 7.1		**16:1–8**			
1aβ	1	*wʿśyt*	C.1	1	c.1aα
1b	3	*ky*	C.2	1	c.1aβ
		hwṣyʾk	Pr.1	1	*yhwh ʾlhyk*
			Pr.2	1	*wʿśyt*
2	3	*wzbḥt*	C.1	N.2	c.1aβ
			Pr.1	1	*hwṣʾyk*
		psḥ lyhwh etc.	L	N.2	*psḥ lyhwh* etc. c.1aβ
3aα	2	*tʾkl*	Pr.1	M.1	*wzbḥt*
		ʿlyw	Pr.2	1	*psḥ lyhwh* etc.
3aβ	3	*tʾkl*	Pr.1	M.2	*tʾkl* → c.2
			L	1	1°
		ʿlyw	Pr.2	M.1	*ʿlyw* → c.2
3bα	2	*ky*	C.2	1	c.3aβ
		yṣʾt	Pr.1	M.3	*tʾkl* → c.2
3bβ	3	*lmʿn*	C.2	N.2	c.3aβ
		tzkr	Pr.1	M.4	*yṣʾt* → c.2
		ṣʾtk mʾrṣ, etc.	L	1	1° *yṣʾt mʾrṣ*, etc.
4a	3	*wlʾ*	C.1	N.3	c.3aβ
		lk	Pr.2	1	*tzkr*
		šbʿt ymym	L	N.3	1° *šbʿt ymym* c.3aβ
4b	4	*wlʾ*	C.1	1	c.4a
		tzbḥ	Pr.1	1	*lk*
			L	N.6	1° *wzbḥt* c.2
		b(h)ywm	D	1	*šbʿt ymym*
5	4	*twkl*	Pr.1	1	*tzbḥ* c.4b'

		lzbḥ	L	1	2° → cc.4b, 2
		ʾt hpsḥ	D	N.8	*psḥ* c.2
		yhwh ʾlhyk	L	N.9	*yhwh ʾlhyk* c.1b
6	8	*ky ʾm*	C.1	1	c.5
		ʾšr ybḥr etc.	L	N.9	*ʾšr ybḥr* etc. c.2
		tzbḥ	Pr.1	M.1	*twkl*
			L	1	3° → cc.5, 4b, 2
		ʾt hpsḥ	L	1	
		bʿrb	L	N.2	*bʿrb* c.4b
		ṣʾtk	L	N.4	2° → cc.3bβ, 3bα
		mmṣrym	L	N.9	*mmṣrym* c.1b
7aα	3	*wbšlt*	C.1	1	c.6
			Pr.1	M.2	*tzbḥ* → c.5
			E	M.1	[*ʾt hpsḥ*] ← c.6
7aβ	5	*wʾklt*	C.1	1	c.7aα
			Pr.1	M.3	*wbšlt* → c.5
			E	M.2	[*ʾt hpsḥ*] ← cc.7aα, 6
			L	N.8	2° → cc.3aβ, 3aα
		bmqwm etc.	L	N.9	*bmqwm* c.2
7bα	3	*wpnyt*	C.1	1	c.7aβ
			Pr.1	M.4	*wʾklt* → c.5
		bbqr	L	N.5	*lbqr* c.4b
7bβ	3	*whlkt*	C.1	1	c.7bα
			Pr.1	M.5	*wpnyt* → c.5
			Ma	1	V Pa / V Pa
8a	4	(*ššt*) *ymym*	L	N.8	2° → cc.4a, 3aβ
		tʾkl	Pr.1	M.6	*whlkt* → c.5
			L	N.3	3° → cc.7aβ, 3aβ, 3aα
		mṣwt	L	N.11	*mṣwt* c.3aβ
8bα	5	*wb(h)ywm*	C.1	1	c.8a
			D	1	*ššt ymym*
			L	N.7	*b(h)ywm* c.4b'
		lyhwh ʾlhyk	L	N.14	2° → cc.2. 1aβ
			Pr.2	1	*tʾkl*
8bβ	2	*tʿśh*	Pr.1	1	*ʾlhyk*
			L	N.17	*wʿśyt*
§7.2		**16:9–12**			
9b	2	*tḥl*	Pr.1	M.1	*tspr*
		lspr šbʿh šbʾwt	L	1	*šbʿh šbʿt tspr*
10	3	*wʿśyt*	C.1	1	c.9b
			Pr.1	M.2	*tḥl* → c.9a
		šbʿwt	L	1	2° → cc.9b, 9a
11	3	*wśmḥt*	C.1	1	c.10
			Pr.1	M.3	*wʿśyt* → c.9a
		yhwh ʾlhyk	L	1	c.10b'
12a	2	*wzkrt*	C.1	1	c.11
			Pr.1	M.4	*wśmḥt* → c.9a

12bα	2	*wšmrt*	C.1	1	c.12a
			Pr.1	M.5	*wzkrt* → c.9a
12bβ	3	*wʿśyt*	C.1	1	c.12bα
			Pr.1	M.6	*wšmrt* → c.9a
			L	N.4	*wʿśyt* c.10
§7.3		**16:13–15**			
14	2	*wśmḥt*	C.1	1	c.13
			Pr.1	M.1	*tʿśh*
15a	1	*tḥg*	Pr.1	M.2	*wśmḥt* → c.13
15bα	2	*ky*	C.2	1	c.15a
		ybrkk	Pr.2	1	*tḥg*
15bβ	3	*whyyt*	C.1	N.2	c.15aα
			Pr.1	1	*ybrkk*
§7.4		**16:16–17**			
16b	3	*wlʾ*	C.1	1	c.16a
		yrʾh ʾt pny yhwh	Pr.1	1	*zkwrk*
			L	1	
17	3	*ʾyš*	Pr.1	1	*yʾrh*
			E	1	[*yrʾh ʾt pny yhwh*]← c.16b
		yhwh ʾlhyk	L	N.2	c.16a
§8		**16:18–20**			
18b	2	*wšpṭw*	C.1	1	c.18a
			Pr.1	1	*špṭym wšṭrym*
19aα	2	*tṭh*	Pr.1	N.2	*ttn* c.18a
		mšpṭ	L	1	
19aβ	2	*tkyr*	Pr.1	M.1	*tṭh*
			Ma	M.1	V O
19bα	2	*tqḥ*	Pr.1	M.2	*tkyr* → c.19aα
			Ma	M.2	V O
19bβ	2	*ky*	C.2	1	c.19bα
		hšḥd	Pr.3	1	*šḥd*
19bγ	2	*ṣdyqm*	L	1	*ḥkmym*
			Ma	1	(S) V O
20a	2	*ṣdq ṣdq*	L	N.6	c.18b *mšpṭ ṣdq*
		trdp	Pr.1	N.3	*tqḥ*
20bα	2	*lmʿn*	C.2	1	c.20α
		tḥyh	Pr.1	M.1	*trdp*
20bβ	3	*wyršt*	C.1	1	c.20bα
			Pr.1	M.2	*tḥyh* → c.20a
		ʾšr yhwh ʾlhyk ntn lk	L	N.9	c.18a
§9		**16:21–22**			
22	3	*wlʾ*	C.1	1	c.21
		tqym	Pr.1	M.1	*tṭʿ*
		mṣbh	L	1	*ʾšrh*

§10		**17:1**			
1b	2	*ky*	C.2	1	c.1a
		hwʾ	Pr.1	1	*šwr wśh*
§11		**17:2–7**			
2	1	*ky*	C.2	N.5	c.5a
4aα	2	*whgd*	C.1	1	c.2
		lk	Pr.2	1	*bqrbk*
4aβ	2	*wšmʿt*	C.1	1	c.4aα
			Pr.1	1	*lk*
4bα	2	*wdršt*	C.1	1	c.4aβ
			Pr.1	M.1	*wšmʿt* → c.4aα
4bβ	1	*whnh*	C.1	1	c.4bα
5a	5	*whwṣʾt*	C.1	N.5	c.2
			Pr.1	N.2	*wdršt* c.4bα
		hʾyš hhwʾ ʾw hʾšh hhwʾ	D	N.5	*ʾyš ʾw ʾšh* c.2
		ʾšr ʿśw ʾt hdbr hrʿ hzh	L	N.5	*ʾšr yʿśh ʾt hrʿ* c.2b'
			D	1	*hdbr* c.4bβ
5bα	3	*wsqltm*	C.1	1	c.5a
			Pr.1	M.1	*whwṣʾt* →c.5a
			Pr.2	1	*hʾyš hhwʾ*, etc.
5bβ	2	*wmtw*	C.1	1	c.5bα
			Pr.1	1	*wsqltm*
6b	2	*ywmt*	L	1	
		ʿl py ʿd ʾḥd	L	1	*ʿl py šnym ʿdym*
7a	1	*bw*	Pr.2	1	*ywmt*
7bα	4	*wyd*	C.1	1	c.7a
			L	1	*yd*
			E	1	[*thyh bw*] ← c.7a
		bʾḥrnh	L	1	*brʾšnh*
7bβ	3	*wbʿrt*	C.1	1	c.7bα
			Pr.1	N.5	*wsqltm* c.5bα
		hrʿ	Pr.3	N.2	*bw* c.7a
§12		**17:8–13**			
8a	1	*ky*	C.2	1	c.8b
8bα	2	*wqmt*	C.1	1	c.8a
			Pr.1	1	*mmk*
8bβ	2	*wʿlyt*	C.1	1	c.8bα
			Pr.1	M.1	*wqmt*
9a	2	*wbʾt*	C.1	1	c.8bβ
			Pr.1	M.2	*wʿlyt* →c.8bα
9bα	2	*wdršt*	C.1	1	c.9a
			Pr.1	M.3	*wbʾt* →c.8bα
9bβ	4	*whgydw*	C.1	1	c.9bα
			Pr.1	N.2	*hkhnym . . . hšpṭ* c.9a
		lk	Pr.2	1	*wdršt*
		dbr hmšpṭ	D	N.5	*dbr lmšpṭ* c.8a

10a	5	*wʿśyt*	C.1	1	c.9bβ
			Pr.1	1	*lk*
		hdbr	D	1	*dbr hmšpṭ*
		ygydw lk	L	1	*whgydw lk*
		hmqwm hhwʾ	Pr.3	N.5	*hmqwm* etc. c.8bβ
10b	2	*wšmrt*	C.1	1	c.10a
			Pr.1	M.1	*wʿśyt*
11a	4	*ʿl py htwrh . . . lk*	L	1	*ʾšr ywrwk* c.10b"
			L	N.2	*ʿl py hdbr ʾšr ygydw lk* c.10a
		tʿśh	Pr.1	1	*wšmrt*
			L	N.2	*wʿśyt* c.10a
11b	2	*tswr*	Pr.1	M.1	*tʿśh* → c.10b
		hdbr ʾšr ygydw lk	L	1	2° → cc. 11, 10a'
12a	4	*whʾyš*	C.1	1	c.11b
		yʿśh	L	N.2	2° *tʾśh* c.11a→ c.10a
		ʾl hkhn . . . ʾl hšpṭ	L	N.7	*ʾl hkhnym . . . wʾl hšpṭ* c.9a
		šm	D	N.4	*hmqwm hhwʾ* c.10a
12bα	2	*wmt*	C.1	1	c.12a
		hʾyš hhwʾ	D	1	*whʾyš*
12bβ	3	*wbʿrt*	C.1	1	c.12bα
			Pr.1	N.3	*tswr* c.11b
		hrʿ	D	1	*hʾyš hhwʾ*
13aα	2	*wkl*	C.1	1	c.12bβ
		yšmʿw	L	N.3	*šmʿ* c.12a"
13aβ	2	*wyrʾw*	C.1	1	c.13aα
			Pr.1	M.1	*wkl hʿm*
13b	2	*wlʾ*	C.1	1	c.13aβ
		yzydwn	Pr.1	M.2	*wyrʾw* →c.13aα

BIBLIOGRAPHY

Achenbach, R. *Israel zwischen Verheissung und Gebot: Literarkritiches Untersuchungen zu Deuteronomium 5–11.* Europäische Hochschulschriften Reihe 23, Theologie; Bd. 422. Frankfurt am Main: Lang, 1991.

Alt, A. "The Origins of Israelite Law." In *Essays on Old Testament History and Religion*, trans. R. A. Wilson, 81–132. Oxford: Blackwell, 1966. First published as *Die Ursprünge des israelitischen Rechts.* Leiden: Hizel, 1934.

Andersen, F. I. *The Hebrew Verbless Clause in the Pentateuch.* SBLMS 14. Nashville: Abingdon, 1970.

———. *The Sentence in Biblical Hebrew.* Janua Linguarum Series Practica 231. The Hague: Mouton, 1974.

Andreasen, N. E. A. *The Old Testament Sabbath.* SBLDS 7. Missoula: Scholars Press, 1972.

Auerbach, E. "Die Feste im alten Israel." *VT* 8 (1958) 1–14.

Avishur, Y. "Expressions of the Type *byn ydym* in the Bible and Semitic Languages." *UF* 12 (1980) 125–33.

———. *Stylistic Studies of Word-Pairs in Biblical and Ancient Semitic Literatures.* AOAT 210. Neukirchen-Vluyn: Neukirchener Verlag, 1984.

Axel, E. "Zur Herkunft und Sozialgeschichte Israels: 'Das Böckchen in der Milch seiner Mutter.'" *Bib* 69 (1988) 153–69.

Baker, D. W. "Further Examples of the *waw* explicativum." *VT* 30 (1980) 129–36.

Balkan, K. "Cancellation of Debts in Cappodocian Tablets from Kültepe." In *Anatolian Studies Presented to Hans Gustav Güterbock.* Uitgaven van het Nederlands Historisch-Archaeologisch Institut te Istanbul 35, 29–41. Istanbul: Nederlands Historisch-Archaeologisch Institut, 1974.

Barr, J. *The Semantics of Biblical Language.* London: Oxford University Press, 1961.

Batto, B. F. Review of Gilmer, *The If-You Form in Israelite Law.* In *CBQ* 39 (1977) 116–17.

Bettenzoli, G. "Deuteronomium und Heiligkeitsgesetz." *VT* 34 (1984) 385–98.

Biblia Sacra iuxta Latinam Vulgatam Versionem. Vol. III, *Numeri-Deuteronomium*, ed. H. Quentin. Romae: 1936.

Blau, J. "Zum angeblichen Gebrauch von את vor dem Nominativ." *VT* 4 (1954) 7–19.

Boecker, H. J. Review of Gilmer, *The If-You Form in Israelite Law.* In *TLZ* 102 (1977) 427–29.

Braulik, G. "Die Ausdrücke für 'Gesetz' im Buch Deuteronomium." *Bib* 51 (1970) 39-60.

———. *Die Mittel deuteronomischer Rhetorik.* AnBib 68. Rome: Pontifical Biblical Institute, 1979.

———. "Die Abfolge der Gesetze in Deuteronomium 12–26 und der Dekalog." In *Das Deuteronomium: Entstehung, Gestalt und Botschaft,* ed. N. J. Lohfink, 252–72. Leuven: University Press, 1985.

———. "Zur Abfolge der Gesetze in Deuteronomium 16,18–21,23. Weitere Beobachtung." *Bib* 69 (1988) 63–92.

Brichto, H. C. "The Golden Calf Episode in Exod 32–34." *HUCA* 54 (1983) 1–44.

Brockelmann, C. *Hebräische Syntax.* Neukirchen: Erziehungsvereins, 1956.

Broide, I. *The Speeches in Deuteronomy, Their Style and Rhetorical Devices.* Unpublished dissertation. University of Tel Aviv: 1970 [Modern Hebrew].

Brown, G., and G. Yule, *Discourse Analysis.* Cambridge Textbooks in Linguistics. Cambridge: Cambridge University Press, 1983.

Budd, P. J. "Priestly Instruction in Pre-exilic Israel." *VT* 23 (1973) 1–14.

Caloz, M. "L'Exode XIII,3-16 et son rapport au Deutéronome." *RB* 75 (1968) 5–62.

Cansdale, G. *Animals of Bible Lands.* Exeter: Paternoster, 1970.

Carmichael, C. M. *The Laws of Deuteronomy.* Ithaca: Cornell University Press, 1974.

———. "A Common Element in Five Supposedly Disparate Laws." *VT* 29 (1979) 129–42.

———. *Law and Narrative in the Bible*. Ithaca: Cornell University Press, 1985.

Cazelles, H. "Droit publique dans le Deutéronome." In *Das Deuteronomium: Entstehung, Gestalt, und Botschaft*, ed. N. J. Lohfink, 99–106. Leuven: University Press, 1985.

Ceriani, A. M. *Translatio Syra Pescitto Veteris Testamenti ex codice Ambrosiano sec. fere VI*. Vol. 1. 1876.

Childs, B. S. *The Book of Exodus: A Critical, Theological Commentary*. OTL. Philadelphia: Westminster, 1974.

Cholewínski, A. *Heiligkeitsgesetz und Deuteronomium*. AnBib 66. Rome: Pontifical Biblical Institute, 1976.

Clark, W. M. "Law." In *Old Testament Form Criticism*, ed. J. H. Hayes, 99–139. San Antonio: Trinity University Press, 1974.

Clarke, E. G., et al. *Targum Pseudo-Jonathan of the Pentateuch: Text and Concordance*. New York: Ktav, 1984.

Cotterell, P., and M. Turner, *Linguistics and Biblical Interpretation*. London: SPCK, 1989.

Craigie, P. C. *The Book of Deuteronomy*. NICOT. Grand Rapids: Eerdmans, 1976.

Dahood, M. Review of *The Torah* (JPSV 1962). In *Bib* 45 (1964) 282–84.

Davidson, A. B. *Hebrew Syntax*³. Edinburgh: T. & T. Clark, 1901 (reprinted 1954).

Day, J. "Asherah in the Hebrew Bible and Northwest Semitic Literature." *JBL* 105 (1986) 385–408.

Dempster, S. G. *Linguistic Features of Hebrew Narrative: A Discourse Analysis of Narrative from the Classical Period*. Unpublished doctoral dissertation. University of Toronto, 1985.

———. "The Deuteronomic Formula KÎ YIMMĀṢĒʾ in the Light of Biblical and Ancient Near Eastern Law." *RB* 91 (1984) 188–211.

De Vaux, R. *Studies in Old Testament Sacrifice*. Cardiff: University of Wales Press, 1964.

De Vries, S. J. "The Development of the Deuteronomic Promulgation Formula." *Bib* 55 (1974) 301–16.

Diem, W. "Alienable und inalienable Possession im Semitischen." *ZDMG* 136 (1986) 227–91.

Diez Macho, A. *Neophyti 1. Tomo V Deuteronomio.* Madrid: Consejo Superior de Investigaciones Científicas, 1978.

Dion, P. E. "Tu feras disparaître le mal du milieu de toi." *RB* 87 (1980) 321–49.

———. "Deutéronome 21,1-9: Miroir du développement légal et religieux d'Israël." *SR* 11 (1982) 13–22.

———. "Deuteronomy and the Gentile World: A Study in Biblical Theology." *Toronto Journal of Theology* 1 (1985) 200–21.

———. "Deuteronomy 13: The Supression of Alien Religious Propaganda in Israel during the Late Monarchical Era." In *Law and Ideology in Monarchic Israel.* JSOTSup 124, eds. B. Halpern and D. W. Hobson, 147–216. Sheffield: JSOT, 1991.

———. *A Student's Guide to Hebrew Poetics*[2]. Mississauga: Benben, 1992.

Doron, P. "Motive Clauses in the Laws of Deuteronomy: Their Forms, Functions, and Contents." *HAR* 2 (1978) 61–77.

Driver, G. R. "Birds in the Old Testament: 1. Birds in Law." *PEQ* (1955) 5–20.

Driver, S. R. *A Treatise on the Uses of Tenses in Hebrew*[3]. Oxford: Clarendon, 1892.

———. *A Critical and Exegetical Commentary on Deuteronomy*[3] (ICC). New York: Scribner's, 1902.

Duke, R. K. "The Portion of the Levite: Another Reading of Deuteronomy 18:6-8." *JBL* 106 (1987) 193–201.

Ehrlich, A. B. *Randglossen zur hebräischen Bibel: Textkritisches, Sprachliches, und Sachliches.* Vol 2. *Leviticus, Numeri, Deuteronomium.* Leipzig: Hindrich, 1909.

Elliger, K. *Leviticus.* HAT 4. Tübingen: Mohr, 1966.

Eslinger, L. "More Drafting Techniques in Deuteronomic Laws." *VT* 34 (1984) 221–26.

Feliks, J. *The Animal World of the Bible.* Tel-Aviv: Sinai, 1962.

Fensham, F. C. "Father and Son as Terminology for Treaty and Covenant." In *Near Eastern Studies in Honor of William Foxwell Albright,* 121–35. Baltimore: Johns Hopkins University Press, 1971.

Fishbane, M. *Biblical Interpretation in Ancient Israel*. Oxford: Clarendon, 1985.

Fisher, L. R. "Literary Genres in the Ugaritic Texts." *Ras Shamra Parallels* 2 (1975) 133–52.

Fohrer, G. "Das sogenannte apodiktisch formulierte Recht und der Dekalog." *KD* 11 (1965) 49–74.

Gerstenberger, E. *Wesen und Herkunft des 'apodiktischen Rechts.'* WMANT 20. Neukirchen-Vluyn: Neukirchener Verlag, 1965.

Gibeathi, M. "The Remission of Money in the Test of Implementation." *Bet Miqra* 25 (1977) 172–80 [Modern Hebrew].

Gibson, J. C. L. *Textbook of Syrian Semitic Inscriptions*: Vol. 2, *Aramaic Inscriptions*. Oxford: Clarendon, 1975.

———. *Textbook of Syrian Semitic Inscriptions*: Vol. 3, *Phoenician Inscriptions*. Oxford: Clarendon, 1982.

Gilmer, H. W. *The If-You Form in Israelite Law*. SBLDS 15. Missoula: Scholars Press, 1975.

Ginsberg, H.L. *The Israelian Heritage of Judaism.* Text and Studies of the Jewish Theological Seminary in America 24. New York: Jewish Theological Seminary, 1982.

Greenfield, J. C. and B. Porten. *The Bisitun Inscription of Darius the Great. Aramaic Version*. Corpus Inscriptionum Iranicarum I.5.1. London: Corpus Inscriptionum Iranicarum, 1982.

Halbe, J. *Das Privilegrecht Jahwes: Ex 34,10–26*. FRLANT 114. Göttingen: Vandenhoeck & Ruprecht, 1975.

———."Passa-Massot im deuteronomischen Festkalender." *ZAW* 87 (1975) 147–68.

———. "Erwägungen zu Ursprung und Wesen des Massotfestes." *ZAW* 87 (1975) 324–46.

Halliday, M. A. K. "Descriptive Linguistics in Literary Studies." In *Linguistics and Literary Style,* ed. D. C. Freeman, 57–72. New York: Holt, Rinehart & Winston, 1970.

———, and R. Hasan, *Cohesion in English.* English Language Series 4. London: Longmans, 1976.

Halpern, B. "The Centralization Formula in Deuteronomy." *VT* 31 (1981) 20–38.

Hals, R. M. Review of Seitz, *Redaktionsgeschichtliche Studien zum Deuteronomium.* In *JBL* 92 (1973) 281–84.

Hamilton, J. M. *Social Justice and Deuteronomy: The Case of Deuteronomy 15.* SBLDS 136. Atlanta: Scholars Press, 1992.

Hempel, J. "Innermasoretische Bestätigungen des Samaritanus." *ZAW* 52 (1934) 254–74.

Hölscher, G. "Komposition und Ursprung des Deuteronomiums." *ZAW* 40 (1922) 161–255.

Horst, F. *Das Privilegrecht Jahwes.* FRLANT 28. Göttingen: Vandenhoeck & Ruprecht, 1930. Republished in *Gottes Recht: Gesammelte Studien zum Recht im Alten Testament,* ed. H. W. Wolff. München: Kaiser, 1961.

Houtman, C. "Ezra and the Law: Observations on the supposed relation between Ezra and the Pentateuch." *OTS* 21 (1981) 90–115.

Humbert, P. "Le substantif *toʿēbā* et le verbe *tʿb* dans l'Ancien Testament." *ZAW* 72 (1960) 217–37.

Ibn Ezra (Abraham ben Meir). *Perush ha–Torah.* Vol. 3, ed. A. Weiser. Jerusalem: Mossad ha-Rav Kook, 1976.

Jagersma, H. "The Tithes in the Old Testament." *OTS* 21 (1981) 116–28.

Joüon, P. *Grammaire de l'hébreu biblique.* Rome: Institut Biblique Pontifical, 1923 (reprinted 1965).

Kaufman, S. A. "The Structure of the Deuteronomic Law." *Maarav* 1/2 (1978-1979) 105–58.

———. "A Reconstruction of the Social Welfare Systems of Ancient Israel." In *In the Shelter of Elyon: Essays on Ancient Palestinian Life and Literature in Honor of G. W. Ahlström.* JSOTSup 31, 277–86. Sheffield: JSOT, 1984.

Kennicott, B. *Vetus Testamentum Hebraicum cum variis Lectionibus.* Vol. 1. Oxford: 1776.

Klein, M. L. *The Fragment-Targums of the Pentateuch*. Vols. 1–2. AnBib 76. Rome: Pontifical Biblical Institute, 1980.

Kline, M. G. *Treaty of the Great King*. Grand Rapids: Eerdmans, 1963.

Knierim, R. Review of Gilmer, *The If-You Form in Israelite Law*. In *JBL* 96 (1977) 113–14.

König, F. E. *Historisch-Comparative Syntax der Hebräischen Sprache*. Leipzig, Hindrich, 1897.

———. *Das Deuteronomium*. KAT 3. Leipzig: Hindrich, 1917.

Kraus, F. R. *Ein Edikt des Königs Ammi-ṣaduqa von Babylon*. Studia et Documenta ad iura Orientis Antiqui pertinentia 5. Leiden: E. J. Brill, 1958.

Kraus, H. J. *Worship in Israel*, trans. G. Boswell. Richmond: John Knox, 1966.

Kugel, J. *The Idea of Biblical Poetry*. New Haven: Yale University Press, 1981.

Lachs, S. T. "Two Related Arameans. A Difficult Reading in the Passover Haggadah." *JSJ* 17 (1986) 65–69.

Langlamet, F. Review of Merendino, *Das deuteronomische Gesetz*. In *RB* 77 (1970) 586–92.

———. Review of Richter, *Exegese als Literaturwissenschaft*. In *RB* 79 (1972) 275–88.

Lemche, N. P. "The Manumission of Slaves—the Fallow Year—the Sabbatical Year—the Jobel Year." *VT* 26 (1976) 38–59.

———. "The Hebrew Slave." *VT* 28 (1978) 129–44.

Levinson, B. M. "Calum M. Carmichael's Approach to the Laws of Deuteronomy." *HTR* 83 (1990) 227–57.

———. *The Hermeneutics of Innovation: The Impact of Centralization upon the Structure, Sequence and Reformulation of Legal Material in Deuteronomy*. Unpublished doctoral dissertation. Brandeis University, 1991.

Lewy, J. "The Biblical Institution of Derôr in the Light of Akkadian Documents." *ErIsr* 5 (1958) 21–31.

Liedke, G. *Gestalt und Bezeichnung alttestamentlicher Rechtssätze*. WMANT 39. Neukirchen-Vluyn: Neukirchener Verlag, 1971.

Lindenberger, J. M. "How Much for a Hebrew Slave? The Meaning of *Mišneh* in Deut 15:18." *JBL* 110 (1991) 479–482.

Lohfink, N. *Das Hauptgebot: Eine Untersuchung literarischer Einleitungsfragen zu Dtn 5–11.* AnBib 20. Rome: Pontifical Biblical Institute, 1963.

———. Review of Richter, *Exegese als Literaturwissenschaft.* In *BZ* 17 (1973) 286–94.

———. "Dt 26,17-19 und die Bundesformel." *ZKT* 91 (1969) 517–33.

———. "Zur deuteronomischen Zentralisationsformel." *Bib* 65 (1984) 297–329.

———. "Distribution of the Functions of Power: The Laws Concerning Public Offices in Deuteronomy 16:18-18:22." In *A Song of Power and the Power of Song.* Sources for Biblical and Theological Study 3, ed. D. L. Christensen, 336–52. Winona Lake: Eisenbrauns, 1993. First published as "Die Sicherung der Wirksamkeit des Gotteswortes durch das Prinzip der Schriftlichkeit der Tora und durch das Prinzip der Gewaltenteilung nach den Amtergesetzen des Buches Deuteronomium (Dt 16:18–18:22)." In *Testimonium Veritati.* Frankfurter Theologische Studien 7, 144–55. Frankfurt am Main: Josef Knecht, 1971.

Longacre, R. E. "The Discourse Structure of the Flood Narrative." *JAAR Supplement* 47B (1979) 89–133.

López, F. G., "'Un peuple consacré': Analyse critique de Deutéronome VII." *VT* 32 (1982) 438–63.

Lundbom, J. R. "Poetic Structure and Prophetic Rhetoric in Hosea." *VT* 39 (1979) 300–8.

Macdonald, J. "Some Distinctive Characteristics of Israelite Spoken Hebrew." *BO* 32 (1975) 162–75.

Manley, G. T. *Deuteronomy—the Book of the Law.* Grand Rapids: Eerdmans, 1957.

Marzal, A. "Mari Clauses in 'Casuistic' and 'Apodictic' Styles (Part I-II)." *CBQ* 33 (1971) 333–364; 492–509.

Mayes, A. D. H. *Deuteronomy.* NCB. London: Oliphants, 1979.

McBride, S. D. "Polity of the Covenant People. The Book of Deuteronomy." In *A Song of Power and the Power of Song.* Sources for Biblical and

Theological Study 3, ed. D. L. Christensen, 62–77. Winona Lake: Eisenbrauns, 1993. First published in *Int* 41 (1987) 229–44.

McConville, J. G. *Law and Theology in Deuteronomy.* JSOTSup 33. Sheffield: JSOT, 1984.

McKay, J. W. "Man's Love for God in Deuteronomy and the Father/Teacher — Son/Pupil Relationship." *VT* 22 (1972) 426–35.

Meek, T. J. "Result and Purpose Clauses in Hebrew." *JQR* 46 (1955-56) 40–43.

Merendino, R. P. *Das deuteronomische Gesetz: eine literarkritische, gattungs– und überlieferungsgeschichtliche Untersuchung zu Dt 12–26*. BBB 31. Bonn: Hanstein, 1969.

Milgrom, J. "Profane Slaughter and a Formulaic Key to the Composition of Deuteronomy." *HUCA* 47 (1976) 1–17.

Moldenke, H. N. and A. L. Moldenke. *Plants of the Bible.* Waltham: Chronica Botanica, 1952.

Moran, W. L. "The Literary Connection between Lv 11,13-19 and Dt 14,12-18." *CBQ* 28 (1966) 271–277.

Morrow, W. "The Composition of Deut 15:1-3." *HAR* 12 (1990) 115–131.

Nachmanides (Ramban). *Commentary on the Torah: Deuteronomy,* trans. C. B. Chavel. New York: Shilo, 1976.

Nebeling, G. *Die Schichten des deuteronomischen Gesetzeskorpus: Eine traditions– und redaktionsgeschichtliche Analyse von Dtn 12–26*. Unpublished doctoral dissertation. Wilhelms-Universität of Münster/Westfalen, 1970.

Nel, P. J. Review of H. Irsigler, *Ps 73—Monolog eines Weisen*. In *WO* 17 (1986) 173–75.

Nicholson. E. W. *Deuteronomy and Tradition.* Oxford: Blackwell, 1967.

North, R. "YAD in the Shemiṭṭa–Law." *VT* 4 (1954) 196–99.

Noth, M. *Exodus*. OTL. London: SCM, 1962.

———. *Leviticus*². OTL. Philadelphia: Westminster, 1977.

O'Connor, M. *Hebrew Verse Structure*. Winona Lake: Eisenbrauns, 1980.

Oesch, J. M. *Petucha und Setuma*. OBO 27. Göttingen: Vandenhoeck & Ruprecht, 1979.

Patrick, D. "Casuistic Law Governing Primary Rights and Duties." *JBL* 92 (1973) 180–84.

———. *Introduction to Old Testament Law*. Atlanta: John Knox, 1985.

Pedersen, J. *Israel: Its Life and Culture*. Vols. 3–4. London: Oxford University Press, 1940.

Perrot, C. "Petuhot et Setumot: Etude sur les alinéas du Pentateuch." *RB* 76 (1969) 50–91.

Petschow, H. "Zur Systematik und Gesetzestechnik im Codex Hammurabi." *ZA* 57 (1965) 146–72.

———. "Zur 'Systematik' in den Gesetzen von Eschnunna." In *Symbolae Iurdicae et Historicae Martino David Dedicatae*, eds. J. A. Ankum, R. Feenstra, and W. F. Leemans, 2:131–143. Leiden: E. J. Brill, 1968.

Preuss, H. D. *Deuteronomium*. ErFor 164. Darmstadt: Wissenschaftliche Buchgesellschaft, 1982.

Rabast. K. *Das apodiktische Recht im Deuteronomium und im Heiligkeitsgesetz*. Berlin-Hermsdorf: Heimatdienstverlag, 1948.

Rashi. *Pentateuch with Rashi's Commentary: Deuteronomy*, eds. M. Rosenbaum and A. M. Silbermann. London: Shapiro, Vallentin, 1934.

Rendtorff, R. *Die Gesetze in der Priesterschrift: Eine gattungsgeschichtliche Untersuchung*[2]. Göttingen: Vandenhoeck & Ruprecht, 1963.

Reuter, E. *Kultzentralisation: Entstehung und Theologie von Dtn 12*. BBB 87. Frankfurt am Main: Hain, 1993.

Richter, W. *Recht und Ethos: Versuch einer Ortung des weisheitlichen Mahnspruches*. SANT 15. München: Kösel, 1966.

———. *Exegese als Literaturwissenshaft: Entwurf einer alttestamentlichen Literaturtheorie und Methodologie*. Göttingen: Vandenhoeck & Ruprecht, 1971.

———. Review of Seitz, *Redaktionsgeschichtliche Studien zum Deuteronomium*. In *BZ* 18 (1974) 142–43.

———. *Grundlagen einer althebräischen Grammatik*. Vols. 1 and 3. ATAT 8 and 13. St. Ottilien: EOS, 1978 and 1980.

———. *Transliteration und Transkription*. ATAT 19. St. Ottilien: EOS, 1983.

Rofé, A. *Introduction to the Book of Deuteronomy*. Jerusalem: Akademon, 1975 [Modern Hebrew].

———. "The Order of the Laws in the Book of Deuteronomy." In *Researches in the Bible* (Cassuto Memorial Volume), 217–35. Jerusalem: Magnes, 1987 [Modern Hebrew]. Published in English as "The Arrangement of the Laws in Deuteronomy." *ETL* 64 (1988) 265–87.

Rogerson, J. W. Review of Richter, *Exegese als Literaturwissenschaft*. In *JSS* 20 (1975) 117–22.

Rücker, H. *Die Begründungen der Weisungen Jahwes im Pentateuch*. Erfuhrter Theologische Studien 30. Leipzig: St. Benno, 1972.

Rüterswörden, U. *Von der politischen Gemeinschaft zur Gemeinde. Studien zu Dt. 16,18–18,22*. BBB 65. Frankfurt am Main: Athenäum, 1987.

Schmidt, J. J. "The Motherhood of Zion and Zion as Mother." *RB* 92 (1985) 557–69.

Schneider, W. *Grammatik des biblischen Hebräisch*. München: Claudius, 1974.

Schoors, A. "Literary Phrases." *Ras Shamra Parallels* 1 (1972) 1–57.

Segal, J. B. "Intercalation and the Hebrew Calendar." *VT* 7 (1957) 250–309.

———. *The Hebrew Passover*. London Oriental Series 12. London: Oxford University Press, 1963.

Segal, M. H. *The Pentateuch*. Jerusalem: Magnes, 1967.

Seidl, T. *Tora für den »Aussatz«-Fall: Literarische Schichten und syntaktische Strukturen in Levitikus 13 und 14*. ATAT 18. St. Ottilien: EOS, 1982.

Seitz, G. *Redaktionsgeschichtliche Studien zum Deuteronomium*. BWANT 13. Stuttgart: Kohlhammer, 1971.

Skweres, D. E. *Die Rückverweise im Buch Deuteronomium*. AnBib 79. Rome: Pontifical Biblical Institute, 1979.

Sonsino, R. *Motive Clauses in Hebrew Law. Biblical Forms and Near Eastern Parallels*. SBLDS 45. Chico: Scholars Press, 1980.

Sperber, A. *The Bible in Aramaic.* Vol. 1, *The Pentateuch According to Targum Onqelos.* Leiden: E. J. Brill, 1959.

Sprecher, M., and S. Sprecher. *The Torah Anthology: Yalkut Me'Am Lo'ez. Deuteronomy vol 3. Book 17: Gratitude and Discipline.* New York: Moznaim, 1985.

Talmon, S. "Double Readings in the Massoretic Text." *Textus* 1 (1960) 144–84.

Talshir, S. "The Detailing Formula *wzh hdbr.*" *Tarbiṣ* 51 (1981) 23–36, IV [Modern Hebrew].

Talstra, E. "Text Grammar and Hebrew Bible 1. Elements of a Theory." *BO* 35 (1978) 169–74.

Van Seters, J. "The Place of the Yahwist in the History of Passover and Massot." *ZAW* 95 (1983) 167–81.

Von Gall, A. F. *Der hebräische Pentateuch der Samaritaner.* Giessen: Töpelmann, 1918.

Von Rad, G. *Studies in Deuteronomy.* SBT 9. London: SCM, 1953.

———. *Das Alte Testament Deutsch 8: Das fünfte Buch Mose, Deuteronomium.* Göttingen: Vandenhoeck & Ruprecht, 1964. Published in English as *Deuteronomy: A Commentary.* OTL. Philadelphia: Westminster, 1966.

Wagner, V. "Zur Systematik in dem Codex Ex 21,2–22,16." *ZAW* 81 (1969) 176–82.

Waltke, B. K. and M. O'Connor, *An Introduction to Biblical Hebrew Syntax.* Winona Lake: Eisenbrauns, 1990.

Wambacq, B. N. "Les origines de la Pesaḥ israélite." *Bib* 57 (1976) 301–26.

———. "Les Maṣṣôt." *Bib* 61 (1980) 31–54.

Watson, W. G. E. "Reversed Word-Pairs in Ugaritic Poetry." *UF* 13 (1981) 189–92.

Watters, W. R. *Formula Criticism and the Poetry of the Old Testament.* BZAW 138. Berlin: De Gruyter, 1976.

Weinfeld, M. *Deuteronomy and the Deuteronomic School.* Oxford: Clarendon, 1972.

———. "Judge and Officer in Ancient Israel and in the Ancient Near East." *IOS* 7 (1977) 65–88.

Weiss, M. *The Bible from Within: The Method of Total Interpretation*. Jerusalem: Magnes, 1984.

Welch, A. C. *The Code of Deuteronomy*. London: James Clarke, 1924.

Wenham. G. J. "Deuteronomy and the Central Sanctuary." *Tyndale Bulletin* 22 (1971) 103–10.

Wevers, J. W. *Deuteronomium: Septuaginta Vetus Testamentum Graecum*. Vol. III, 2. Göttingen: Vandenhoeck & Ruprecht, 1977.

———. *Text History of the Greek Deuteronomy*. Abhandlungen der Akademie der Wissenschaften in Göttingen, Philologische-Historische Klasse. Dritte Folge 106 (= Mitteilungen des Septuginta-Unternehmens 13). Göttingen: Vandenhoeck & Ruprecht, 1978.

———. *Leviticus: Septuaginta Vetus Testamentum Graecum*. Vol. II, 2. Göttingen: Vandenhoeck & Ruprecht, 1986.

White, H. A., "Leaven." In *A Dictionary of the Bible*, ed. J. Hastings 3:90. New York: Scribners, 1911.

Williams, R. J. *Hebrew Syntax*[2]. Toronto: University of Toronto Press, 1976.

Wright, W. *A Grammar of the Arabic Language*[3]. Vol. 2. Cambridge: University Press, 1967 (first published 1898).

Zakovitch, Y. *The Pattern of the Numerical Sequence Three-Four in the Bible*. Unpublished doctoral dissertation. Jerusalem: 1977 [Modern Hebrew].

Index of Textual References in Chapter Four: Literary Unity in the Clause Rows of Deuteronomy 14:1–17:13

Biblical References

Genesis

2:5 122
3:23 122
4:2 122
8:3 95
15:31 81
16:5 188
17:13 81
18:25 160
20:14 130
24:6 97, 106
24:8 97, 106
24:35 130
27:37 164
29:18 122
29:20 122
29:25 122
30:26 122
31:44 82
31:24 106
33:10 160
35:1 189
35:3 189
42:25 165
44:4 78
44:9 182
44:10 182
45:10 126
45:11 87
47:3 65
47:24 83

Exodus

1:11 152
1:14 121
9:29 78
9:33 78
10:24 126
12:1–20 130
12:6 137, 147
12:8 131, 147
12:9–10 97
12:9 131, 132, 141, 142
12:10 137, 148
12:11 66, 136
12:15 136, 147, 148
12:17 136, 149
12:18 137
12:32 126
12:38 130
12:43–47 95–96
12:43 95
12:48 136
13:2 123, 124, 126
13:3 136, 147, 149
13:4–7 148
13:4–6 149
13:4 149
13:6 137, 146, 148, 149, 150
13:7 135, 136, 148, 161
13:9 82, 136, 149
13:12 123, 124
13:13 80, 126
13:15 123, 124, 126
15:26 94, 97, 98

Extra Biblical References

Akkadian

Aramiac

Hebrew

Phoenician

Ugaritic

Index of Bibliographic References